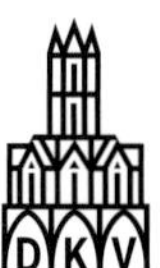

Dirk Syndram

Jutta Kappel

Ulrike Weinhold

The Historic
Grünes Gewölbe
at Dresden.
The Baroque Treasury

DEUTSCHER KUNSTVERLAG

STAATLICHE
KUNSTSAMMLUNGEN
DRESDEN

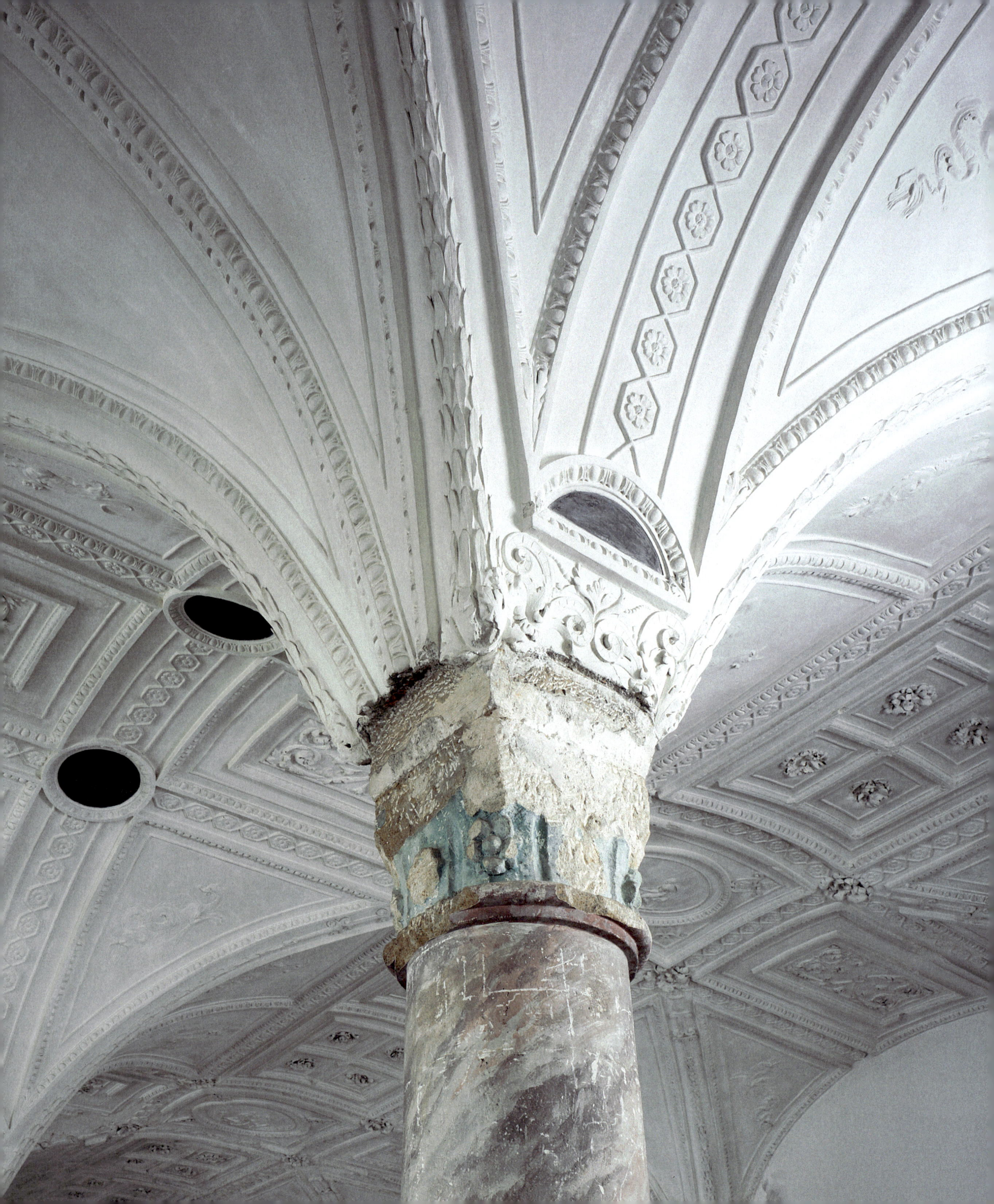

Monument to a Royal Collector:
the Grünes Gewölbe of Augustus the Strong

»In Dresden there is one thing that you should endeavour to do and that is to visit the so-called Grünes Gewölbe or Schatzkammer (Treasury).«[1] This still apposite advice is to be found as early as the second half of the 18th century in Johann Georg Keyssler's much read travel guide for Germany, Bohemia, Hungary, Switzerland, Italy and Lorraine. Keyssler visited the treasury art collection in October 1730 a few months after the building had been completed and was very impressed. The well-travelled writer ends his detailed description with the words: »This is a general survey of what the Grünes Gewölbe contains and can be seen while walking round. It is not possible to mention all the precious objects and this becomes more difficult from year to year, because the number of exhibits multiplies. The Florentine Tribuna and what goes with it, perhaps surpasses the treasures listed here in value: however, it cannot be denied that the mounts and well-thought arrangement of the objects and the impression they make, are far more striking than the Florentine collection.« This assessment would have greatly pleased Augustus the Strong as the Tribuna of the Uffizi in Florence was at that time the undisputed yardstick of magnificent presentation and the fusion of material and artistic wealth. It is not only the present-day visitor for whom the name of the Dresden treasury (Grünes Gewölbe = Green Vault) is not self-explanatory. In the Baroque period it also required explanation. Johann Georg Keyssler comments: »A number of rooms are green but the whole furnishing has been changed and expanded so that this treasury now consists of seven rooms and one cabinet.«[2] In 1730 what had given rise to the strange name had already disappeared behind the mirrors of the display architecture. Although the vaulted ceilings and the opulent stucco in the Hall of the Precious Objects were visible, the capitals and wall surfaces painted in malachite green were not (Ill. 1). From the end of the 16th century the name Grünes Gewölbe was used for a suite of rooms consisting of two large rooms and a room with an adjacent »cabinet« in the tower on the ground floor in the representational west wing of the Dresden Palace. Until the beginning of the 18th century this self-contained suite served the Saxon electors as a »Geheime Verwahrung« – a secure and somewhat mysterious treasury.

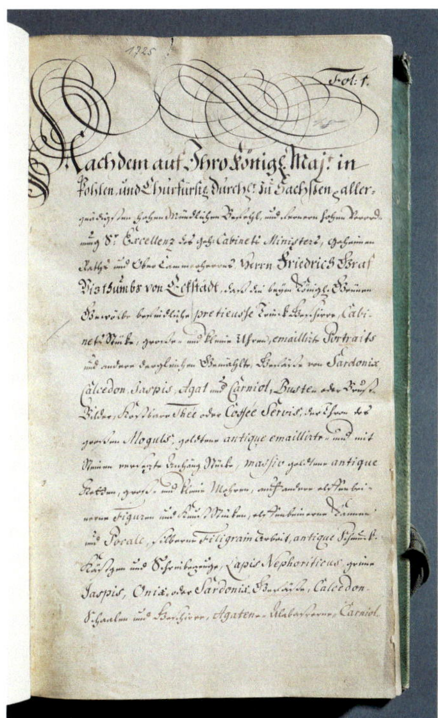
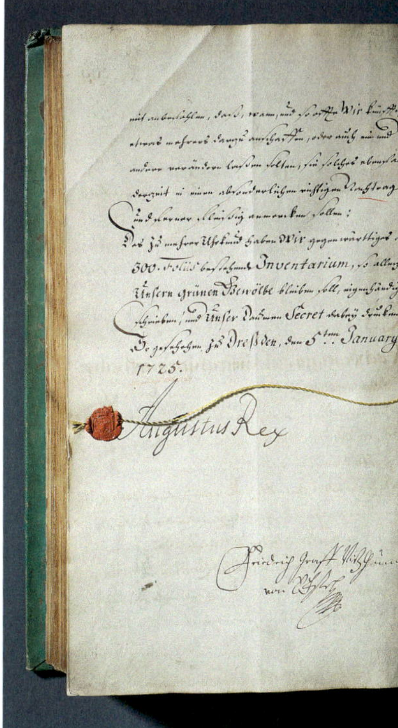

Ill. 2   First and last page of the inventory of the pretiosa of 1725

The History of the Rooms of the Collection

All this changed when in June 1723 Augustus the Strong ordained the construction of splendid rooms to display the collection. The Oberlandbauamt (office of buildings) directed by Matthäus Daniel Pöppelmann was responsible for the supervision of the building works. The Elector was, however, able to bring his ideas for the design to bear. In late autumn 1723 the area in front of the double staircase on the Zwinger side of the west wing, which was the new means of access, had already been paved. In March 1724 the Silver Room in its function as the entrance hall to the new treasury had been largely completed. In the summer of that year the court goldsmith Johann Heinrich Köhler restored a large number of older nautilus and precious stone vessels in silver-gilt mounts. In September a large number of lathe-turned works in ivory came from the Kunstkammer to the Grünes Gewölbe. When Augustus the Strong signed off the inventory of the pretiosa on 5 January 1725 (Ill. 2), in which the large number of exhibits in the Hall of the Precious Objects and the Corner Cabinet were listed the first building phase was regarded as completed.

Ill. 1   Hall of the Precious Objects in the Grünes Gewölbe,
         capital with traces of painting in malachite green, 1999

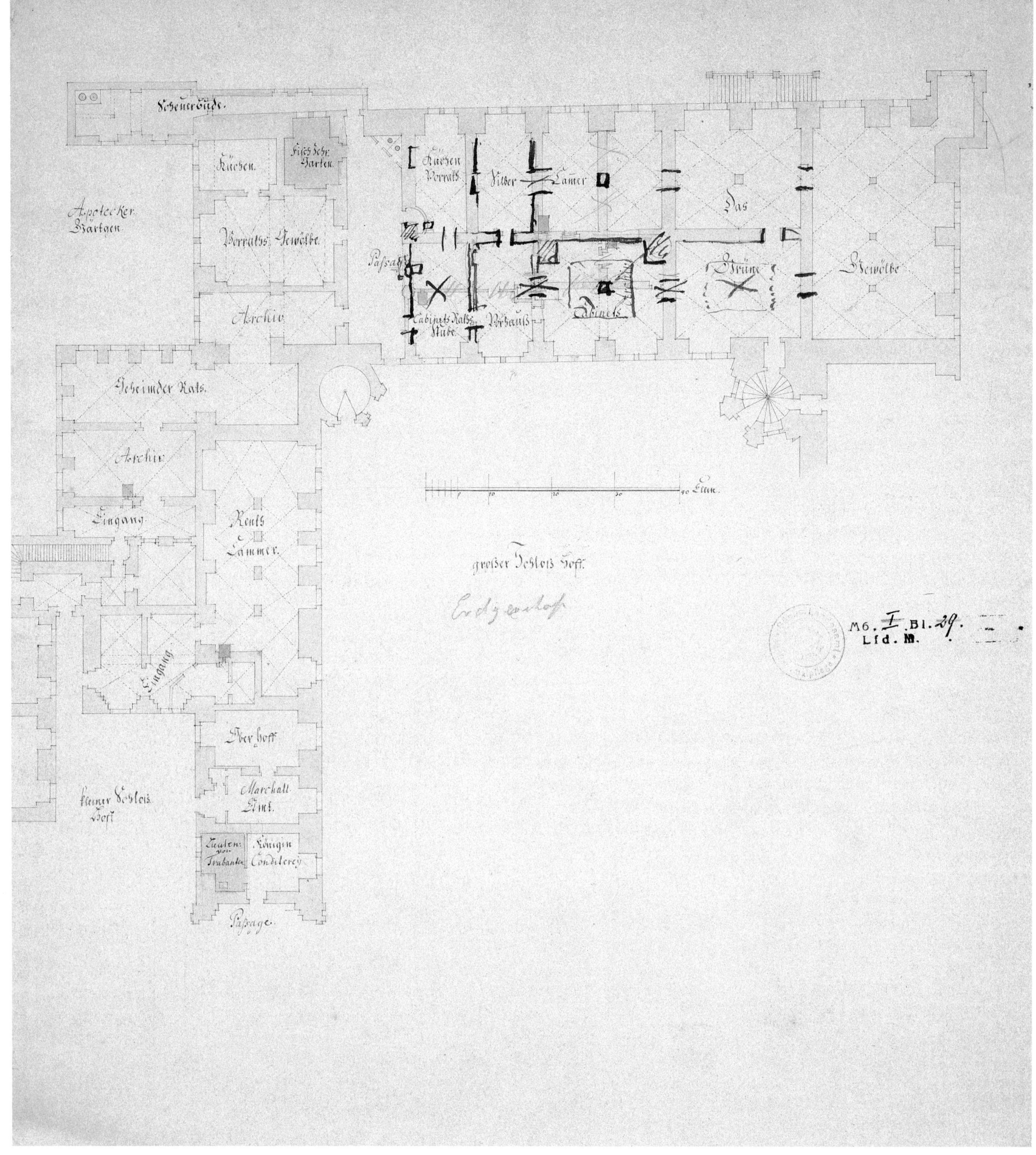

Ill. 3   Plan of the ground floor of the west wing of the Dresden Palace with handwritten notes by Augustus the Strong
in connection with the expansion of the Grünes Gewölbe
Warsaw 1727
Pen and ink in black and brown, red, yellow and ochre wash on drawing paper
47.6 x 52.5 cm

These two rooms largely had their present-day form in the first construction phase. Only the large room was to see a number of alterations a few years later. In 1724 access was only from the Silver Room to the Hall of the Precious Objects and on the narrow end wall there was still the large jewellery cupboard which had been installed in 1719. The Silver Room was to be changed considerably a few years later. In the first building phase it was painted lime green and had far fewer mirrors than today. An »Inventarium über dasjenige Massiv Goldtene, Vergoldtete und weiss Silberne Geschirre, so sich bey dem Königl. Grünes Gewölbe be-findet.« (an inventory of the solid gold, gilded and white silver vessels which are in the royal Grünes Gewölbe) signed on 30 June 1723, i.e. shortly after building began, brought the silver together which in an administrative sense was the responsibility of this treasury room. To judge by this, the Silver Room must have been overflowing with vessels, candelabra and other objects. In general the first display in the Baroque Grünes Gewölbe was much larger and less structured than now. Dishes in precious stones stood next to ivory vessels, the Baroque indoor replica of an equestrian statue between wall panels filled with Renaissance ostrich egg and nautilus cups. All in all, the first treasury museum in the Grünes Gewölbe was not exactly what Augustus the Strong had in mind.

Thus, in spring 1727 the Elector-King decided on expansion. In a ground plan that has been preserved he demonstrated his ideas with boldly drawn lines, and Pöppelmann and the other architects of the Oberlandbauamt of the Saxon Electorate went to work again (Ill. 3). The second building phase began in April 1727 with demolition work and bricklaying. This time, the entire wing of the palace was to be altered. In September 1729 the King's ideas had been realised. The structure of a museum with eight display rooms and a functional area with a cloakroom, foyer and office for the »inspectors« and a large storage area anticipated the functional structure of a modern museum. From 1732 a royal directive regulated visits in groups of up to five persons led by a royal inspector.[3] What Keyssler was the first to describe, was an unprecedented innovation in the Baroque period: at the end of his reign which lasted almost four decades Augustus the Strong made his crown treasures and his personal collection of pretiosa together with the inherited treasures of the Wettin electoral dynasty accessible to the public.

The Theatrical Tour

From the outset the collection and the design of the museum formed an indivisible whole. The presentation of the collection was materials-based and the interior decoration of the rooms of differing sizes was adapted both in colour and form to the exhibits. Display walls, painted and partly fitted with mirrors, with consoles arranged symmetrically and tables in front of them served to present the treasures. (Ill. 4) The individual rooms were juxtaposed in a theatrical mise en scène, so that walking through the rooms a gradual crescendo, decrescendo and another crescendo of sensual experiences was created.

The beginning and end of the tour was the Room of Bronzes. More than one hundred small bronzes were placed on numerous consoles

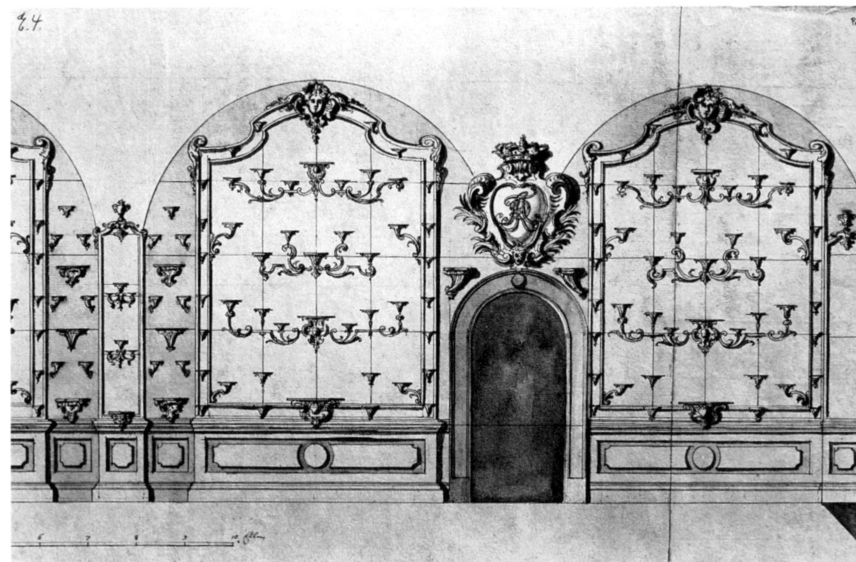

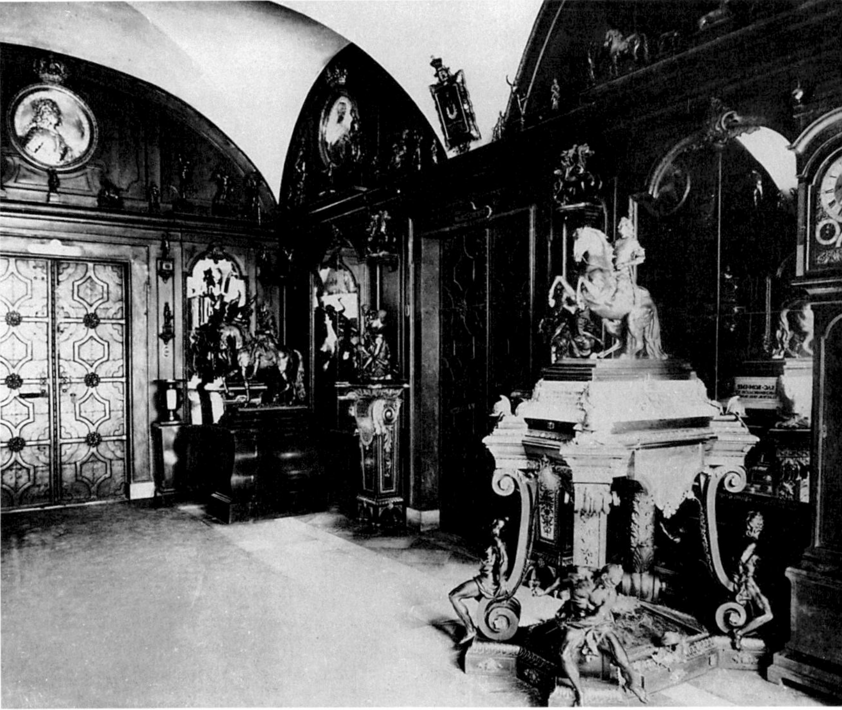

Ill. 4   Draft of the west part of the south wall of the Hall of the Precious Objects, Carl Friedrich Pöppelmann, 1723
Original drawing burnt in 1945 in the Grünes Gewölbe

Ill. 5   Room of Bronzes in the Grünes Gewölbe 1904
(SLUB / Abt. Deutsche Fotothek)

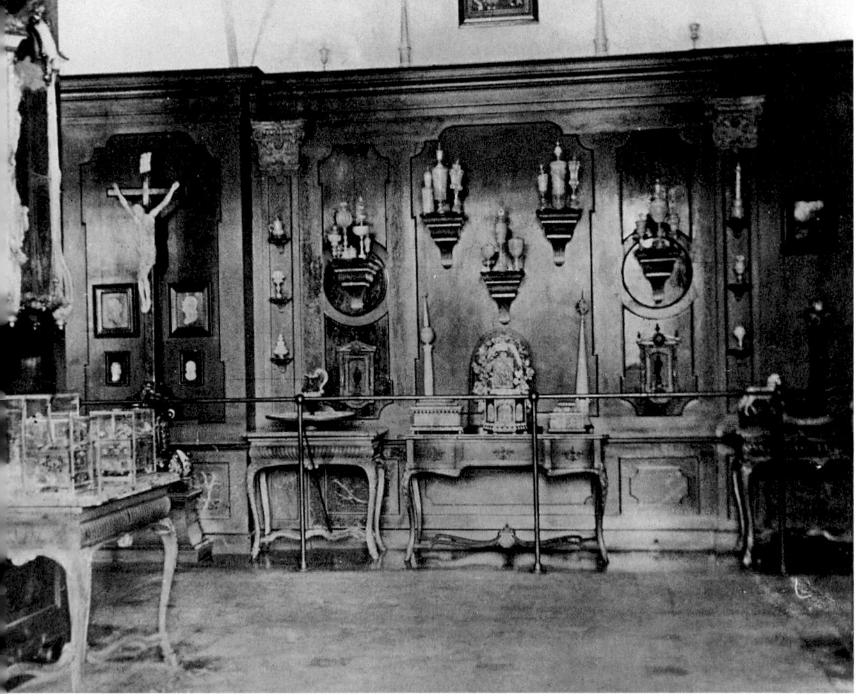

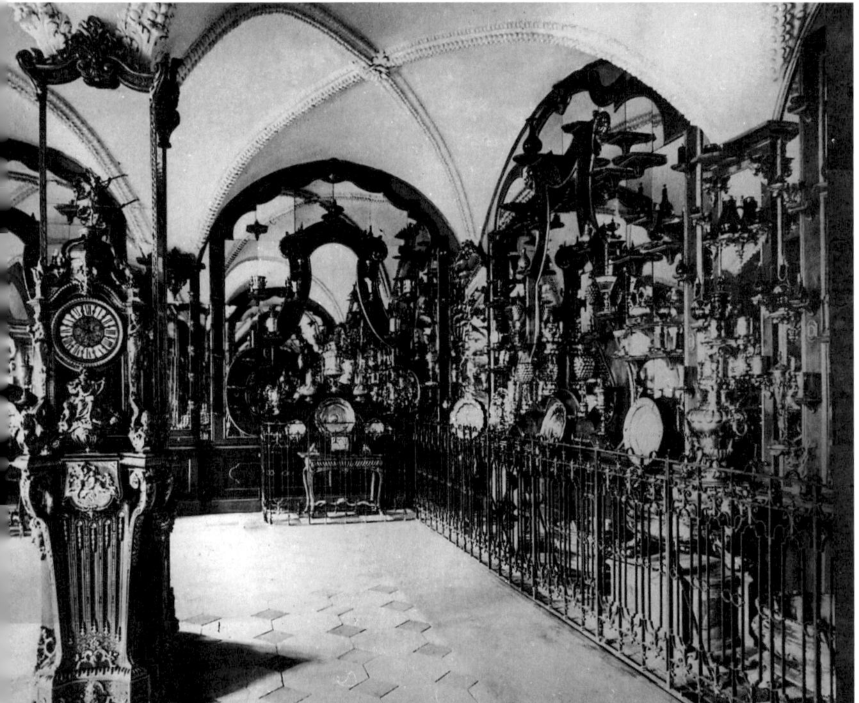

and a dado shelf running round the room against oak-panelled walls relieved by only a small number of mirrors (Ill. 5). The exhibits were above all small bronzes from France. These works of contemporary Baroque art were complemented by important Renaissance bronze statuettes from the existing collection. For ten larger bronze groups there were precious boulle pedestals. However, small replicas of well-known marble sculptures of French courtly art and famous sculptures from Antiquity predominated thematically. Two relatively large »room monuments«, one after the model of an equestrian statue of Louis XIV, the other after a type of picture created for Augustus the Strong dominated the room which was only 45 square metres in size – and a wooden white eagle – the symbol of the Kingdom of Poland – hung from the ceiling. The small Ivory Room with its marbled walls adjoined the Room of Bronzes. It displayed the unusually large and varied collection of turned works of art, ivory tankards embellished with reliefs, ivory reliefs and carved statuettes (Ill. 6). The works of the 17th and 18th centuries usually came from the private Saxon collection and were once the pride and joy of the Dresden Kunstkammer. The next room that the visitor entered was the vermilion painted White Silver Room which housed the ungilded tableware silver of the Saxon-Polish rulers. According to the inventory of 1733, 377 items in ungilded silver were arranged in the form of a pyramid and displayed as a permanent silver buffet on and in front of the six wall panels (Ill. 9). They were almost without exception late Baroque tableware. This included ice jugs, cooling kettles and kettles for glasses, dishes for pies or soups, chain bottles and multi-armed girandoles, and also dozens of garnitures of bowls and ewers, most of which had been bought only a short time before 1719 on the occasion of the marriage of the crown prince. The material value was enormous. The vases and cauldrons standing on the floor had a total silver weight of 925 kilograms alone. With the exception of three silver statuettes these splendid objects were melted down in 1772 in the aftermath of the Seven Years' War, turned into coins and brought into circulation again. At that time almost two thirds of the exhibits in gilded silver and pure gold, which had been displayed in the next room, the Silver Gilt Room, disappeared. Originally almost three hundred

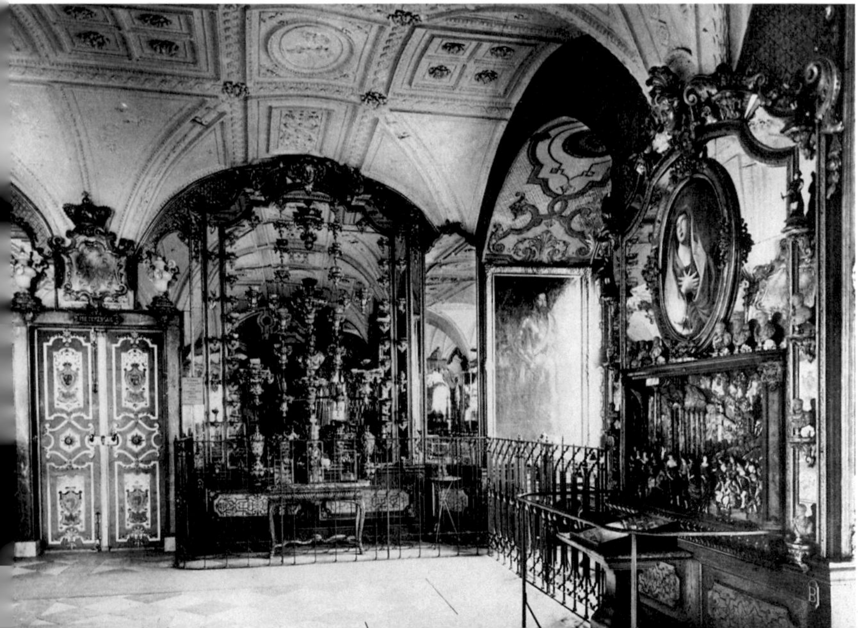

Ill. 6   Ivory Room in the Grünes Gewölbe, before 1938

Ill. 7   Silver Gilt Room in the Grünes Gewölbe, 1904

Ill. 8   Hall of the Precious Objects in the Grünes Gewölbe, 1904

Ill. 9   White Silver Room (Enamel Room) in the Grünes Gewölbe, 1933

Ill. 10   Draft of the south part of the east wall of the Hall of the Precious Objects
with the arrangement of the cabinet piece
›Throne of the Grand Mogul‹
Dresden 1728/29
Original 1945 burnt in the Grünes Gewölbe

Ill. 11   Corner Cabinet in the Grünes Gewölbe, 1973

Ill. 12   Jewel Room in the Grünes Gewölbe, 1933

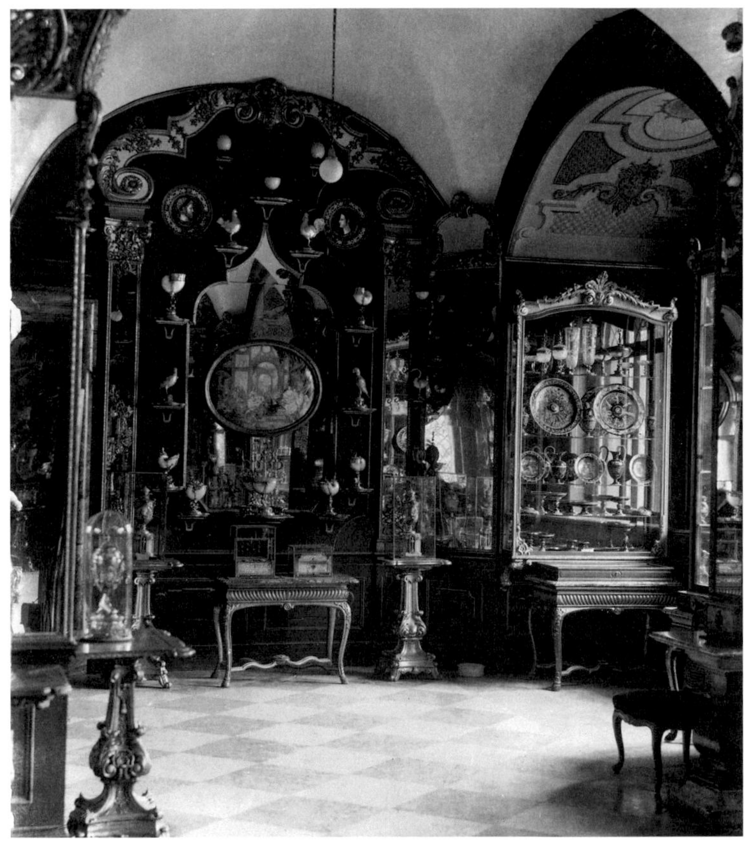

Ill. 9

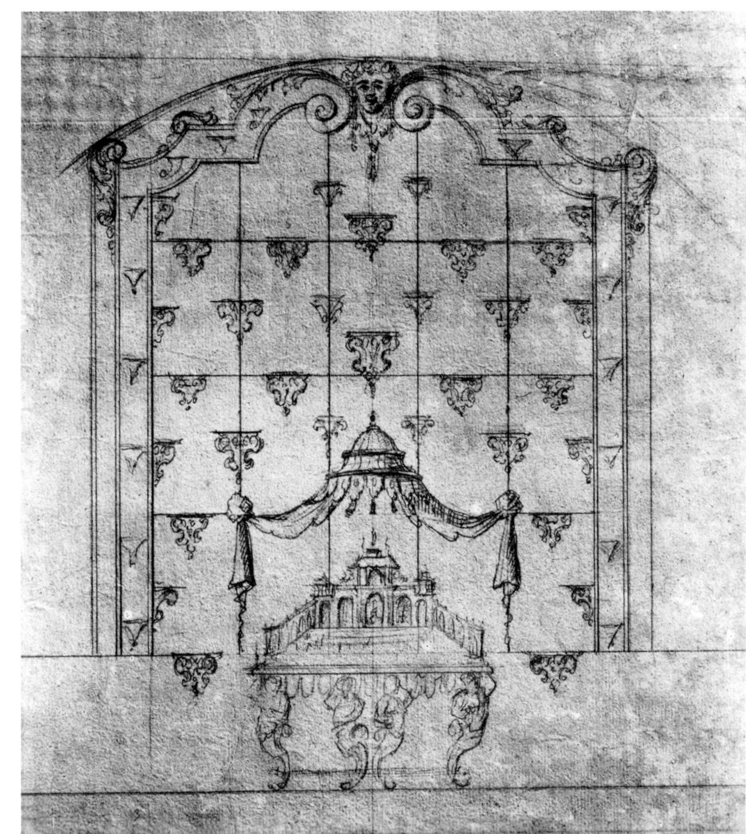

Ill. 10

Ill. 11

Ill. 12

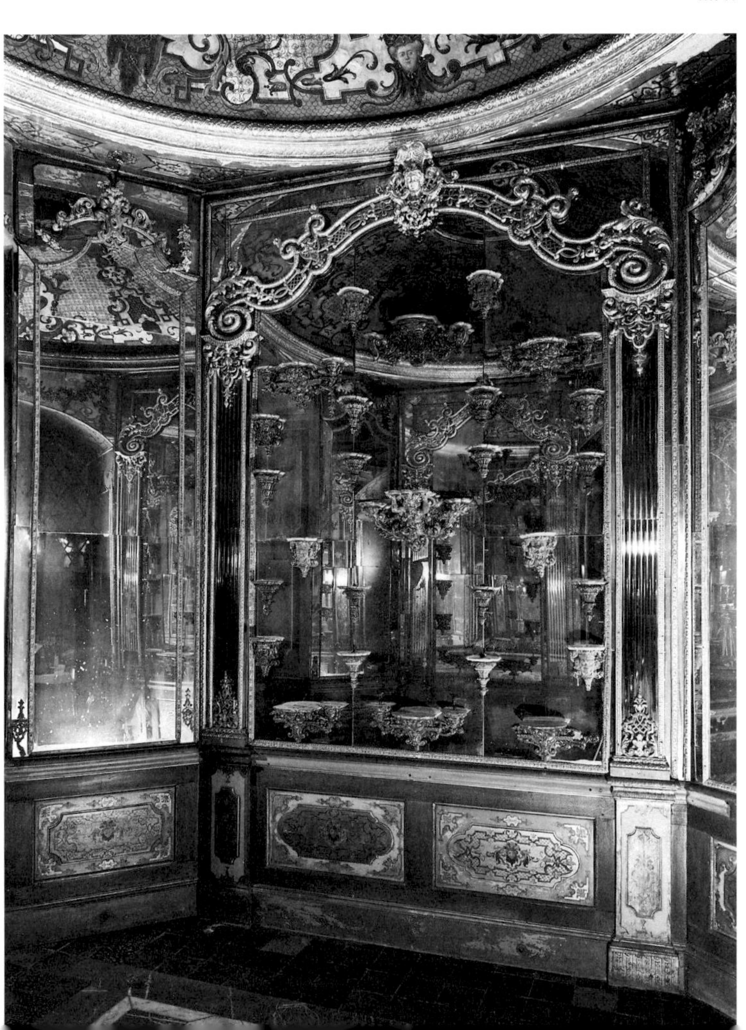

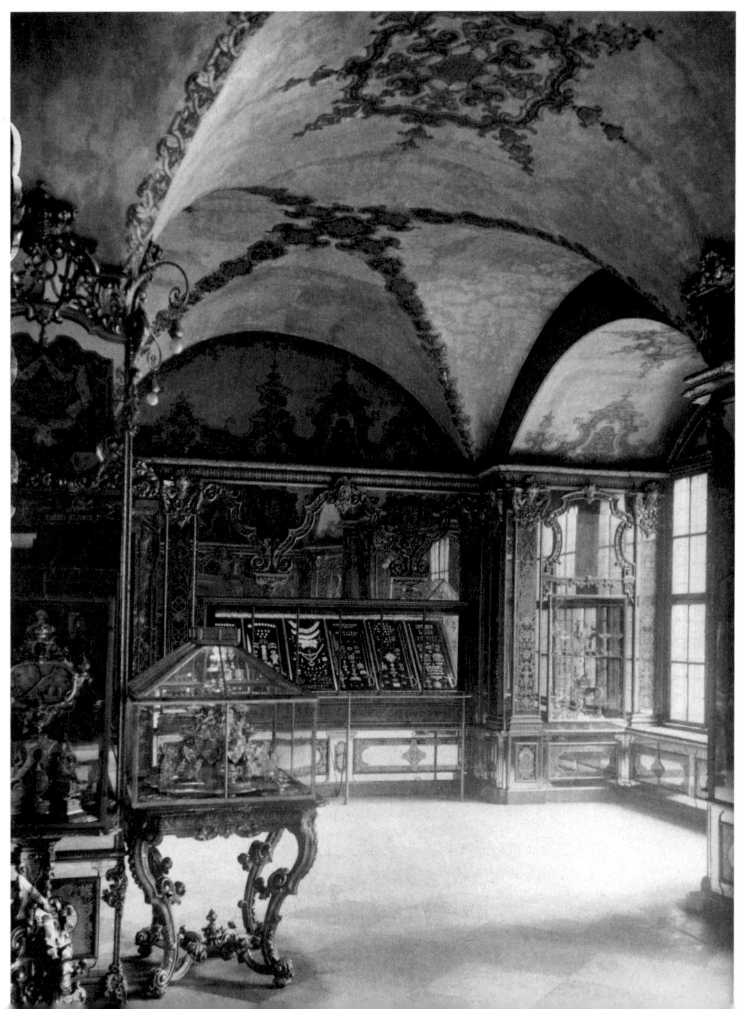

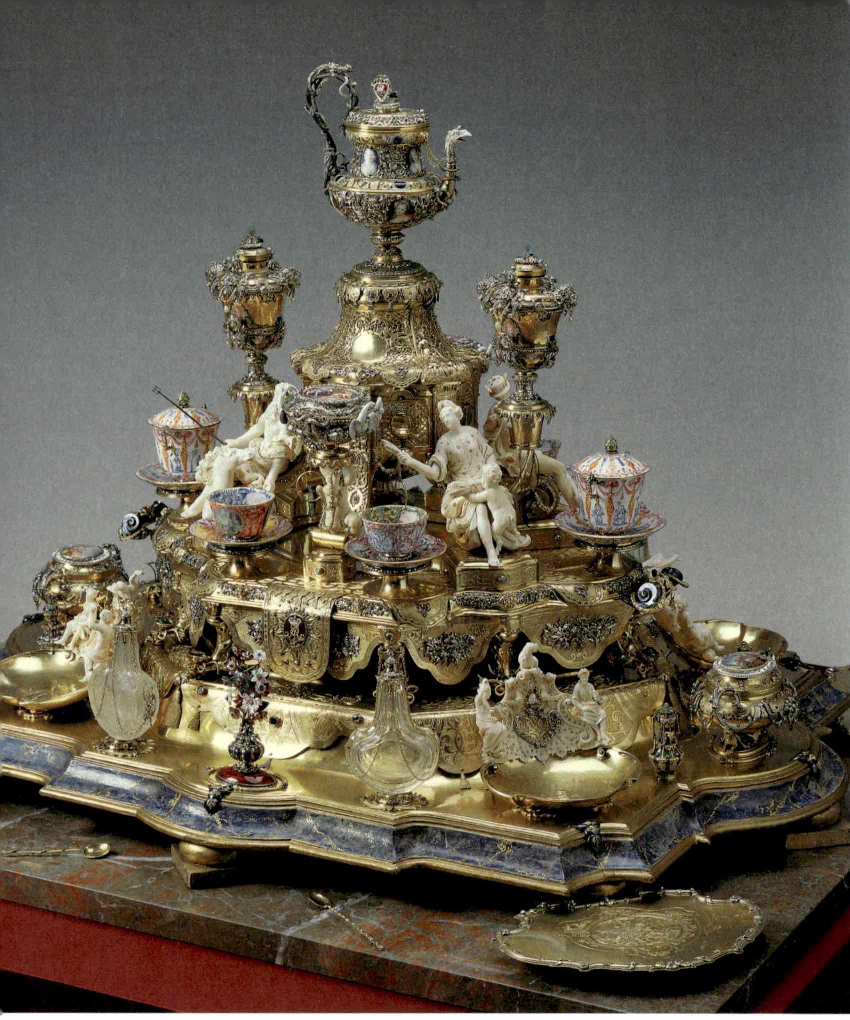

Ill. 13 ›Golden Coffee Set‹
Design and goldsmith work: Johann Melchior Dinglinger
Enamel work: Georg Friedrich Dinglinger
Ivory sculptures: Paul Heermann
Dresden 1697–1701
Wooden core, gold, silver-gilt, enamel, ivory, precious stones
H. 96 cm, w. 76 cm, d. 50 cm
Dresden, Grünes Gewölbe, Inv. no. VIII 203

drinking vessels, pouring garnitures and other artistically designed parade vessels were displayed on more than 250 consoles and eight tables. A variety of inherited shapes and modern formal severity were united in this room and displayed against walls painted copper oxide green and fitted with a wealth of mirrors. A special effect was achieved in the Silver Gilt Room when all the doors fitted with mirrors and small consoles were closed. The visitor then found himself in a room without visible exit, which was filled to the ceiling with a profusion of gleaming gold precious objects and their reflections.

The splendour and exclusiveness increased from room to room as the visitor reached the Hall of the Precious Objects, almost 200 sq metre in size (Ill. 9). There were several hundred objets d'art displayed on gilded consoles painstakingly carved by sculptors on the wall panels of the room, which was almost entirely fitted with mirrors. However, the Hall of the Precious Objects was arranged systematically. The two wall panels to the left and right of the entrance to the Silver Gilt Room were reserved for mounted and unmounted works in lapis lazuli, agate, jasper, chalcedony, alabaster and serpentine. On the next two panels to the left and right of the door to the Coats of Arms Room an unusual number of vessels made of nautilus and turbo snail shells and the proud collection of ostrich-egg cups were displayed. The narrow wall panel between the colourful dishes in precious stones and the gleaming white mother of pearl and ostrich-egg vessels was used to display amber objects. The almost 10 metre long narrow wall of the Hall of the Precious Objects served to present the highly regarded vessels and objects in rock crystal (Ill. 10). The whole of the artistic and material wealth, which had been inherited or acquired in the last few decades, took on almost fairytale proportions in the endless reflections in the ubiquitous mirrors. At the same time the room had a strong dynastic link. A series of portraits of Saxon rulers hung in the deep window recesses linked Elector Moritz, the founder of the electoral dynasty in the middle of the 16th century to the son of Augustus the Strong, crown prince Friedrich August (II). Augustus the Strong did not alter the richly stuccoed ceiling with Renaissance ornamentation from the middle of the 16th century, which in both a physical and aes-thetic sense linked the late Baroque collection of the Elector-King with the origins of his role as an elector in the middle of the 16th century.

The Corner Cabinet installed in a tower room was linked in theme to the Hall of the Precious Objects and separated from it only by a Ren-aissance wrought iron screen (Ill. 11). The small room of only 14 sq. metre provided an experience of its own in spite of the fact that it was not entirely separated from the large room. A large part of Augustus the Strong's collection of several decades was displayed on more than one hundred consoles, fashioned as expressive faun masks, and on five ornately carved side tables. Almost five hundred miniature-like works made of pearls, precious stones, ivory, enamel, silver and gold present-ed an almost overwhelming profusion of forms and colours. As no oth-er room in the Grünes Gewölbe the Corner Cabinet managed to retain the intimate character of the earlier presentation of the collec-tion.

The visitor, whose senses were overwhelmed by the splendid colours preciousness and artistic virtuosity, could gain some respite in the next room – the Coats of Arms Room. Three walls of the room were lined with fitted cupboards in which in accordance with tradition secret documents and similar things were kept. 44 gilded coats of arms in beaten copper were affixed to the doors of the cupboards so that the room had a distinctly dynastic and political function as a result of the coats of arms of the hereditary possessions of the house of Wettin and those to which they lay claim, the coats of arms of the King-dom of Poland and the Grand Principality of Lithuania and shields with the ornamentally interlaced initials of various Saxon electors.[4]

In the Jewel Room, the last room of the suite, the largest concen-tration in Central Europe of material and artistic wealth to which the public had access, awaited the 18th century traveller (Ill. 12). The splen-

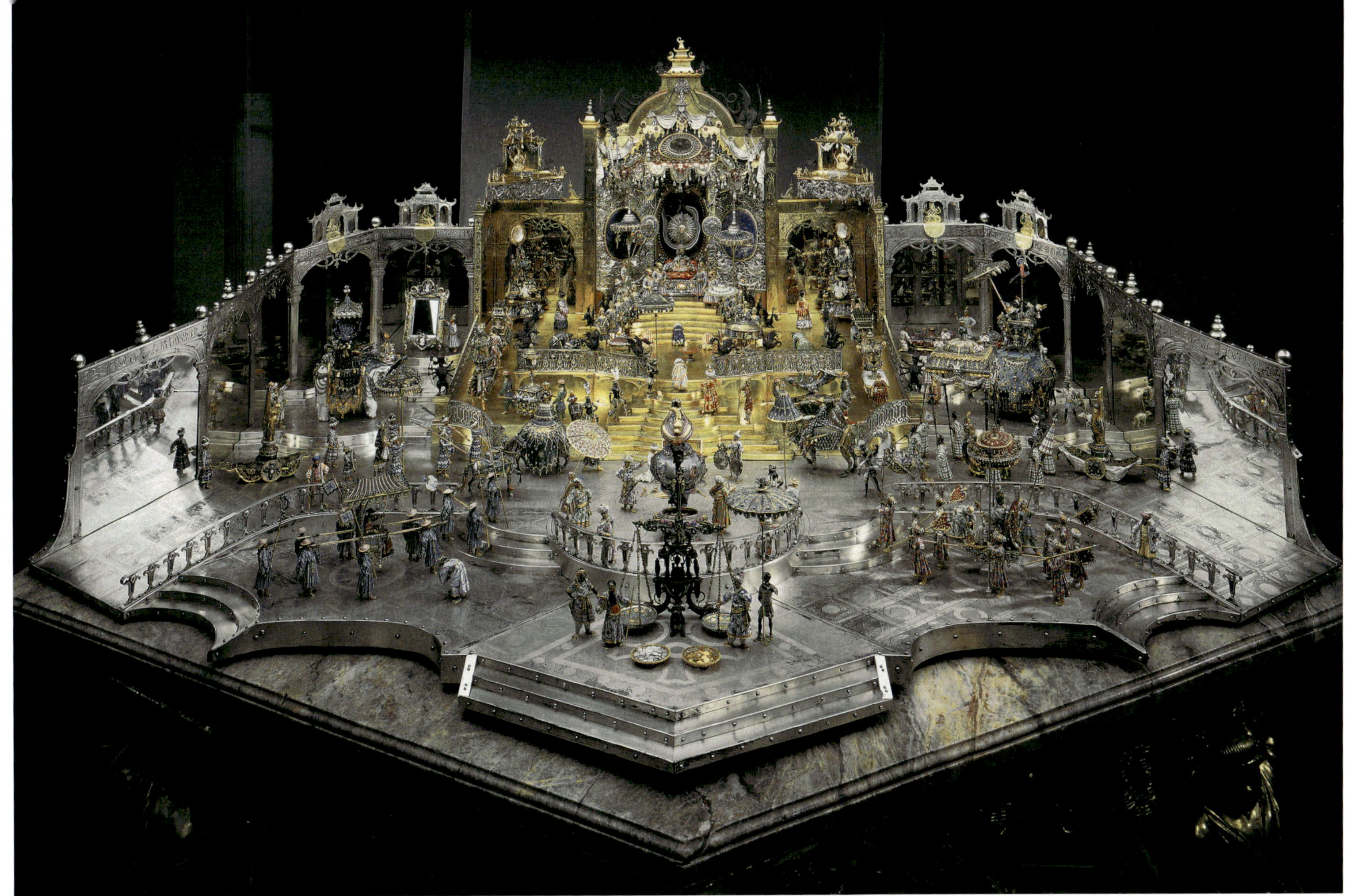

Ill. 14   ›Throne of the Grand Mogul‹
Design: Johann Melchior Dinglinger
Goldsmith work: Johann Melchior Dinglinger and workshop
Enamel work: Georg Friedrich Dinglinger
Dresden 1701 – 1708
Wooden core, gold, silver, partly gilded, enamel,
precious stones, pearls, lacquer work
D. 114 cm, w. 142 cm, h. 58 cm
Dresden, Grünes Gewölbe, Inv. no. VIII 204

dour of the fittings of the Jewel Room in the form of a treasury was outstanding. From the floor to the display shelf the walls consisted of mirrors and verre églomisé mirrors on which ornamental panels in gold engraving on a blue and crimson ground alternated with emblems of orders, state coats of arms and initials. The carved and gilded ornamentation crowning the wall panels and the door surrounds were of a high artistic quality. Four large glass cabinets let into the walls contained the jewels of the Saxon-Polish Elector-Kings. They were to increase in number and quality until the middle of the 18th century. In 1733 the following were displayed here: two large modern jewel garnitures of diamonds with a brilliant and rose cut, a further eight in gold and silver with emeralds, sapphires, rubies, agates, carnelians and tortoiseshell. This collection of jewels was in itself overwhelming, its artistic and monetary value inestimable. Inherited jewellery, and symbolical and ceremonial swords were also displayed in the four jewel cabinets. This magnificent collection of jewels was complemented by cabinet pieces by Johann Melchior Dinglinger: the ›Golden Coffee Set‹ (Ill. 13) and the ›Throne of the Grand Mogul‹ (Ill. 14), the ›Three Phases of Life's Pleasures‹ and a number of ingenious parade dishes, the two blackamoors with the Emerald and cluster of local stone and finally, rising heavenwards between two glass cabinets and dominating the room, the ›Obeliscus Augustalis‹.

The Collections of the Treasury Museum

Even by the standards of the late baroque period the Grünes Gewölbe housed a wide variety and superabundance of princely collector's items. Among them there were also works of art which would not have been out of place in other types of collection. Small bronze sculptures, for example, had been part of the collections of picture galleries in Northern Europe since the 17th century. Thus Augustus the Strong had had most of the statuettes displayed in the treasury (which he had opened to the public) acquired in Paris for the art galleries of his palaces by his art chamberlain Baron Raymond Le Plat. In 1707 more than six hundred paintings had been collected to form a picture gallery in the Redoute of the Dresden Palace. In 1712 28 bronzes were transferred from the Kunstkammer to the royal ›Bilder-Cabinets‹ (picture cabinets).[5] Some of them were displayed in the Bronze Room a few years later. The same was the case with the huge accumulation of functional or decorative silver objects. Administratively they were generally the responsibility of the princely Silberkammer. This institution continued to exist at the Dresden court and was also »royally« expanded when Augustus became king. However, the parade silver whether »antique« or »modern« was listed in the inventories of the Grünes Gewölbe from 1723.[6] The Dresden »Schatzgewölbe« (treasure vault) owed (and still owes) its fame to two genres, which were an essential part of the courtly self-presentation of a prince in the late Baroque period. This was on the one hand the collection of jewellery which was unique in its size and consisted of modern precious stone garnitures of the Elector-King, which were adapted in accordance with changing fashions. The second area was treasury art. Both were regarded shortly after 1700 as the personal possession of the sovereign and at other princely courts they usually remained at the disposal of the prince – especially since treasury art involved objects created exclusively for princely or royal collectors. These splendid, highly artistic and masterly objects usually consisted of precious and frequently exotic materials. The predominantly small-scale objects were connoisseurs' pieces of an intimate nature intended to stimulate the observer to discover them in a playful fashion and to examine their details closely. Their small size and delicate design made them private collectors' pieces which were concealed from the public and housed in secure rooms or in locked ›Cabinet‹ cupboards complete with metal grille. From the beginning of the Renaissance treasury art was one of the elite forms of princely collecting. In the course of the 16th and 17th centuries specific fashions evolved so that works of stone-cutting or ivory, jewellery sculpture and fashionable accessories each had their demand cycle at any given time.

The Tradition of the Kunstkammer
and Sources of Inspiration

Before the installation of the Grünes Gewölbe, north of the Alps there was only one form of museum-like collection, in which rare naturalia, which awakened curiosity, technical innovations – craftsmen's tools and scientific instruments, complicated clocks and automata – were presented alongside treasury art works in a form accessible only to courtly society. This was the Kunstkammer. At the time of Augustus the Strong the Dresden Palace contained one of the oldest collections of this kind, which was famous far beyond the borders of Saxony. Founded in 1560 by Elector August as a technological ›Wunderkammer‹, it initially contained perfectly formed tools and instruments and hardly anything else. Examples of artistic virtuosity (›artificialia‹) and miracles of nature (›naturalia‹) were originally scarcely represented. Between 1586 and 1591 Christian I began to adapt his father's Kunstkammer to the new standard and after 1600 the collection of the Saxon electors rose to become one of the most magnificent in the Holy Roman Empire. Almost one hundred years later its fame cast its spell on Tsar Peter I who was touring Europe. In June 1698 he could not wait to see it and spent the first night after his arrival in Dresden in the rooms of the Kunstkammer. Peter I was to return several times and finally founded his own Kunstkammer on the Dresden model in his new residence St Petersburg.

Augustus the Strong had travelled through Europe a decade before Peter I. The impressions he gained in Versailles, Madrid, Lisbon, Turin, Genoa, Florence and Vienna between 1687 and 1689 profoundly influenced him as a collector, builder and ruler. The court of the French king made the strongest impression.[7] Thus, three decades after his grand tour, when refurnishing the Dresden Palace, Augustus the Strong referred to the silver furniture he had seen in the ›grands appartements‹ of Versailles – at the court of a »prince très magnifique, de très bon goût« – to justify his own idea of such parade furniture.[8] In Versailles the young duke learnt from Louis XIV not only the majestic use of jewellery, he also saw a highly effective way of displaying royal treasury art collections – and this in a differentiated form. In several rooms accessible only to a precisely defined class of visitors splendid vessels in precious stones served to underline the majesty of the ruler.[9] Displayed on bronze consoles against the almost completely mirrored walls the splendour of their colours and wealth of forms could be admired in their reflections from all angles. Louis XIV and his son the Dauphin were extremely ambitious collectors of ›gemmes‹, cut stones mounted in gold and enamel. The king especially loved coloured stone cuts of which he had inherited a considerable number. Later Louis XIV also acquired historic and contemporary hard stone vessels of outstanding quality in the European and Middle East art trade. Some of them were given new mounts in jewellers' workshops in Paris.[10] Together with important paintings the largest part of this treasure was displayed on gilded wooden consoles on three levels one above the other and adorned the walls of the richly furnished ›Petite Galerie du Roi‹. The gallery, completed in 1686, was one of the most modern and magnificent rooms that Augustus the Strong saw in Versaillles.[11] The impression it made on the visitor from Saxony was so strong that it was reflected in the Hall of the Precious Objects of the Grünes Gewölbe forty years later. Finally, the much more intimate ›Cabinet des Médailles et Bijoux‹, which was adapted solely to the requirements of the royal collector and which similar to the German concept of the ›Kunst- und Wunderkammer‹ was also called ›Cabinet des Curiosités‹ or ›Cabinet des Raretés‹, formed the bridge between the modern display form on consoles against mirrored walls and the older method of keeping objects in cupboards or on open shelves.[12] The interiors of the appartements of Louis XIV, which in their day were extremely influential, are no longer in existence and can only be reconstructed from records.

The other two princely treasuries which influenced the design and above all the function of the later Grünes Gewölbe are no longer in existence in an architectural sense, either. One of them was the Tribuna of the Uffizi in Florence. This heart of the grand ducal art collections of the Medici – in contrast to the official private nature of the rooms of the royal collection of Versailles – served consciously to demonstrate the splendour, wealth and power of the dynasty. It enjoyed well-orchestrated international fame. The young duke from Saxony visited the »raritaetengallerie« in Florence in March 1689. At that time the octagonal Tribuna still largely existed with the original display form and composition of objects of the late 16th century, and was not dissolved until the end of the 18th century. The octagonal room was roofed with a gleaming cupola with a mother of pearl effect. A display sideboard crowded with dishes in precious stones and bronze statuettes ran round the walls covered in red velvet. There were further treasures in two hidden fitted cupboards. The floor was in precious red and green porphyry. The splendour of the display in the mannerist style probably did not seem very modern to the young duke. The overwhelming profusion and intoxicating splendour of the dishes in precious stones and rock crystal in their golden mounts, their integration into the highly symbolical backdrop of the room in combination with the bronze statuettes and paintings by Rafael, Andrea del Sarto, and Fra Bartolomeo created an extraordinarily delightful mise en scène.[13]

The third collection that impressed Augustus the Strong as a young man and which was the yardstick for every princely treasury in Europe, was the treasury gallery of the Hapsburg imperial family in Vienna. Access to the treasures of the highest European noble family was even more restrictively regulated than in Versailles. The secular treasury of the »Casa d'Austria« was installed between 1640 and 1642 in a long gallery in the Hofburg. The strict arrangement of the inestimable treasures assembled there corresponded to the Hapsburg court ceremony. 13 tall cupboards crowned by imperial eagles served to house the precious objects. Arranged systematically by groups of materials, the sequence began with exotic materials, continued with ivory turned objects and carvings leading to clocks and automata and then increased in material value to the overwhelming in the precious mounted vessels in gemstones from the collection of Rudolf II and highly valued rock crystal vessels. The climax was reached with the last cupboard with the imperial state jewellery and modern crown insignia. This imperial treasury in which old and modern treasury art was used in a theatrically impressive display to glorify supreme royal power, posed in spite of its hermetically sealed appearance the greatest challenge for princes of the Holy Roman Empire, among whom the Elector of Saxony ranked high.

The Sovereign-collector

Four years after he had completed his journey through Europe Friedrich I inherited the title of elector from his brother who died unexpectedly in 1694. Immediately afterwards Augustus the Strong began the systematic expansion of his treasury art collection as befitted his princely rank. When in 1697 he was elected King August II of Poland-Lithuania, this private collection rapidly took on royal dimensions. It is not so much the fact that Augustus the Strong started a collection of this kind that is remarkable. The astonishing thing is the number and quality of the objects collected. The collector, who personally had a great affinity to material beauty and artistic mastery, took advantage of this elite form of collecting to attain the top position among his princely rivals with the splendour, uniqueness and variety of his collection. Although today there are only isolated examples of late Baroque treasury art in a few historic collections, evidence from archives shows that a collection of pretiosa or treasury art was to be found at almost all the courts in Germany and beyond.[14] Among the royal art treasures from that period are works of sculptural jewellery made of pearls and precious stones, luxuriously mounted statuettes made of ivory and rare woods, magnificent clocks and complex showpieces. ›Galanterien‹ were also included. This was taken to mean smallscale luxury items: decorative dishes, small boxes, sal volatile and perfume bottles, seal holders, cases and writing implements. All these things could be closely scrutinised or held in the hand and thus sensually experienced.

One of the oldest datable works of the pretiosa collection of Augustus the Strong is a cabinet piece 15 cm in height which is a miniature display wall with consoles on which a tea service is exhibited (Ill. 15). The piece, which is now displayed in the Grünes Gewölbe, is crowned by an electoral cap. This clearly indicates that the small work of art was created between 1694 and 1697, as after that the Polish crown assumed the function of a symbol of power for Augustus the Strong.[15] What is above all unusual is the representation of an architectural motif. The choice of a theme cultivated a few years before in Versailles, almost 30 years before it was further developed in the Grünes Gewölbe shows that the collector devoted a great deal of thought over a long period of time to the best possible way of displaying such objects. Small cabinet pieces usually tell a story, which is explained by their function as a form of ›recreation‹ or to divert. The ingenious objects intended to stimulate the imagination gave their princely owner personal pleasure and served as a cultivated conversation piece in the presence of guests.

One of the great achievements of the art collector Augustus the Strong is the creation of a pretiosa cabinet over a period of more than four decades. The Elector-King created conditions at his court under which outstanding goldsmiths, among them above all the jewellery artist Johann Melchior Dinglinger, were able to produce unique works. Alongside this court jeweller, who was supported by his two younger brothers, the enamel painter Georg Friedrich and the ›gold worker‹ Georg Christoph Dinglinger, goldsmiths such as Gottfried Döring and above all Johann Heinrich Köhler and also the sculptors Paul Heermann and Balthasar Permoser were active in the service of

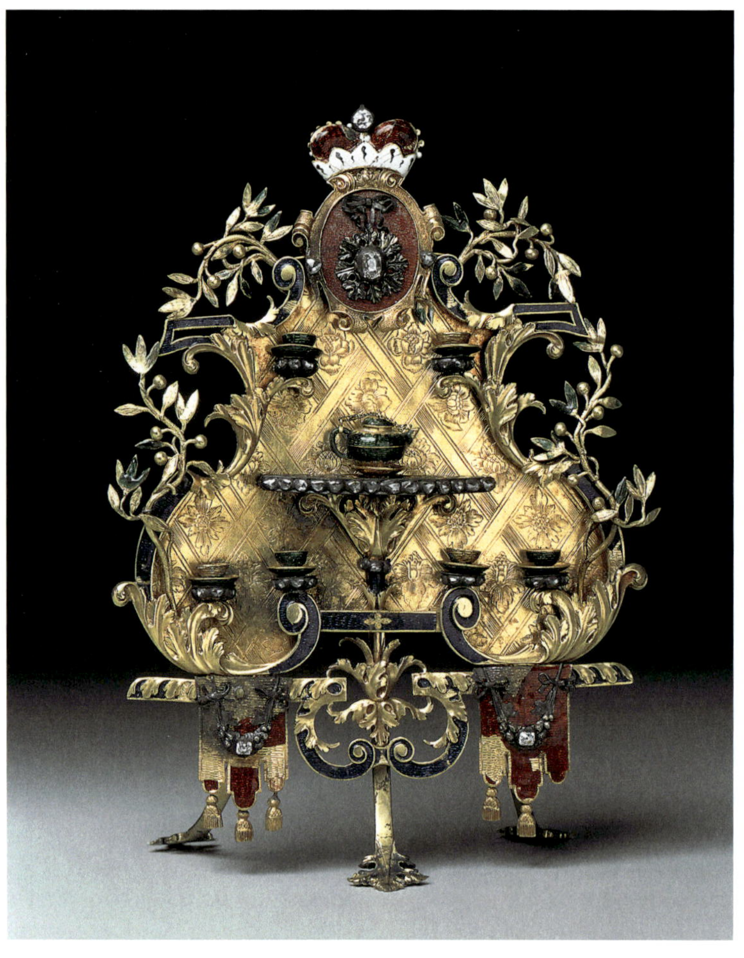

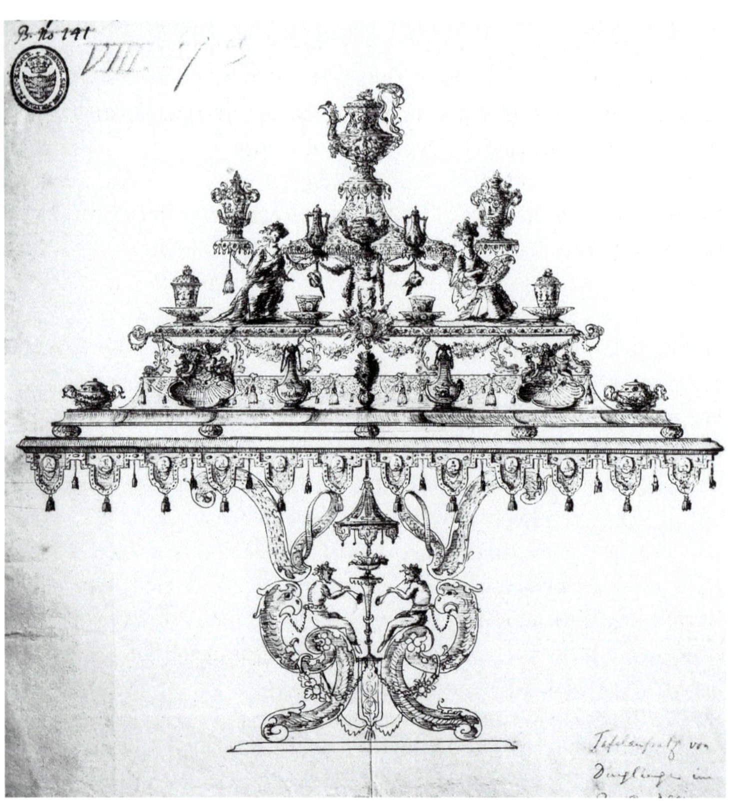

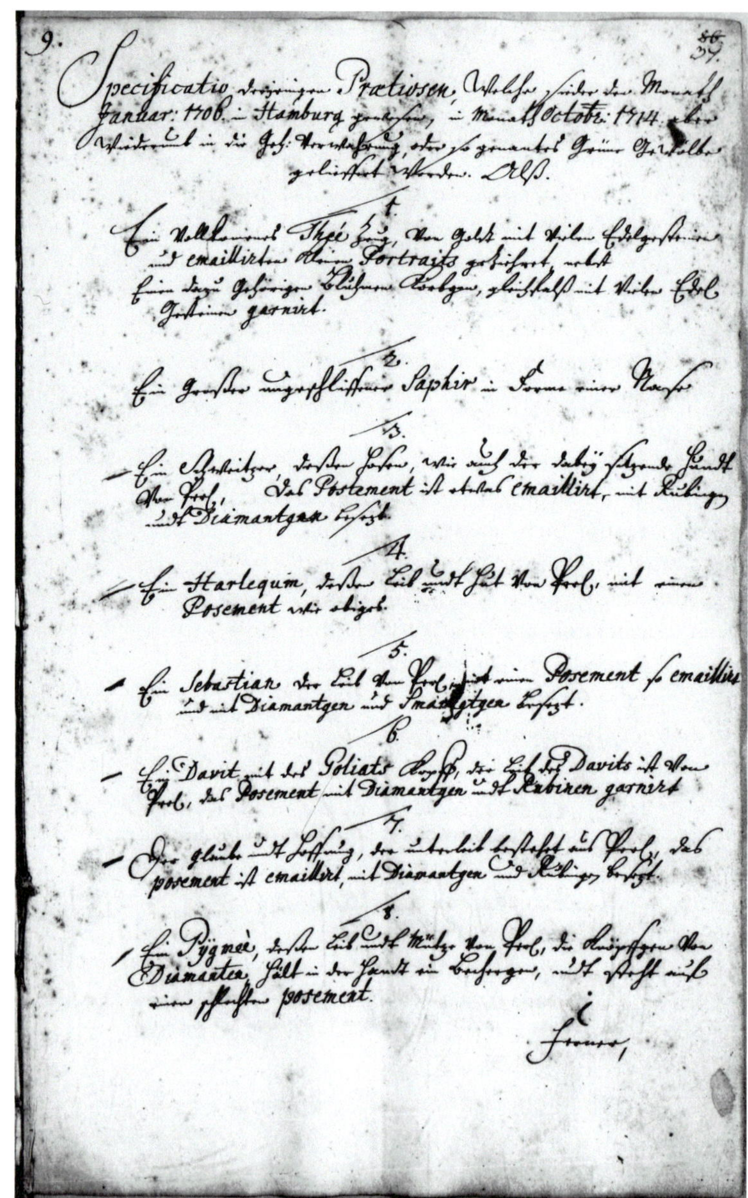

Ill. 15 Cabinet piece in the form of a display wall with a tea service
Dresden 1694–1697
Silver gilt, enamel, diamonds, glass paste
H. 14.8 cm, w. 10.7 cm, d. (with feet) c. 5 cm
Dresden, Grünes Gewölbe, Inv. no. VI 133

Ill. 16 The ›Golden Coffee Set‹ in its original condition
After 1701
Pen and ink drawing in sepia
H. 33.2 cm, w. 36.1 cm

Ill. 17 First page of the list with the Pretiosa mortgaged in Hamburg in January 1706

Saxony. Within a short time Dresden evolved into the treasury art centre of Baroque art.

After his coronation the treasury served to make Augustus the Strong's political successes shine all the more radiantly. On the occasion of his coronation in Cracow and his ceremonial entry into Warsaw the city of his new royal residence he presented himself not only with jewellery made of diamonds, rubies and sapphires. He also had impressive goldsmith works and rock crystal vessels brought to Poland from the Grünes Gewölbe and his private treasury »Kabinett«.

During the ceremonial coronation banquet and after, they were designed to document his majestic power. For the same reason at the beginning of winter 1701 he called on Dinglinger to bring the ›Golden Coffee Set‹ which had been completed a short time before from Dresden to Warsaw (Ill. 16). At that point, in the first phase of the Nordic War against Sweden, which brought the Elector-King great losses, he planned to use this cabinet piece, which was extravagant both in dimensions and splendour, to win over the Polish aristocracy. This first great masterpiece of Dinglinger and the ›Throne of the Grand Mogul‹, which followed by 1709 (Ill. 14) indisputably raised the pretiosa collection of the Elector-King to a leading position among comparable collections of the time. The same objective was behind the appointment of his highly paid court official, the Privy Counsellor Georg Freiherr von Rechenberg as his authorised art buyer in 1701. He was to scout for suitable objects at the Leipzig Fair, at that time the largest trading centre in Germany, on behalf of the collector, who was usually in Poland. With Rechenberg's help a treasury art collection came into being in a short space of time, some of which are on a list compiled in 1706, which has been preserved (Ill. 17).[16] 102 cabinet pieces, gems and pretiosa, among them the ›Golden Coffee Service‹, ›Diana bathing‹, 34 pearl figures and numerous inherited pieces of jewellery. These were mortgaged in Hamburg between 1706 and 1714 on account of the Nordic War.

The Precursors of the Grünes Gewölbe in the Dresden Palace

Before these objects were pawned they were kept in the »praetiose Kabinett« of the Elector-King. Their owner had arranged them »in einen express dazu Verferttigten Schranck mit eigener Hoher Handt rangiret« (in a specially made cupboard with his own hands) on one of his brief visits to Dresden in November 1704.[17] It was a private room in which to display a collection and was part of the appartments of the king. He always carried the key on his person. As the Privy Chamberlain responsible reported, Augustus the Strong »bißweilen gantz alleine, auch zum öfteren mit Damens und Cavalliers hinein gegangen, ihre Praetiosa besehen, unter weilen verändert und einige anders fassen« (went in there sometimes quite alone, often with ladies and gentlemen, to look at the pretiosa, which were sometimes changed around.[18]

The purchase in February 1709 of the ›Throne of the Grand Mogul‹ for the first time caused problems as far as space was concerned as the stage, which was 142 cm wide and 114 cm deep and which was displayed on a special table, was simply too big for a small cabinet room. The lack of space caused by this purchase meant that the focus was again on the traditional treasury of the Saxon electors, which was installed by Christian I towards 1586 as the ›Geheime Verwahrung‹ in the suite of rooms of the Grünes Gewölbe. It is quite clear that the presentation of the ›Throne of the Grand Mogul‹ in the Grünes Gewölbe was only a temporary solution.

After the pawned pretiosa had been redeemed in October 1714 and a further large work – the ›Golden Coffee Set‹ – also required space a suitable place had to be found for the meanwhile considerably expanded collection of the king. For practical reasons this should be adjacent to the private apartments of the Elector-King on the first floor of the royal palace. The royal apartments in which court protocol applied were situated in the south wing, the present day intermediate north wing. The southernmost room served as a parade bed-room. Adjacent to this were the private living quarters of the king in the first large room of the west wing which today houses the ›Hall of the Kunststücke‹ of the New Grünes Gewölbe (Ill. 18). Around 1714 this room was referred to as the »gallery« and there is a note on the floor plan that this is the room where the Elector-King took his meals privately. The room also had an alcove, a vaulted niche for a bed, which Augustus the Strong probably used as his actual bedchamber at that time. On the side of the Zwinger, where the Sophienstrasse is today, Augustus the Strong had access to the small ›cabinet de retirade‹, which probably contained his private writing-desk, from his dining room and bedchamber. The next room – a good 45 sq metre in size – which today is used as the ›Crystal cabinet‹ of the New Grünes Gewölbe, was remodelled in 1716 as a ›cabinet de glasse pour les joyaux du Roy‹. Baron Le Plat bought not only a large number of French bronzes, important paintings and porcelain in Paris in 1715 but also the entire fittings for a mirrored cabinet room. After the French mirrors had been fitted to the walls and the ceiling, Augustus the Strong had his large and precious jewellery placed in a smaller glass cabinet in this room. The gilded bronze consoles fitted in front of the mirrors were suitable for displaying rock crystal vessels or other stone cut works.[19]

However, the Jewel »Kabinett« was not big enough for the large treasury art collection. In 1715 Augustus the Strong allocated an additional room on the same floor, the marble room of ›Mother‹, a rarely used room in the suite of the electoral widow Anna Sophia. There he had »Praetiosa und Christall Geschirre« displayed on a newly made table. The collection of objects displayed in this »Praetieusen Cabinett« can be successfully reconstructed from a claim for damages as a result of a building accident which occurred in the night of 2 to 3 April 1716. Many objects were damaged and had to be repaired by the court jewellers. Most of the treasury art works repaired in this context are still to be found in the collection of the Grünes Gewölbe.[20]

It is typical of Augustus the Strong's behaviour as a collector that changes in the presentation of his treasury art collection were always triggered by considerable purchases. Thus, in 1715, when for the first time there was a suite of rooms available for these precious objects, he bought three splendid cabinet pieces from Dinglinger, among them the ›Children's bacchanalia‹ for 9,000 thalers, which appeared in the bill as »Dish with billy goa«. At the same time works by other artist-jewellers were bought at the Leipzig Fair and a number of the last works by the stonecutter Giovanni Battista Metellino, who had worked for Louis XIV, were brought from Milan to Dresden via an agent.

A Decision in Favour of the Grünes Gewölbe

Around 1715 the Dresden palace was for over one and a half decades the scene of a princely architectural vision. After a large part of the palace burnt down in the spring of 1701 the Elector-King who loved architecture was only too pleased to consider the possibilities of a completely new building. For financial and finally for political reasons Augustus the strong decided in spring 1717 to keep the outer shell and modernise the interiors. Before building work was quickly begun in February 1718, the King himself noted down ideas for the use of the rooms. Among these there is a plan for the first floor already used for the pretiosa collection, which records the ideas of the Elector-King in the form of a sketch for the installation of a mixture of a pretiosa collection and a Kunstkammer.[21] At that time the collections in Dresden were in flux. Shortly after 1720 many of the now existing collections evolved – the picture gallery, the Kupferstich-Kabinett (collection of prints and drawings), the porcelain collection, the collection of sculpture and the Mathematisch-Physikalischer Salon. The event which triggered the rebuilding of a prestigious royal residence was the marriage of Prince Friedrich August to the Archduchess Maria Josepha of Austria in 1719. In two respects these celebrations which fascinated the whole of Europe also affected the future development of the Grünes Gewölbe. On the one hand, Augustus the Strong had a silver buffet installed in one room of the newly created parade suite – the tower room – which was overflowing with a wealth of design (Ill. 19). The large collection of precious metal vessels was displayed to great effect on consoles against wooden painted walls.[22] In addition, the jewellery was modernised and added to considerably at great expense for the wedding festivities lasting several weeks. At the end of the celebratory year of 1719 the king personally arranged this part of his treasure in a newly created jewel cabinet in the future Hall of the Precious Objects of the Grünes Gewölbe (Ill. 20). After the palace was wholly used again as the royal residence and had to accommodate not only the monarch but also the heir to the throne and his family, the ›Geheime Verwahrung‹ in the Grünes Gewölbe was given a new function – and was finally opened to the public.[23]

The treasury, which was evolving into a museum, initially made a rather temporary impression, which was not satisfactory. Again, it was a large-scale purchase in February 1722 from Johann Melchior Dinglinger, which pointed the way in which the Grünes Gewölbe was to develop. In this year Augustus the Strong bought the majestic ›Obeliscus Augustalis‹, the cabinet piece with the cameo of a Roman emper-

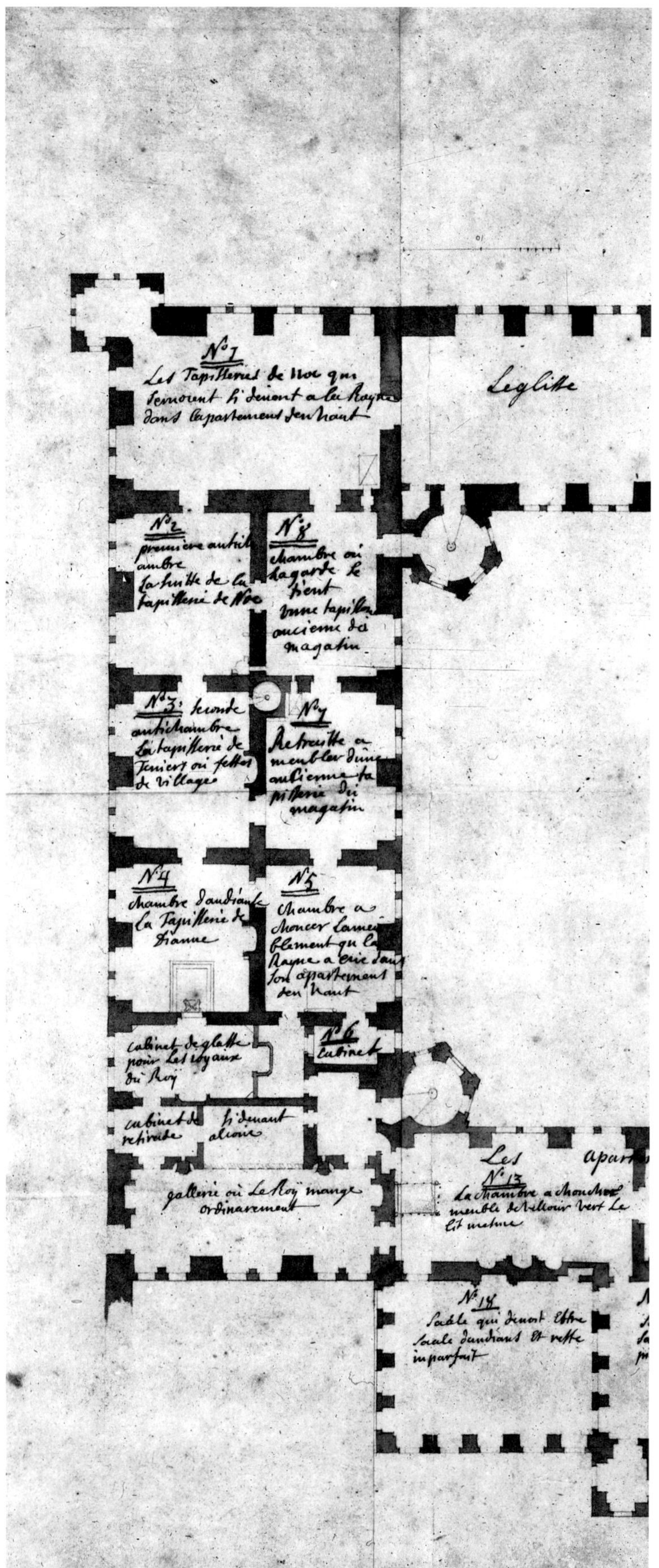

Ill. 18 Plan of the first floor of the west wing of the Dresden Palace
with notes on the furnishings of the rooms
Dresden, c. 1718

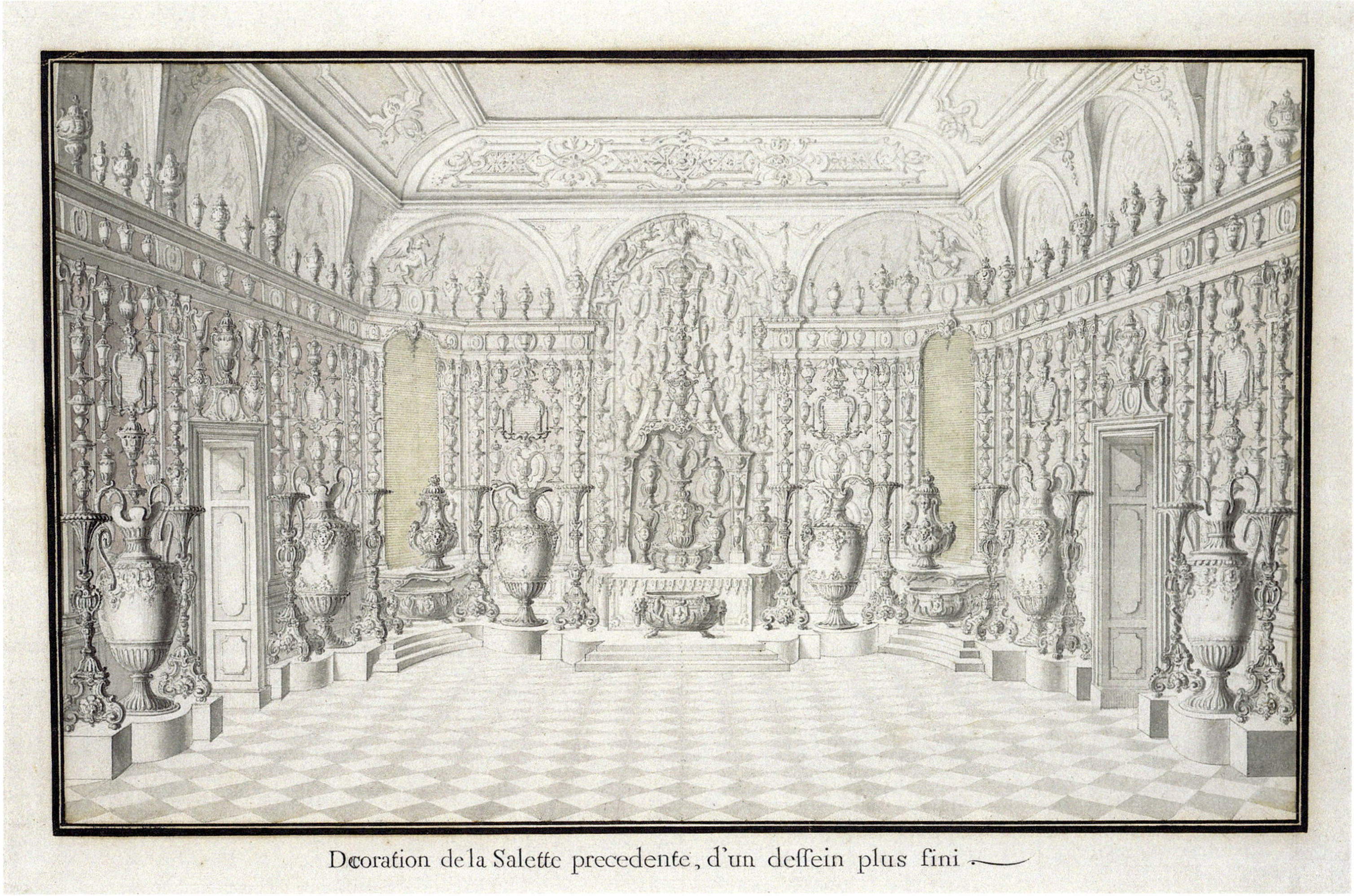

Ill. 19   View of the tower room with the silver buffet
          Presumably Zacharias Longuelune
          Pencil, brush, gouache
          H. 30.2 cm, w. 46.7 cm,
          Dresden, Kupferstich-Kabinett, Inv. no. C 6754

Ill. 20   Draft design of a jewel cabinet, c. 1719, original drawing
          burnt in 1945 in the Grünes Gewölbe

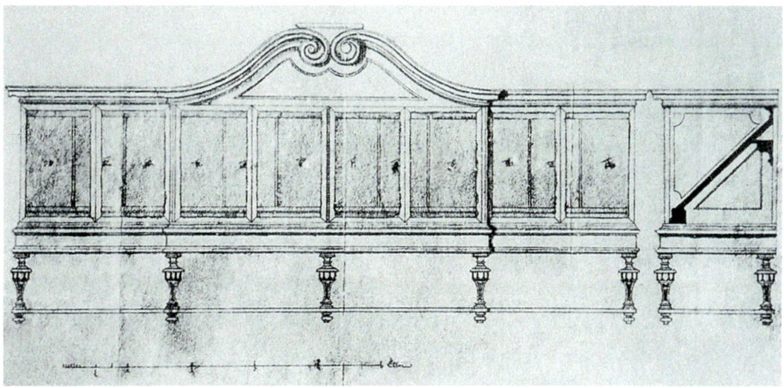

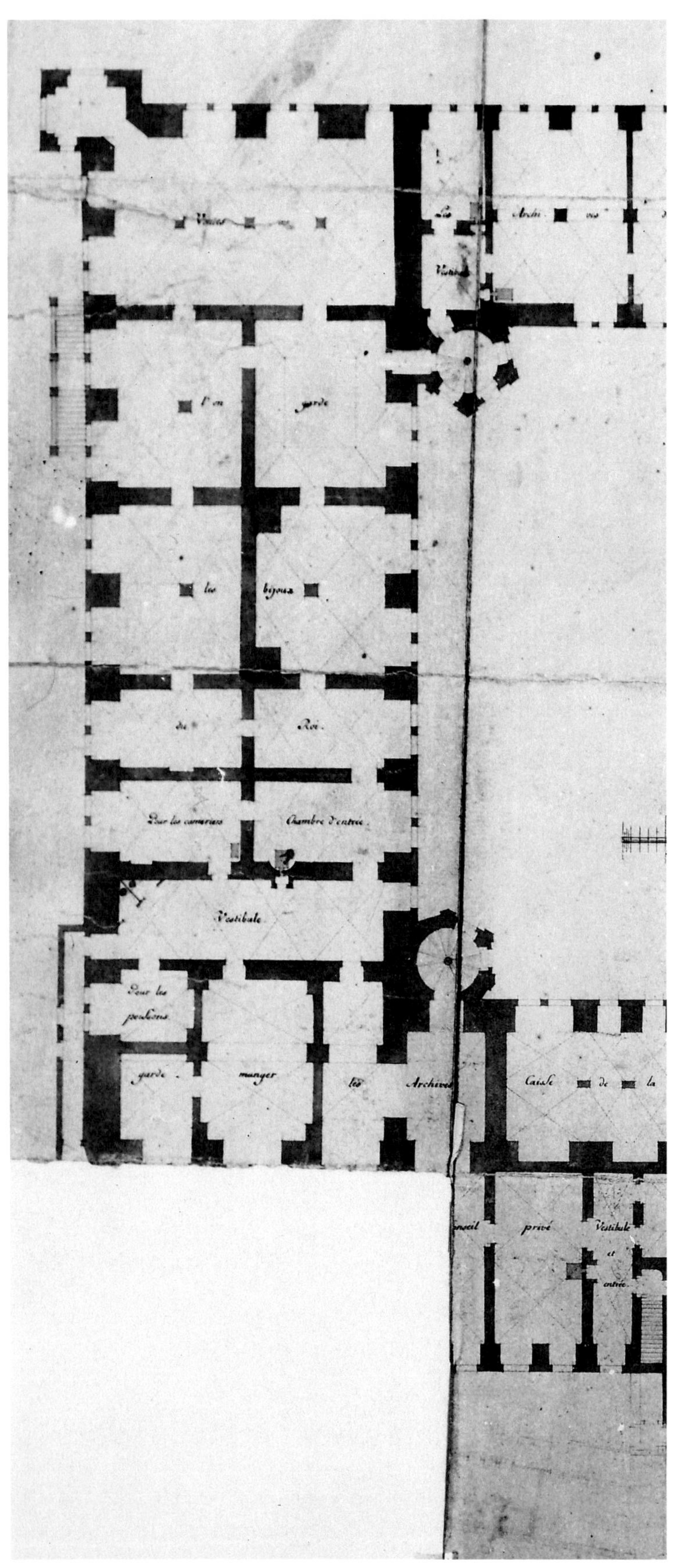

Ill. 21   Plan of the Royal Palace in the mid-18ᵗʰ century

or and a pair of parade bowls with horses saddled in the Polish fashion, 73 unmounted precious stone dishes in oriental agates, carnelians and garnets from Dinglinger.[24] Together with other precious objects there were 120 »geschnittene Schalen und andere Curiosa« (cut bowls and other curiosities), highly colourful material for an eye-catching presentation, which have now again taken up their place on two walls in the Pretiosa Room.

If the ›Golden Coffee Set‹ in 1701 marked the beginning of an at that time unrivalled collection, the ›Obeliscus Augustalis‹ of 1722 stands for the opening up of this collection of treasury art to visitors and expanded thoughtfully and sensitively to include inherited objects. In June 1723 work began to convert the rooms previously allotted to the ›Geheime Verwahrung‹ – the Silver Gilt Room and the Hall of the Precious Objects with the Corner Cabinet – into the future treasury museum. In June 1724 Monsieur de Prohengue was one of the first guests to visit the still unfinished display rooms. The Privy Chamberlain Starcke responsible for the Grünes Gewölbe reports in a letter to Augustus the Strong: »(…) habe ich ihn in das Grüne Gewölbe geführet und so wohl alle Praetiosen und Cabinetstücke, alß auch besonders den gantzen Königl. Schmuck gezeiget, worüber er sehr vorwundert war, und zum öfftern sagte, daß er Zuvor viel schon darvon gehöret, sich aber doch nicht einbilden können, daß alles so Subberbe, und in der allergrösten Magnificence undt Vollkommenheit wär, alß er es nun selbst sähe (…).« (I led him into the Grünes Gewölbe and showed him all the pretiosa and cabinet pieces; he said several times that he had heard a great deal about it, but had never imagined that everything would be so superb and of such magnificence and perfection, as he now saw it).[25] The Elector-King might well be pleased with these comments. It would have made him more pleased if he had read the verdict of King Friedrich Wilhelm I after he had seen the jewellery of his Saxon rival in the new Jewel Room of the Grünes Gewölbe. The King of Prussia wrote laconically to his friend, Prince Leopold zu Anhalt-Dessau in his own particular style: »(…) was das grüne gewelbe ist cella ebl(o) ist meine(n) vatter seine Juvehlen ist nits dagegen (…).« (my father's jewels are nothing compared with this).[26]

The Development from a Public Treasury to a Museum 1732 – 1942

The Grünes Gewölbe had passed the test. Augustus the Strong had installed it as a political instrument, for the demonstration of extravagant wealth and as a secure place for the safe keeping of the family treasures. In December 1732 he appointed two administrative officials alongside the already existing privy chamberlains whose task it was to guide the crowds of curious visitors of high social standing in small groups through the unimaginably splendid collection. In the instructions of their contract of employment Augustus the Strong laid down what he wanted the tour to be like: (English paraphrase) »Although We should permit tourists and local people to see the precious objects in the Grünes Gewölbe, we should ensure that not anybody and not too many people at any one time are shown around. In order that the »Inspectors« should know how to proceed, they should report anybody who requests to see the collection to the senior chamberlain, and in his absence to the chamberlain, and if both are absent to the majordomo, and in his absence to the governor. No-one else is authorised to permit access to the collection«.[27] Three months later the founder of the collection died in Warsaw, the city of his official royal palace in Poland.

The Grünes Gewölbe had been created for just such a moment. It was to guarantee his only legitimate son and heir to the title of the Saxon elector the best chance of following in the office of elected king of Poland and Grand Duke of Lithuania. Augustus III who was above all interested in paintings and the graphic arts, profited longest from the impact of the well-ordered and richly filled treasury museum. Although he was not so fascinated by small-scale treasury works, he did complete the collection with important purchases from the estate of the court jeweller Johann Melchior Dinglinger, who died in 1731. Other works were also added to the collection. Augustus III above all increased the jewellery, among other things by purchasing the »green diamond«, the value of which exceeded that of all the works by Dinglinger. (Ill. 22) Augustus the Strong's great achievement had been to keep the treasures together. The detailed inventories in which he had all the rooms individually listed topographically (with the exception of the Ivory Room) made an important contribution to this end. They served as a guideline for the new installation of the Grünes Gewölbe.

The perils to which the treasury museum was exposed in the 18th century appeared for the first time in summer 1744 with the beginning of the Second Silesian War. The most precious part of the collection, the jewellery, was packed up to be evacuated to the Fortress of Königstein where it would be safe from the invading troops. On 29 August 1756 the worst fears were fulfilled. In the first days of the Seven Years' War Prussian troops began to occupy Saxony. When they entered Dresden on 9 September without encountering any resistance, the display cabinets of the Jewel Room were already empty and their contents already in Poland. This meant the end of the Grünes Gewölbe as created by Augustus the Strong and August III in its traditional form.

In September 1759 the Prussian occupation force had to surrender Dresden to their imperial enemies. Immediately, the works of treasury art were packed up. The most precious parts of the collection that remained were taken to the Fortress of Königstein. The other parts were protected in the cellars of the palace against further risks of war.[28] Not a minute too soon, for in the summer of 1760 the Prussians laid siege to Dresden using heavy artillery, to which large parts of Baroque Dresden fell victim. At the beginning of 1758 a box with pure gold and 62 boxes with works in silver-gilt and ungilded silver were taken from the Grünes Gewölbe and pawned in Amsterdam at the behest of Queen Maria Josepha.[29] It was the entire collection of the White Silver Room and the Silver Gilt Room, altogether 37 kilograms of gold vessels and 3,235 kilograms of silver. Very little finally returned to the treasury. With the exception of three silver sculptures the ungilded silver was melted down in 1772 in the Dresden Mint and turned into thalers.[30] Thus, the collection of the White Silver Room disappeared and only roughly a third of the original collection of the Silver Gilt Room was preserved. The losses of that time are still visible. Until the beginning of the 20th century this was the biggest loss of substance and the only one that could not be compensated for.

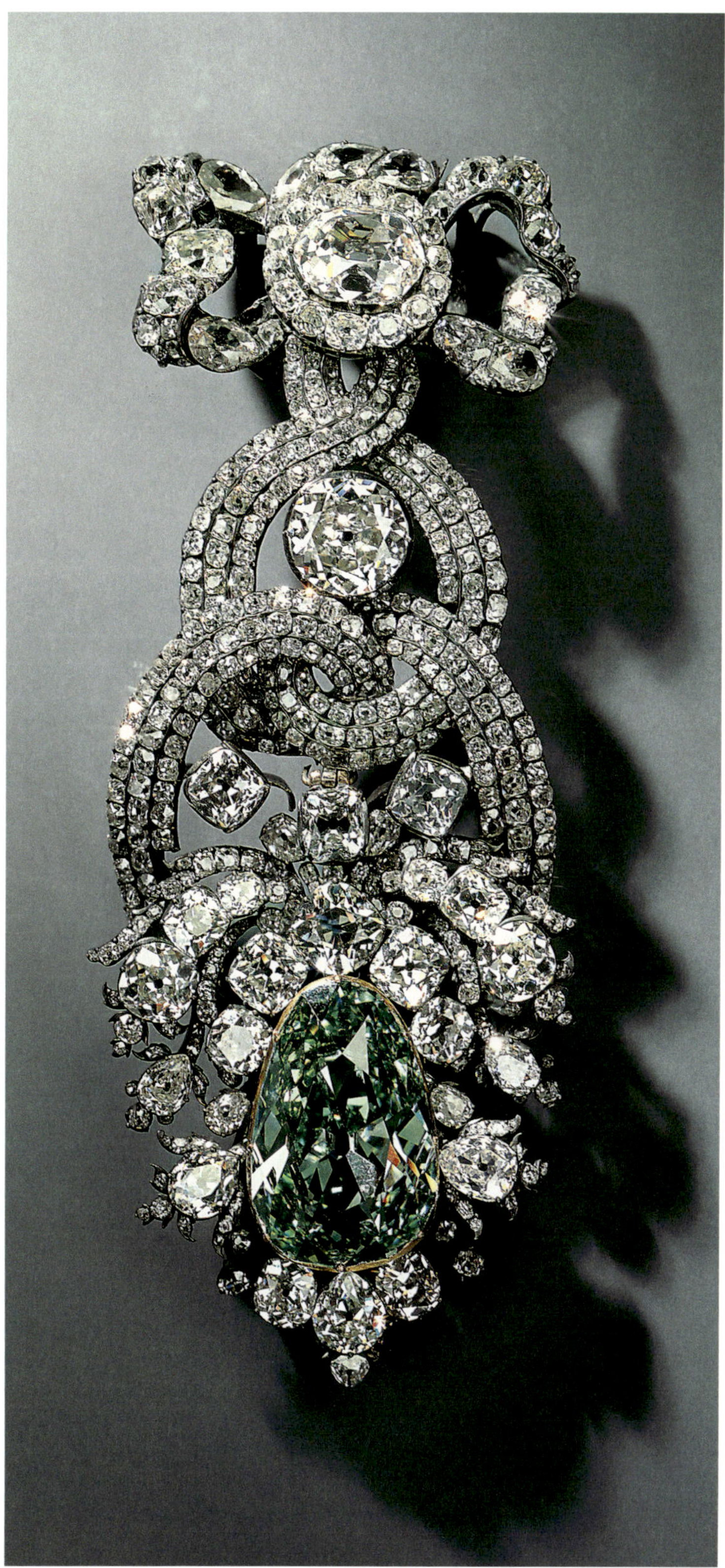

Ill. 22 Hat brim with the ›Dresden green diamond‹ from the brilliant cut diamond garniture
Franz Michael Diespach, Dresden/Prague 1796,
using parts by Jean Jacques Pallard, Vienna 1746
Diamonds, silver, gold, h. 14.1 cm, w. 5 cm
Dresden, Grünes Gewölbe, Inv. no. VIII 30

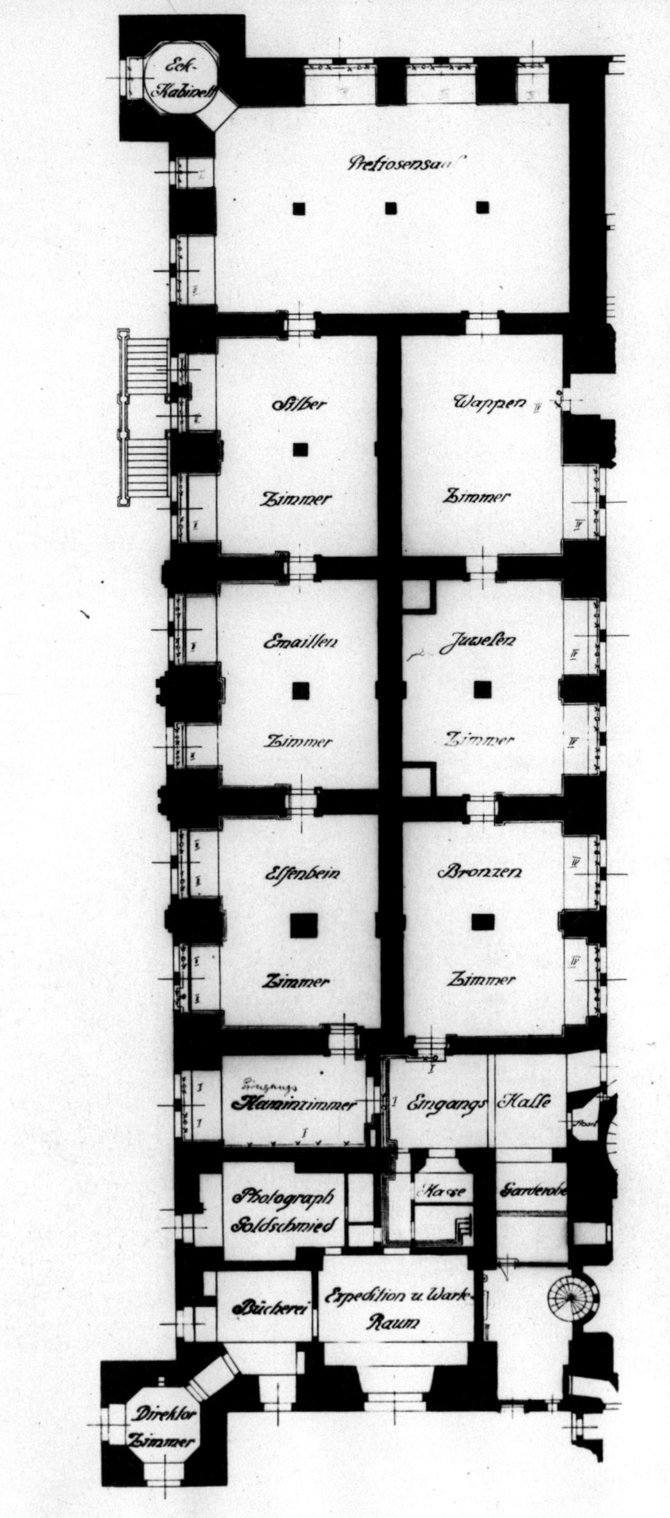

Ill. 23   Plan of the Grünes Gewölbe, 1913

The next important event took place in 1831/32. At that time the Grünes Gewölbe was declared by law to be the inalienable possession of the Crown and received roughly a further five hundred objects from the dissolution of the Kunstkammer. After 270 years this oldest collecting institution in Dresden with its wealth of traditions was abandoned as a result of a decision of the parliament. The same fate might easily have threatened the Grünes Gewölbe in the preceding decades. The dramatic defeat in the Napoleonic Wars again meant that the collection was banished to the Fortress of Königstein several times over. In 1817 a severe case of theft shook the reputation of the collection. Above all, the Enlightenment, which abhorred these »princely baubles«, and neo-classicism which tolerated no other styles were the worst enemies of almost all the collections of treasury art of the Baroque period. They were dissolved, sold, melted down. The new acquisitions which made up almost one sixth of the original collection, were able to fill the gaps on the consoles but they fitted only imperfectly into the Baroque picture.

From the middle of the 19th century visiting patterns to the treasury also changed. As a result of its growing popularity the tradition of the expensive guided tours in small groups was discontinued and visitors could walk round as they pleased. For this purpose the display walls with the freely accessible objects standing on them had to be protected by high small-mesh grilles. This aesthetically somewhat dubious measure in no way dampened the growing enthusiasm of the visitors. In the historicist period the playful pretiosa were again the focus of visitors interested in art. Roughly at the same time towards 1860 the deteriorating state of the rooms became a problem. Unheated and with only inadequate lighting the treasures could only be seen well in summer. In autumn and winter visitors moved through cool, semi-dark rooms. This also caused damage.

When the west wing of the Dresden royal palace was given a new façade between 1890 and 1892, considerable changes also took place in the Grünes Gewölbe. These not only affected the windows to the west and north but also the Ivory Room and the Corner Cabinet. The former was eaten away by woodworm so that the wall panelling had to be completely replaced and it was painted in more subdued colours in keeping with the times. The Corner Cabinet was also thoroughly renovated and restored.

With the directorship of Jean Louis Sponsel (1908 – 1923) the works of art began to dominate the theatrical Baroque arrangement. From 1910 display cabinets were built into the deep window-recesses in suitable rooms, which made it possible to view particular works of art in the collection independently of the mirrored walls. In September 1912 Sponsel received authorisation to expand the exhibition space which dated from 1729. The changes were radical. Construction work was started in June 1913. The suite, which had hitherto consisted of eight rooms now got a ninth room in the form of the Kaminzimmer. At the same time the Bronze Room and the Ivory Room were doubled in size (Ill. 23) and the panelling of the wooden arches was removed to improve the lighting. When the museum opened to the public at the end of January 1914, it had under floor heating, which was intended to make winter visiting a more pleasant experience, electric light in the rooms and much more space for the works of art. However, the atmosphere of the

Baroque treasury had changed. In the following years, which were already affected by the First World War, Sponsel continued his modernisation programme. Electric lighting was installed in the jewel display cases and the arrangement was changed so that the focus fell on the most interesting works.

This modernised ensemble remained in place until 1938. In the course of the »Sudeten crisis« the first works of art were removed in 1938. In 1939, five days before the invasion of Poland, almost all the works of the Grünes Gewölbe followed suit (Ill. 24). Carefully packed in boxes they were stored in the cellar of the Royal Palace where they were safe in a conservational sense and safe from bombs. By June 1942 the bombing of German cities had become so destructive that it was decided to evacuate the transportable collection in a specially fitted out casemate in the Fortress of Königstein. There it remained until 14 May 1945. The treasures of the Grünes Gewölbe were seized by the spoils of war commission of the Red Army and taken to the Soviet Union for 14 years. The baroque display rooms in the Royal Palace fell victim to war damage. In the night of 13 to 14 February, 1945 the Royal Palace was destroyed (Ill. 25). The rooms facing the courtyard of the palace, the Room of Bronzes, the Jewel Room and the Coats of Arms Room were consumed with their furnishings in the conflagration. The other rooms survived the demise of the old part of Dresden thanks to the iron doors and iron shutters. There was considerable damage to the Silver Gilt Room but part of the original substance was spared.

From 1945 to 1999 the idea of rebuilding the historic Grünes Gewölbe in its original form grew stronger and stronger. After the return of the art treasures from the Soviet Union in the year 1958 (Ill. 26) the resurrection of its former splendour was no longer a utopian dream. The permanent exhibition of the treasury museum (Ill. 27) in the Albertinum designed in 1974 by Joachim Menzhausen pointed the way, which in the last few years was completed. In 2004 a modern treasury, the New Grünes Gewölbe was created, in which the focus is on individual works of art in all their beauty, magic and opulence (Ill. 28). The large numbers of visitors can view the splendour of the details in antireflective glass cabinets with optimum lighting in an atmosphere conducive both to a pleasant visit and to the well-being of the exhibits. It is astonishing how extensive a treasury collection could have been compiled by Augustus the Strong with inherited objects and objects which he himself acquired. What is unique, moreover, is that the Elector-King had them displayed in a magnificent suite of rooms. It is, however, nothing short of a cultural and historical miracle that this collection has managed to survive for almost three centuries despite crises and wars and that its famous architectural frame could be restored despite

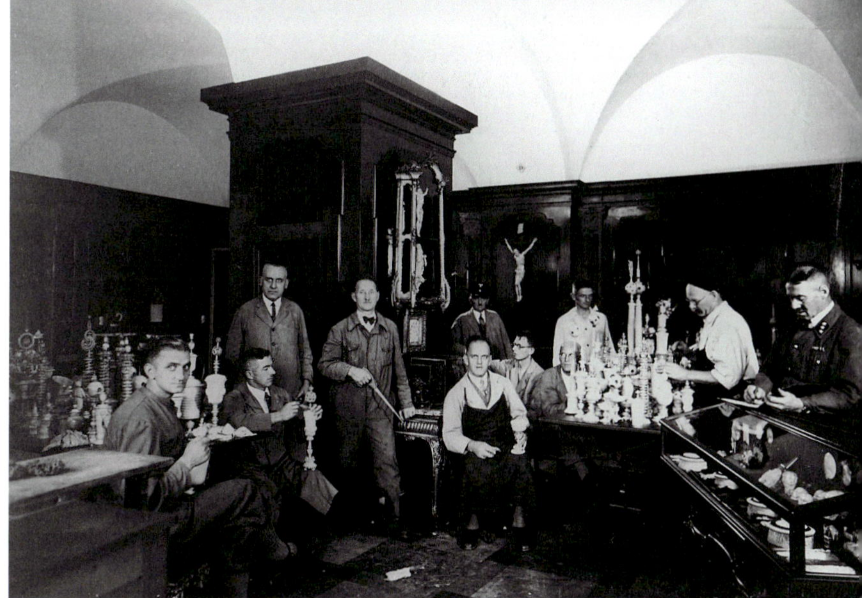

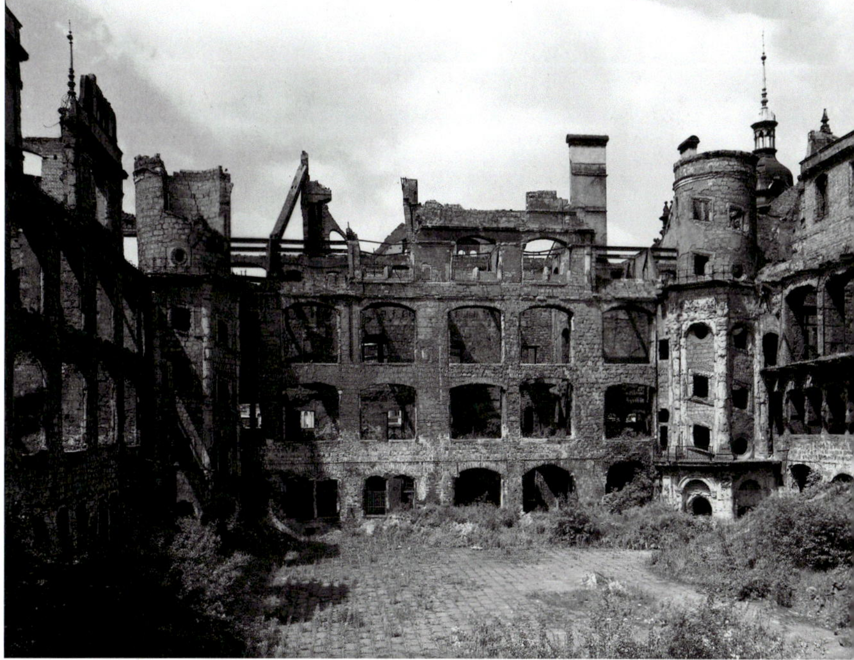

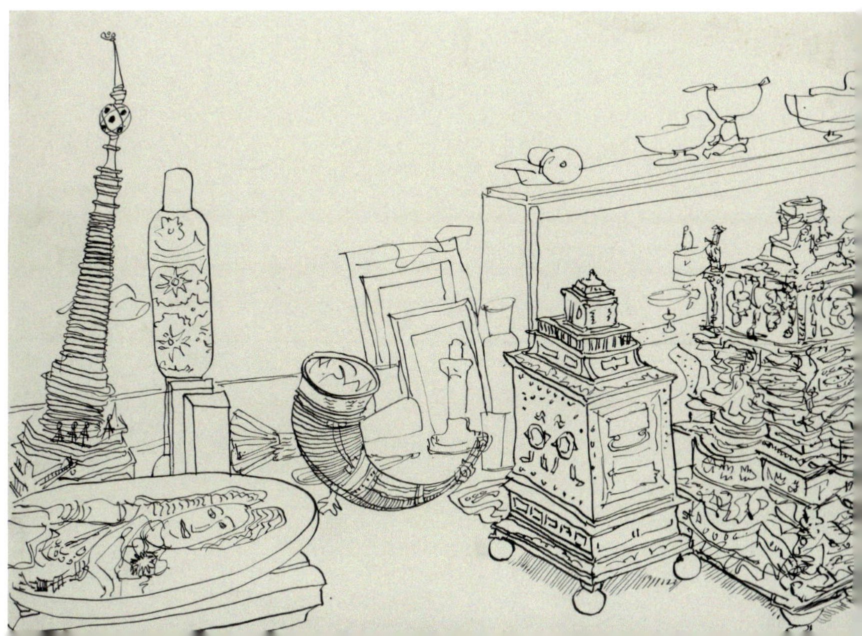

Ill. 24 Packing the objects of the Grünes Gewölbe, September 1938

Ill. 25 Great Courtyard of the Dresden Palace, 1957

Ill. 26 Group of works from the Grünes Gewölbe after unpacking, 1958/59
     Ernst Hassebrauk
     Dresden, Kupferstich-Kabinett, Inv. no. 1988 – 807

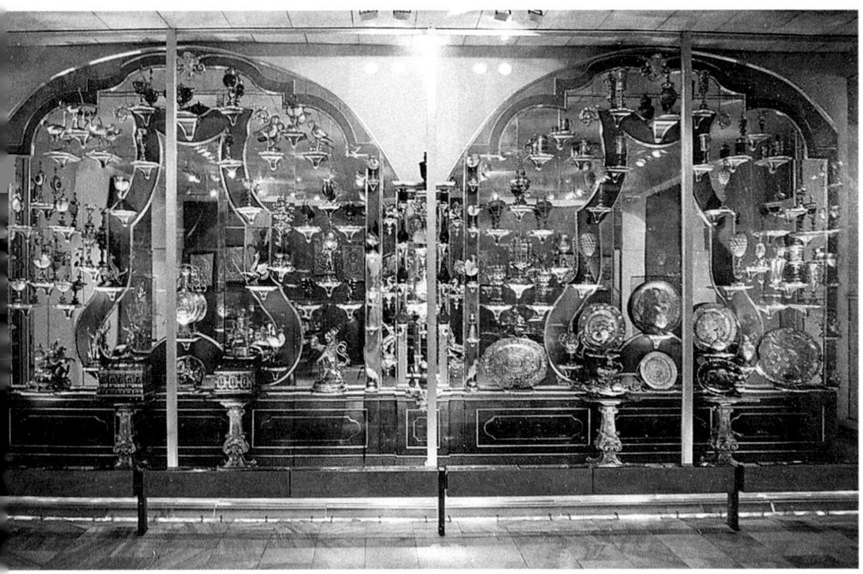

the extensive damage. Today, it is again possible to experience the Grünes Gewölbe as the young philosopher Arthur Schopenhauer described it in 1804: »Auch jetzt nachdem ich so viele Schatzkammern gesehen habe, finde ich doch noch dass es alle an Reichthum weit übertrifft. Man glaubt sich in einen Feen-Palast versetzt, u. wird von der unendlichen Pracht geblendet, wenn man die glänzenden Zimmer betritt, in denen sich die kostbaren goldenen Gefäße u. Spielwercke von Diamanten, an den Spiegelwänden vervielfachen.«[31] (Even now after I have seen so many treasuries, I find that it far surpasses all others in opulence. One feels transported to a fairy palace and is dazzled by the infinite splendour on entering the glittering rooms in which the precious golden vessels and diamond playthings are multiplied in the mirrored walls …)

DS

1 Johann Georg Keyßler, *Schweiz, Italien und Lothringen, worinnen der Zustand und das Merkwürdigste dieser Länder beschrieben…, Neue und vermehrte Auflage,* Hanover 1751, p. 1299.

2 Keyßler 1751, p. 1299.

3 Dirk Syndram, *Die Schatzkammer Augusts des Starken. Von der Pretiosensammlung zum Grünen Gewölbe,* Leipzig 1999, p. 172.

4 Under Augustus the Strong the so-called »Oraculum«, an automaton in the form of a female bust, which could roll its eyes and murmur something incomprehensible stood in the middle of the room. This gave the Coats of Arms Room an almost theatrical character. Viz. Syndram 1999, p. 201.

5 Gerald Heres, *Dresdener Kunstsammlungen im 18. Jahrhundert,* Leipzig 1991, p. 64.

6 Inventarium über dasjenige Massiv Goldtene, Vergoldtete Silberne und weiss Silberne Geschirre, so Sich bey dem Königl: Grünen Gewölbe befindet. 1723, Staatliche Kunstsammlungen Dresden, Inventories no. 21

7 Duke Friedrich August was in Paris from 24 June to 26 September 1687 and from 20 May to 7 November 1688. During his first stay he visited Versailles nine times. He was frequently able to admire the French king in all his splendour. During his second stay, which was overshadowed by the outbreak of the Palatinate Wars of Succession, he was in Versailles only seven times and only twice met Louis XIV. Cf. Katrin Keller (ed.), »Mein Herr befindet sich gottlob gesund und wohl«. *Sächsische Prinzen auf Reisen,* Leipzig 1994.

8 Friedrich August O'Byrn, *Die Hofsilberkammer und die Hof-Kellerei zu Dresden,* Dresden 1880, p. 91–93.

9 Stéphane Castelluccio, *Les Collections royales d'objets d'art de François Ier à la Révolution,* Paris 2002, pp. 95–97, P. Verlet, *Les gemmes du Dauphin,* in: Art de France, III, 1963, p. 138.

10 Verlet 1963, p. 139.

11 Castelluccio 2002, pp. 104–107, Ill. p. 106.

12 Castelluccio 2002, pp. 112–115.

13 Detlef Heikamp, *Zur Geschichte der Uffizien-Tribuna und der Kunstschränke in Florenz und Deutschland,* in: Zeitschrift für Kunstgeschichte, Vol. 26, 1963, pp. 200–205.

14 The most important surviving examples of princely treasury art today are to be found in museums in Brunswick, Florence, Kassel, Copenhagen, Munich, St Petersburg and Vienna.

15 Dirk Syndram, *Schatzkunst der Renaissance und des Barock. Das Grüne Gewölbe zu Dresden,* Munich/Berlin 2004, p. 91.

16 Syndram 1999, p. 72, 82f.

17 Syndram 1999, p. 76.

18 Syndram 1999, p. 76.

19 Syndram 1999, pp. 116–121.

20 Syndram 1999, pp. 107–115.

21 Heres 1991, p. 41f., Syndram 1999, p. 125.

22 Syndram 1999, pp. 125–129.

23 Iccander (Johann Christian Crell) in a publication presumably from 1772, *Das fast auf dem höchsten Gipfel seiner Vollkommenheit und Glückseligkeit prangende Königliche Dreßden in Meissen, Oder ICCANDERS Kurtze doch deutliche Beschreibung … Die aufs neue übersehen, revidiret, corrigiret und mit einem starcken Zusatz durch und durch bis aufs Jahr 1723. vermehret,* 2. Auflage, Leipzig 1723, was the first to write on the coming treasury museum: »Unter Ihrer Maj. der Königin Zimmer ist das grüne Gewölbe, in welchem der Landes=Fürst iederzeit den grössten Schatz und Vorrath von denen pretieusesten Curiositäten und sinn-reichesten Erfindungen derer berühmtesten Künstler Europä verwahren lässet, deren Beschreibung kein Mensch nach Vermögen dar zuthun capable; und muß sich derjenige Ausländer glücklich schätzen, welcher in diesem so genannten grünen Gewölbe die von vielen Churfürsten mit unsäglichen Kosten und Mühe zusammen gebrachten Kunst=Wercke und pretieuse Wunder=Stücke anschauen zu können, Erlaubniß bekommen. Die

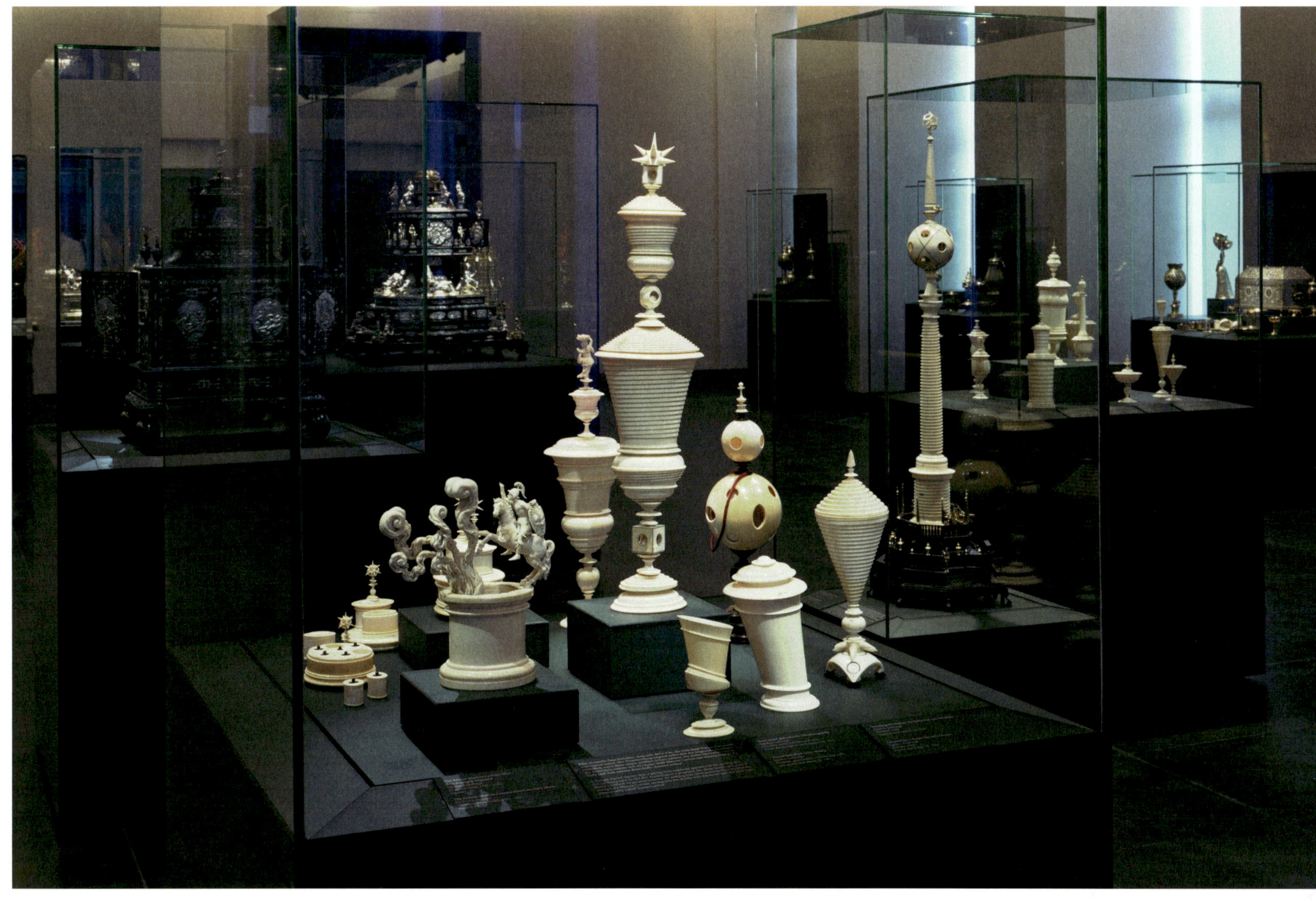

Ill. 28   View of a room, New Grünes Gewölbe, Hall of the Kunststücke

Direktion und Auffsicht über diese Königlichen Pretiositäten hat der Herr Accis-Rath und Geh. Cämmerier, Gottfried Lange.« (p. 27).

24   Syndram 1999, p. 139f.

25   SächsHStA Dresden, Loc. 354, Acta Chatoullen-Sache betr. 1718–1728, 1742–1746, vol. I, fol. 276v.

26   *Briefe König Friedrich Wilhelms I. an den Fürsten Leopold zu Anhalt-Dessau*, bearb. von O. Krauske, Berlin 1905, no. 470.

27   SächsHStA Dresden, Geheimes Kabinett, Loc. 896, Sachen das Grüne Gewölbe, Deßen Revision, und denen geheimen Cämmerieren Starcke und Marchen (...) betr. Ao. 1687–1704 seg., fol. 76r–78r.

28   Ulli Arnold, *Der historische Bestandsverlust an Silber im Jahre 1772. Ein Beitrag zur Geschichte der Schatzkammersammlung ›Grünes Gewölbe‹*, in: Jahrbuch der Staatlichen Kunstsammlungen Dresden, vol. 21, 1989/1990, p. 59.

29   See on this and on the further development of the pawning of the silver: Arnold 1989/1990, p. 59.
An itemised list giving the weights of the precious metals is to be found in: SächsHStA Dresden, Geheimes Kabinett, Loc. 896, Sachen das Grüne Gewölbe, Deßen Revision, und denen geheimen Cämmerieren Starcke und Marchen ... betr. Ao. 1697–1704 seq., fol. 94i–k.

30   Older inventories of the Staatl. Kunstsammlungen no. 14, Journal 1733–1782, fol. 220r.
On 4 August 1772 the boxes of silver, »qui sont arrivé d'Hollande«, were checked and compared with the inventories by the court official Leschke.

31   Arthur Schopenhauer, *(Reisejournal IV) Juni–August 1804*, manuscript: Schopenhauer-Archiv, Frankfurt a.M. IX, 4. I should like to thank Herr Jochen Stollberg for drawing my attention to this quotation.

Entrance Vault

It was only with the newly planned Grünes Gewölbe in the 1990s that the south part of the west wing was given its present form and transformed into a large vaulted hall. This »Vorgewölbe«, a name that goes back to the 18th century, now houses a special part of the collections of the Grünes Gewölbe.

In 1727 Augustus the Strong had an existing group of small rooms in this part of the palace allotted to the treasury museum as storage space. The group of rooms had for more than 270 years been part of the palace kitchen where stores were kept. Roughly where today the late Gothic drinking horns called »griffon's claws« are displayed, there was the water bowl of the »Fisch Zehr Garten« where live fish were kept before they were cooked. There was a small building attached to the façade of the west wing which was roughly on the spot where the south west late nineteenth century corner tower stood. This was the »Scheuer Bude« or scullery where the dishes were washed. The »Passage« or corridor was accessible by a door from the Great Palace Courtyard of the palace. The door, which still exists at the same spot, was used as the main entrance to the treasury museum from 1729 to 1942. The passage separated the publicly accessible part of the Grünes Gewölbe from the storage area, the »stores« which were kept in the large »storage vault«, the »side vault« and the »last vault«. Initially, these rooms took over the function of the ›Geheime Verwahrung‹, the state treasury, in which important archives and valuable goods were kept. There were cupboards in these rooms, some of them built-in cupboards, and the rooms were lit by chandeliers. Stoves made it possible to work here even when it was cold. The inventory of the »stores« drawn up in 1733 mentions 149 pieces of the most varied kind, which were of some value but which could not be integrated into the structure of the Baroque collection. Towards the end of the 18th century these rooms were more and more neglected, until in 1877 the Coin Cabinet moved into this rather confined part of the palace. After this museum had moved to the administrative building the plan to re-install functional rooms for the Grünes Gewölbe in this part of the west wing could be implemented. Until the Second World War the ticket office and cloakroom, the »Expedition« (mail office) and the wardens' office, the goldsmiths' restoration room, the museum library and the director's room – in the southwest tower – were situated here.

Today the 280 sq. metre Entrance Vault serves as a treasury-like introduction to the historic Grünes Gewölbe. It houses the numerically small but important collection of treasury art of the Middle Ages and the early Renaissance. At the same time it houses the precious collection of enamel works from Limoges. Commemorative artifacts from the Saxon electoral house, dating to the period of the Reformation and characterized by Lutheran piety, are shown in the southwest tower. The passage has regained its original function as a foyer for visitors to the Baroque treasury. In the place of the paintings of valuable horses and Polish allies originally hung on the walls there are now large-format photographs as a reminder of the pre-war condition of the Grünes Gewölbe.

DS

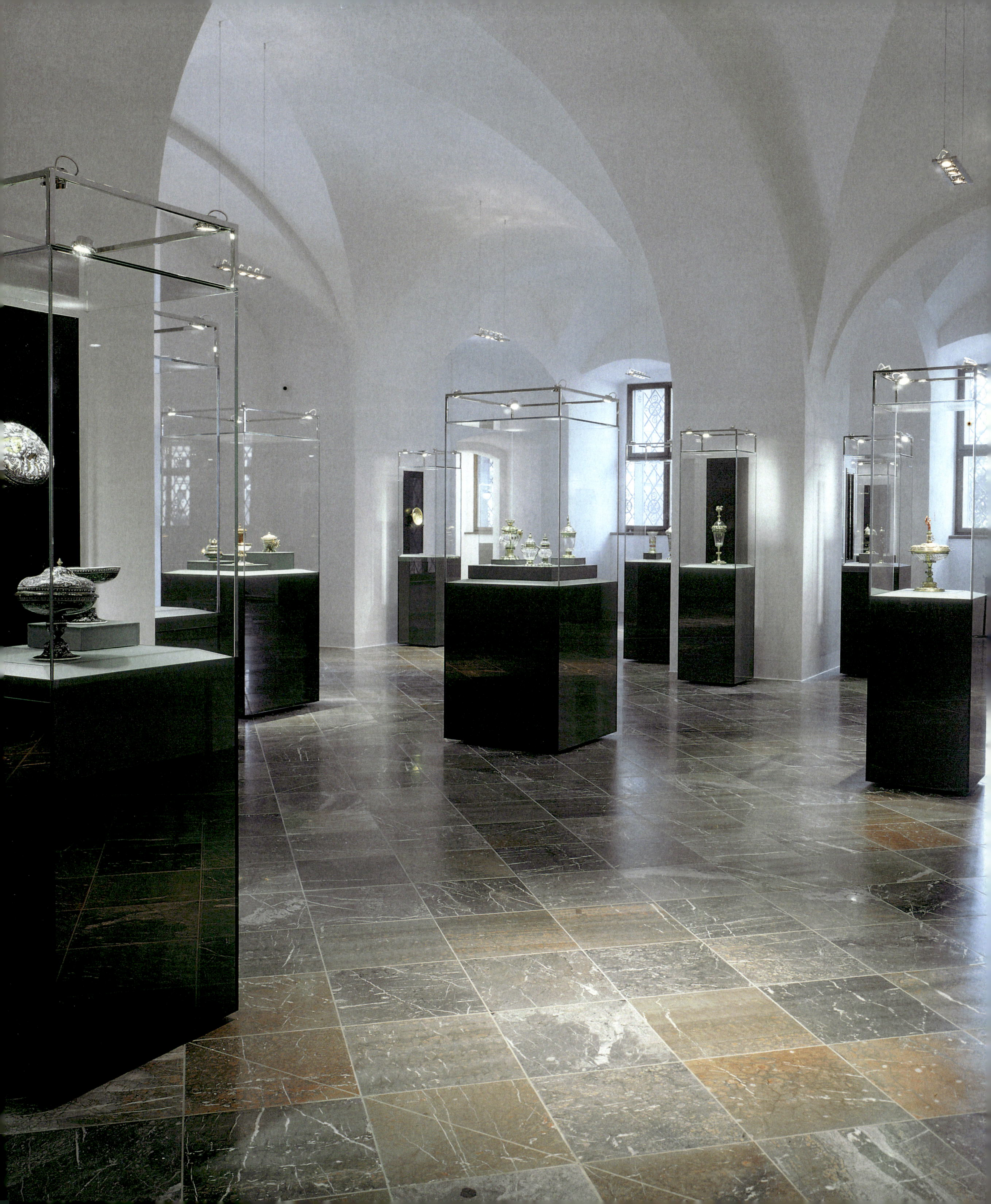

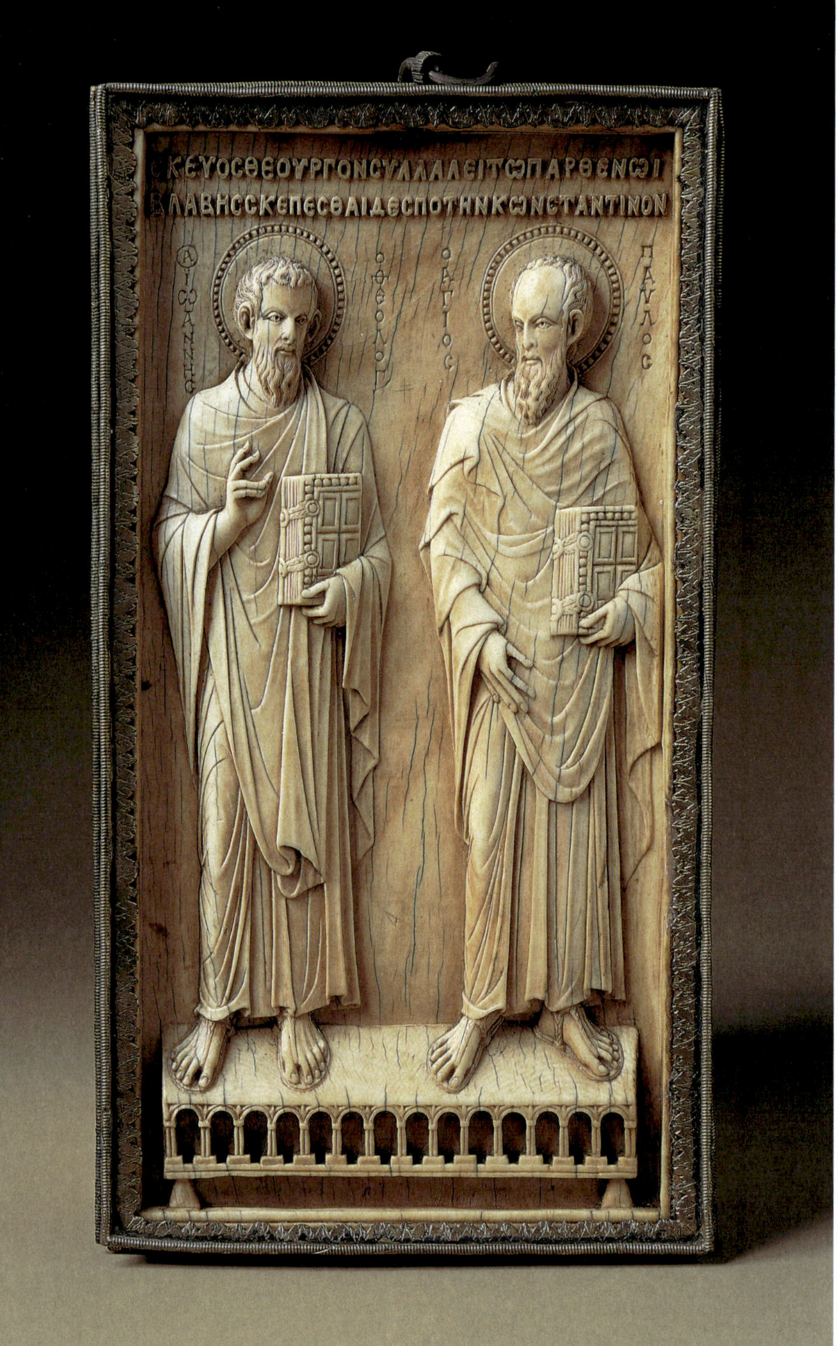

St John and St Paul

Ivory, silver-gilt frame (17th century addition)
Constantinople, middle of 11th century
H. 24.5 cm, w. 12.9 cm (without frame), Inv. no. II 52

According to the inventory of the Ivory Room of the Grünes Gewölbe from 1876 this ivory icon came from the Church of San Giovanni di Verdura near Padua. Maria Antonia of Bavaria (1724–1780), from 1747 wife of the Elector Friedrich Christian of Saxony who reigned briefly in 1763, received the precious object as a gift in 1752. With the permission of the bishop, King Johann of Saxony (ruled: 1854–1873) had the ivory relief removed in 1855 from the sacristy of the chapel of the Taschenbergpalais in Dresden, the representational residence of the couple, to the treasury of the palace only a few yards away.

The ivory panel from Constantinople, which is one of the most important masterpieces of Byzantine court art, portrays the evangelist John (left) and the apostle Paul (right) full face and clad in long garments, holding a richly decorated manuscript in their left hand with their names inscribed vertically. The text above their haloed heads describes their close friendship in Greek, cut in raised letters. Translated it says that the »instrument of God« (Paul) with the »unsullied youth« (John) are deliberating how to protect King Constantine from disaster. The same message is conveyed by an ivory panel – which differs in only a very few details – of John and Paul at the Museo Archeologico in Venice, which in turn is very similar in carving technique to an ivory panel in Vienna (Kunsthistorisches Museum, Kunstkammer) showing St Andrew and St Peter. All three reliefs of roughly the same size form a homogeneous group both in iconography and style. The inscriptions on the panel in Venice and on that of the Grünes Gewölbe suggest a ruler threatened by disaster, in whose name the apostles are asked for help. If the generally accepted dating of the reliefs in the middle of the 11th century is followed, this must have been the Emperor of the Byzantine Empire, Constantine X Dukas (reign: 1059–1067), who was already old and ill when he ascended the throne and narrowly escaped assassination in 1060.

JK

Two Glass Beakers with enamel Decoration

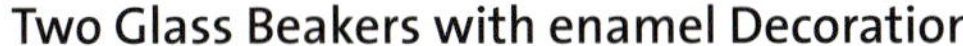

Colourless glass, enamel, silver gilt mount
Glass: Syria, c. 1300
Mount: Germany, late 15th or early 16th century
Left: H. (with cover) 34.9 cm, Ø of cover 13.2 cm, Inv. no. IV 192;
right: H. 19.9 cm, Ø rim of vessel 11.2 cm, Inv. no. IV 193

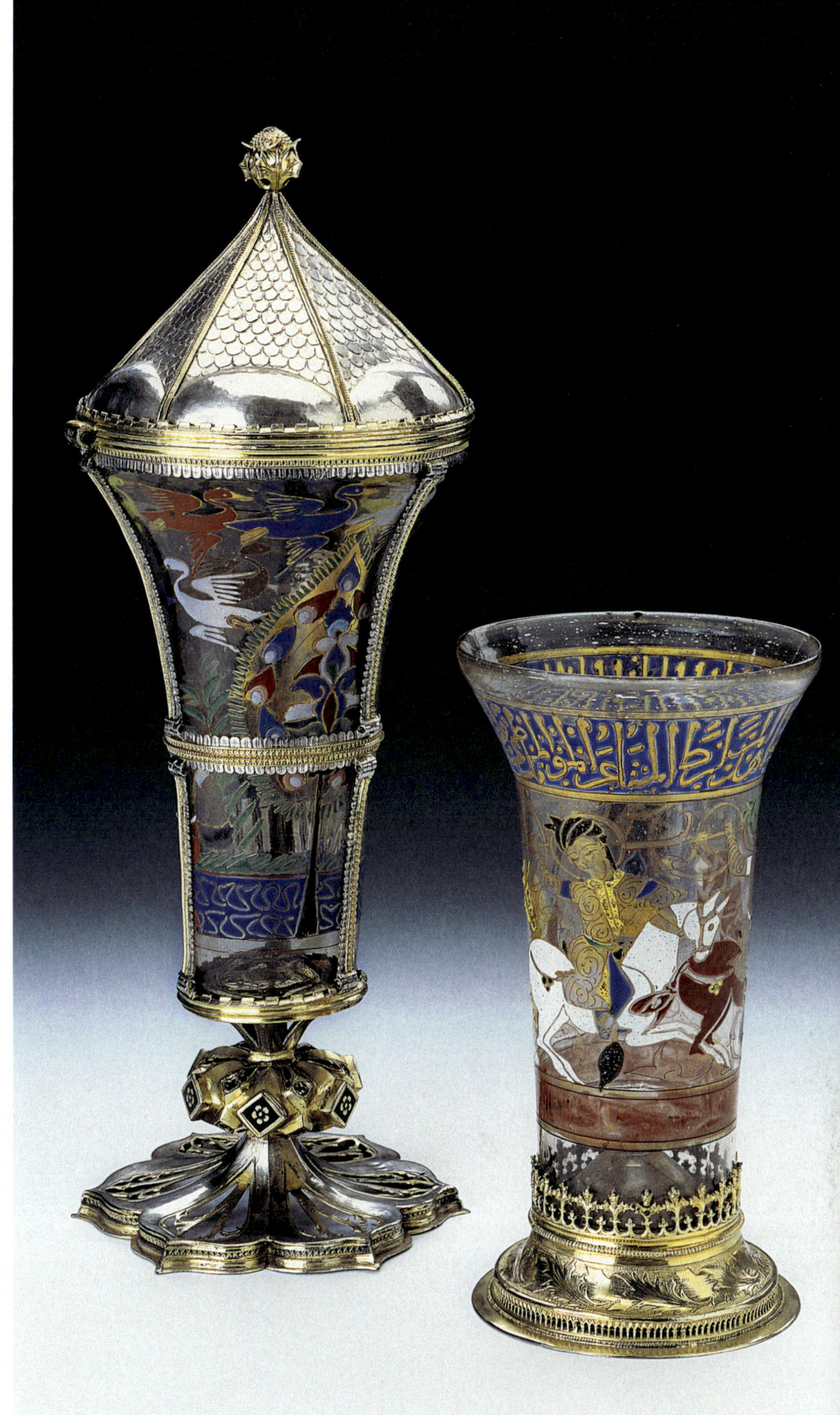

For almost the whole of the Middle Ages the southern Mediterranean region, which was under the influence of Islam, was culturally far superior to the west. This is borne out by these two masterpieces with enamel painting, which were made around 1300 in the heyday of the Syrian glass industry. The cylindrical drinking beaker form with a broad rim and a fused-on footring is typical of the Islamic Middle Ages. Such glass beakers with a colourful enamel decoration were made not only for the wealthy courts of the luxurious cities of Samara, Baghdad and Cairo, these fragile precious objects also came to Europe as ›souvenirs‹ with the crusaders and wealthy pilgrims or were literally imported via Venice. This may have been how these two beakers came to Europe. They were given their richly decorated silver mount only in the fifteenth or early sixteenth century in northern Europe.

The figural ornamentation of the much older glasses conveys the aristocratic way of life of oriental rulers. On the wall of the smaller of the two beakers three horse-riders gallop between friezes with ornament-like inscriptions. They are playing polo, the courtly game that came from Persia. In their long wide-sleeved garments reaching down to the knees, voluminous trousers and a large turban the colourfully clad polo-players ride on a white, a yellow and a red horse. An Arabic inscription which frames this pictorial section, extols the fame of the Sultan – not mentioned by name – at the upper rim in ancient Naskhi script and at the lower edge the same text in italics. The decoration of the taller beaker with an aquatic hunting scene is sufficiently identical in figural style to the smaller beaker to assume that they come from the same workshop. An aristocratic hunter is portrayed shooting cranes and wild geese with a bow and arrow, while a second hunter shoos the birds out of a thicket of reeds with a cloth. The records show that the two beakers were in the possession of the Dresden Kunstkammer from 1640, from where they were transferred to the Grünes Gewölbe in 1832.

DS

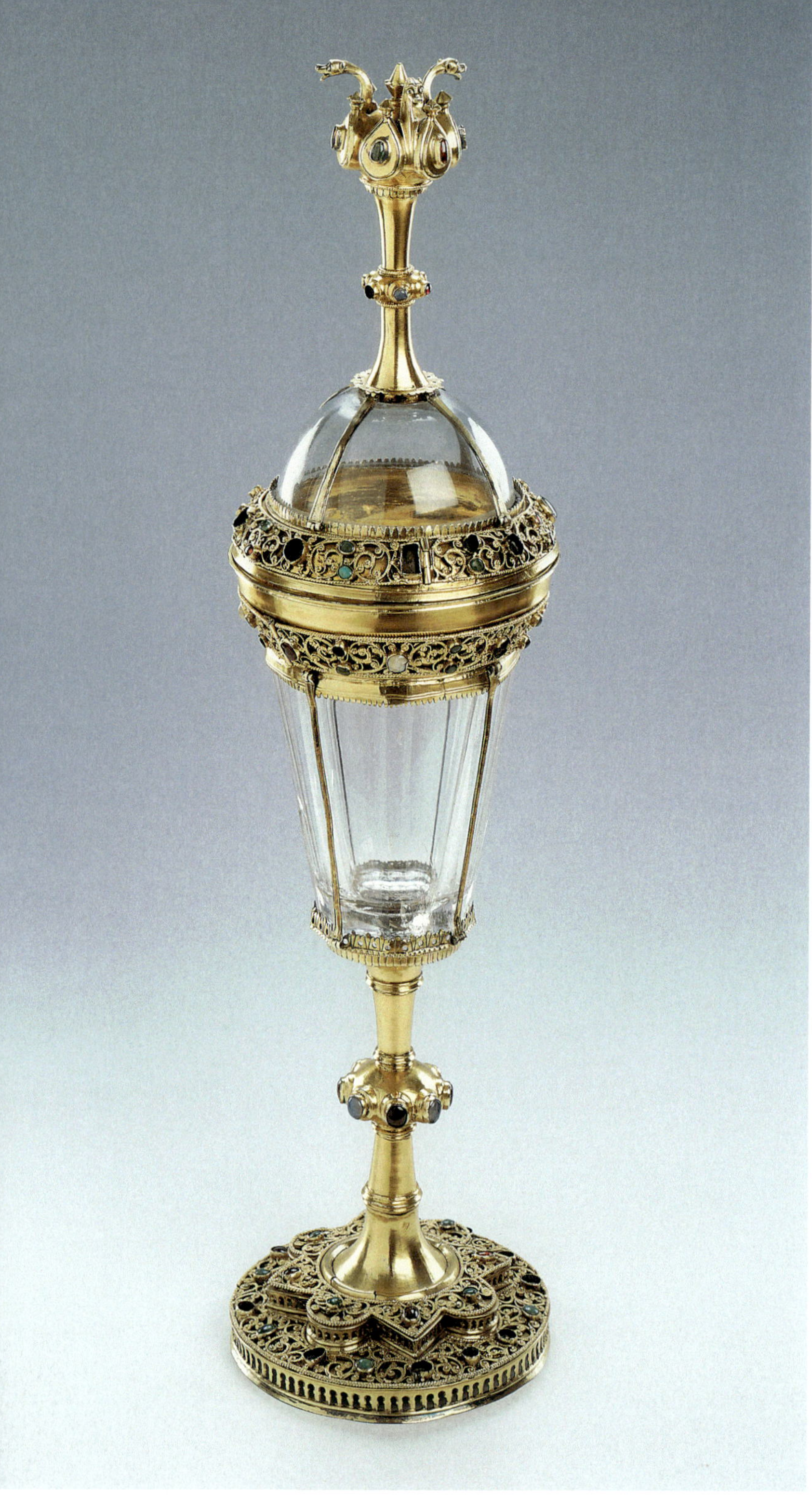

Eleven-sided covered Vessel

Agate-amethyst, silver gilt
Stone cut: Prague, 1350–1375
Mount: probably Burgundy, end of 15th century
H. 13.8 cm, Ø of cover 11.5 cm, w. (with handle) 14.3 cm, Inv. no. IV 343

Historically the covered cup, which is impressive in its enormous size alone, dates from the beginning of Venetian rock crystal cutting. The conical cuppa with 16 alternating narrow and broad facettes makes it the oldest preserved rock crystal cup with a facetted cut. This technique, which greatly enhanced the gleam and reflection of light, appeared in the 13th century in Europe. Records in the archives of facetted cups with a cut well date from the end of the 13th century at the earliest. At that time Venice alongside Paris became a centre of European vessel cutting. The large rock crystal cup also has a particularly splendid mount of Venetian silver filigree in the typical style of the time. The double foot is decorated in this technique with high gothic ornamental forms. It is also embellished like the shaft with a flat, depressed node with cabochon gemstones in a high box-mount. The cover crowned by a high finial embellished with three serpents' heads takes up the ornamental techniques and inset precious stones of the foot. The fact that the hemispherical cover is made of glass does not necessarily point to a repair; there may also have been technical reasons for this. The painstaking design and the size of this rare drinking vessel from the late 13th century point to a royal owner. The rock crystal cup was already listed in the Dresden treasury inventory of 1586/87.

The eleven-sided drinking vessel with an unusually opulent mount may also have come from a royal collection. The precious stone used for the body of the vessel is of a special nature. The stone comes from the mine in the Bohemian Erzgebirge mountains at Ciboušov north west of Prague opened up at the behest of Emperor Karl IV. Some of the stones found there were used in the decoration of the Wenceslas chapel in the cathedral of St Vitus in Prague and the Katharinenkapelle at Karlstein Castle. However, parade vessels were also made and a group of eleven objects have been preserved in various important international museums and collections. The form of the precious stone bowl with its attached handle is typical of this group of works. It was probably given its rich mount interspersed with various profane symbols in coarse individual devices roughly one hundred years later in a cultural region influenced by Burgundy. There is said to have been a medallion with the Saxon coat of arms on the cover of the parade bowl, which was listed for the first time in the Kunstkammer inventory of 1640.

DS

Tall covered Cup

Rock crystal, glass, silver gilt, pearls, turquoises, chrysoprases, garnets
Cut and mount: Venice, c. 1290
H. 48.2 cm, Ø of cover 12.8 cm, Inv. no. V 231

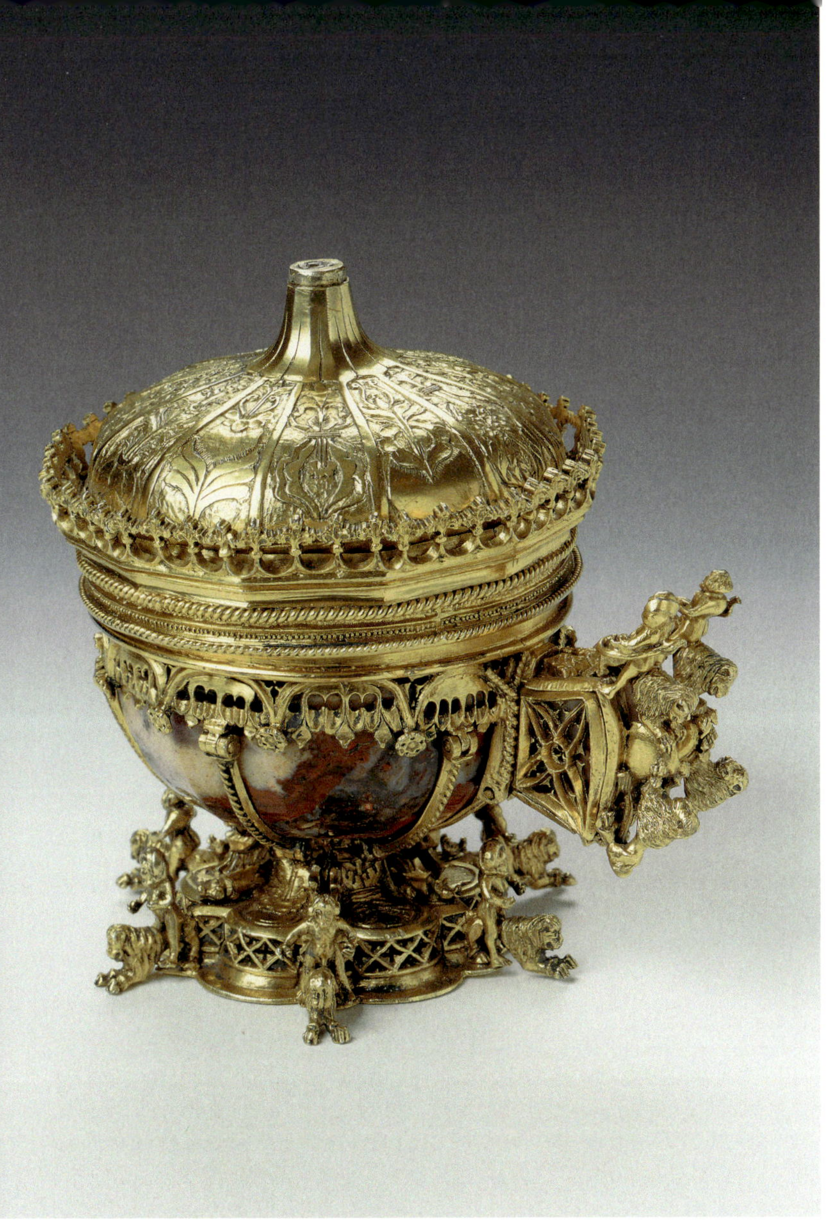

beaker which made it possible to use it as a welcome cup for guests and also for festive occasions such as the »Minnetrinken« in honour of particularly revered saints, at weddings, signing contracts, celebrating reconciliations and funerals. The silver-gilt mount with its hollow cast figural support in fashionable dress from the period around 1400 is meticulously finished. On the high rim there are seven medallions connected by a broad band. Between three medallions with blooms on a gold ground there are two shields with coats of arms, one with the Bohemian lion, and reliefs with Christ giving blessings and a saint with a book who can be interpreted as the Virgin Mary. Vestiges of the heavily damaged opaque enamelling suggest that the drinking horn once had a much more splendid appearance. Inside the cover that belongs to it there is another medallion with a deer resting in a wooded landscape. The solidly fashioned point of the horn ends in a clearly defined miniature piece of architecture. This consists of an enclosing wall behind which a cross-shaped building rises with a crossing tower in a slanting position. The floral and scroll ornamentation on the clasps and mounts of this impressive late gothic piece of secular goldsmith work was decorated with similar care as the figurative parts. The particularly splendid ornamentation of the buffalo horn is akin to the »beautiful style« of the Prague court workshop and can be dated around 1400. It is possible that there is a close link between the drinking horn and the Bohemian king Wenceslas IV.

Altogether eight of these ancient drinking vessels found their way over the centuries into the Dresden Kunstkammer and from there into the Grünes Gewölbe in the 19th century. Their romantic name »griffons' claws« is derived from the unusual material and their form and size. It can no longer be said when this term arose. But one of the drinking horns of the Grünes Gewölbe which was also made at the beginning of the 15th century, rests on a monster which apart from its bird-like head has all the characteristics of a griffon.

DS

Drinking Horn on a crouching Man with a Castle

Horn, silver-gilt, enamel
Probably Prague, c. 1400
H. 34.2 cm, l. 48.5 cm, Ø cover 12.3 cm, Inv. no. IV 333

»Halt veste uns/komen geste« (hold us firmly, guests are coming) – this exhortation which was engraved on the branch which supports the creeping, bearded bearer of the ancient drinking horn, clearly defines its function. It is a ceremonial vessel containing a silver-gilt

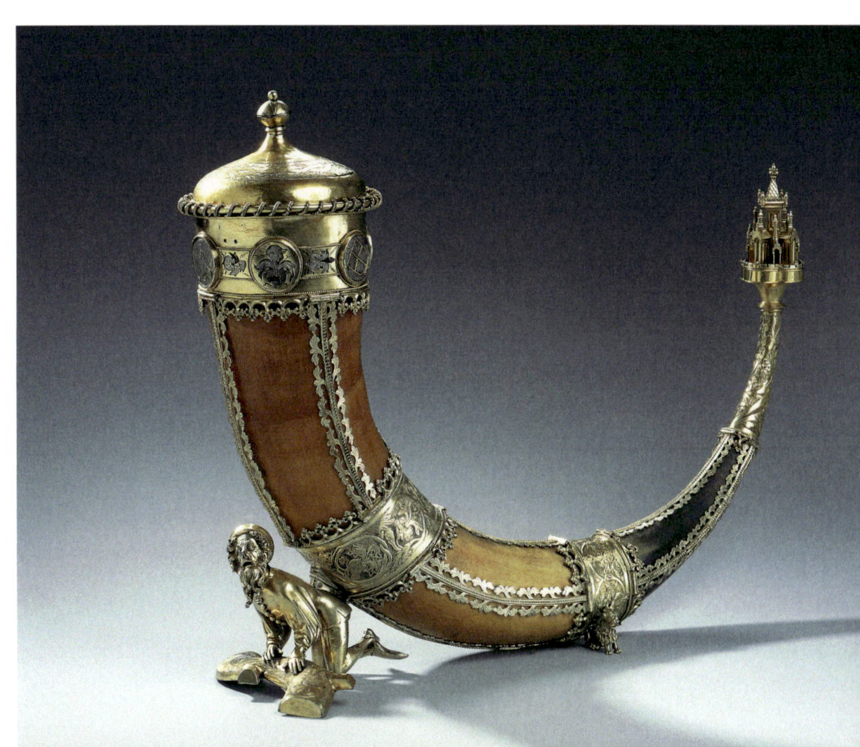

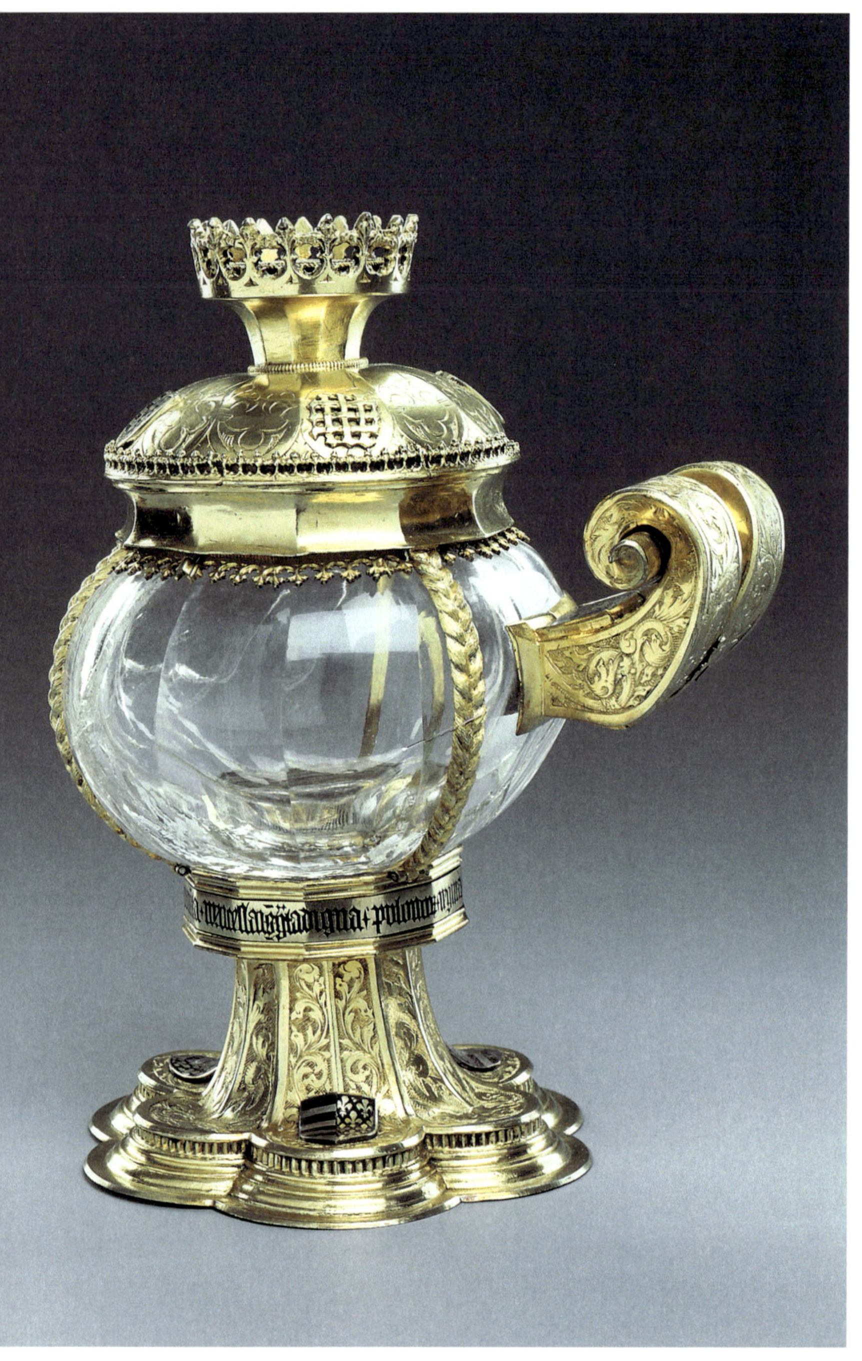

Vessel of Queen Jadwiga of Poland

Rock crystal, silver gilt, enamel
Cut: probably Paris or Venice, middle to second half of the 14th century
Mounts: foot and handle by a goldsmith from the Rhineland,
Cracow, shortly before 1399
Cover: later addition, Cracow, beginning of 15th century
plait-like braces in the neo-gothic manner were added before 1725
in Dresden after the vessel had been damaged.
H. 24.1 cm, w. (with handle) 18.6 cm, Inv. no. V 294

The vessel that was presumably cut in Paris or Venice from rock crystal and which received its ornate precious-metal mount in Cracow, was already listed in the inventory of the treasury of the Dresden Palace drawn up in 1586/87. Friedrich August I, Elector of Saxony and from 1697 Augustus II King of Poland, had this heirloom displayed in the Hall of the Precious Objects of the Grünes Gewölbe although the rock crystal body of the vessel was damaged. Did the King of Poland know the history of the vessel? The early inventories of the treasury and the Grünes Gewölbe do not recount its impressive dynastic history. It was commissioned by Jadwiga, who was crowned Queen of Poland as a ten year-old girl in 1384. The coats of arms on the foot and cover give details of the young queen's noble origins in the powerful Anjou dynasty. Her marriage in 1386 made the Lithuanian Grand Prince Jogaila King of Poland and founded the Jagiellon dynasty in Poland with its wealth of traditions.

The Latin inscription engraved in abbreviations on the ring of the mount above the stem says that Jadwiga had intended the vessel as a votive gift for the Wawel cathedral in Cracow to honour St Wenceslas, the patron saint of the cathedral and to request that she, the Polish Queen, might ascend to the kingdom of heaven. Apparently, as a result of the early death of Jadwiga in 1399 this gift was never made. The coats of arms and the monograms consisting of the letter ›m‹, which may be construed as ›Mater Maria‹ or ›Memento Mariae‹ were later appliquéd on to the lid with the lightly engraved fleur de lys décor. A stylised crown enclosing the white eagle on a red enamelled shield – the coat of arms of the kingdom of Poland – was also added. This must have taken place after the death of Jadwiga at the behest of her husband Władisław II.

It is only possible to surmise how this work of art, which was of such significance for the Polish crown, came to Dresden. Perhaps the vessel with its rich symbolism was intended to celebrate the marriage in 1496 of Princess Barbara of Poland from the Jagiellon dynasty to Duke Georg the Bearded of Saxony.

JK

Covered Dish with Coral

Rock crystal, silver gilt, coat of arms in verre églomisé, coral
Cut: Paris, 1st half of 14th century
Mount (foot and cover): Egidius Blanke, Szczecin 1583
H. 37.9 cm, Inv. no. V 260

The cover of the oval dish in clear, ice-cold rock crystal is crowned by a brilliant piece of red coral. This combination of two natural materials, which harmonise superbly with the matt gleam of the silver gilt mount, was quite in keeping with Renaissance taste. ›The wonders of nature‹ seemed mysterious and enigmatic. Thus, towards the close of the 16th century bizarrely branching precious corals were among the highly prized naturalia and rare objects of a princely Kunstkammer. It was thought that rock crystal, which was interpreted in ancient Greece as water frozen into eternal ice and in the Christian liturgy of the Middle Ages as a sign of divine purity and strength of faith, possessed magical and healing properties. Rock crystal vessels cut in facets had a central position in the art of stone-cutting at that time. Often they were not given a mount in precious metal. Some of them were fitted with a mount very much later. This was also true of this rock crystal dish decorated with a swirl design forming the body of the parade vessel with a coral branch. This particularly attractive cut for rock crystal vessels was probably invented in Paris in the first half of the 14th century and then adopted by Venetian stonecutters. Only roughly 15 dishes executed in this complicated technique are known so far. Those at the Grünes Gewölbe are among the best. The mount can be attributed to the goldsmith Egidius Blanke (died 1609) who was active for the court in Szszecin. The preciously appointed dish once belonged to Erdmuthe of Brandenburg (1561–1623), wife of Duke Johann Friedrich of Pommern-Stettin (1542–1600). Her name is to be found on a verre églomisé medallion on the underside of the crystal bowl. The year 1583, which is difficult to decipher, makes it possible to date the mount precisely. It can only be surmised how the dish came to Dresden. It might have been a gift from Erdmuthe to her sister Sophia of Brandenburg (1568–1622), from 1582 wife of Christian I of Saxony (reigned 1586–1591). It is possible, however, that the piece found its way to Dresden three years after the death of Erdmuthe. A source in the archives reports that on 12 November 1626 a part of her estate came to Dresden and was received by Johann Georg I, who was now the ruling elector of Saxony.

JK

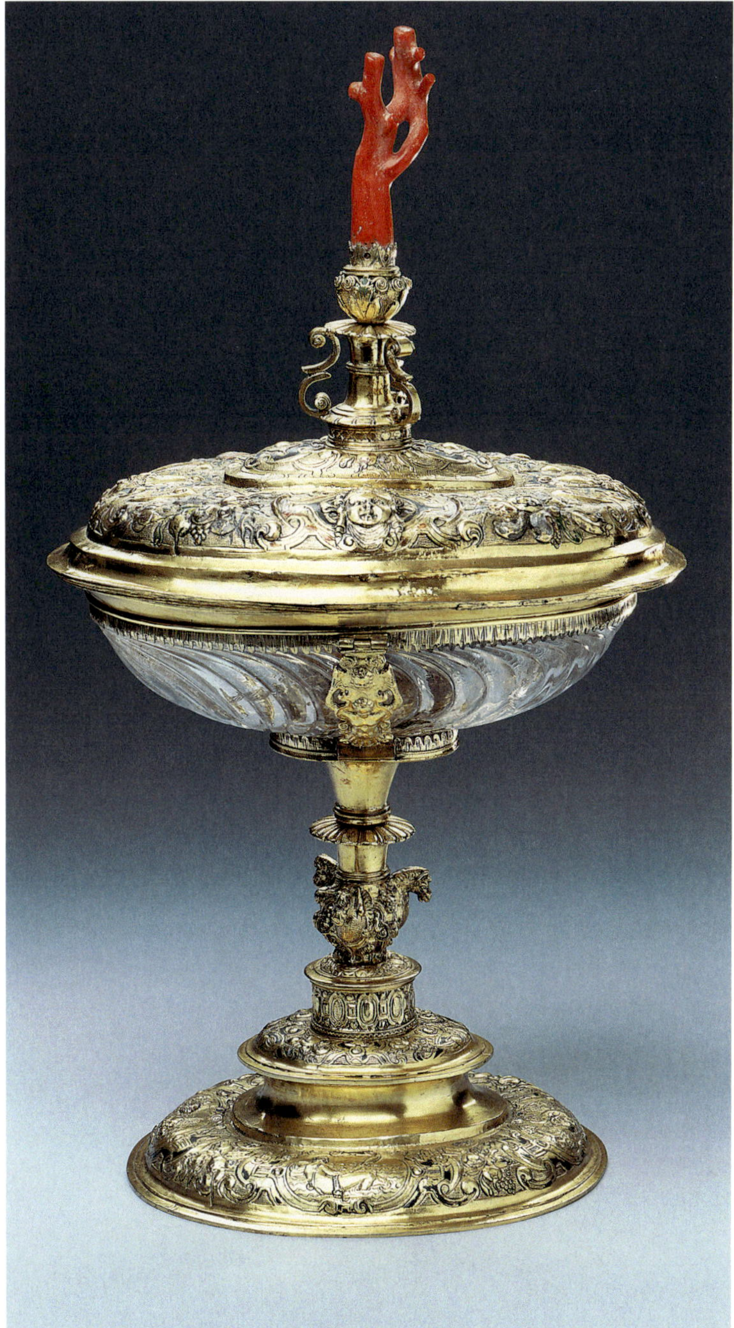

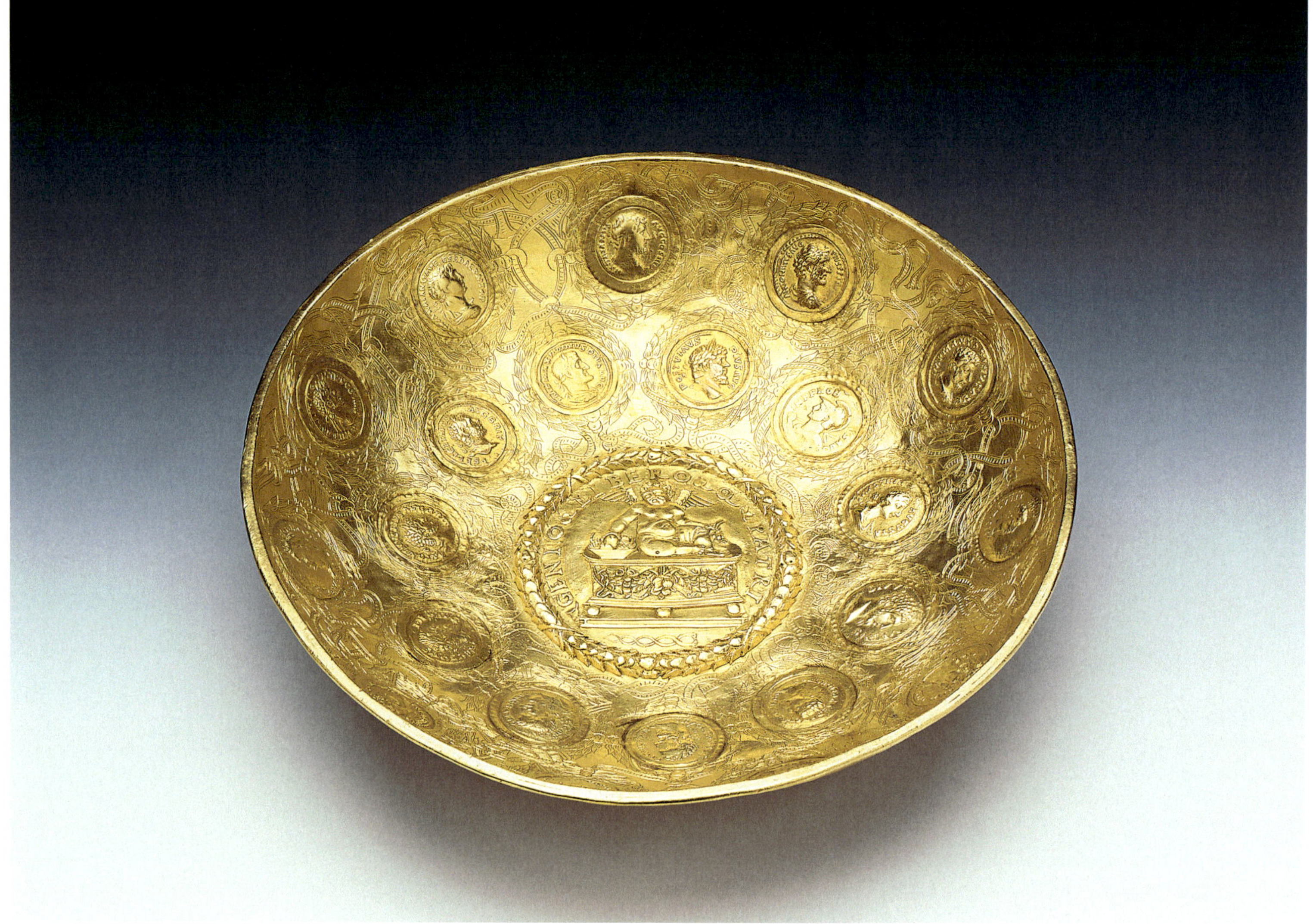

Drinking Bowl of Augustin Kesenbrot

Gold, 22 Roman coins
South Germany, dated 1508
H. 5.1 cm, Ø 18.5 cm, Inv. no. IV 40

Provost Augustin Kesenbrot (1467 – 1513) from Olmütz in Northern Moravia was as Chancellor of King Władisław II the most powerful official in Hungary. In his time he must have been a very modern thinker as he was a member of the humanist societies for the support of the sciences and arts, which at that time were also being founded outside Italy. He donated this gold bowl in 1508 which with a gold content of 882 grams was unusually valuable at that time. Latin inscriptions on the underside and inside of the middle of the bowl record the circumstances of the gift and its intended use. On the rim of the bowl there is the inscription: »may the sacred host of the sons of Phoebus and the Order of the Initiate donate an abundance of gifts with this patena of Bacchus. You are far from here, O Uniniated ones«. On the well the »Sodalitas litteraria Danubiana« »The learned society of the Danube«

in what was formerly Pest, now Budapest, is named as the recipient of the gift. The form of the vessel follows the classical patena, a special kind of bowl for libations. Only a very small number of goldsmiths' works deal so clearly with humanist thinking around 1500 as this gold bowl. Its classical form, decoration of coins and inscriptions reflect the rebirth of Antiquity in the early Renaissance north of the Alps. According to tradition after the benefactor's death the precious vessel was kept in the burial chapel in the city of his birth. There it is said to have fallen into the hands of plundering Turkish soldiers in the 17th century. When the Russian troops of Tsar Peter I stormed the Turkish fortress of Asow on the Black Sea, the humanist vessel resurfaced. A few years later the Saxon Chancellor Count Beichlingen acquired it for Augustus the Strong and brought it to Dresden. The very rare 22 coins from Imperial Rome were removed from the bowl and placed in the collection of the Elector-King. Some of them are still in the Dresden Kupferstich-Kabinett. Augustus the Strong had them replaced by less rare originals and copies of classical coins.

DS

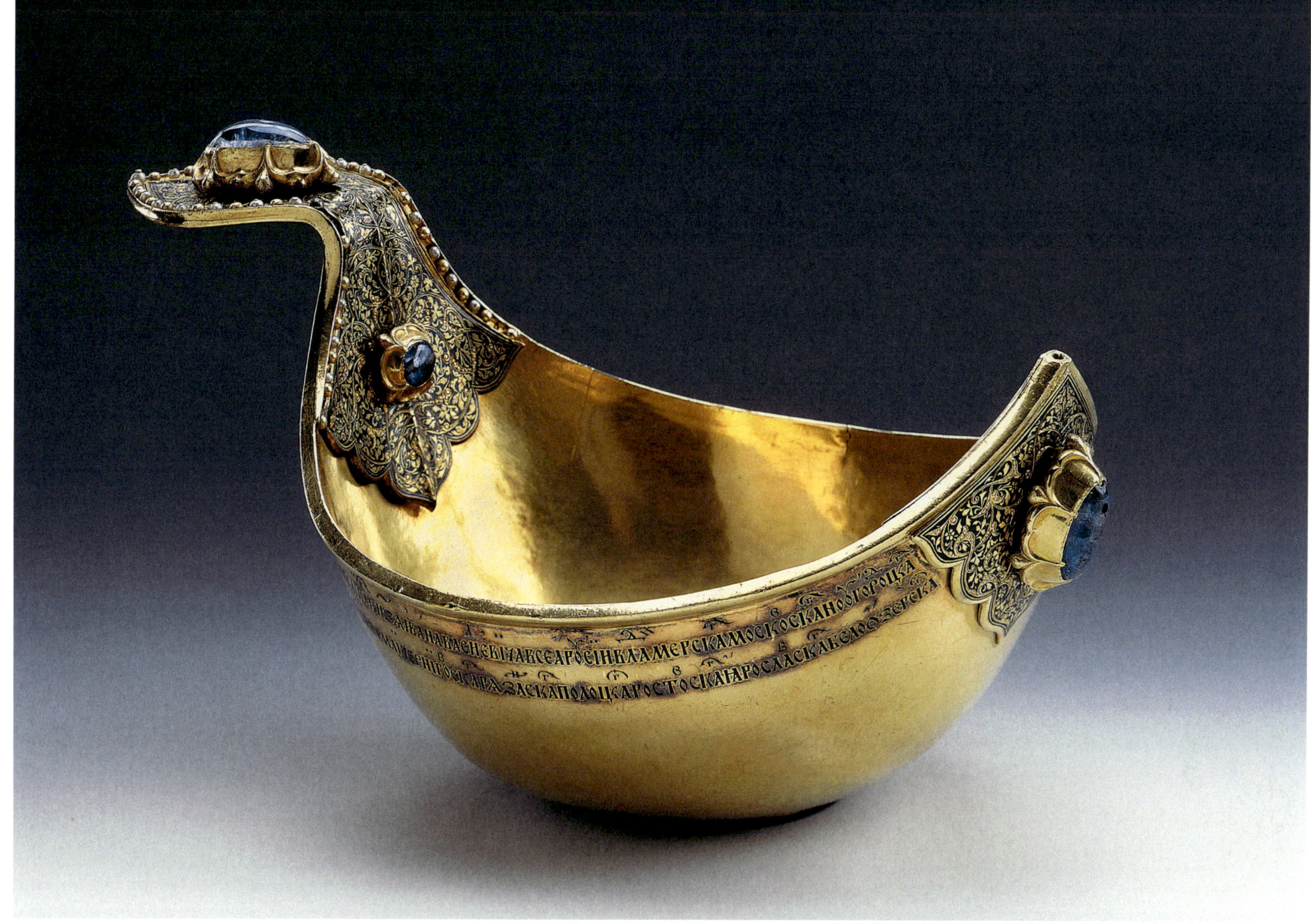

Drinking Bowl of the Tsar Ivan the Terrible

Gold, niello, sapphires, rubies, pearls
Workshops of the Kremlin, Moscow, after 1563
H. 12.4 cm, w. 23 cm, d. 13.8, Ø foot 5.4 cm, weight 1946 grams, Inv. no. IV 43

On the 15th February 1563 Tsar Ivan IV Wassiljewitsch, known as »Grosnyj« or the »Terrible«, accepted the capitulation of the important trading city of Polozk on the Düna. For the Tsar this military success was a climax in the gruelling war, which he fought in 1561 and 1583 against Poland-Lithuania and was at the same time an important step in his aim of »bringing together Russian lands«.

Ivan IV commanded that a bowl should be made of the looted gold from Polozk. This is far more than an imperial drinking vessel. The bowl fashioned in the tradition of the old Russian ladle, the ›koffsch‹ is rather a memorial to victory and at the same time a symbol of the new majesty of the first Russian Tsar. The four large sapphires in cabochon cut on the decorative plate, the largest of which is framed in small rubies on the handle, also contribute to this effect. On the outer rim of the drinking ladle there is the full title »Great Ruler, Tsar and Grand Prince« in two lines. In addition, a gold disk engraved with the Russian double-eagle in niello technique is appliquéd on the well of the vessel. A further plate under the base gives the date and reason for its manufacture.

With its rhythmic, balanced and flowing form the vessel is one of the outstanding examples of European goldsmiths' art in the 16th century. It can be assumed that this unusually high koffsch was created by a west European artist in the Kremlin. All the other vessels in silver and gold in the treasury of the Kremlin are much shallower and wider. To this day it has not been possible to determine under what circumstances the koffsch of Ivan the Terrible came into the possession of the Saxon Electors. A precious work of art of such national importance can only have been removed by the Tsar himself from his Treasury for a very important reason and given as a present. The thick-walled koffsch accompanied Augustus the Strong in 1697 to the celebrations on the occasion of his coronation as King of Poland and Grand Duke of Lithuania. It stood in the Grünes Gewölbe with the other gold vessels near the shaft between the windows in the Silver Gilt Room.

DS

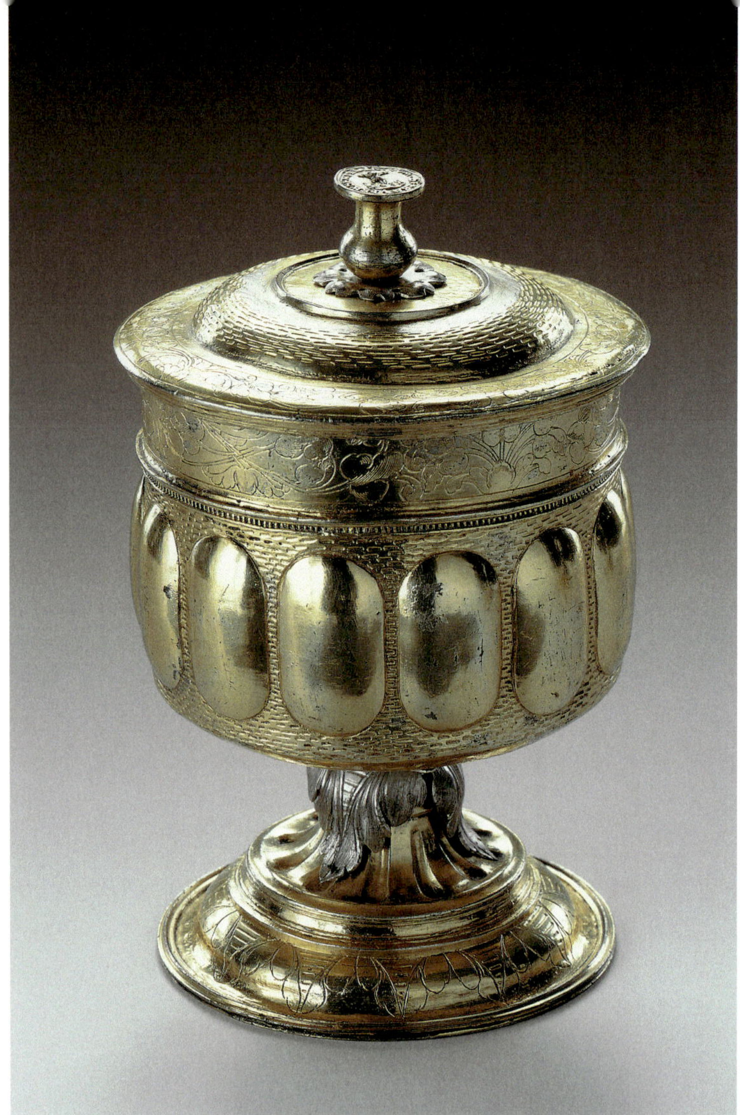

Martin Luther's Signet Ring

Gold, carnelian cameo
Augsburg, c. 1530
H. 2.8 cm, w. 2.8 cm, Inv. no. VIII 97

Covered Beaker from Martin Luther's Estate

Silver gilt
South Germany, c. 1540
H. 14.3 cm, Inv. no. IV 313

The goldsmith, who commissioned by Duke Johann Friedrich (the Generous) mounted a carnelian with the newly cut signet of Martin Luther in a gold ring on the occasion of the Augsburg Imperial Diet was not aware of the size of the fingers of this Wittenberg professor of theology, and thus based his work on the usual way his aristocratic clientele wore their rings. In September 1530 Martin Luther gave his friend Philipp Melanchthon an account of his experiences with this signet ring: »But so that I was to notice that I was not born to wear gold it soon slipped from my thumb and fell to the ground, because it is too big for my finger«. The great reformer wore his ring next to the skin whereas gentlemen wore theirs over their gloves, which necessitated a larger size. This simple gold ring widens to enclose an oval carnelian in which the coat of arms designed by Luther himself – the Luther rose with a heart and the cross and the mirror-image initials ›M.L‹ – were engraved. Before 1650 Martin Luther's signet ring came into the possession of Elector Johann Georg I via the great grandson of the highly respected founder of the Reformation. The strict Lutheran thanked Johann Martin Luther for the precious gift by giving him an aristocratic estate and kept the signet ring on his finger until his dying day. For several decades the ring then went to the Electoral Saxon Kunstkammer until Johann Georg III removed it in 1679. This simple precious object has been listed in the inventory of the Jewel Room of the Grünes Gewölbe since 1733.

Apart from the golden signet ring, Martin Luther had a sizeable collection of silverware, of which several drinking vessels have been preserved. Alongside the ›Lutherbecher‹ at the Stadtgeschichtliches Museum in Leipzig, this small covered beaker from the Grünes Gewölbe are among the silver objects that can clearly be attributed to the reformer. It was presented to him around 1540 by his friend and fellow reformer, the Wittenberg theologian and provost Justus Jonas. A small medallion on the finial is decorated with Jonas's coat of arms. A larger medallion from 1538 with a likeness of Luther is inscribed with the motto »Im Stillsein und Hoffen werdet Ihr stark sein« (serenity and hope will be your strength) on the underside of the lid. This beaker was presented on 29 August by the pastor and Superintendant General Calovius to Elector Johann Georg II, who displayed the vessel nine months later in his Kunstkammer.

DS

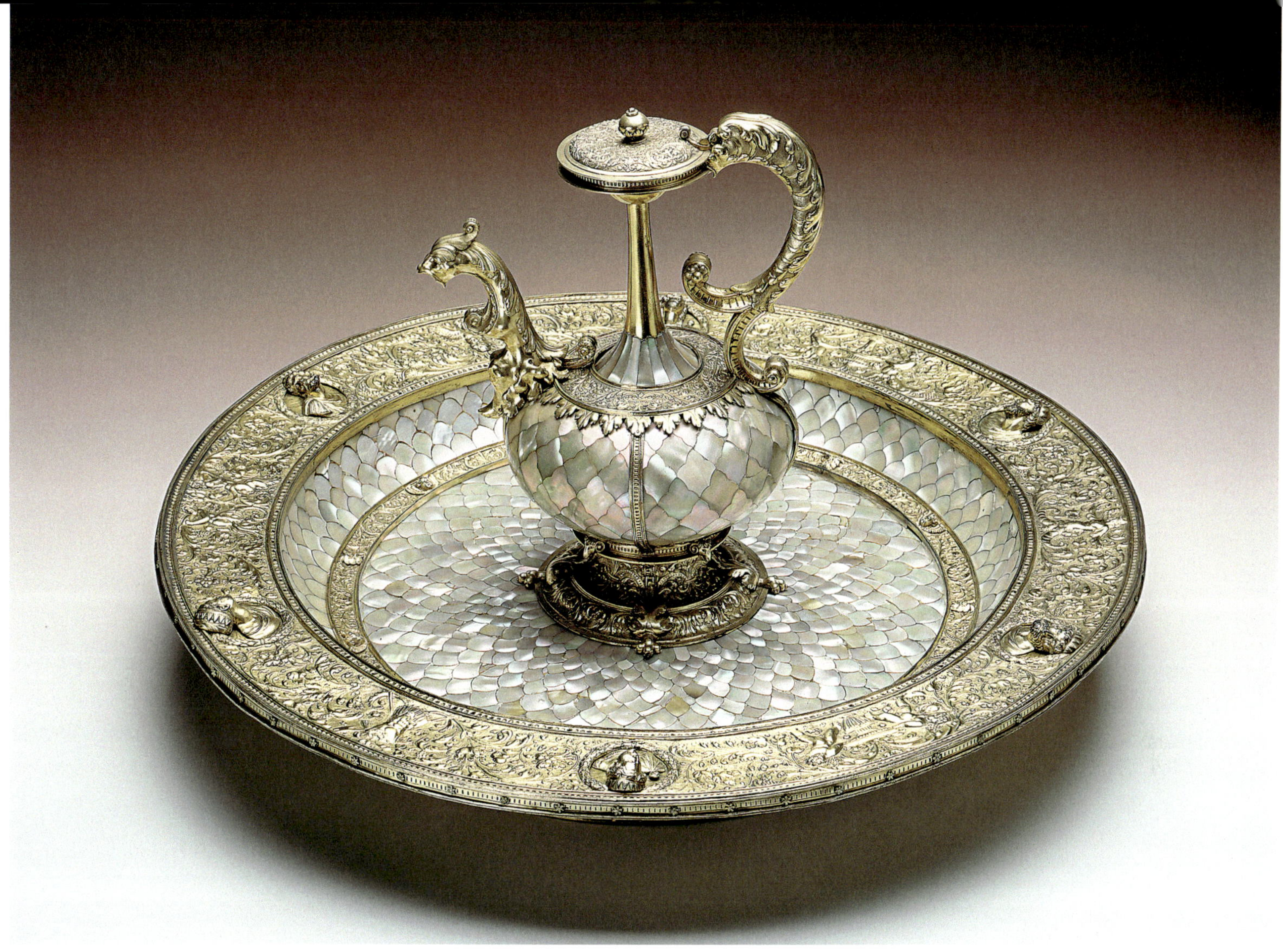

Mother of Pearl Basin and Ewer

Wooden core, mother of pearl, copper, silver gilt, vestiges of paint
Mother of pearl work: Gujarat (India)
Mount: probably Nuremberg, c. 1540
H. 8.6 cm, Ø (basin) 56 cm, H. 29 cm, w. top 23.3 cm, Ø foot (ewer) 15.9 cm,
Inv. no. IV 181 (basin), IV 256 (ewer)

A reflection of the fairytale splendour of the orient, this parade basin densely covered in mother of pearl tesserae and the ewer made of the same material were imported to Southern Germany from Gujurat in north west India via Portuguese dealers. The two exotic vessels were probably fitted with a matching mount by a technically and artistically outstanding goldsmith in Nuremberg around 1540, which adapted them to the luxurious requirements and way of life of German Renaissance princes. The ewer, whose original copper core is hidden beneath the new silver mount, had a neck section with a bird-like spout superimposed, plus a high scroll-like handle and a tall well-formed foot. All the newly added parts are artistically joined together with clasps. The European mount remained surprisingly close to the tradition of Indian vessels. Even the flat cover of the Nuremberg silver mount is to be found in the popular rose water garnitures of the Mughal palaces. The artist decorated the broad rim of the basin with appliquéd sculptural busts of princes embellished in the latest fashion with ornamental friezes after models by Peter Flötner. This superimposed rim was attached to the gilded strips of precious metals in the well of the bowl and the footring and to the wooden core by means of an adhesive agent and pegs. If the superimposed silver stand is removed from the body, a ground in bright red lacquer emerges such as is generally found in these Indian mother of pearl pieces. As a result of its considerable age and superb goldsmith work, this pouring garniture was regarded as the first baptismal font of the Wettin dynasty. There is no record of this in the archives, however. This piece of goldsmith's work from the early German Renaissance was transferred to the Grünes Gewölbe from the Kunstkammer which was dissolved in 1832.

DS

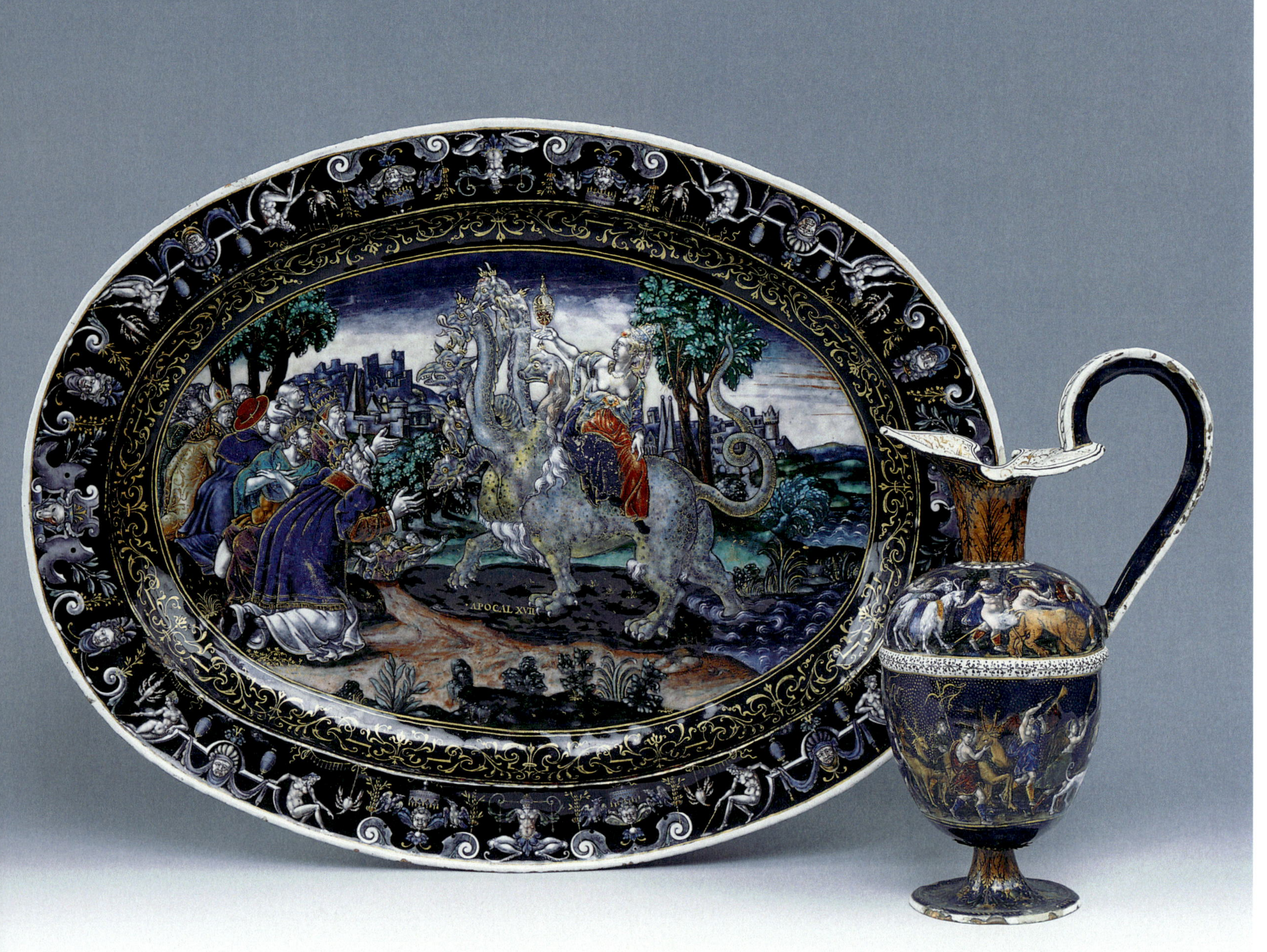

Basin with the Representation of the Whore of Babylon

Copper, enamel
Martial Courteys (designated on the reverse side »Courtois«)
Designated on top »APOCAL XVII«
Limoges, c. 1570
L. 54.9 cm, w. 40.7 cm, Inv. no. III 8

The city of Limoges in central France, located on important trading and pilgrimage routes became a centre of enamelling whose importance extended beyond its immediate region as early as the 12th and 13th centuries. The city saw a second heyday in the 16th century. The highly specialised Limousin workshops developed a complex process by means of which they covered even large copper vessels and panels with complex narrative décors which rivalled panel painting both in colour and composition. The precious gleaming devotional paintings, portraits,

parade vessels and other luxury articles were extremely popular not only among the French aristocracy and saw a renaissance in the 19th century.

The oval basin of the Grünes Gewölbe, which is remarkable in its dimensions alone, is among the masterpieces of its genre. It is characterised by a wealth of opaque and translucent enamels and their luminous quality is enhanced by the gold and silver foil beneath them. There are two almost identical works by Martial Courteys at the National Gallery of Art, Washington and at the British Museum, London. The upper side of these basins is decorated with dignitaries both worldly and spiritual paying homage to the whore of Babylon riding on a seven-headed monster. This figure from the Apocalypse of St John which originally symbolised pre-Christian imperial Rome was re-interpreted in the age of the Reformation as a comment on Papism. This vessel, like most objects from Limoges, is modelled on a print. It is based on an illustration in the Lutheran Bible of the 1520s and 30s, which was strongly influenced by Albrecht Dürer's famous woodcuts. While some woodcuts clearly emphasise their anti-papal message by depicting the whore wearing the papal tiara, in this work the Pope is not directly identified with the »great whore«. He begs forgiveness from her with whom the kings on this earth have fornicated. Against this background, the provenance of this basin from the estate of Queen Christiane Eberhardine from 1727 thus seems logical. While her consort Augustus the Strong converted to Catholicism to become King of Poland, the Queen a devout protestant, refused to follow suit. She refused steadfastly to visit Poland and bore the title of Queen without being crowned.

UW

Archangel Michael struggling with Satan

Lime wood
Munich or Augsburg, c. 1595 – 1600
H. (with staff) 63.6 cm, w. 32.8 cm, d. 16.5 cm,
pedestal: H. 16.4 cm, w. 16.7 cm, d. 15 cm
Inv. no. 141

This portrayal of the decisive battle between good and evil makes a light and airy impression. The Archangel Michael uses a long spear to push Satan lying below him out of heaven, as can be read in the revelation to John (12,7 – 12): »The great dragon was thrown down, that ancient serpent, who is called the Devil and Satan, the deceiver of the whole world – he was thrown down to the earth, and his angels were thrown down with him.«

St Michael, the leader of the heavenly host, was regarded as the protector of the Church, patron of Christian armies and patron saint of the Germans. In this function he adorns the façade of the Jesuit church of St Michael in Munich, which was built as a militant symbol of the beginning of the counter-reformation. Between 1588 and roughly 1590 Hubert Gerhard, the Dutch-German sculptor and pupil of Giovanni da Bologna active in Florence, received a commission to furnish this programmatic edifice. The somewhat severe but at the same time dramatic monumental bronze group of St Michael is closely akin to the highly detailed, brilliantly carved lime wood statuette in the Grünes Gewölbe. As Lorenz Seelig has demonstrated, the silver sculpture of the fighting archangel by the Augsburg goldsmith Christoph Lencker, which was formerly in the treasury of St Michael, is also closely related. The Dresden group in lime wood must have been made by this circle. The contortion of the body of Satan who has been defeated, the even greater lightness of movement in the Archangel, his subtly fashioned garment, the otherworldly calm in the face of the victorious angel make this wood sculpture an independent work of art of the first rank. It was probably originally intended as a Kunstkammer piece. This splendid

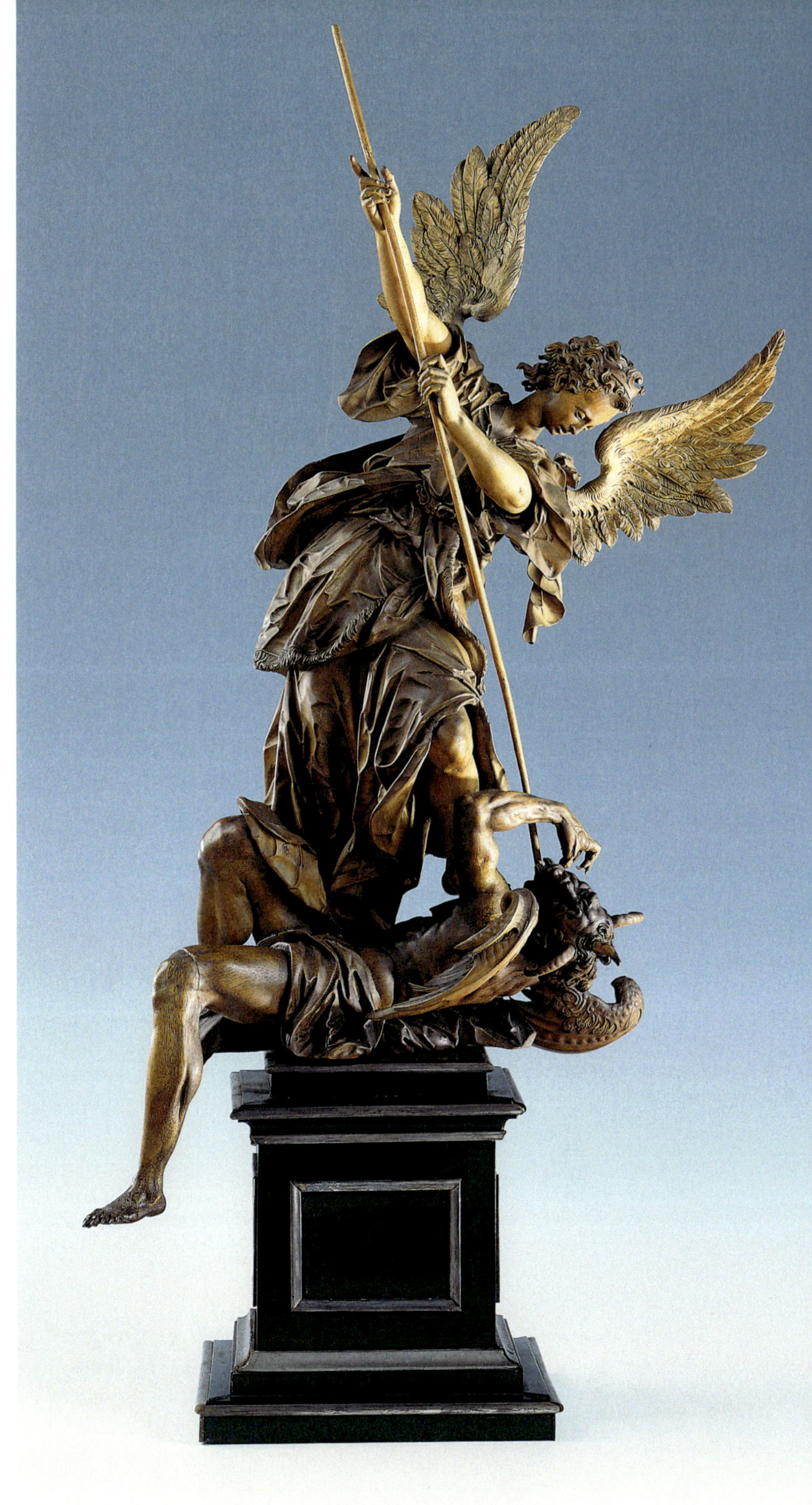

piece of carving, which was made shortly before 1600, was bought in the Hamburg art trade on behalf of Augustus the Strong in 1732. Because of its outstanding artistic quality it was displayed in a prominent position on a table in the first niche of the Hall of the Precious Objects at the Grünes Gewölbe beneath the portrait of the Elector Augustus, a determined defender of the protestant faith.

DS

Amber Cabinet

After a brief 6 seconds' wait in the security lock the visitor enters the Amber Cabinet. This room has been restored to its original proportions of the time around 1700, when it served as an office for the staff of the Grünes Gewölbe. Previously, until 1727, it had been part of the pantry. At that time a spiral staircase at the southeast corner of the room led into the cellar. Augustus the Strong had the room which was designated »pantry vault« fitted out with a stove, which could be heated from the »passage«, chandeliers, a set of scales on which silver works could be weighed, fitted cupboards and an escritoire. Thus the duty inspectors in the rank of privy chamberlains could work here until visitors came to be accompanied through the treasure rooms.

Today, the entire displayable collection of amber objects of the Grünes Gewölbe is exhibited in glass cabinets some of which are placed in what were originally doorways. The collection of works of art made of this »magic stone« from the Baltic is unusually diverse and of very high quality. From the Renaissance to the end of the Baroque period luxury objects made of Baltic amber came as precious acquisitions and also as diplomatic and state gifts to the Kunstkammer and the treasury of the Saxon electors. Among them there is the parade ewer with a gold mount embellished with precious stones from the beginning of the 17th century by Georg Schreiber from Königsberg and the large amber cabinet which Augustus the Strong received in 1728 as a gift from the Prussian king. It is the largest extant work of art in this fragile material.

Originally Augustus the Strong had 19 amber works displayed on the central wall panel of the east wall of the Hall of the Precious Objects. For reasons of conservation this is no longer possible. Amber, a fossilized resin, requires special protection from sunlight and a constant temperature and particular humidity level. This is guaranteed in the Amber Cabinet of the Grünes Gewölbe in special air-conditioned display cabinets with fittings in Saxon serpentine. This room designed by Horst Witter is plunged mysteriously into semi-darkness with its golden-shimmering collection of delightful amber objects« and is today located at the beginning of the tour of Augustus the Strong's treasury museum.

DS

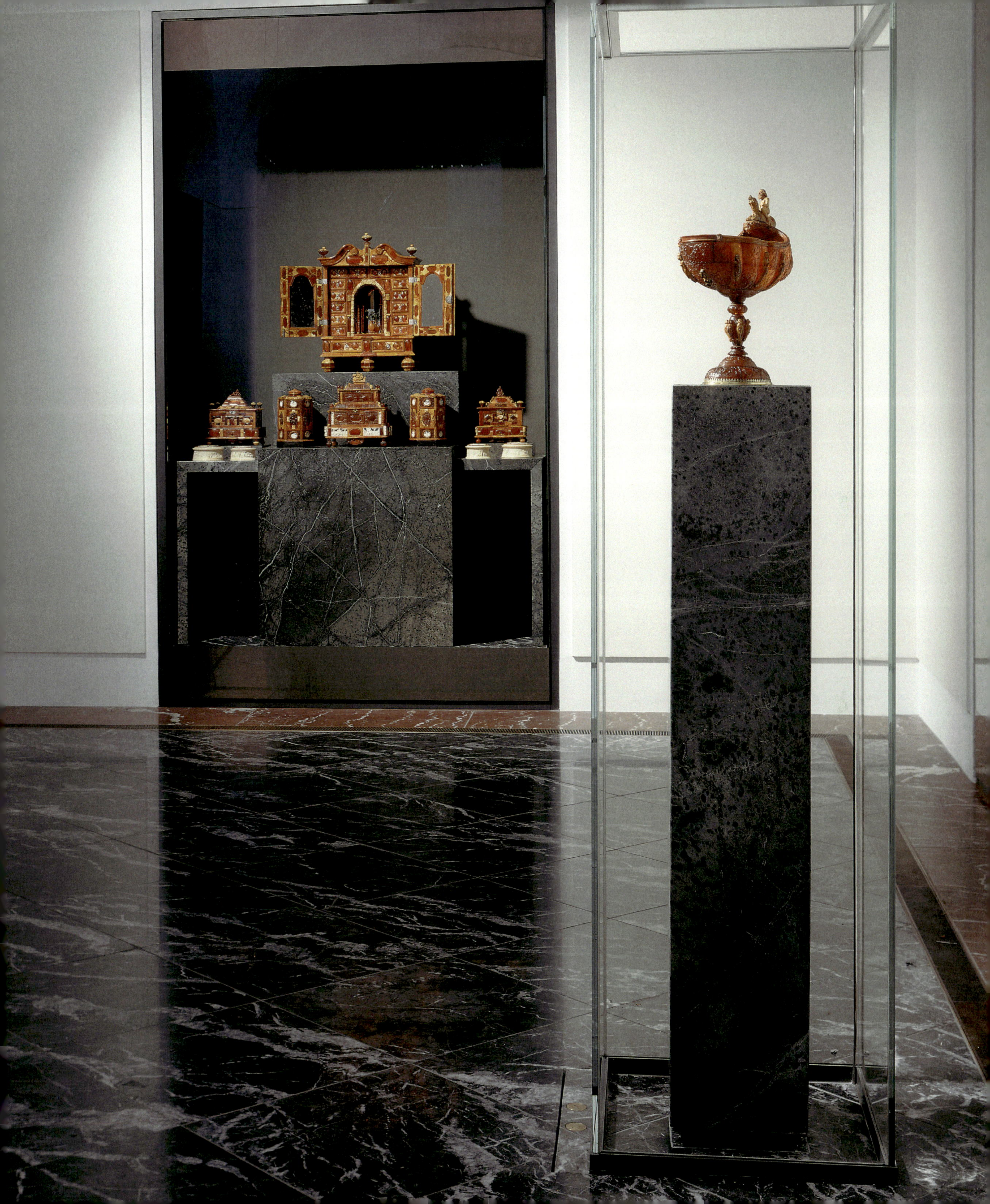

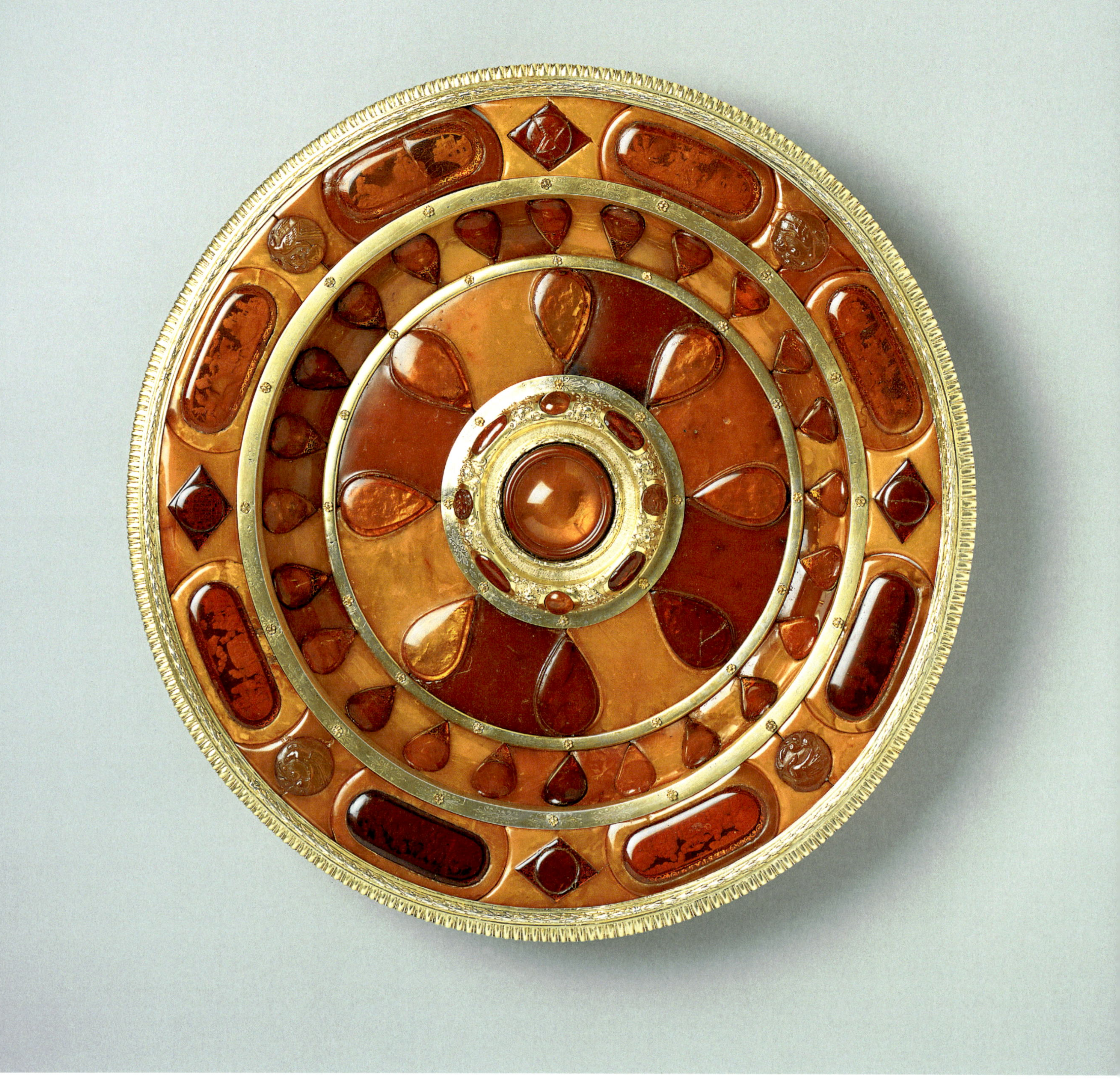

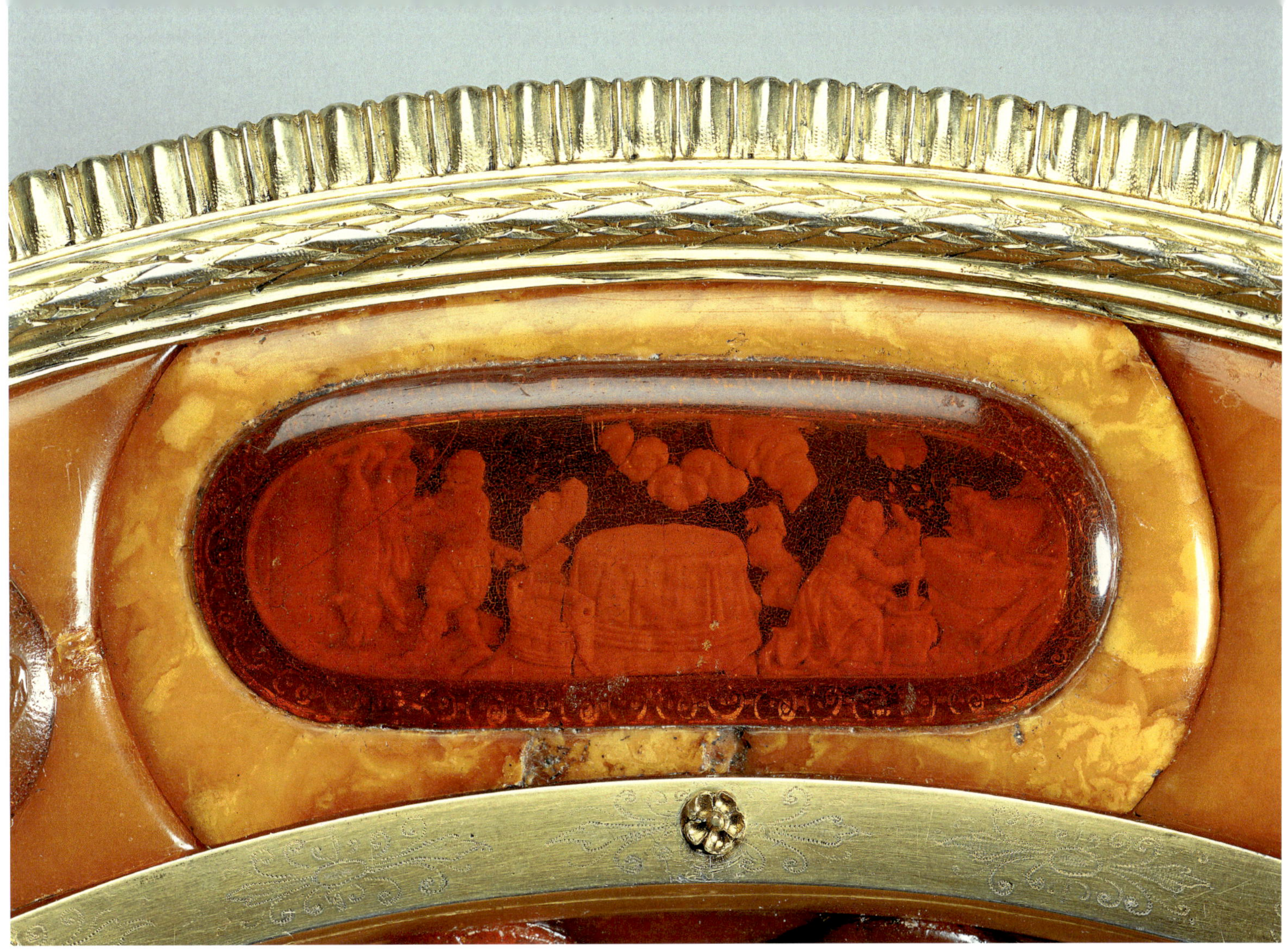

Large Basin

Amber, different varieties, metal foil, silver gilt
Königsberg, presumably c. 1605–1607
Ø 46 cm, Inv. no. III 76

Magdalena Sibylla (1586–1659), consort of the Elector, had her own Kunstkammer collection, which was distributed over four rooms. In all probability, the large amber basin was exhibited there as well. Magdalena Sibylla, daughter of the Marchgrave Albrecht Friedrich von Brandenburg, born in Königsberg, may have received this precious piece on the occasion of her wedding to the Elector Johann Georg I (reigned 1611–1656), which the coat of arms of Brandenburg and the loving couple in relief suggest. The lovers, reclining opposite each other, were carved on the rim of the vessel and overlaid with convex amber plaques.

The extensive restoration of the bowl revealed that it had been manufactured using a fascinating technique that made extremely economical use of the precious material with its rich palette of shades. Pieces of amber in different shapes were inserted into an elaborate silver-gilt ›frame‹, which is only visible on the reverse side. The pieces, placed close together, combine to form a splendid unity, which is given stability and support by means of a compact rim mount. The rim of the bowl is embellished with eight elongated oval amber cabochons over tiny relievos in pale bone amber. The tiny scenes in relief are only discernible with a magnifying glass and represent the four seasons as the cycle of birth and death in nature. These depictions of rural scenes alternate with the likenesses of the founders of the four great empires in classical antiquity (Julius Caesar as ruler of the Roman Empire, Alexander the Great representing the Hellenic Empire, Ninos of Assyria and Cyrus of Persia). They symbolize the transience of worldly power, the portraits being modelled on a series of etchings by Adriaen Collaert after Marten de Vos. Some of the 24 drop-shaped pieces of amber are placed over diminutive half-length portraits in bone amber.

This parade bowl basin came to the Electoral Kunstkammer in 1687, 28 years after the death of Magdalena Sibylla from the estate of the wife (also called Magdalena Sibylla) of Johann Georg II of Saxony (reigned 1656–1680). In 1832 it was given to the Grünes Gewölbe.

JK

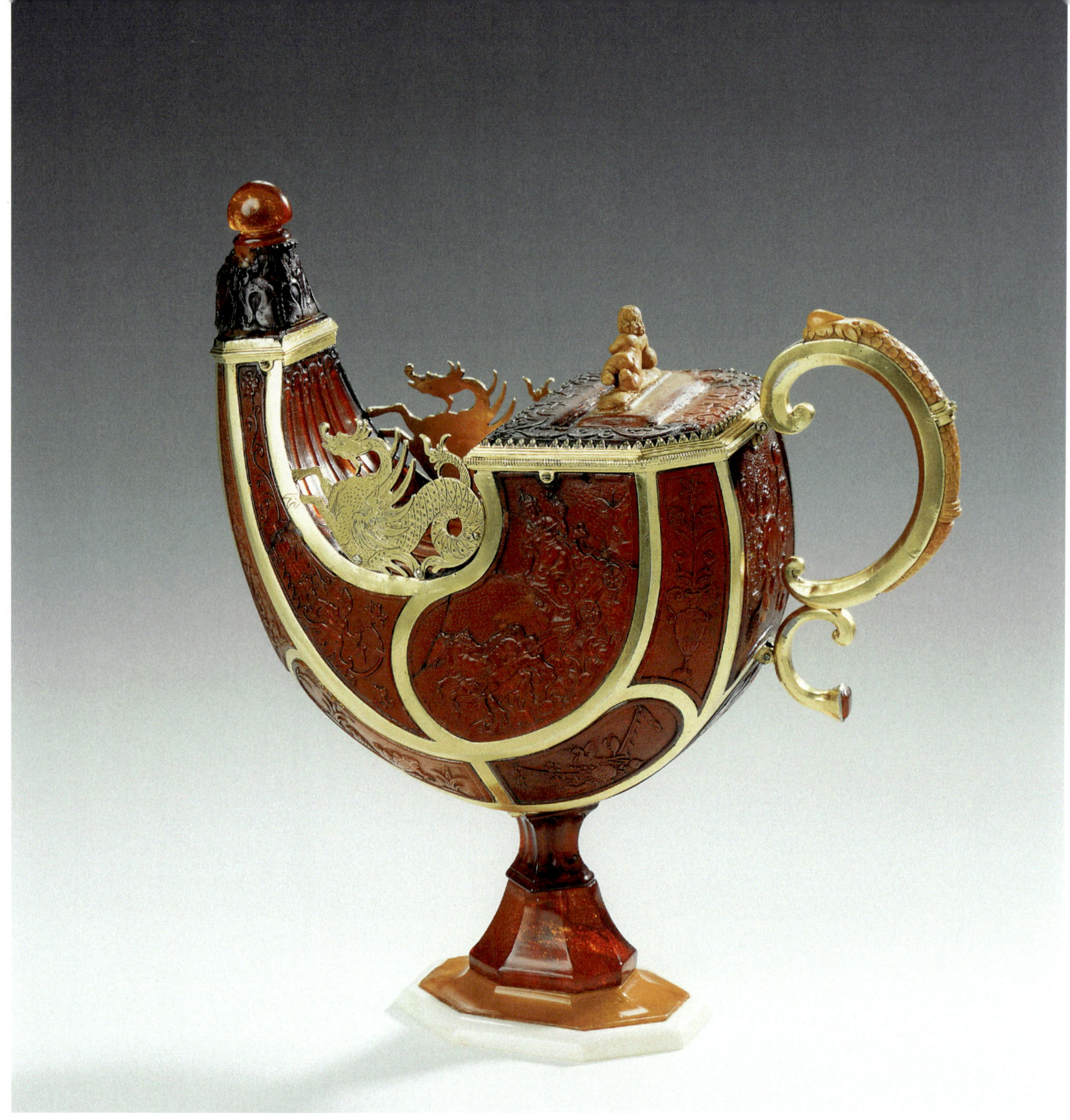

Ewer

Amber, different varieties, ivory, silver-gilt
Georg Schreiber
Königsberg, c. 1620 – 1630
H. 22.2 cm, Inv. no. III 82

Ewer

Amber, gold, enamel, silver, diamond roses
Königsberg, c. 1640 – 1650
Silver mount with diamonds: addition by Heinrich Köhler,
Dresden 1724
H. 20.5 cm, Inv. no. III 78

The inventory of the Dresden Kunstkammer records in the year 1662 the receipt of a ewer in the shape of a »Schnecke oder Schifflein« (snail shell or a small ship). It is made from thin amber plaques, which are given their unusual shape by means of a framework of slender silver-gilt strips which also serve to stabilise the vessel. The amber plaques are decorated with flowers, fruit, grotesqueries and garlands in relief and then fitted into the frame. The larger plaques on either side of the opening, which never actually served a practical purpose, are adorned with allegorical representations of Europe and Asia. The curved silver spout is decorated with two exactly identical dragons, cut from thin silver foil and delicately engraved and gilded. The figures of Neptune and

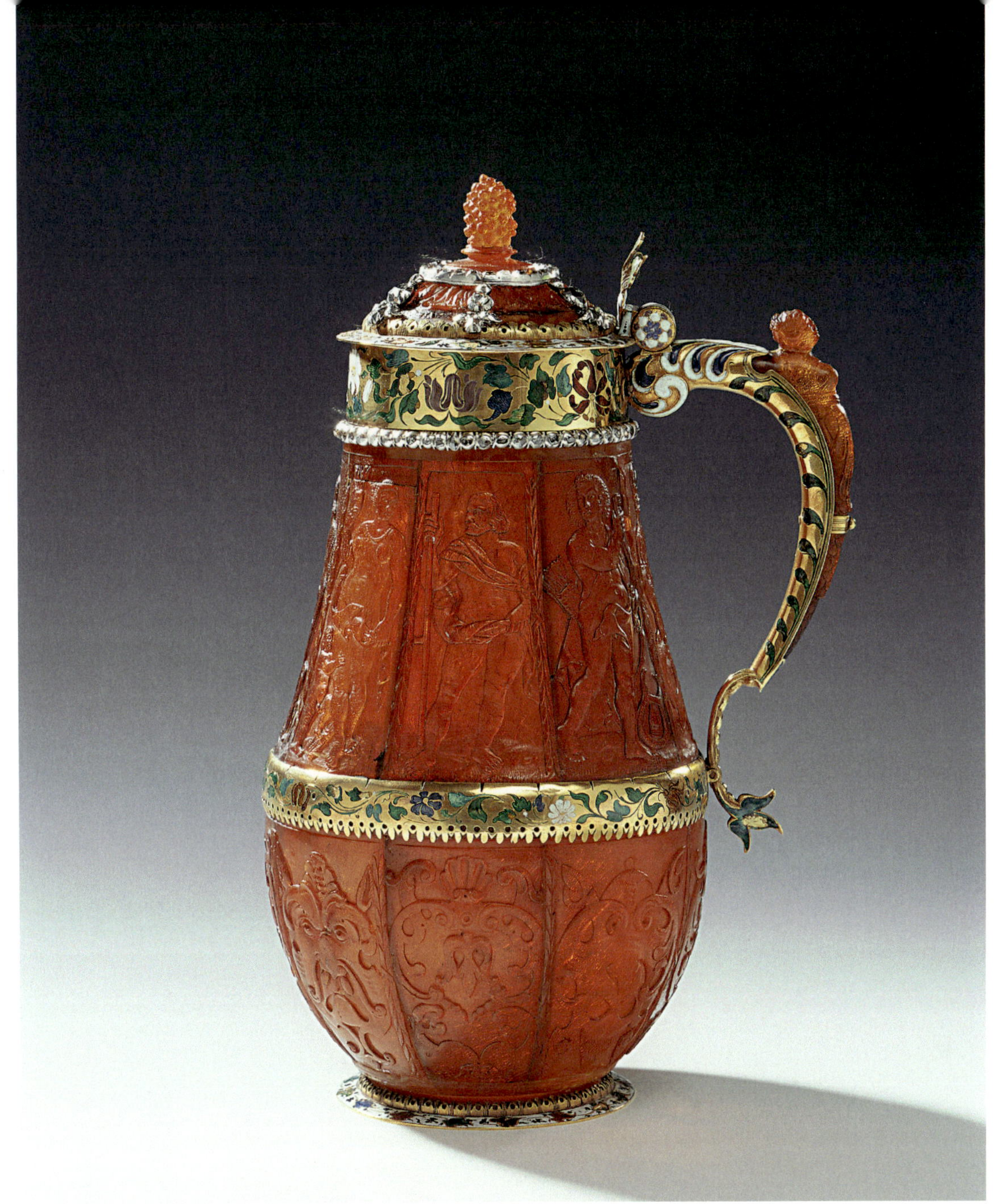

Orpheus, worked in bone amber, originally embellished the cover. These figures have sadly been lost or damaged. They were replaced by the small reclining figure of Cupid in or after 1880. This ewer and a matching basin, also part of the amber collection of the Grünes Gewölbe, are among Georg Schreiber's most beautiful works. So far, four signed and dated works by Schreiber, manufactured in the brief period between 1614 and 1619, have been identified. Schreiber was a prolific artist who was much in demand and was one of the first two master craftsmen who were members of the guild of amber turners in Königsberg, founded in 1641 with the permission of Friedrich Wilhelm of Brandenburg (reigned 1640–1688).

The second ewer made from amber segments was also created in Königsberg. The upper zone is decorated with deities from classical antiquity, the bottom one with mascarons and an ornamental décor. The gold mount decorated in colourful enamels was inspired by south German and Danish floral enamel decoration. French engravings from the same period show floral motifs of similar elegance and delicacy and may also have served as models. The silver-mounted diamonds at the rim of the spout and on the lid were added by the Dresden court jeweller Johann Heinrich Köhler in 1724, to which an invoice that has been preserved testifies.

JK

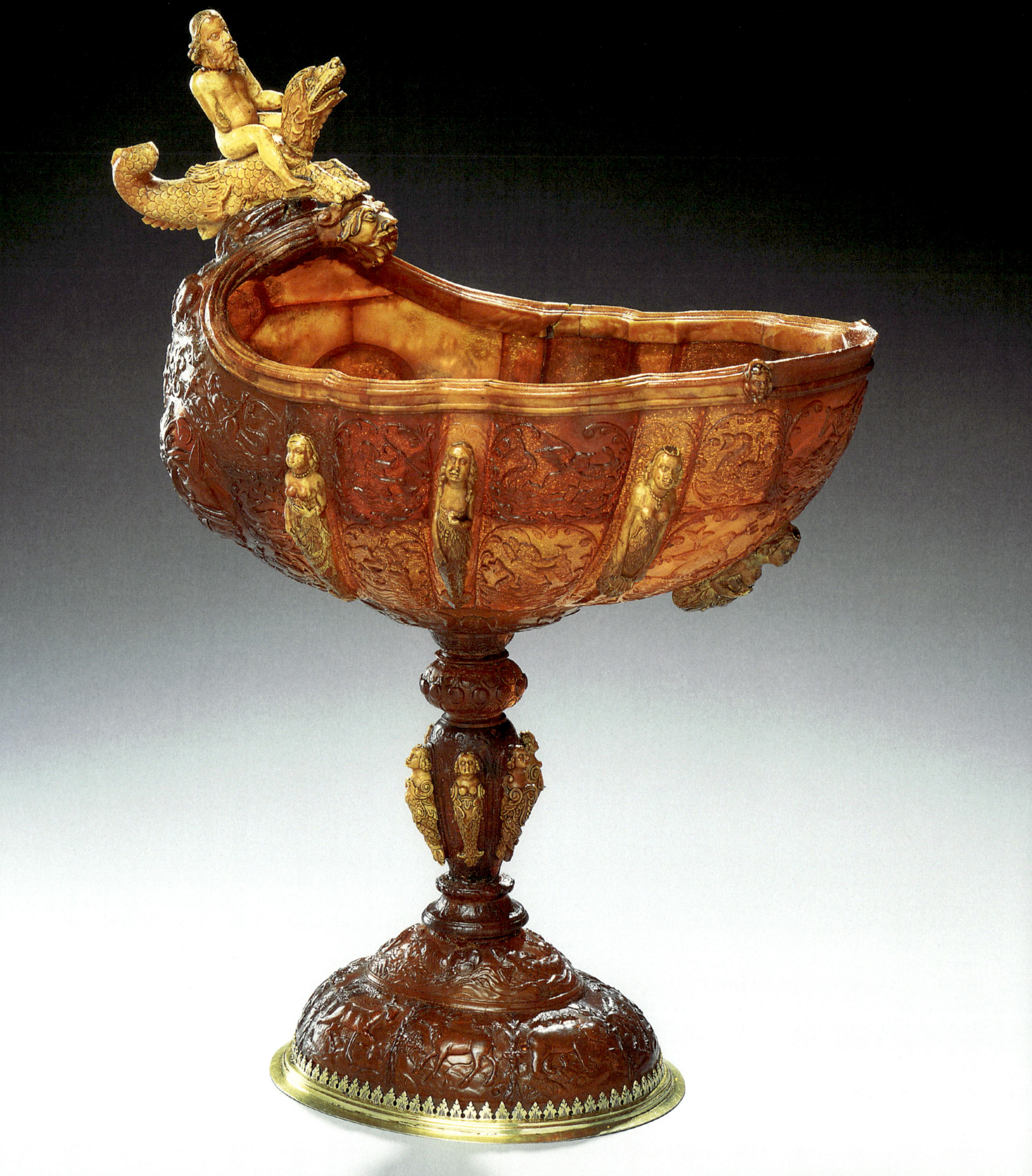

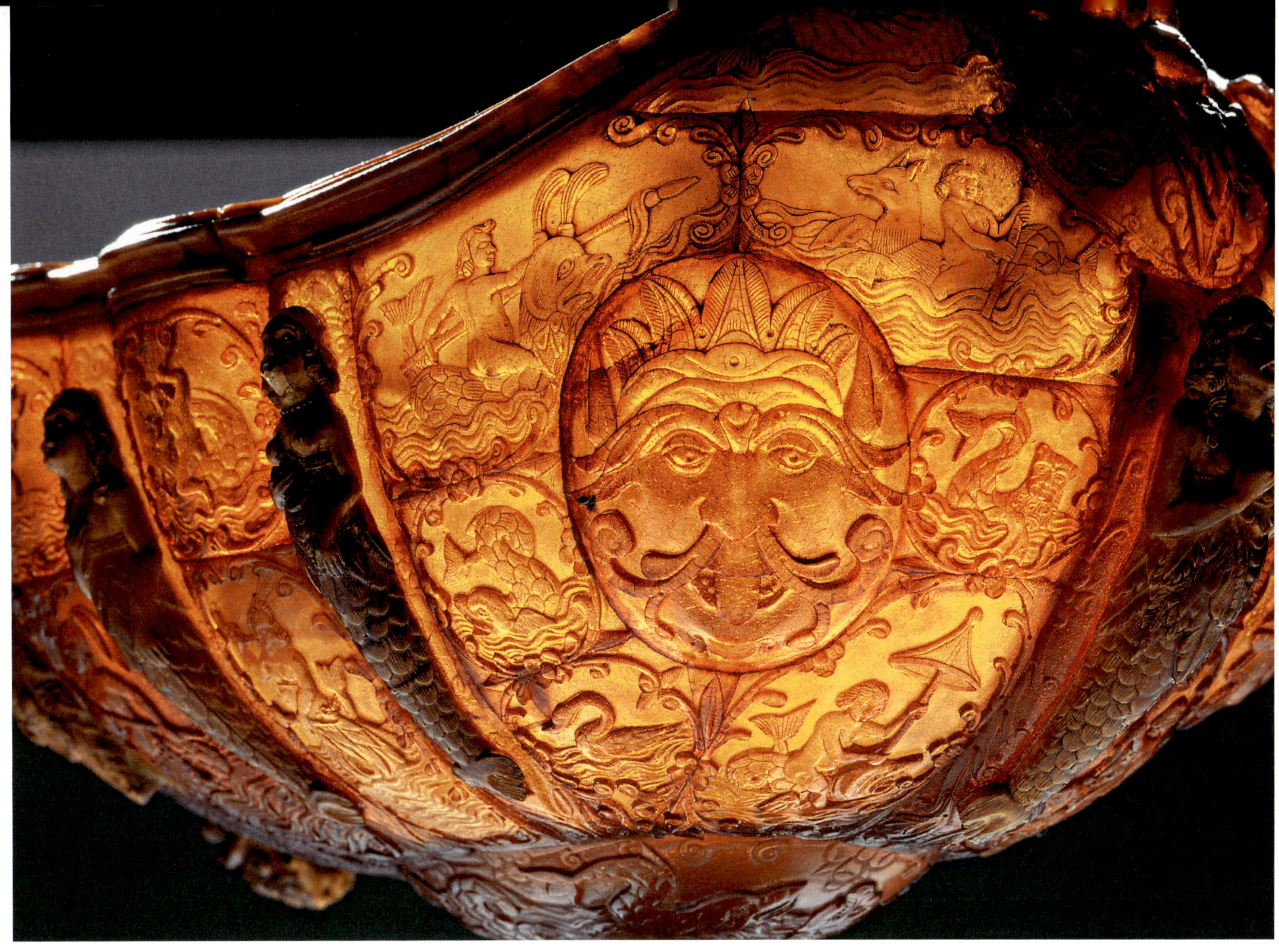

Parade Vessel in the Form of a Nautilus Shell

Amber, different varieties, ivory, silver-gilt;
foot, shaft and cuppa linked by means of a wooden rod
Jacob Heise
Königsberg 1659
Signed on the underside of the foot (in verre églomisé):
JACOB HEIS FECIT KONIGSBERG ANNO 1659
H. 34.5 cm, Inv. no. IV 340

Elector Friedrich Wilhelm of Brandenburg (reigned 1640–1688), the ›Great Elector‹, made precious gifts in amber not only to the German Emperor, but also to the Russian Tsar and the King of Denmark. Johann Georg II of Saxony (reigned 1656–1680) was also among those receiving gifts from Friedrich Wilhelm. In 1662 he was presented with this amber bowl, signed in detail and dated 1659 by the Königsberg amber cutter Jacob Heise. This parade vessel is modelled on the shell of the nautilus, a marine animal. It can also be regarded as an adaptation of a popular and widespread type of vessel in early 17th century stone-cutting. At first glance, one may be tempted to assume that the cuppa was cut from one large piece of amber, as the compact and homogenous wall of the vessel suggests. But its outward appearance is deceptive. The body of the vessel is composed of more than thirty differently curved, transparent amber plaques decorated with maritime scenes in alto rilievo. In addition, there are depictions of maritime mythical creatures, both male and female, and in the well of the vessel a minuscule representation in relief of Bacchus as a child with grapes and a drum. This tiny likeness is overlaid with an oval amber plaque. A curved treaded border in very light amber forms the rim of the bowl. This border consists of several parts and ends in a dynamic volute with a mascaron on which Neptune, God of the Oceans, is shown seated on a scaly sea monster. With this bowl, Jacob Heise gave impressive evidence of his activity as a stonecutter in Königsberg. A similar vessel from the year 1654 signed by Heise (originally at the palace in Königsberg) was destroyed in the Second World War, which makes this bowl and a second one, dated 1663, from the treasury of the Esterházy (Budapest, Museum of Applied Art) such a valuable source of information for the identification and attribution of other works in amber to Jacob Heise and his workshop.

JK

Casket

Amber, different varieties, softwood, ivory, copper, plated brass, iron pins
Gdansk, c. 1675 – 1680
H. 32.3 cm, w. 25.9 cm, d. 18 cm, Inv. no. III 91

Unlike the famous amber boxes by Michel Redlin and his Gdansk workshop, the walls of this three-tiered container consist, from the base zone upwards, of transparent pieces of faceted amber or segments with incised decoration. The wooden base zone is encrusted with amber and appliquéd with ivory ornamentation in relief. The main tier consists of a casket made of amber segments in groove and tongue technique. It is a »cantilever« construction without any supporting wooden elements. This enhances the brilliance of the transparent amber in a fascinating way, especially when light falls on the casket. The bottom and the inside of the lid are decorated with ivory carved in relief. When the lid of this casket is shut, the second casket, which is mounted on top, can be opened. The bottom of the much smaller second casket in transparent amber is also adorned with ivory in relief. The two small drawers on the narrow sides contain a surprise. Their inside is decorated with ivory relievos ›en miniature‹ showing loving couples. Thus the box only reveals all its splendour and its gallant secret when it is opened and more closely inspected. That was exactly what the artist had in mind when he created this casket. It had never been intended for practical use.

The ivory decoration in relief plays a crucial role in the design concept of this parade casket. The four relievos on the base zone with allegorical representations of the four continents are modelled on copperplate engravings by Cornelis Visscher from the early 17th century. Nicolaus Turau (Turow) in Gdansk used the same prints as models for four relievos in amber which originally adorned the armrests of the splendid amber throne. This throne was completed in 1677, and in 1678 it was taken to Vienna to be presented as a diplomatic gift to Emperor Leopold I (reigned 1658 – 1705) from Friedrich Wilhelm of Brandenburg (reigned 1640 – 1688).

JK

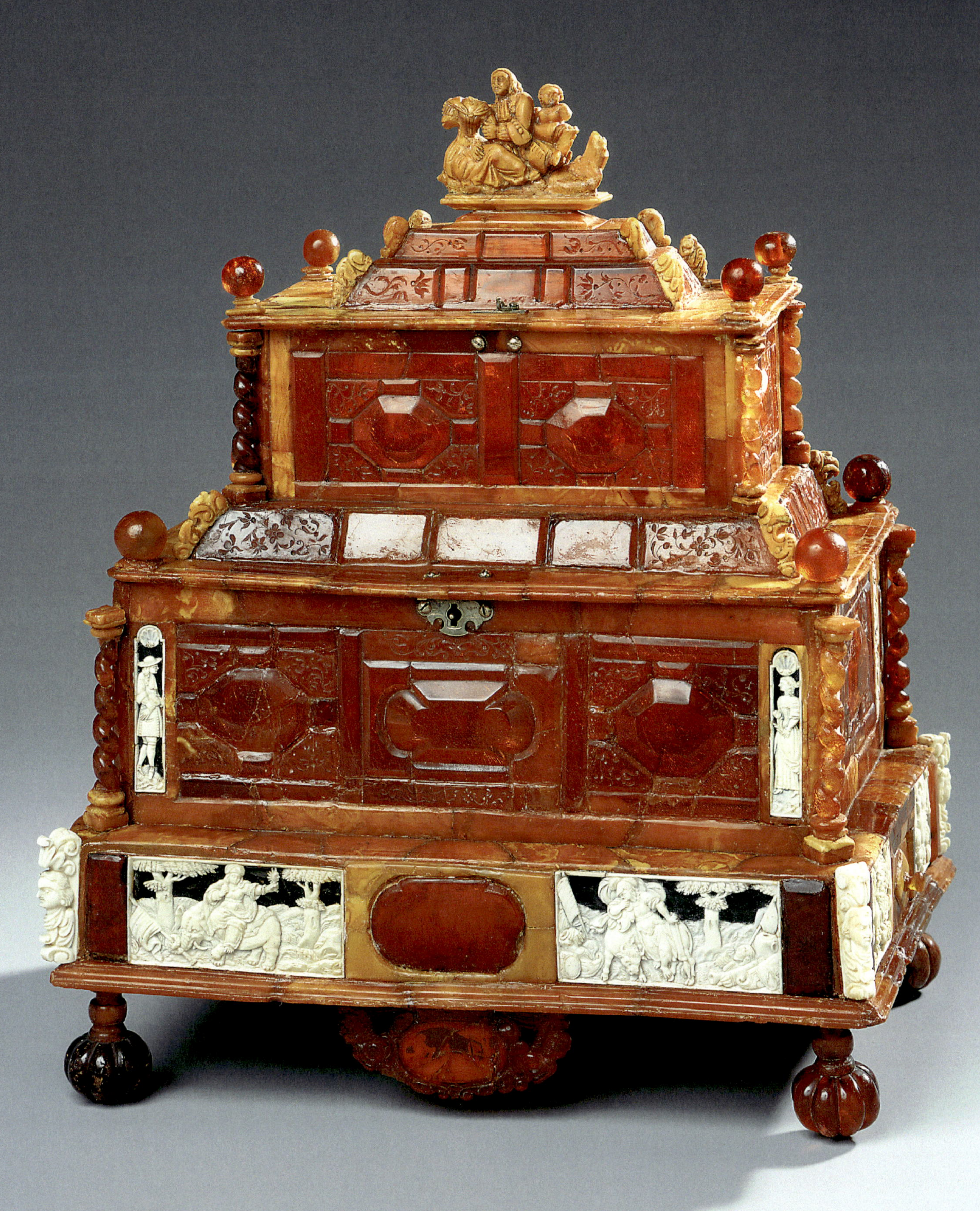

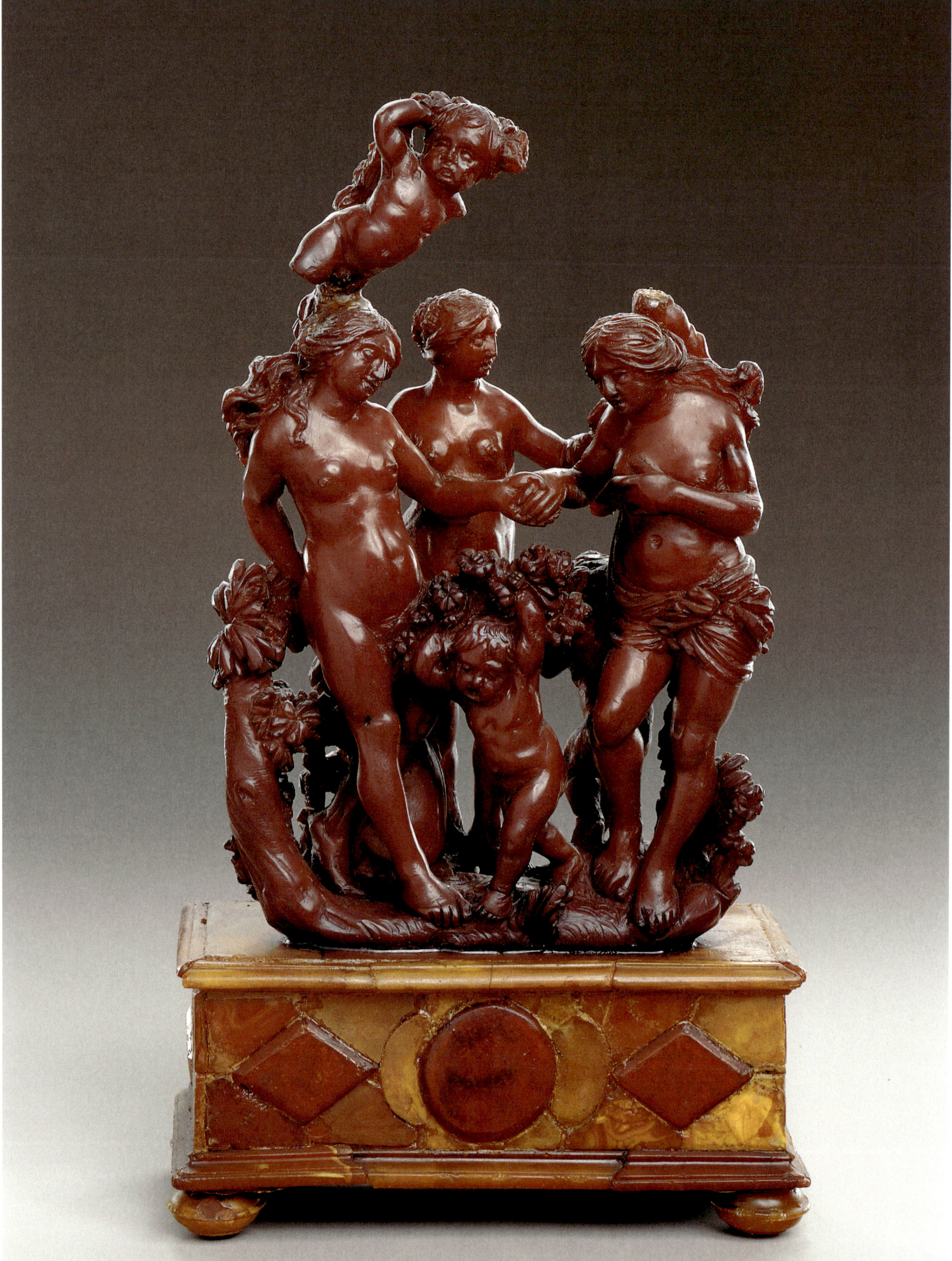

Group with the Three Graces

Amber, different varieties, wood
Christoph Maucher
Gdansk, c. 1680
H. (incl. pedestal) 25 cm, Inv. no. III 64

Female Figure with Loincloth (Lampetia?)

Amber, different varieties, wood, gilded sun not preserved
Jacob Dobbermann
Kassel, c. 1725
H. (incl. plinth) 16 cm, Inv. no. III 94

The three graces was carved from one single large piece of amber, which is very unusual. The women are rather plump and radiate a somewhat homespun charm, not at all the divine appeal that would be appropriate. They are the three Graces, Aglaia, Euphrosyne and Thaleia, daughters of Zeus, whose task is to propagate grace, joy and beauty. The group was created by Christoph Maucher, who made a name for himself as an ivory worker and amber carver alike. He was born in Schwäbisch Gmünd, but worked as a freelance artisan in Gdansk from 1670 or earlier. The fact that he was independent of the guild meant freedom but also envy and resentment. The statuettes and groups created by this extremely talented artist who possibly did his apprenticeship with Nicolaus Turau (Turow) in Gdansk can be seen in Vienna (Kunsthistorisches Museum, Kunstkammer), Modena (Galleria e Museo Estense), London (Victoria & Albert Museum), Künzelsau (Sammlung Würth) and Berlin (Skulpturensammlung).

The figurine of a woman in a loincloth is among the best amber sculptures that were ever created. Originally, this graceful beauty wore »eine vergoldete Sonne« – a gilded sun – on her head as the inventory of 1879 states. This attribute makes it easier to identify the figure, which was for a long time thought to be the goddess Diana. It may be a representation of Lampetia, the shining one. In Ovid's *Metamorphoses* she is referred to as one of the Heliads (daughters of Helios and Clymene), lamenting the death of their impetuous brother Phaeton. The mourning sisters were transformed into poplar trees and tears streamed from their barks which congealed in the sun and fell to the ground as amber. The creator of this delicate figurine was Jacob Dobbermann, known above all as an ivory turner, who had a predilection for depictions from classical mythology. He entered the service of Count Carl of Hessen in Kassel and, until his death in 1745, he remained court artist »in Birnstein«. Dobbermann's signed amber group ›Chronos and Cybele‹ and a statuette representing Cleopatra are part of the collection of the Staatliche Museen, Sammlung für Kunsthandwerk und Plastik in Kassel.

JK

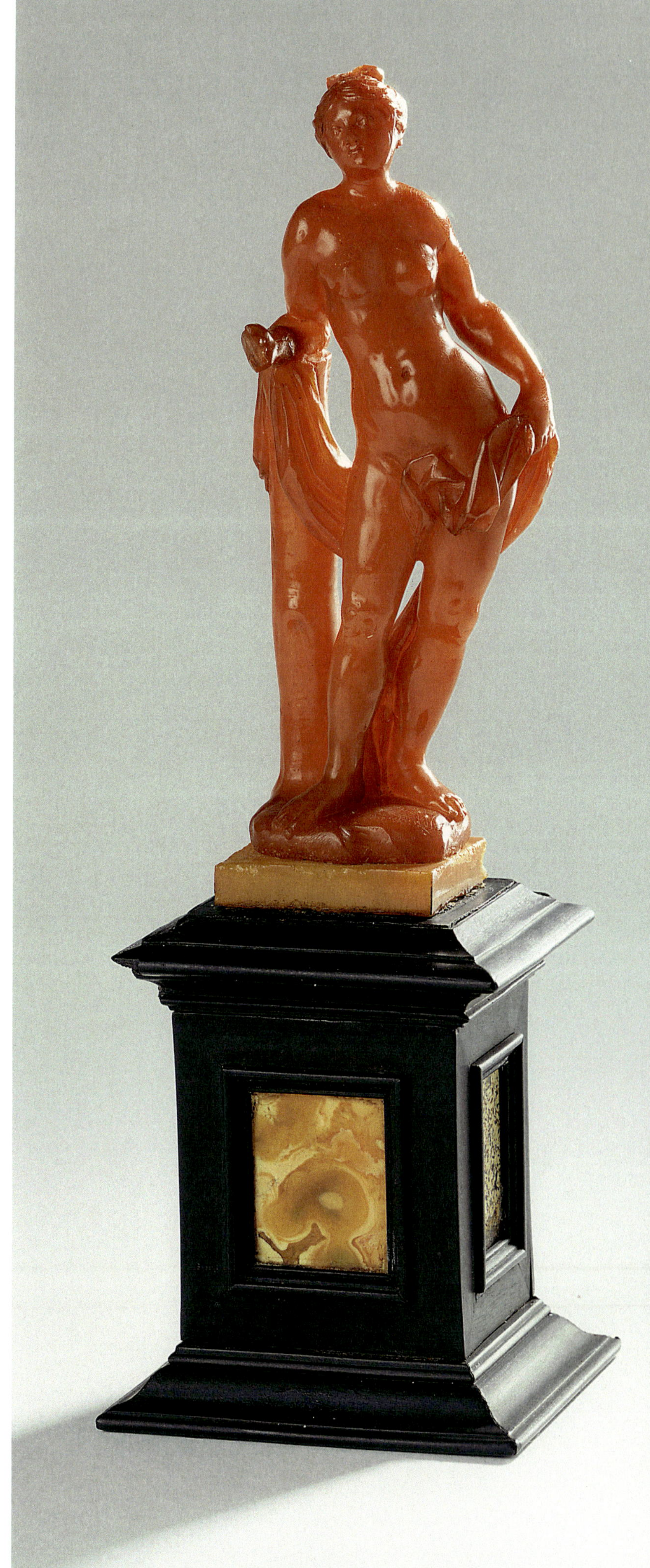

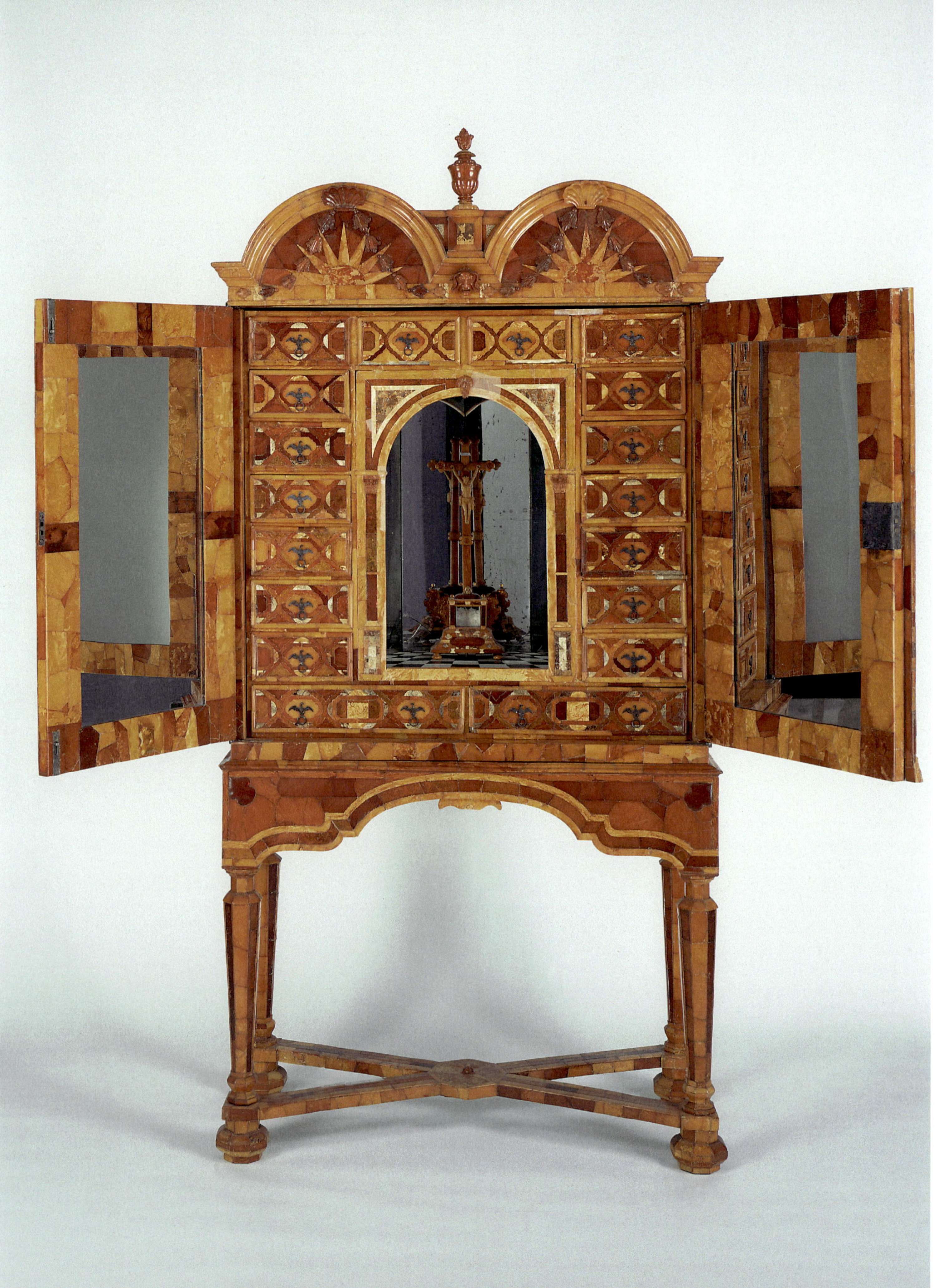

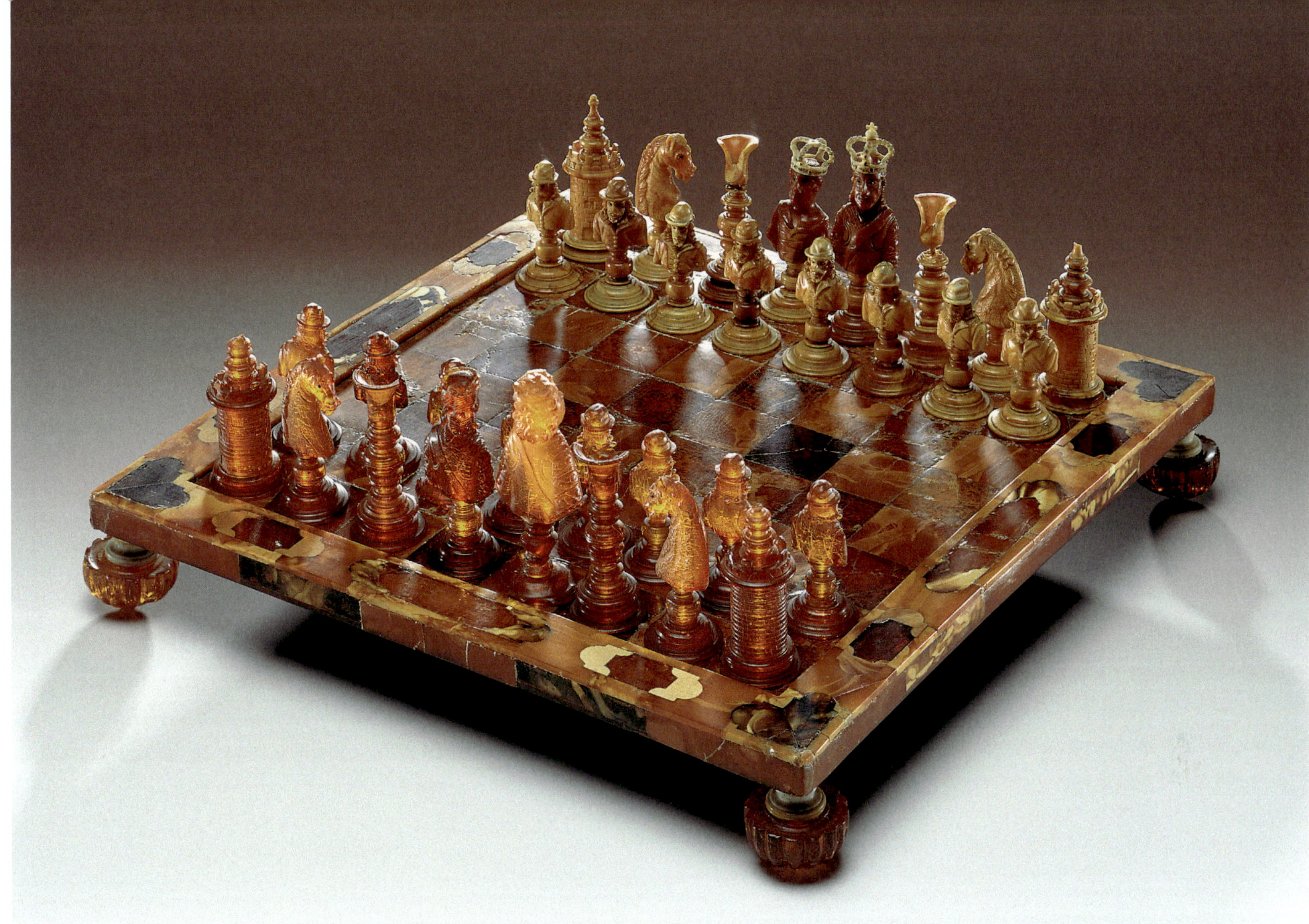

Cabinet

Wood; amber, different varieties; ivory; metal foil;
silver, blackened; mirror glass
Königsberg 1728
H. 212 cm, w. 107 cm, Inv. no. III 88

The large amber cabinet at the Grünes Gewölbe is an impressive example of the Prussian policy of donating gifts. In the years from 1719 onwards, relations were not very good between the Electorate of Saxony and Prussia. The relationship between these two countries was characterised by tensions and conflicts. Friedrich Wilhelm I of Prussia (reigned 1713 – 1740) travelled to Dresden in 1728 in an act of political diplomacy. He was treated to all kinds of courtly entertainment and stayed for almost a month. Elector Friedrich Augustus I, also known as Augustus the Strong, the powerful king of Poland reciprocated the visit in May of the same year when he went to Potsdam and Berlin. This visit merited a very special gift. Friedrich Wilhelm I decided on a cupboard in amber with two doors, which was hastily manufactured in Königsberg, as letters which have been preserved show. A piece of furniture of that size could only be manufactured in the incrustation technique. This means that polished segments of amber of different varieties were appliquéd to the wooden cabinet in such a way that they gave the impression that the entire object was made of amber.

The cabinet was presented – according to a chronicler of the festivities – on 2 June 1728 at the royal palace in Berlin. Johann Heinrich Köhler, court jeweller of Augustus the Strong, took the cupboard to Dresden immediately after its presentation and had it exhibited at the Amber »Kabinett« which was a part of the »Naturalienkabinett« at the Dresden Zwinger. It was only in 1789 that the cupboard eventually came to the Grünes Gewölbe. It was not only praised because of its size and beauty, but also because of the contents of its drawers. Augustus the Strong must have been amazed by the variety of precious objects revealed on opening the drawers, which were covered with mirrors. There were boxes for pins and needles, scissors and bangles for the ladies. For the gentlemen there were tabatières, buttons and tampers in the shape of attractive female legs. There was also a chess board in one of the larger drawers as well as a game of solitaire and a box of chips in amber. The crucifix was added after 1760 and placed in the niche of the cupboard.

JK

Ivory Room

For the 18th century visitor the Ivory Room was the second display room. It was entered from the Bronze Room. The Ivory Room, which was only one window section wide, was created in the first building phase. Painting and decorating began in winter 1727/1728 and took until February 1729. Together with his staff Christian Reinow created the colour décor »[…] auf italienischer marmor art von zwölfferley Sorten gemahlet, hernachmals Lackiret […]« (in the style of Italian marble of twelve different kinds, then lacquered) of the small room with an area of 44 sq. metre. The court lacquer master received the not inconsiderable wage of 3,500 thalers. The use that the »marbled room« was to be put to seems initially not to have been decided. Thus the travel writer Georg Keyssler reported after his visit in 1730 that he had seen automata there. However, only a few years later it had been decided to display here the existing collection of ivories of the Grünes Gewölbe, whose number was increased by others from the Dresden Kunstkammer. In order to round off and complement the Room of Bronzes, late Baroque imagery and the artistic virtuosity of the late Renaissance have been illustrated here since that time in ivory, a precious and optically highly attractive material. Both with regard to conservation and aesthetics a more beautiful solution for a Baroque presentation of ivories cannot be imagined than on tables, consoles and the dado shelf of a cabinet room in a décor of faux marbre.

Only a few capitals, consoles and the panelling of the entrances to the Bronze Room and the White Silver Room have been preserved from the original interiors. In 1860 the then director of the Grünes Gewölbe complained that the lacquered wood panelling was infested with woodworm. When the west façade of the Royal Palace was remodelled between 1890 and 1891 the entire panelling of the Ivory Room was removed and replaced by a copy. During the modernisation of the Grünes Gewölbe by Jean Louis Sponsel a quarter of a century later the intimacy of this display area was destroyed. The Ivory Room was extended to the south and doubled in size and the present Amber Cabinet was also integrated. From 1914 until 1942 when the Grünes Gewölbe was finally closed, not much of the original character of the Ivory Room was visible and the collection was displayed in a much less structured fashion. The decision in the course of refurnishing the Grünes Gewölbe to highlight the Baroque structure of the collection meant that Renaissance ivory turned objects and carved sculptures, reliefs and vessels were again presented in their original context. The small dimensions of the Ivory Room and the open display is one of the reasons why only a limited number of visitors per hour are admitted to the treasury museum.

The reconstruction of the Ivory Room was based on the wall panels made in 1891 and the consoles and architectural elements that still existed. The lost décor of the »zwölfferley Marmorart« was reconstructed from surviving fragments and a similar décor created by the same artist for the altar of the Stadtkirche Hohenstein. Thus, the present Ivory Room is a receptacle in the spirit of the late Baroque period for one of the most comprehensive historic collection of ivories in the world created by the restorer Hans-Christoph Walther, who took his inspiration from Christian Reinow.

DS

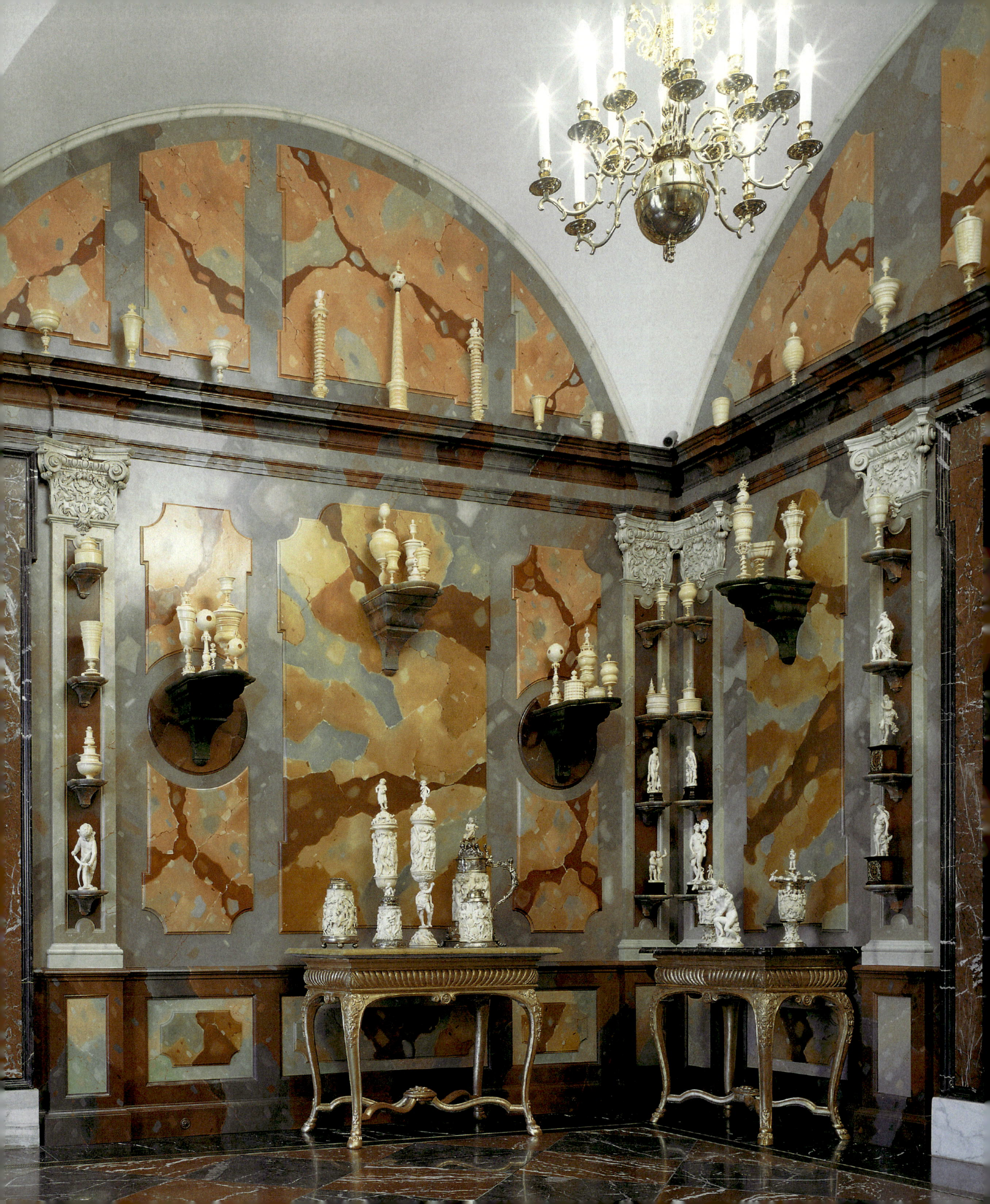

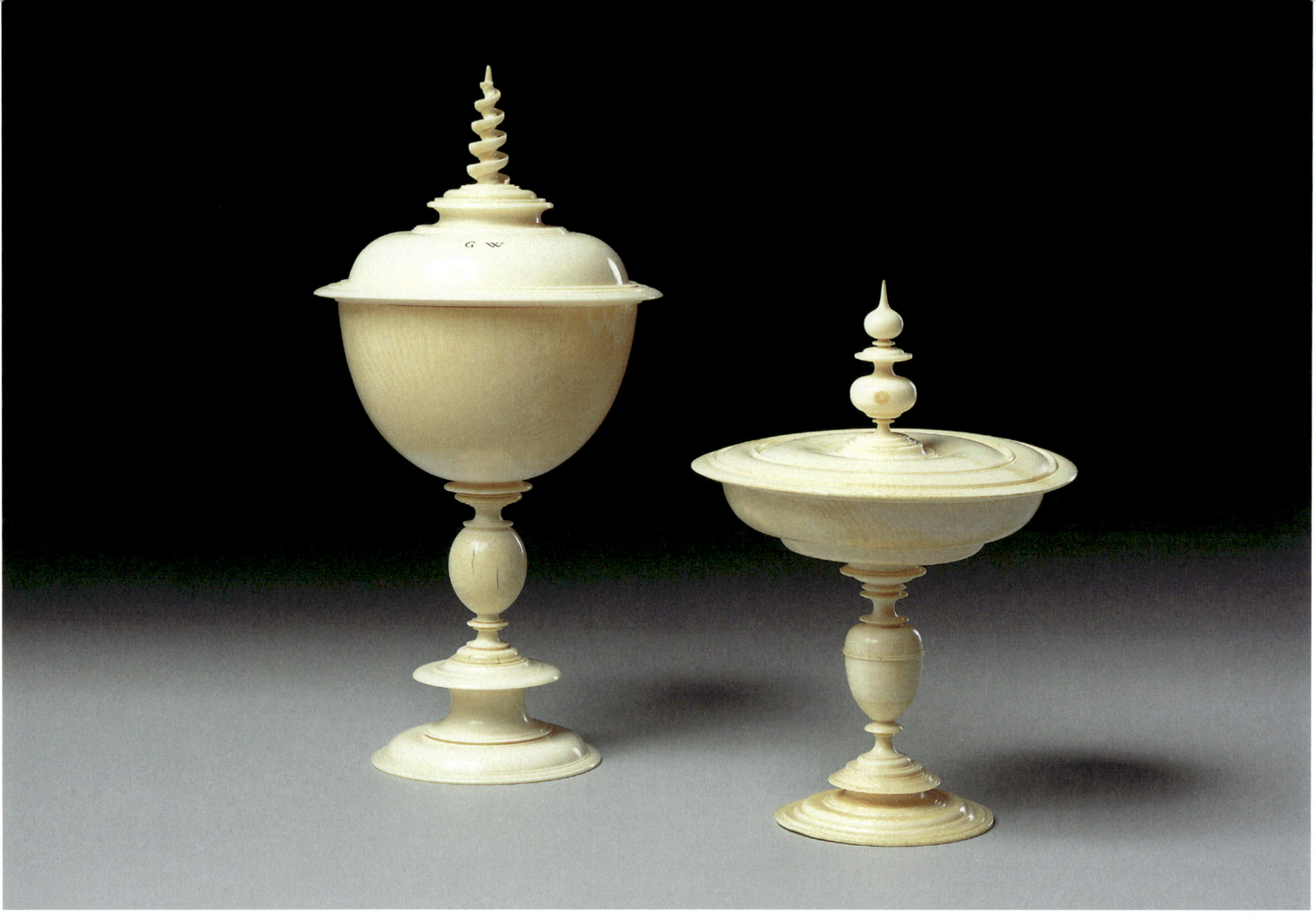

Two covered Bowls

Ivory
Left: signed and dated by Georg Wecker
Dresden 1588
H. 22.3 cm, Inv. no. II 260
Right: signed by Georg Wecker
Dresden, presumably between 1588 and 1590
H. 16.2 cm, Inv. no. II 162

These two signed covered bowls by Georg Wecker came to the Dresden Kunstkammer in 1590. Their simple elegance epitomises the restrained, well-proportioned style of Wecker's works in turned ivory. A type of vessel that will certainly have influenced his works is the so-called »tazza«, which was an extremely popular and modern vessel in goldsmiths' work in the last third of the 16th century. Another, more obvious reason for the shape of these clearly structured vessels with their wide cuppas, torus profiles, grooves and smooth baluster shafts is the technology used in ivory turning. The highly artificial character of these mechanically created works of art was the reason for their extreme popularity as exhibits of the Kunstkammer. The material used and the design of the vessels, however, made it impossible to use them as drinking or serving bowls.

A comparison of works signed by Georg Wecker and dated between 1586 and 1589 reveals an amazing stylistic continuity on the highest artistic level. Wecker, who was originally from Munich, was employed as court turner for Elector Augustus of Saxony on a permanent contract from early 1578 onwards, which means that the bulk of his work, carried out with immense zeal, was not produced until after the death of Wecker's great patron. Together with the court turner Egidius Lobenigk he transformed the turning room near the Kunstkammer at the palace in Dresden into an efficient and productive workshop that soon became famous. Elector Augustus and his son and successor Christian I both took a keen interest in ivory turning. Augustus himself worked at the lathe in his rare leisure hours and Christian was also well versed in the art of ivory turning. As a result, lathe-turned ivory became an art form that was held in high esteem at the court. The objects created in Dresden, together with gifts and acquisitions, eventually made ivories one of the largest groups of items in the collection of the Electoral Kunstkammer. Consequently, Augustus the Strong had a room furnished in the Grünes Gewölbe specially devoted to turned works in ivory.

JK

Column with Icosahedron and Columns with Tetrahedon

Ivory
Left: signed and dated by Egidius Lobenigk
Dresden 1591
H. 70.6 cm, Inv. no. II 99
Right: signed and dated by Egidius Lobenigk
Dresden 1588
H. 52.5 cm, Inv. no. II 7

Egidius Lobenigk from Cologne was taken on as court turner in Dresden in 1584. Lobenigk's stylistic preferences differed from those of Georg Wecker and his designs were more experimental, yet for more than ten years the two craftsmen worked in Dresden alongside each other as highly prolific artists of the same artistic calibre. The works by Lobenigk that were part of the collection of the Kunstkammer bear his monogram, »EL«, and usually the year in which they were produced.

In the years 1588/89 and 1591, Lobenigk turned eight large ivory columns. They are all preserved in the Grünes Gewölbe. The two columns illustrated here highlight the principles of design and construction in ivory turning: turned hollow cylinders form the stable base. The columns were turned separately from one piece of ivory. They are oval in cross section and taper towards the top. The spirals cut into the body of the works are reminiscent of those of screws and contribute to the unusual appearance of these columns. The spirals are executed in such a precise and accurate fashion suggesting that a lathe was used which Lobenigk had designed specially for the production of these works of art with their »streifig« (striped) decoration. The accuracy and precision of the columns, a type of ivory object he himself had invented, are the features of the works which bear his signature.

Looking at the finials of the columns, it is easy to see that Lobenigk seems to have regarded his invention as an opportunity to perfect his skills and demonstrate the whole range of his artistic creativity. The large and impressive works are crowned with absolute masterpieces of the art of lathe working. The representation of geometric objects penetrating each other is, however, not an invention of ivory turning, but an element of theories on design and perspective in the second half of the 16th century. In 1568 Wenzel Jamnitzer published his *Perspectiva corporum regularium*, and Hans Lencker had his *Perspectiva corporum* printed in 1571. Both books were available in the court library. They are mentioned in the inventory of the Dresden Kunstkammer of 1587 and might be used, in this or another edition, by the court turners for design models and as a source of inspiration.

JK

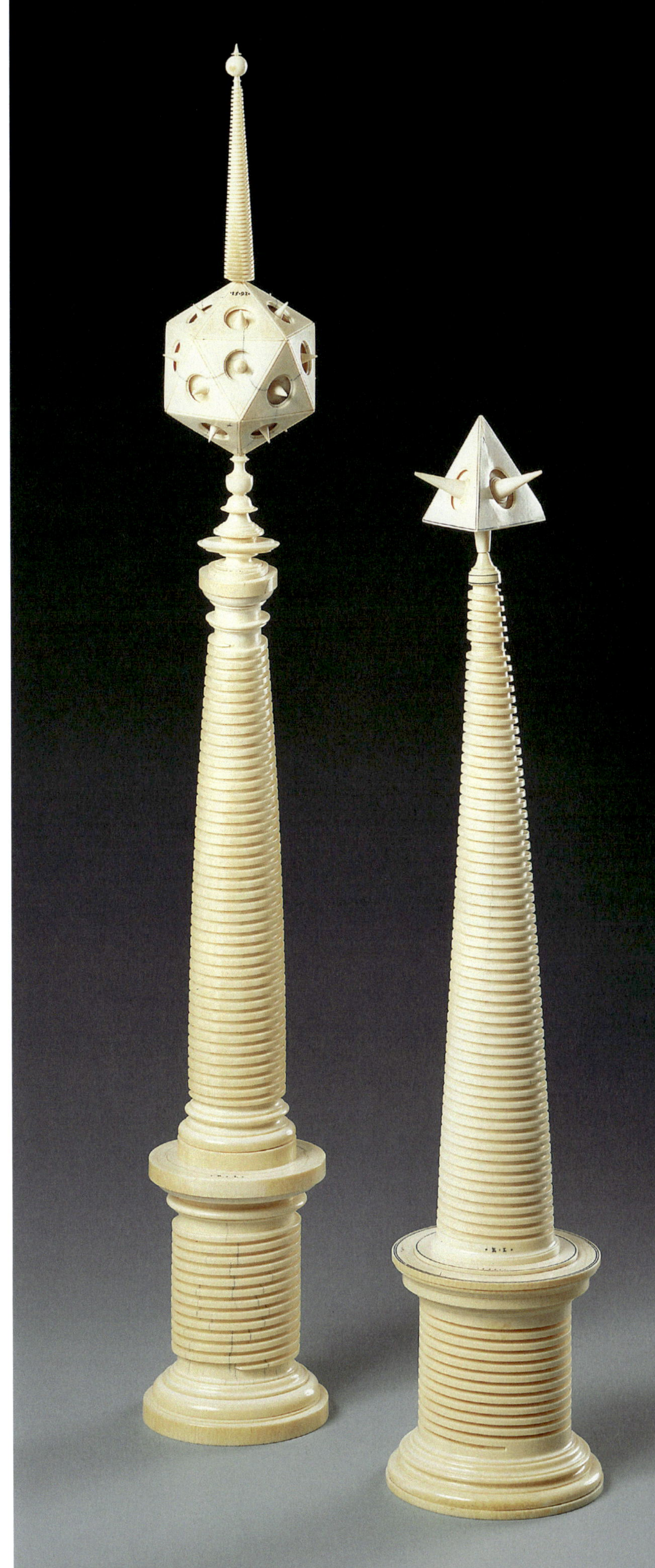

Cup and Cover Crowned with a Figure of Minerva

Ivory; in the cover the electoral coat of arms in the form of a medallion
in verre églomisé and the circumscription V.G.G.CHRISTIA: C.F.Z.S
Signed and dated by Egidius Lobenigk
Dresden 1590
H. 50 cm, Inv. no. II 9

This cup belongs to the group of works from 1590 signed and dated by Egidius Lobenigk. It is turned in a bulbous shape, with only a few slender torus elements giving the vessel structural articulation. Inside the cover there is a verre églomisé medallion with the coat of arms of the Electorate of Saxony and the circumscription »V.G.G. (von Gottes Gnaden – by the grace of God) CHRISTIA: C.F.Z.S (Christian Churfuerst zu Sachsen – Christian Elector of Saxony). This is a clear reference to Elector Christian I who supported and encouraged the art of ivory turning at the Dresden court until his early death in 1591.

Not all elements of Lobenigk's cup were turned on the lathe. The figure of Minerva, originally holding a lance and a shield, was carved by hand. There are four other examples of carved figures complementing a lathe-turned work – a stylistic feature which is completely absent in the work by court turner Georg Wecker which has been preserved. Lobenigk mounted the figures of a Roman warrior and of a woman with a fruit basket on the covers of two turned cups from 1590 and in 1591 he used statuettes representing Mercury and Sol as finials for a tall column with a contrefait sphere. In the last phase of his career, between 1591 and 1595, he created a sequence from the life of Marcus Curtius that is exhibited at the New Grünes Gewölbe. He mounted the figure of this brave young hero on a cylindrical turned ivory plinth. According to the legend, Marcus Curtius sacrificed his own life for Rome by hurling himself into a fiery abyss. These works mark Lobenigk's first steps towards a new stylistic concept in ivory working in the late 16th century, which was to move away from purely mechanical production in favour of a combination of turning and figurative carving, used in moderation. Lobenigk's skills as an ivory carver were, however, limited and he lacked stylistic dexterity. As a turner he was, by contrast, both extremely skilled and highly prolific.

JK

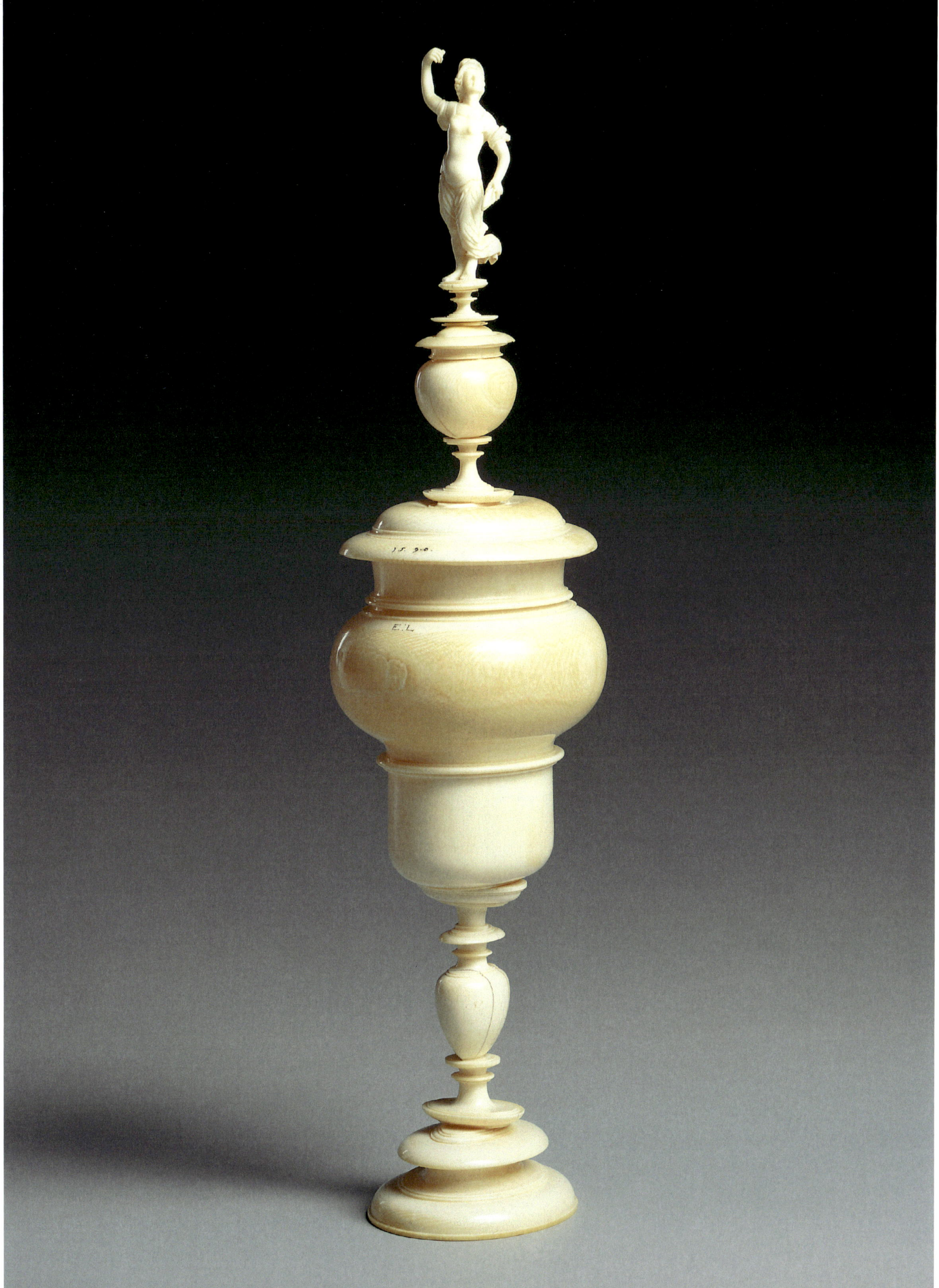

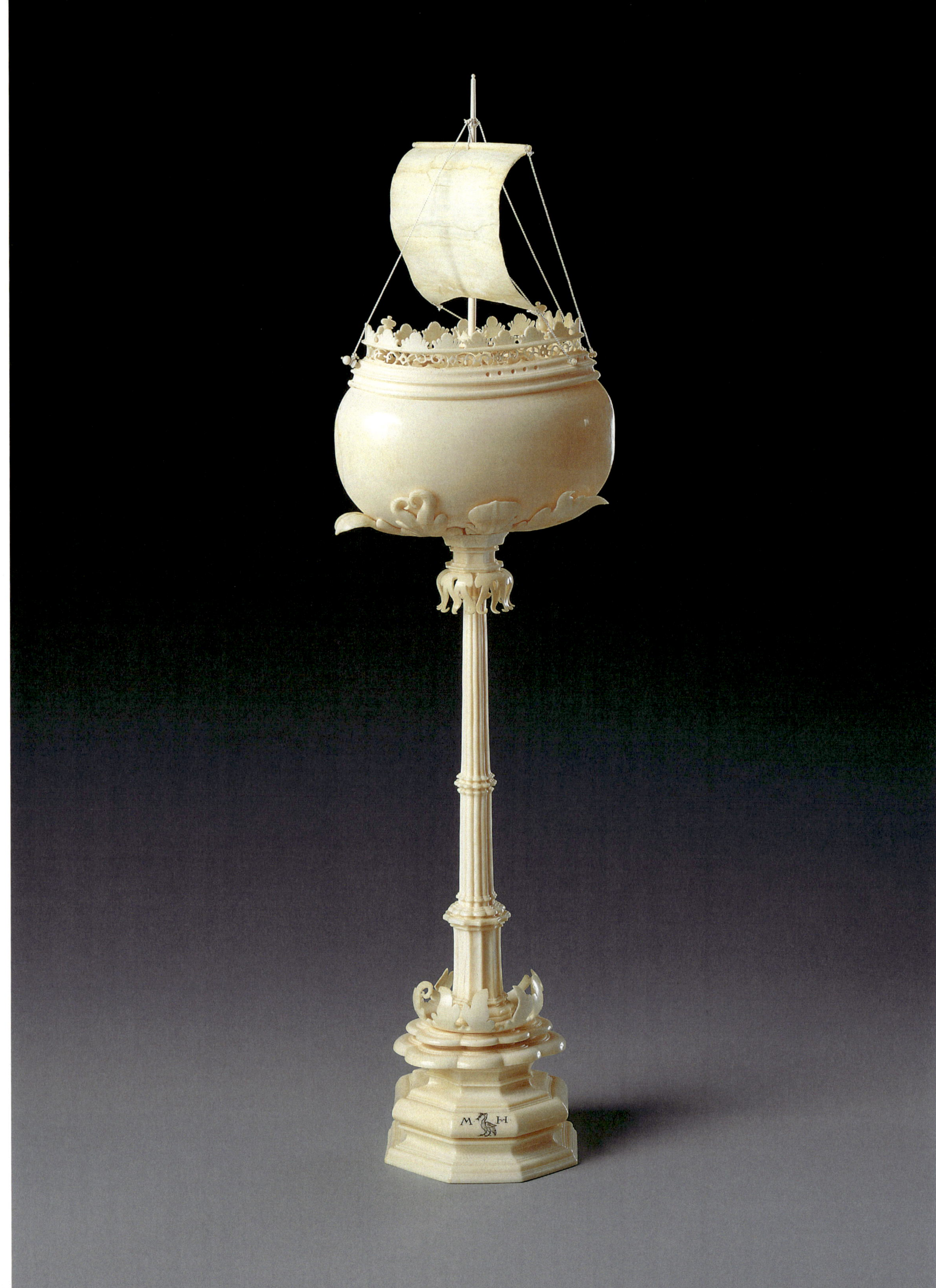

Turned Object in Ivory with a Sailing Boat

Ivory
Attributed to Marcus Heiden and Georg Friedel
Inscription on foot: MH framing the figure of a heron
Dresden, presumably between 1617 and 1619
H. 36.8 cm, Inv. no. II 233

Goblet

Ivory
Marcus Heiden
Inscription on the inside of lid below the finial:
MARCVS HEIDEN FECIT ANNO 1623
Coburg, 1623
H. 38.5 cm, Inv. no. II 354

Marcus Heiden's skillfully turned ivory goblets, often embellished with figural carvings, are in the tradition of Jacob Zeller who was court turner in Dresden from 1610 onwards. It is not unlikely that Heiden, born 1597/98, came to Dresden as a young man to learn ivory working at Zeller's workshop. One object in the collection of the Grünes Gewölbe, a work in ivory crowned by a boat with billowing sails made of wafer-thin, turned ivory, may serve as evidence for this assumption. On its footring there is an incised, blackened monogram. The letters M and H frame a tiny heron. This bird was part of Georg Friedel's signature, who between 1610 and 1619 was employed at Zeller's workshop in Dresden and supplied numerous turned objects to the Kunstkammer. The monogram »MH« can only be attributed to Marcus Heiden. Thus, the skilfully crafted object preserved in the Dresden collection may well be the result of the fruitful cooperation between the experienced Friedel and the apprentice Heiden. The ivory goblet from the Grünes Gewölbe, dated 1623, is the earliest of the signed and dated works which Marcus Heiden created while working for Duke Johann Casimir von Saxony-Coburg (reigned 1569–1633). The inscription »CHRISTVS SPES MEA« on the underside of the foot shows that Heiden was a deeply religious, steadfast Protestant who adorned some of his works with Christian tenets written in Latin.

A small book written by Marcus Heiden in 1640 – *Beschreibung eines Helffenbein gedrehten Kunststücks ... beneben desselben geistliche Bedeutung* (Landesbibliothek Coburg) – provides moving insights into the work and thoughts of the artist, who was active during the Thirty Years' War as court turner in Coburg, then in Eisenach and from 1639 in Weimar.

JK

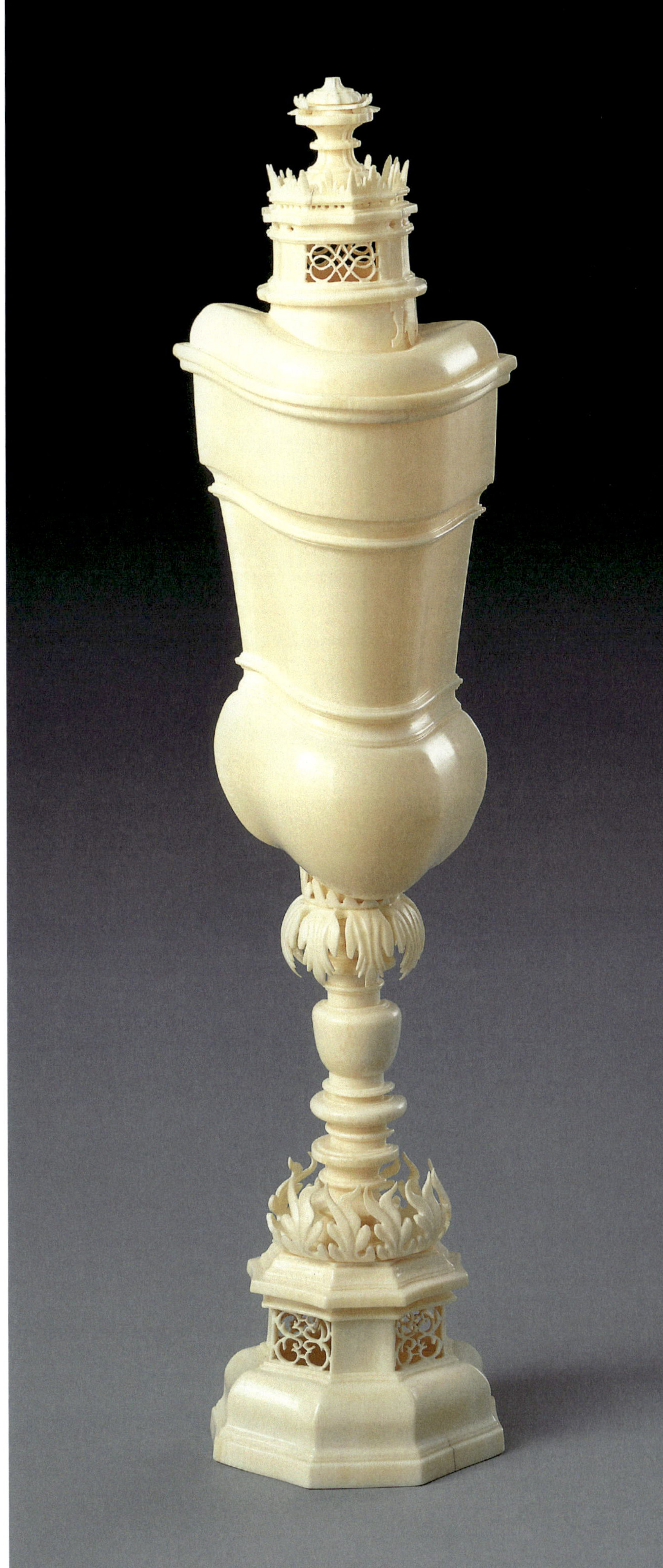

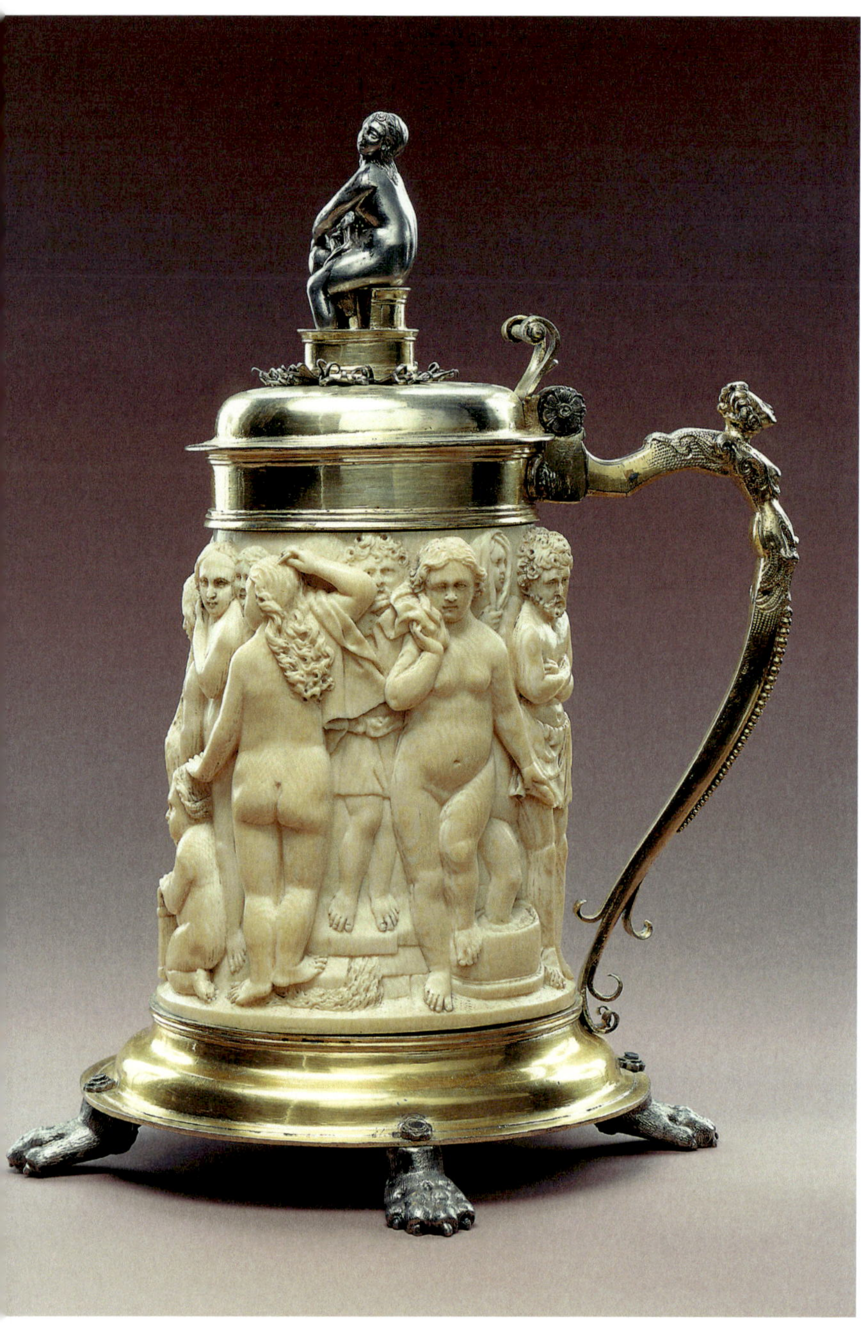

Tankard with Bathing Scene

Ivory, silver-gilt
Carving: workshop of Leonhard Kern
Schwäbisch Hall, c. 1640 – 1645
Mount: Martin Borisch
Dresden, before 1649
H. 33.2 cm, Inv. no. II 22

Leonhard Kern's small sculptures and reliefs in wood, stone, and above all ivory, won him artistic renown and recognition from his contemporaries. After his sojourn in Italy between 1609 and 1614 where he had an opportunity to study the works of numerous artists in Venice, Rome and Naples and try his hand at nude drawing, he settled in Schwäbisch Hall in 1620 and remained faithful to his adoptive town. He died in 1662, a highly respected, very well-to-do burgher. It was here that he developed his unmistakable style and opened a workshop. Depictions of nudes are a recurring theme in his work and are incorporated into religious, mythological and also secular contexts. Kern's typical female figures are sturdy, tense and at the same time calm, hardly ever displaying any sign of emotion, neither pain nor joy. In spite of their nudity they almost completely lack erotic appeal.

Men and women bathing were a popular motif in the work of Leonhard Kern and his workshop in the 1640s, which this opulent tankard from the Grünes Gewölbe exemplifies. The massive ivory wall of the vessel is densely decorated with more than twenty men and women bathing. This slightly risqué scene is depicted in two relief levels. The women are naked, while the men are only sparsely clad in loin-cloths. Engravings by Hans Sebald Beham served as an inspiration for the bathing scene.

The vessel has some stylistic weaknesses, and details of the carving are not very carefully executed. Yet, it is a sound workshop product that reveals the influence of Leonhard Kern. The ivory wall for the vessel was probably sent to Dresden soon after it was manufactured. Here, Martin Borisch's mount transformed it into a tankard. On the lid of the vessel, the goldsmith appliquéd the small figure of a bathing woman in cast silver and thus made a very personal and imaginative comment on the scenes in ivory.

JK

Tankard with the Wise and the Foolish Virgins

Ivory, silver-gilt
Carving: Johann Georg Kern
Öhringen, 1650s
Mount: Andreas I Wickert
Augsburg, 1650s, 1661 at the latest
H. 58 cm, Inv. no. II 399

This impressively large tankard was first mentioned in the inventory of the pretiosa of the Grünes Gewölbe in 1725. The wall in ivory shows the wise and the foolish virgins in alto rilievo standing very close to each other. The parable of the ten virgins waiting for their bridegroom (Christ) is narrated in the New Testament (Matthew; 25,1–13). The five wise virgins were well prepared and had brought enough oil for their lamps, while the five foolish ones had forgotten to bring spare oil. As a result, they could not find their way in the darkness, came too late and found the door to their bridegroom's house locked. The ivory carver clearly gave his work moralising overtones in his interpretation of the parable by juxtaposing the virtuous wise virgins and the immoral foolish ones. The domed lid of the tankard is adorned with a statuette of St John the Baptist as a young man in a seated position. He gives the impression of balancing on a stylised calyx of leaves in silver as his legs are bent backwards with his feet dangling in the air. Both the figural finial and the relief on the wall of the tankard can with a high degree of certainty be ascribed to Johann Georg Kern, nephew of the famous artist Leonhard Kern. Kern the Younger lived in Öhringen/ Hohenlohe from 1650 until his death in 1698. Although he was not active in the workshop of his uncle in Schwäbisch Hall, his work – which is still not very well known – shows that he belonged to a group of ivory artists whose style was strongly influenced by Leonhard Kern.

The date ante quem of the completion of the tankard is indicated by the hallmark of the silversmith Andreas I Wickert from Augsburg who died in 1661. Wickert specialised in sumptuous silver mounts for tankards with an ivory body as is shown by several examples which have been preserved in Vienna (Kunsthistorisches Museum, Kunstkammer), Kassel (Staatliche Museen, Sammlung für Kunsthandwerk und Plastik), Karlsruhe (Badisches Landesmuseum), Copenhagen (Rosenborg Slot), Gotha (Schloss Friedenstein) and Berlin (Staatliche Museen zu Berlin, Kunstgewerbemuseum). Stylistically, however, the mount for the tankard illustrated here is much closer to that of the tankard at the Victoria & Albert Museum in London, the carved ivory body of which was signed and dated in 1651 by Bernhard Strauss.

JK

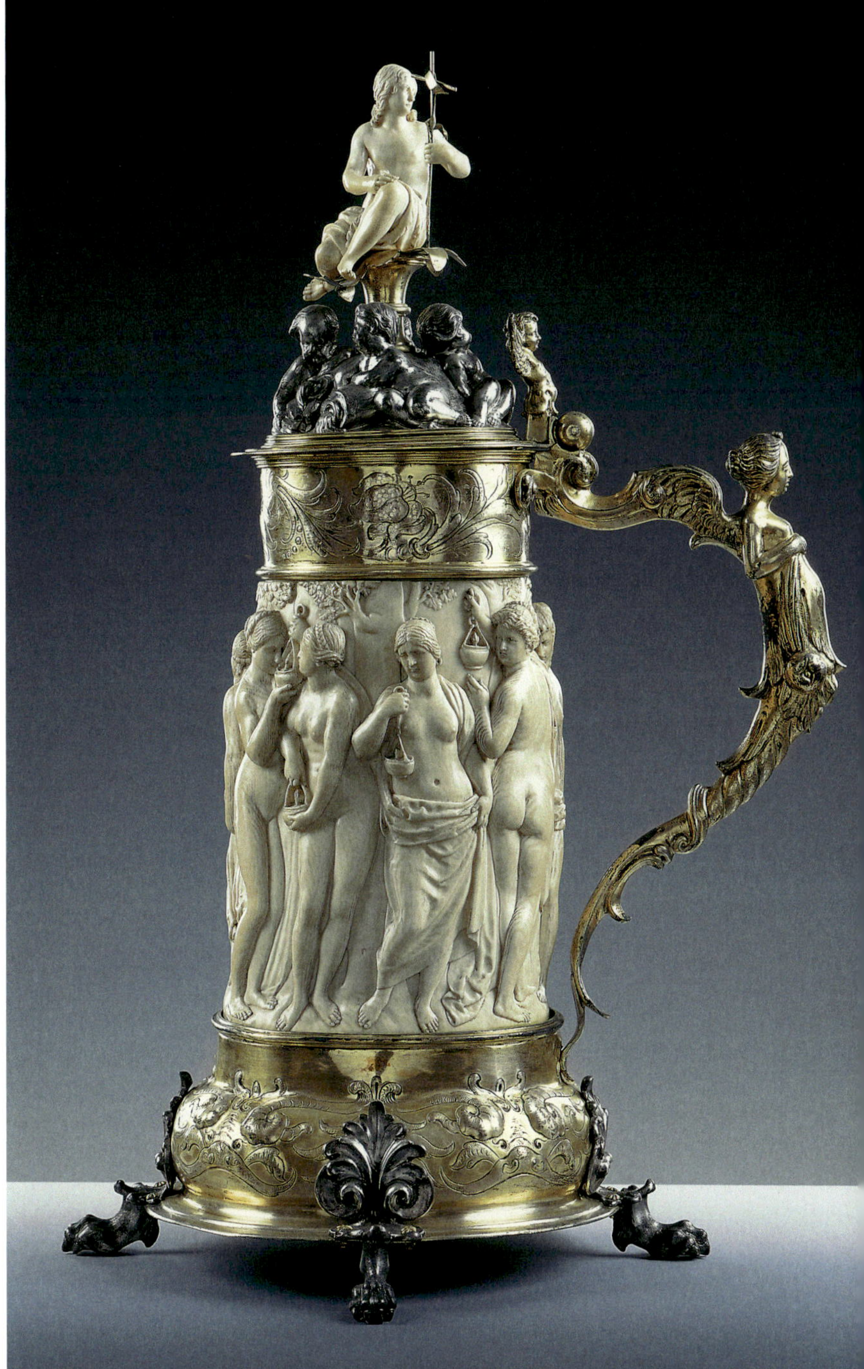

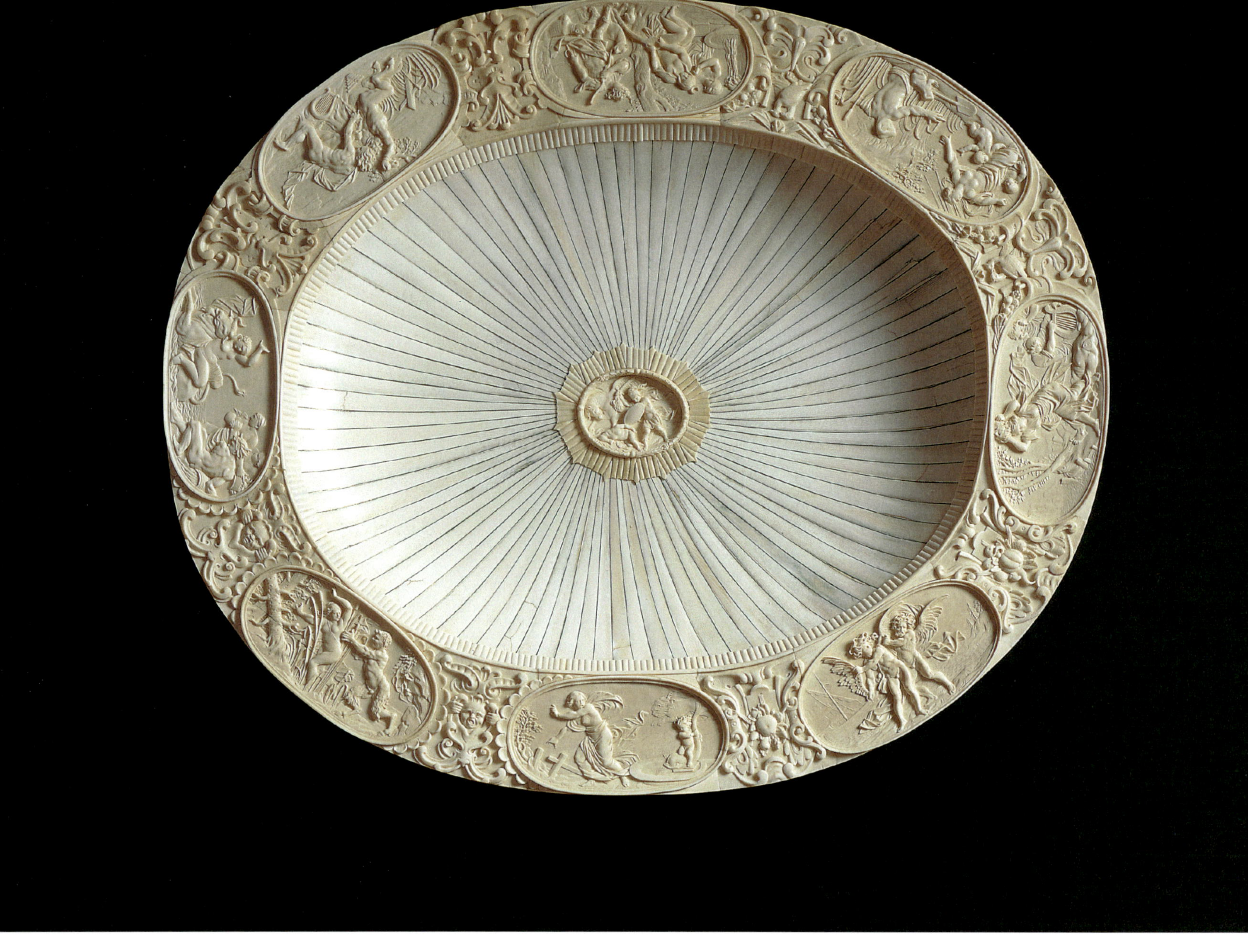

Basin and Ewer

Ewer: horn, ivory, silver
Basin: ivory, wood, originally horn (lost in war),
2001: new body with veneer strips in maple wood, glued in three layers
Ewer: Johann Michael Maucher
Schwäbisch Gmünd, c. 1670 – 1680
Basin: Germany (possibly circle of Balthasar Griessmann, Salzburg),
c. 1670 – 1680
Ewer: H. 32.7 cm; basin: H. 7.8 cm, l. 58.6 cm, w. 47.8 cm; Inv. no. II 245

Duke Heinrich von Saxony-Merseburg was the owner of this set and it came to the Grünes Gewölbe from his estate in 1738. The ewer, made from individual pieces of horn is embellished with a figural freeze in ivory showing peasants hunting. The inside of the spout is also lined with ivory. The handle in the shape of a fruit garland is also made of this precious material. Vessels of this type – clearly not intended for everyday use, but exclusively as precious collectors' items – became Johann Michael Maucher's »hallmark« and are among the most important examples of his creative years between 1668 and 1688 in Schwäbisch Gmünd. Johann Michael Maucher also mastered the complicated working of large-scale dishes in ivory and horn. Magnificent examples have been preserved in Neuenstein (Hohenlohe Museum), Vienna (Kunsthistorisches Museum) and Brunswick (Herzog Anton Ulrich-Museum).

For stylistic reasons, this basin from the Grünes Gewölbe cannot clearly be attributed to Johann Michael Maucher. It is obviously the product of a different artist of excellent skills as an ivory turner who must have had access to a state-of-the-art workshop. Other works that may be attributed to this artist are: the parade dish in Stockholm (Nationalmuseum) and Paris (Bibliothèque Nationale, Cabinet des Médailles).

These conditions were a prerequisite for executing the various different steps in the process of working a basin like this one with a body in horn, the strips of ivory radiating from a central medallion and the rim made from individually worked segments.

Each of the nine oval reliefs in the Dresden dish show a different episode from Ovid's *Metamorphoses*, who was the most popular poet from Greek antiquity in the 16th and 17th centuries. Numerous illustrations, such as those by Hendrik Goltzius of the first four books of the *Metamorphoses*, were popular and widespread and constituted the basis of the mythological knowledge which was indispensable at that time.

The parade basin from the Grünes Gewölbe was severely damaged during its post-war exile after 1945. The body of the vessel in horn was lost. The ivory parts were kept in a leather satchel specially designed for this bowl, and most of the parts have been preserved. After comprehensive restoration work in 2000/2001 the vessel experienced an almost miraculous »resurrection«.

JK

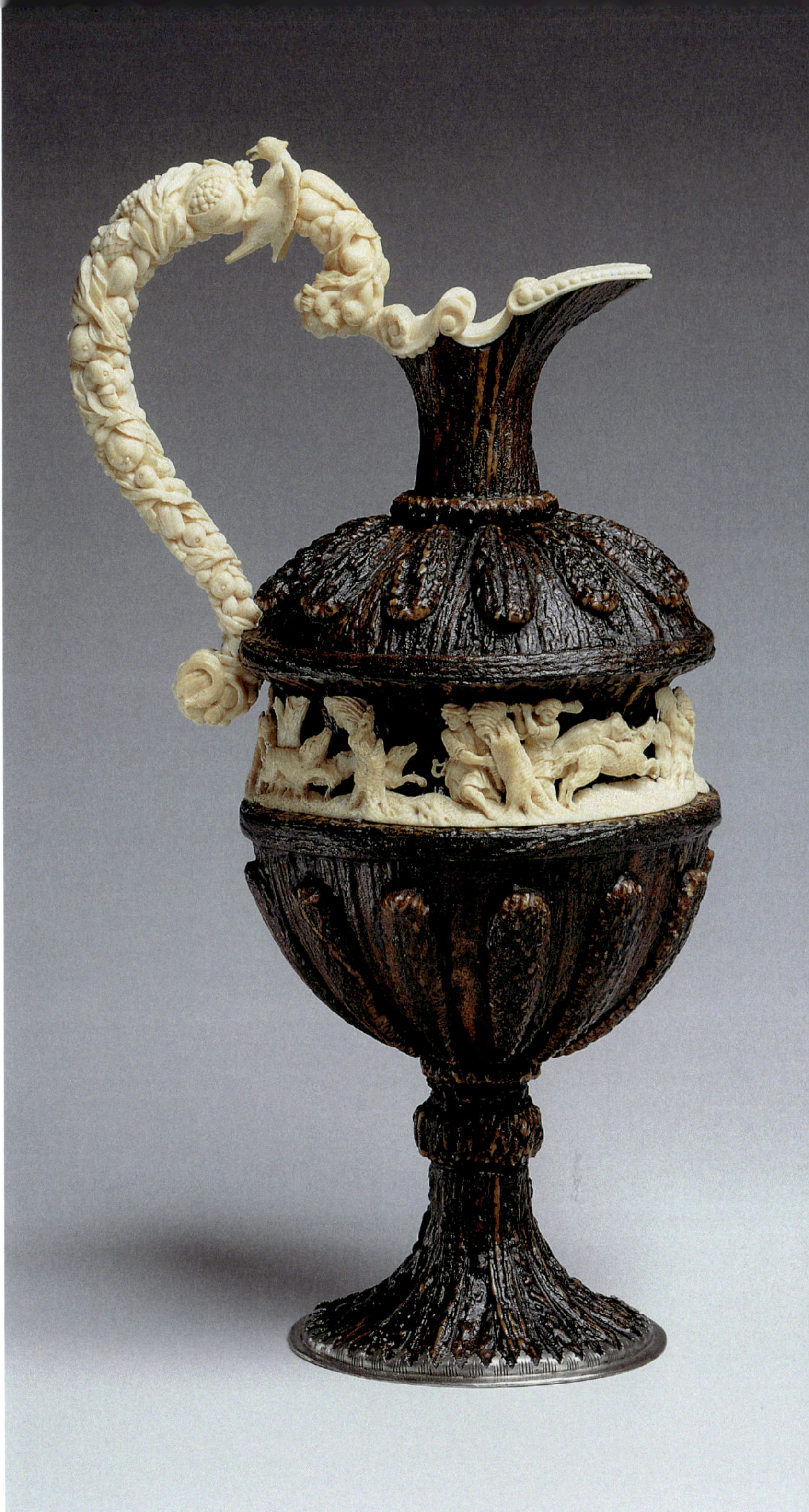

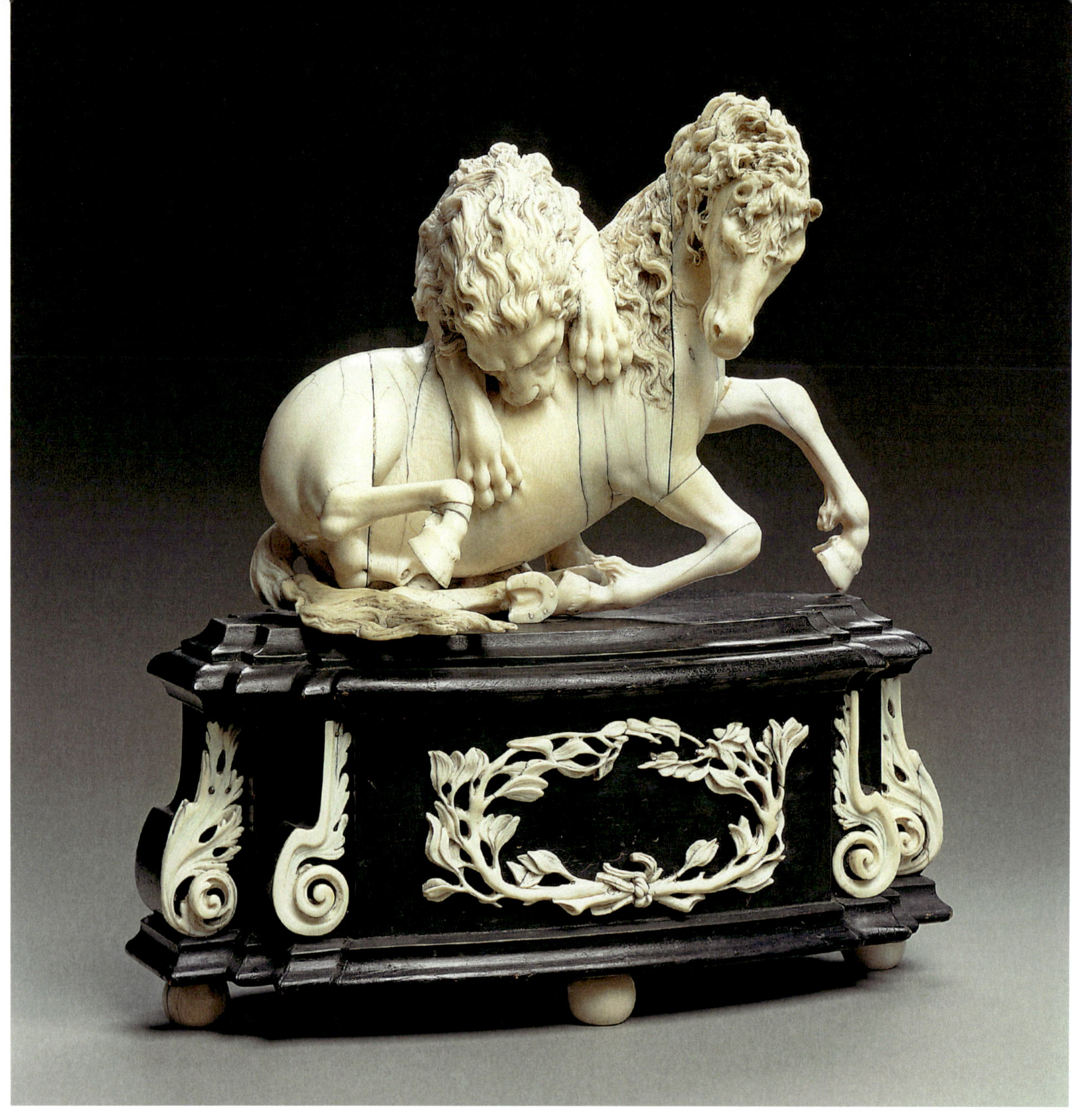

Horse and Lion

Ivory, plinth in wood with ivory appliqués
Melchior Barthel
Venice and Dresden, shortly before 1670 – 1672
Ivory group: H. 21.5 cm, Inv. no. II 342

This dramatic ivory carving of a scene with animals fighting did not belong to the Saxon king. It came from the estate of Heinrich Count of Brühl (1700 – 1763) who had risen to power under King Augustus III of Poland (reigned 1733/34 – 1763) to become the second most powerful person in the Electorate of Saxony and the Kingdom of Poland. A wealth of posts and offices – among them that of prime minister – gave him immense prosperity and influence. His fall was as dramatic as his rise to power when he returned to Dresden from exile in Warsaw after the Seven Years' War in 1763, shortly before his death. In keeping with his former status, Brühl started to build up his own art collection around the year 1740. Within a decade this collection had reached dimensions which made it comparable in quality and function to that of the king. Part of Brühl's private collection was a small and exquisite range of ivories. The pieces which have been preserved in the Grünes Gewölbe show that Brühl was a collector well versed in the field of ivories who owned masterpieces of the highest quality. His large estate lists, among other works, the ivory group after the so-called Farnesian Bull and Horse and Lion. Both works, the former exhibited in the ivory room at the Grünes Gewölbe, are by Melchior Barthel. This artist left Dresden as a young man to go to southern Germany and Rome and eventually to spend 17 creative years in Venice. It was only in 1670, two years before his premature death, that he returned to Dresden, where he was recommended to Johann Georg II (reigned 1656 – 1680) by Oberlandbaumeister Wolf Caspar von Klengel. As a result, Barthel became court sculptor. The ivory group Horse and Lion belongs to the group of later works by the artist. It is modelled on the colossal Roman marble group (Rome, Palazzo dei Conservatori) which also inspired the sculptor Giambologna whose work was cast in bronze by Antonio Susini and Giovanni Francesco Susini. Among these casts are the signed works in Detroit (The Art Institute), Rome (Museo di Palazzo Venezia) and the Louvre in Paris.

JK

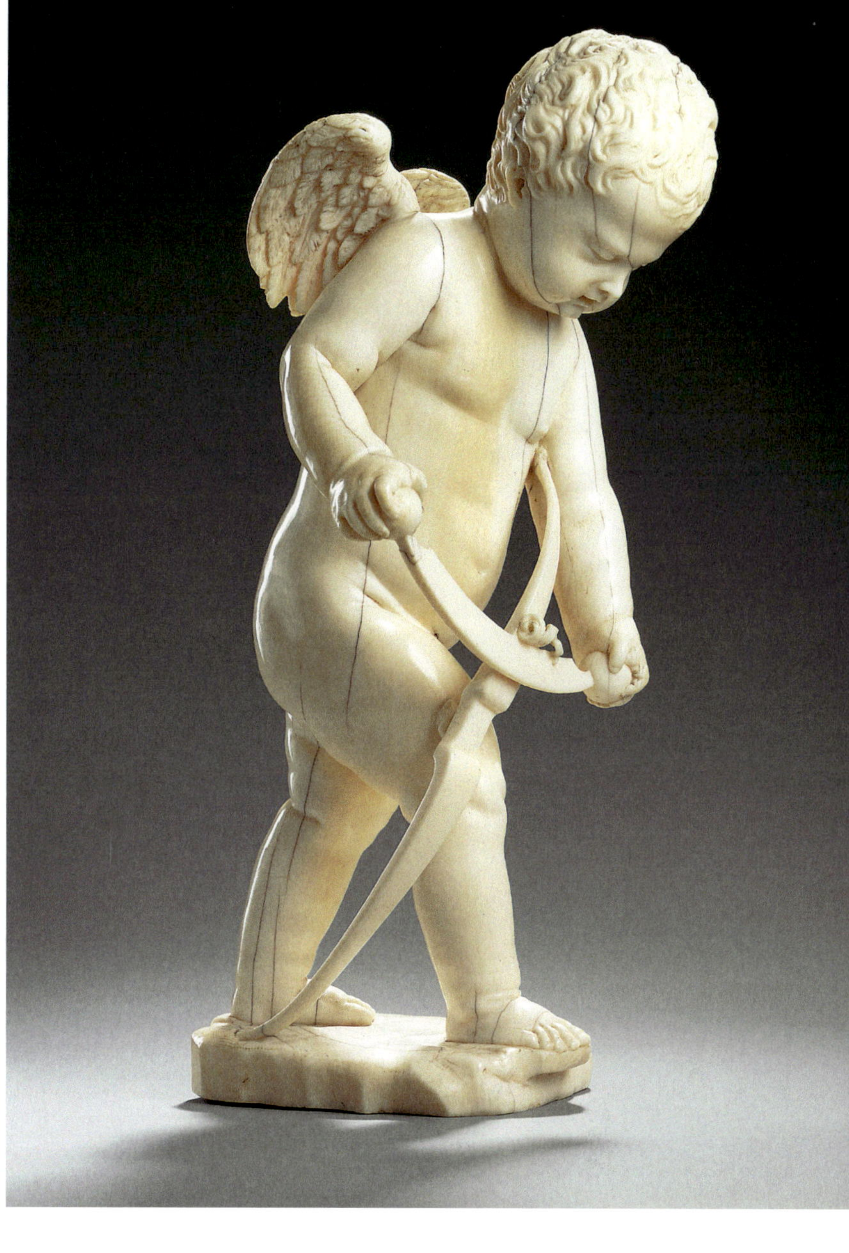

Cupid Carving a Bow

Ivory
Balthasar Permoser (after François Duquesnoy)
Probably Berlin, between 1706 and 1708
H. 27 cm, Inv. no. II 334

Cupid, the god of passionate love, appears as a well-fed infant with wings in this ivory statuette. He pursues his arduous work with dexterity and patience, carving his bow – the indispensable tool of the harbinger of love – with which he could shoot his golden arrows to kindle love in gods and men alike. The motif, although original, is not Permoser's invention. Francesco Mazzola (known as Parmigianino) had depicted a very similar scene in his famous painting »Bogenschnitzender Amor« c. 1532/33 (Vienna, Kunsthistorisches Museum, Gemäldegalerie). This ivory figure, however, is not based on the painting, but on a detailed copy of a marble sculpture roughly twice the size which was created by François Duquesnoy around 1626 – an artist who came from Brussels and worked in Rome. This work had a very varied history: it came into the possession of the Dutch merchant based in Venice Luc van Ufflen in 1629 through the agency of the painter and biographer Joachim von Sandrart. After van Ufflen's death, the city of Amsterdam acquired the work in 1637 to present it to Princess Amalie von Oranien.

In 1689 this work in marble came to the electoral Kunstkammer in Berlin from her estate and the court sculptor Michael Döbel, the Younger, immediately made a copy of it (both works: Staatliche Museen zu Berlin, Skulpturensammlung). The ivory statuette of Cupid would have been unthinkable without the in depth study of Duquesnoy's sculpture. But who was gifted enough to carve the marble model in ivory? After working in Rome and Florence, Balthasar Permoser came to Dresden in 1689 and became a much admired court sculptor whose art was promoted and held in high esteem by Augustus the Strong. Permoser remained close to him all his life, yet worked for a short period in Berlin between 1706 and 1708. This may have been the period in which he had the opportunity to study Duquesnoy's Cupid and make a copy in ivory. Permoser who was wont to follow his own artistic ambitions, may have been tempted to copy the child-like Cupid of his great predecessor Duquesnoy as accurately as possible.

JK

The White Silver Room

The White Silver Room was installed in 1727 in the area, which had hit-herto served as the Court Silver Chamber of the electoral family. This was moved into the ground floor of the then south wing and now intermediate north wing presently used as a cloakroom. The White Silver Room preserved the character of a representational Silver Chamber until the Seven Years' War. According to the inventory drawn up in 1733, 377 objects in ungilded silver were displayed in pyramid form on more than 130 consoles on six wall panels and ten tables. Without exception they were almost all ›modern‹ late Baroque silver, which shortly before 1719 had been bought from Augsburg and Dresden master craftsmen on the occasion of the marriage of Prince Friedrich August to the Hapsburg Archduchess Maria Josepha. Some of the vessels were huge. There are records of ›extra large‹ vases that each weighed 85 kilograms. The huge parade vases and cauldrons that stood on the floor of this room had a total silver weight of more than 925 kilograms. The other silver objects were mainly tableware: centrepieces consisting of several parts, ice jugs, cooling vessels and vessels for glasses, bowls for pies or soup with spoons. 65 garnitures consisting of basins and ewers, two »Coffé Maschinen«, 36 chain bottles and 16 multi-armed girandoles stood on the tables. The latter perhaps stood on the 16 large guéridons in this room, which were placed on the floor against the display walls. The whole of this splendid collection of silver with the exception of three silver statuettes from the middle of the 17th century was melted down in 1772.

The intense colour of the walls with the carpentry consoles painted in a mixture of mineral vermilion, red lead and red coloured lacquer was preserved. In spite of the considerable damage to the display walls in the last war it was possible to preserve and reinstate the original surface by painstaking restoration. Even the traces of centuries of cleaning became visible.

Today only one of the six wall panels demonstrates the festive effect of ungilded silver before a vermilion ground. In addition to the three silver statuettes, ungilded silver works from the Grünes Gewölbe were united with basin and ewer garnitures from the Saxon electoral silver chamber bought in the last few decades. As a result of the destruction of the original exhibits, the White Silver Room had been a problem from the end of the 18th century for presentation as a museum. Initially, the neo-classical parade fireplace surround with precious stones by Johann Christian Neuber, which is now in the New Grünes Gewölbe, was displayed from 1786 against the central column. The White Silver Room changed its name and was known henceforth as »Kaminzimmer«. Solutions were sought for the unoccupied consoles, which were, however, not entirely convincing. At the beginning of the 20th century this room focussed on the collection of Limousin enamel works highly valued at that time, while the fire surround was displayed elsewhere. The name of the room was changed to »Enamel Room«.

With the refurbishment of the Baroque Grünes Gewölbe this room is to be given its original name. The works displayed on the long east wall – figures made of a combination of wood and ivory – mostly came to the collection after the death of Augustus the Strong. This is also true of the much older cups and vessels made of coconuts and rhinoceros horn, which came from the Kunstkammer after it had been dissolved in 1832. Important works of the serpentine collection of the treasury museum are displayed against the wall panels of the south wall. The northwest wall presents mounted nautilus dishes and mother of pearl works, some of which used to be displayed in the Hall of the Precious Objects but which can no longer be presented in the same numbers in a safe and secure manner.

DS

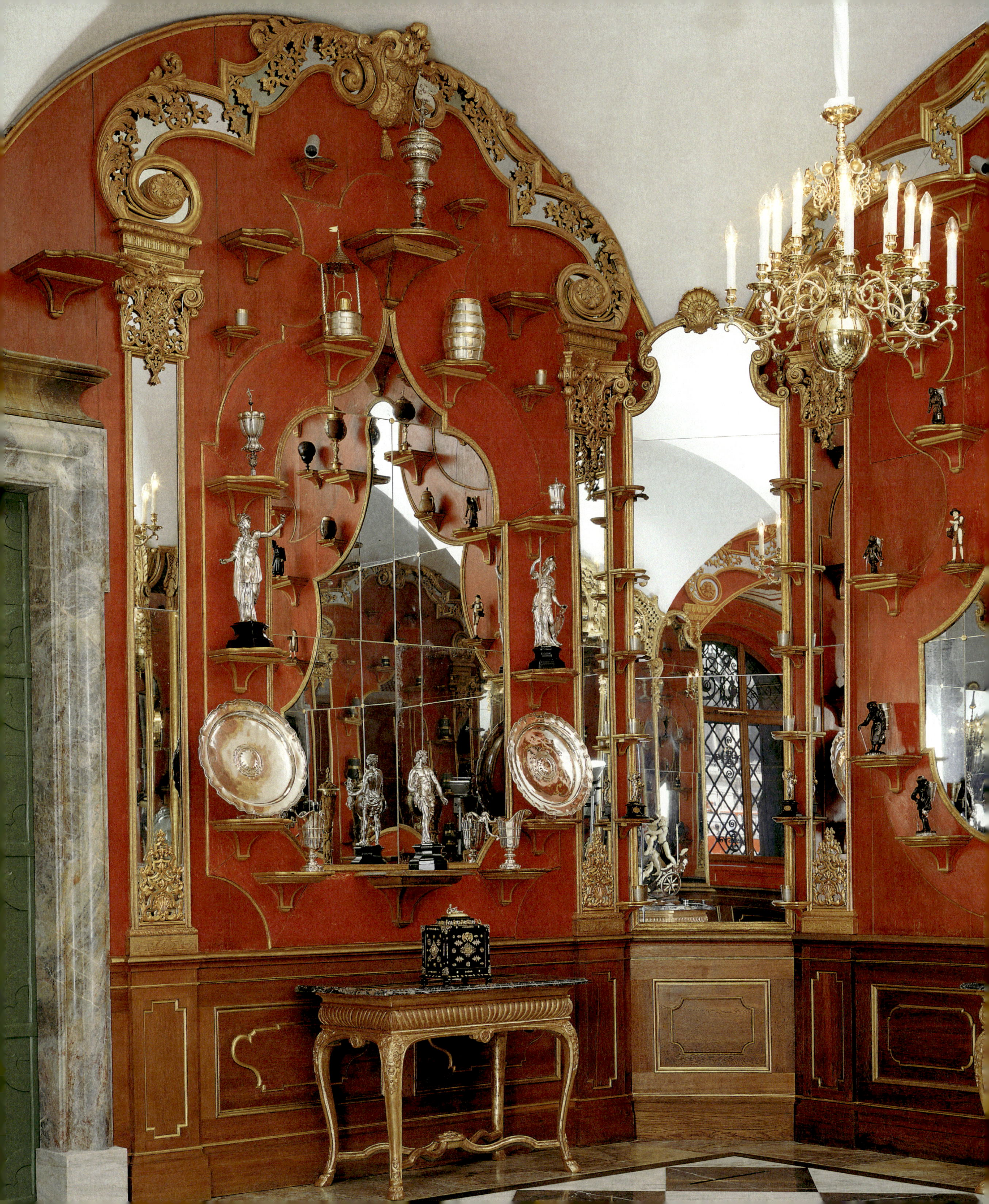

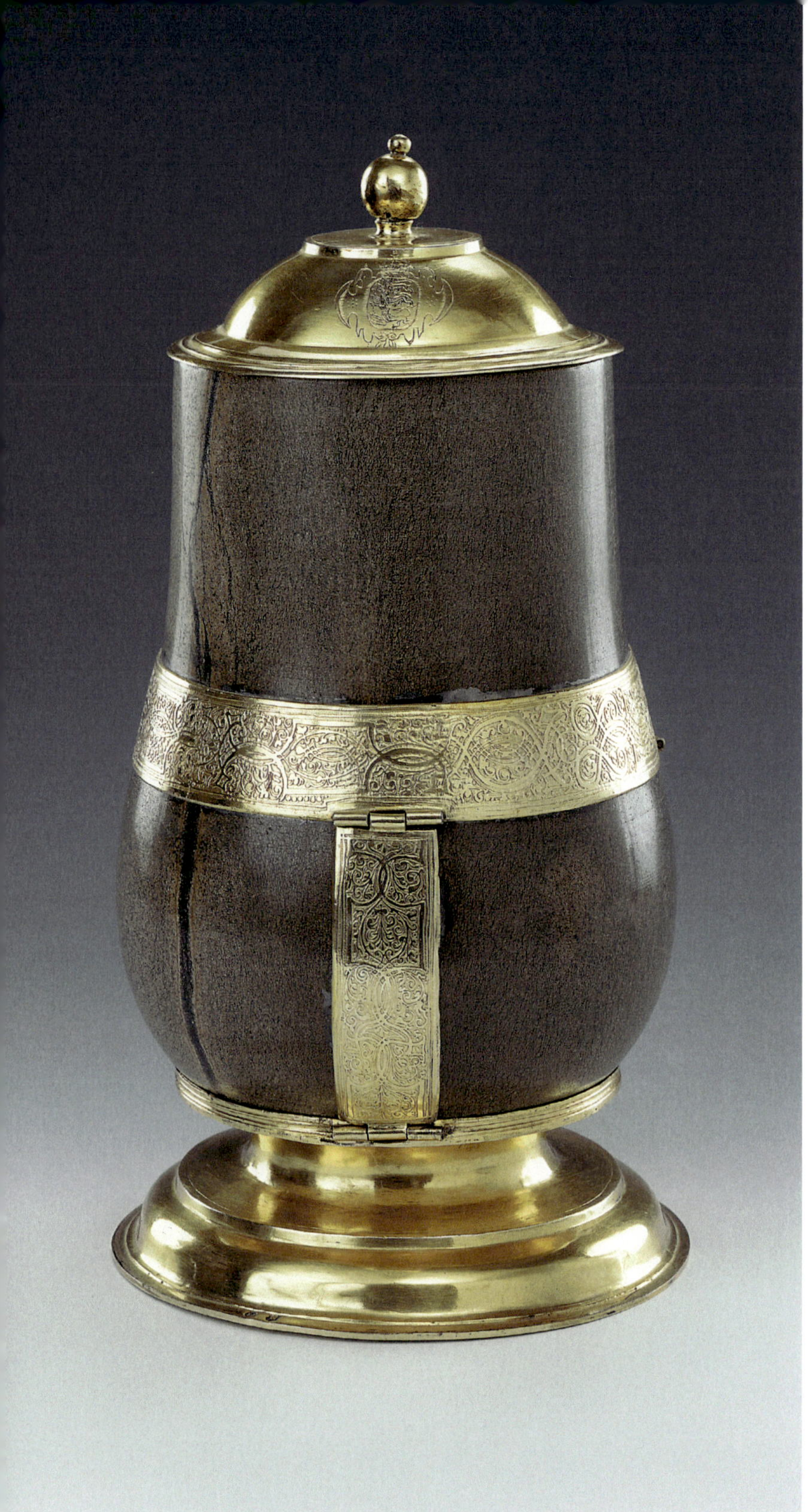

Six Parade Tankards

Serpentine, silver-gilt
Design: Giovanni Maria Nosseni
Goldsmith's mount: Urban Schneeweiss
Dresden, before 1585
H. between 29 and 31.5 cm,
Inv. nos. V 397, V 389, V 390, V 386, V 399 and V 380
(individual photograph)

Serpentine was among the gemstones from Saxony that were highly prized in Europe during the 16th and 17th centuries. Serpentine was quarried near Zöblitz in the Erzgebirge mountains from the middle of the 15th century onwards. It is an unusual gemstone whose colour palette ranges from an almost black dark-green to a light pine green, occasionally even porphyry red. Almost all these colour variants can be seen on the display walls of the White Silver Room. Serpentine is sufficiently soft immediately after quarrying to be turned on the lathe. In 1575 Elector Augustus sent the sculptor, architect and master of ceremonies, Giovanni Maria Nosseni from northern Italy, who had just joined the court service, to the area where serpentine deposits had been found in order to ensure an optimum yield and to examine to what extent the material lent itself to the manufacture of high-quality vessels.

As a result of Nosseni's visit, serpentine working improved significantly. Vessels in serpentine with precious goldsmith's mounts were created that found their way into the princely Kunstkammer collections

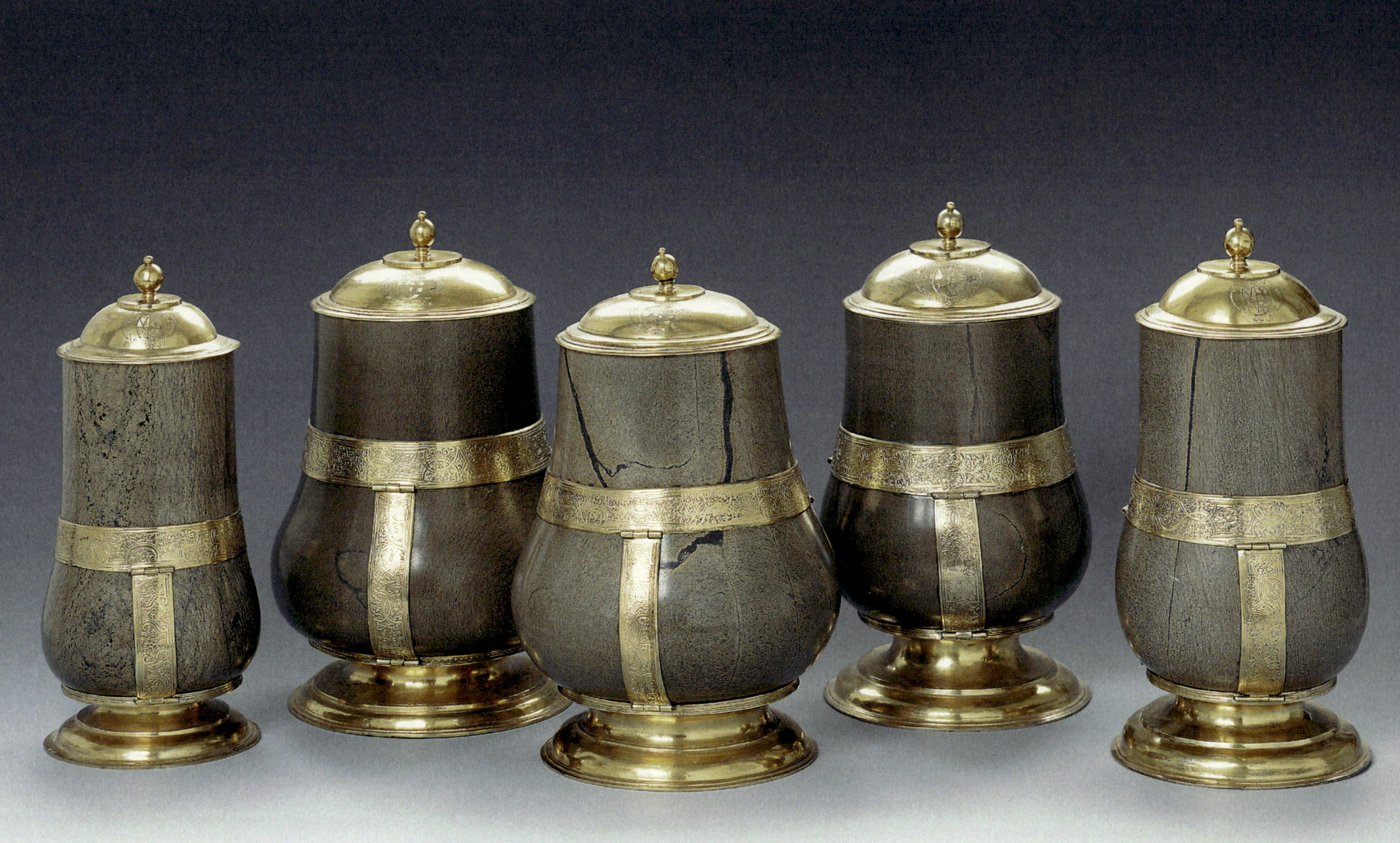

of the Holy Roman Empire. The popularity of the stone was due to its rarity and to its typical grain, which is reminiscent of snakeskin. This association may have led to the assumption that serpentine could repel poison. There are beautiful examples of serpentine works from the period shortly before 1600 at the Grünes Gewölbe. Of particular importance is a group of six parade vessels, which are first mentioned in the 1586/87 inventory of the treasury. They have a smooth wall with an almost cylindrical upper part and a bulbous lower part. The vessels are of almost the same height whereas their diameters are different so that they appear, depending on their circumference, slender or squat. Each vessel was given an identical mount by the Dresden goldsmith Urban Schneeweiss. This mount includes a simple footring, two clasps with a carefully engraved arabesque ornamentation and a horizontal band with the same décor which serves as a visual border between the cylindrical upper part and the bulbous lower part. The domed covers are engraved with the coat of arms of the Elector Augustus and his wife Anna, Princess of Denmark.

This ensemble of serpentine tankards with their precious mounts had a purely decorative function and served no practical purpose. Even in this context, the manufacture of a set of six different, but formally related vessels is unusual. The group appears to be a playful formal study, an étude in design, the creation of which was motivated purely by artistic reflection. Beyond doubt, this impressive ensemble was made by the extremely creative artist Giovanni Maria Nosseni.

DS

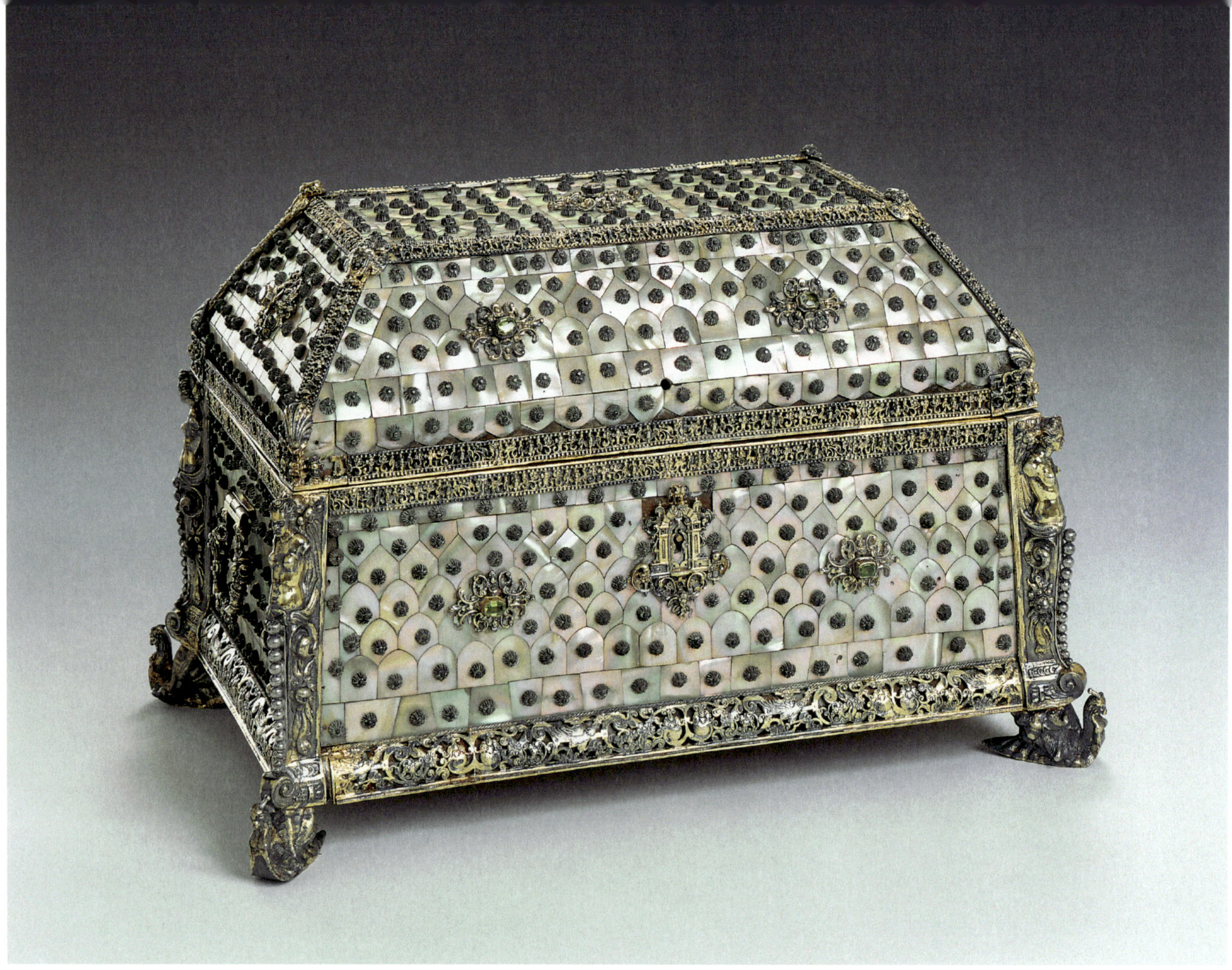

Parade Casket

Mother of pearl, painted wood, silver-gilt, velvet, silk, gold braid trimming,
chrysolites, amethysts
Mother of pearl work: Gujarat (India), late 16th century
Mount: Nicolaus Schmidt
Nuremberg, c. 1600
H. 22.7 cm, w. 35.5 cm, d. 21.5 cm, Inv. no. III 244

Parade Casket

Mother of pearl, painted wood, silver-gilt, velvet
Mother of pearl work: Gujarat (India), late 16th century
Mount: Nicolaus Schmidt
Nuremberg, c. 1600
H. 17.1 cm, w. 27.5 cm, d.18 cm, Inv. no. III 55

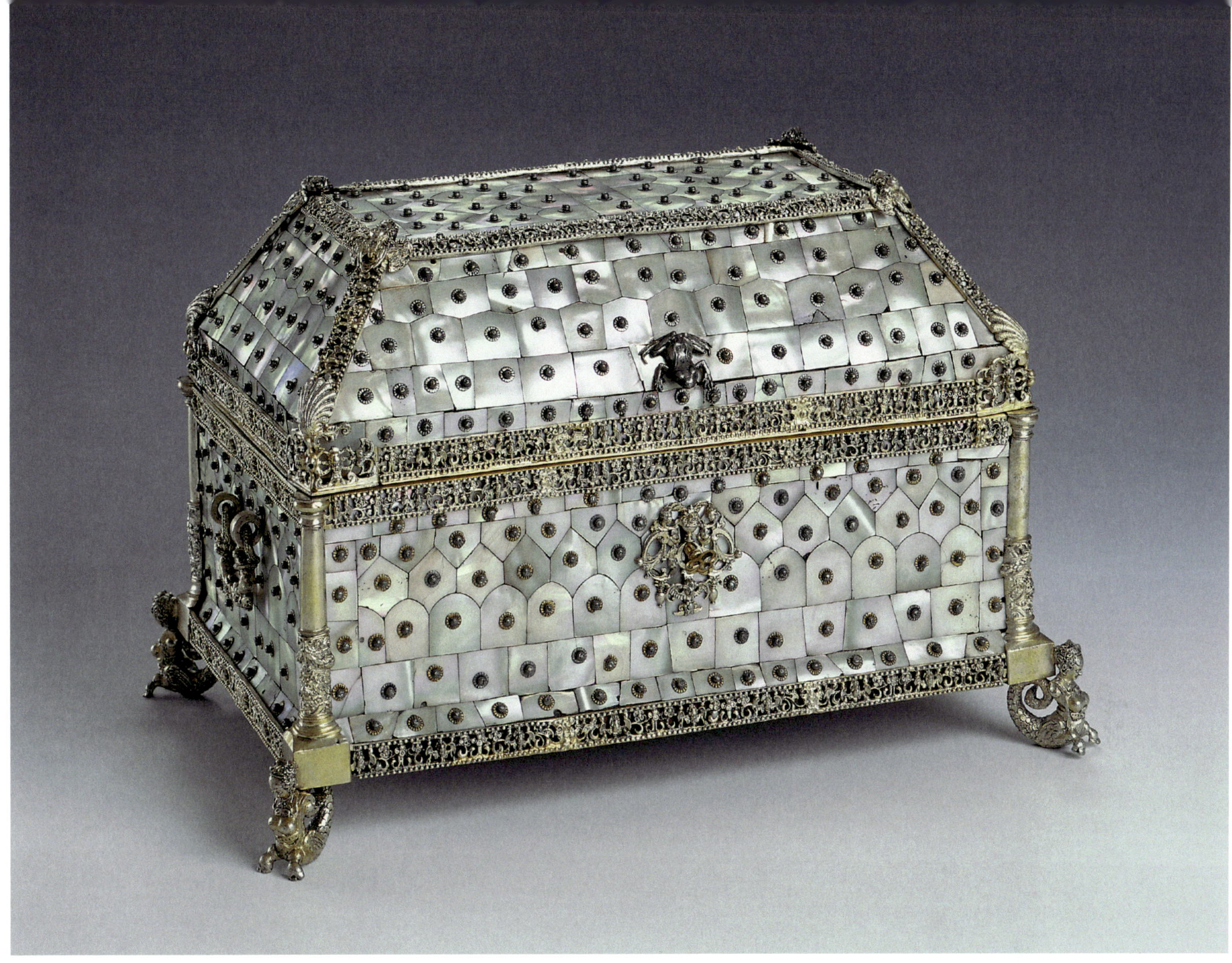

There is no other collection worldwide in which such an abundance of attractive 16th century mother of pearl works from India with European goldsmiths' mounts has been preserved as in the Grünes Gewölbe. In the 16th and early 17th century, the mother of pearl works from Gujarat – ewer and basin garnitures, caskets and bowls – were brought to the European market by Portuguese seafarers. The iridescent shimmer of the Indian mother of pearl plaques was at that time – and still is – irresistible. Three of these caskets with their magical sheen are today exhibited on the tables of the White Silver Room. They belong to a group of seven precious parade caskets from the Dresden Kunstkammer acquired for the Elector between 1589 and 1609. Five of them remained in the Grünes Gewölbe. The two other caskets were transferred to the ›Familienverein Haus Wettin‹ in 1924 in connection with the compensation of the German aristocracy.

Two of the remaining mother of pearl caskets, which have been in Dresden for 400 years, are from the workshop of the Nuremberg goldsmith Nicolaus Schmidt. He was active as a goldsmith in Nuremberg between 1582 and 1609 and was one of the pupils of Wenzel Jamnitzer, the great master of goldsmith's art. The Saxon Electors around the year 1600 seemed to have appreciated his splendid mounts as they acquired, alongside the two caskets mentioned, numerous other works like the large parade casket, modelled on a design by his mentor Jamnitzer, and a very imaginative mother of pearl ewer and basin garniture, which are today both part of the collection of the Grünes Gewölbe. The two caskets are made of rectangular and lanceolete mother of pearl plaques, cut in India, assembled to form the body and lid of the object. Schmidt affixed the plaques to the wooden body of the casket using a small, decorative metal pin. Compared with the mounts of the smaller caskets with their more restrained decoration, this richly ornamented casket, studded with precious stones, demonstrates the variety of forms in the period around 1600. The two mother of pearl caskets have been comprehensively restored and are on display for the first time since a good half century.

DS

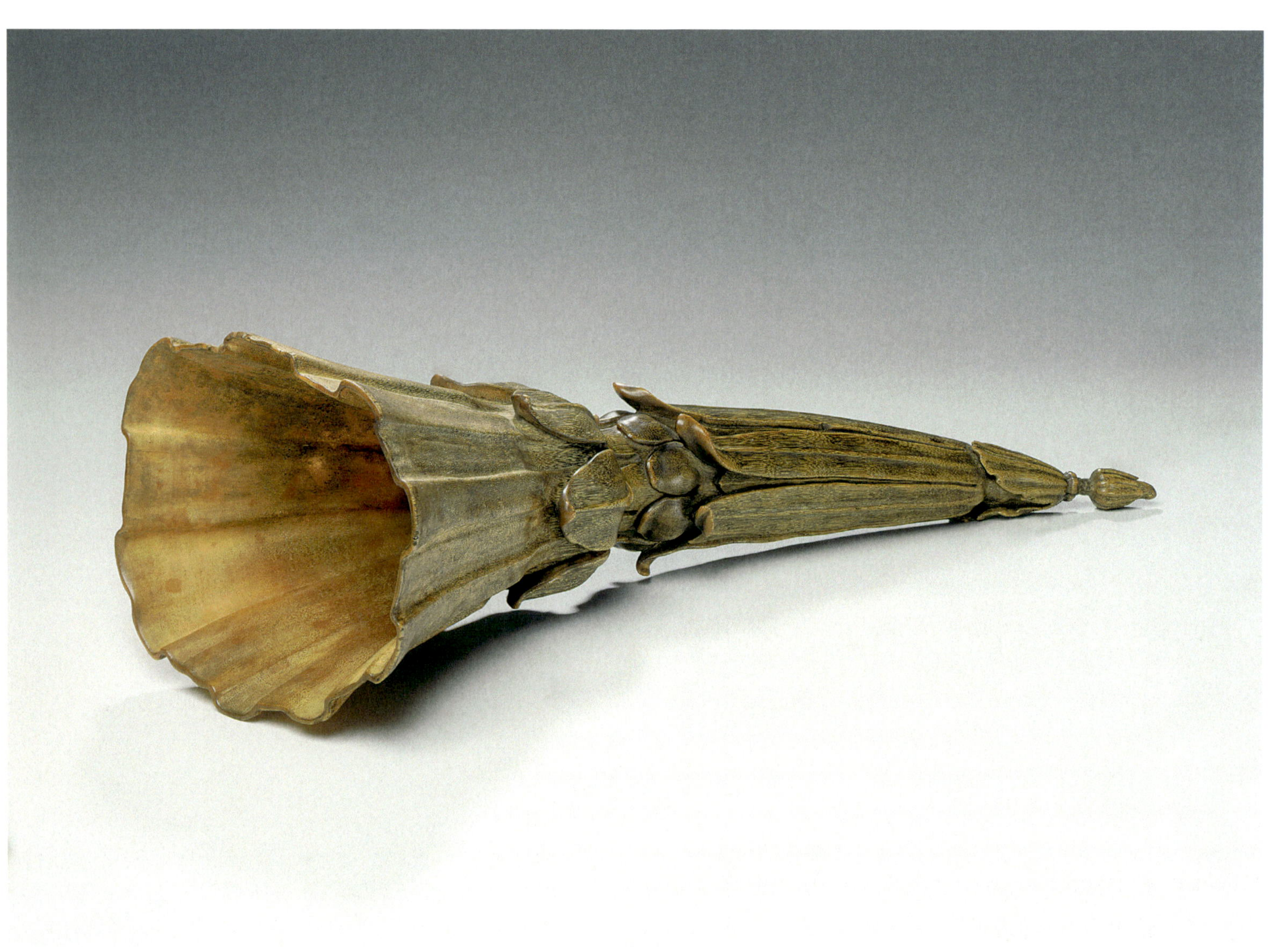

Drinking Horn in the Shape of a Calyx

Rhinoceros horn
Probably Nicolaus Pfaff
Prague, before 1612
L. 46.5 cm, Inv. no. IV 348

Goblet with Cover

Rhinoceros horn, silver-gilt, carnelians, agates, turquoises
Carvings in the manner of Georg Pfründt
Goldsmith mount: Hans Jakob Mair
Augsburg, before 1678
H. 61 cm, Inv. no. VI 245

The horns of Asian or African rhinoceroses were particularly wondrous and admired objects for European rulers of the 17th century. The horns were believed to have magical properties and only a relatively small number, carved and partly used in parade vessels, found their way into princely collections. The Kunstkammer inventory of Emperor Rudolf II in Prague listed 13 mounted horns and eleven unmounted, partly carved horns. They occupy an outstanding position among the ›naturalia‹ from this world-famous collection. The exceptionally long (46.5 cm) drinking horn in the shape of a calyx made from the main horn of an African rhinoceros is in the tradition of Rudolfinian court art. This attractive, unmounted drinking vessel with a decoration of leaves was first recorded in the Kunstkammer inventory of 1640. Its powerful vegetal shape with its lobed, individually carved acanthus leaves and naturalistic design of the ornamental leafstalk are very similar to a horn at the Kunsthistorisches Museum in Vienna, which suggests that both vessels were created at the workshop of the woodcarver Nicolaus Pfaff who worked for the imperial court. Both objects have in common that they are unmounted and that the artist only used the partly polished surface of the horn with its characteristic texture for the carving work. The dense keratin of the horn with its layered, fibrous structure is an extremely challenging material for an artist. As a result, the works in rhinoceros horn that appeared around the middle of the 17th century, most of them probably made by south German ivory cutters, are generally rather coarse and rough-hewn. The horn goblet with its simple silver mount by the Augsburg goldsmith Hans Jakob Mair stands out from these works for the high quality of its carving. The depiction of intertwined sea creatures on the steep foot, the shaft formed by a man in a feather loin-cloth and a naked woman, and the cuppa with its rich figural ornamentation in low relief showing a group of sea gods, tritons and naiads are of high sculptural quality. The detailed representation of the couple forming the shaft and the seated nymph with a dolphin as a finial are reminiscent of works by the ivory carver Georg Pfründt who died in 1663. According to entries in the inventory in 1678, this outstanding goblet came to the Kunstkammer as a gift from Electress Magdalena Sybille to her consort Johann Georg II.

DS

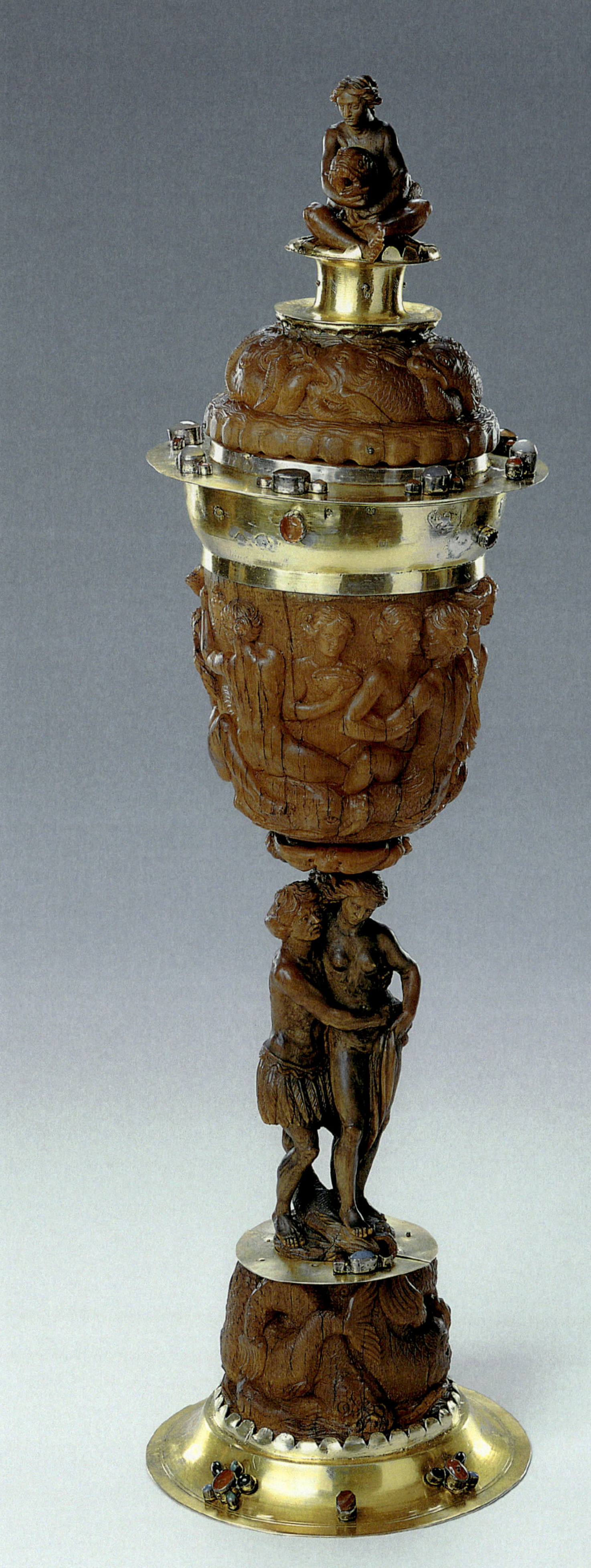

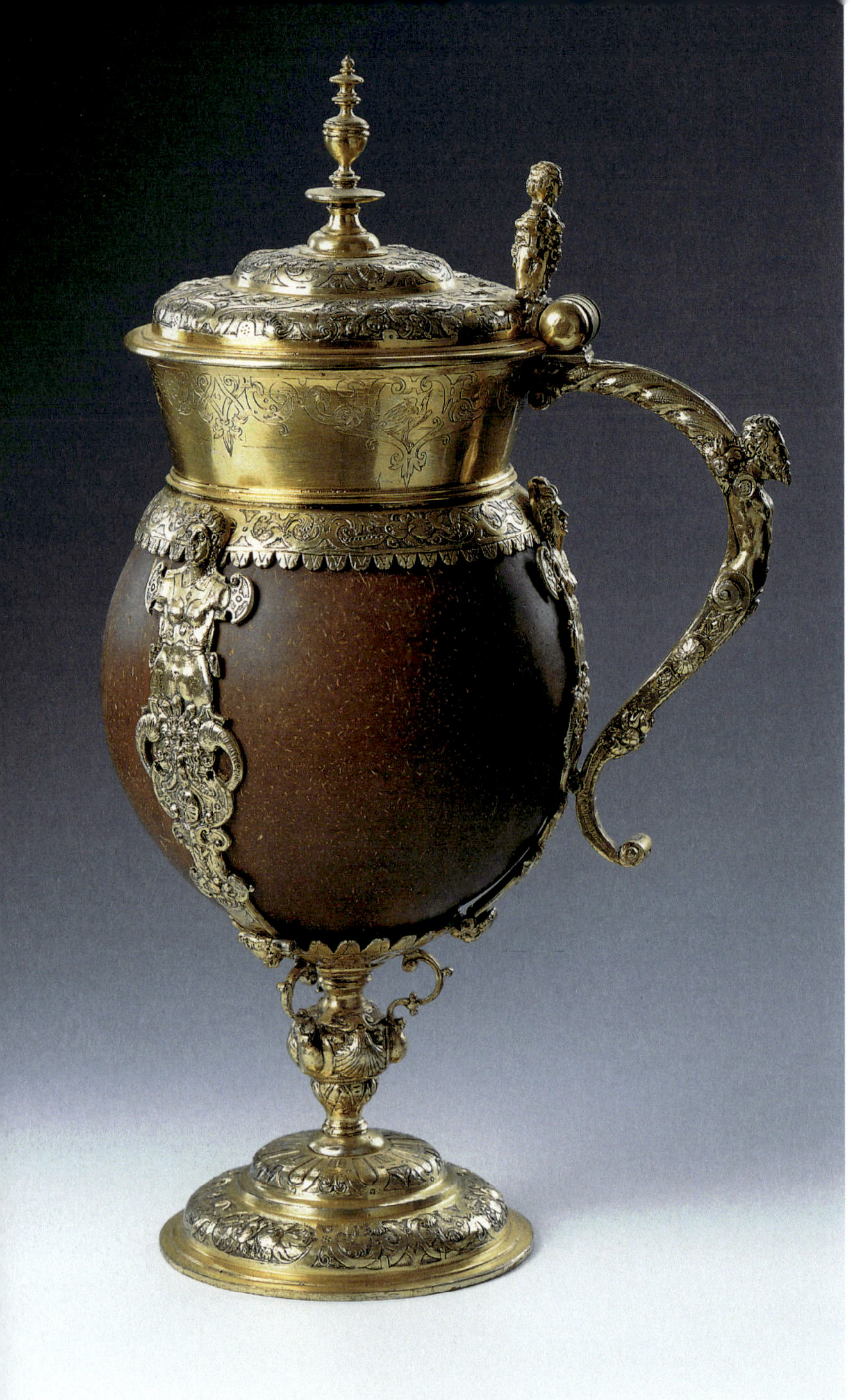

Ewer

Coconut, silver-gilt
Nuremberg or Leipzig, late 16th century
H. 30.7 cm, w. (incl. handle) c. 18 cm, ø coconut 13 cm, Inv. no. IV 328

Welcome Goblet for the »Neuer Stall« (new stables)

Coconut, silver-gilt, verre églomisé
Valentin Geitner
Dresden, c. 1586–1588
H. 48.1 cm, ø coconut 17.6 cm, Inv. no. III 257

Among the objects that Augustus the Strong had selected for display at the Grünes Gewölbe there was only one coconut cup. The numerous other coconut vessels were traditionally kept at the Kunstkammer. They had silver-gilt mounts and in some cases the coconut was decorated with carved ornaments or figural representations in relief. It was only after the Kunstkammer collection had been dissolved that the representational collection of coconut cups came to the Grünes Gewölbe in 1832.

This ewer-like vessel with a cuppa made from a coconut with a polished surface typical of the 16th century can be dated to the last two decades before the year 1600, judging by its ornamentation and design. Its slightly squat shape with the short shaft, the twisted handle, bearded head of a herm and the thumb-rest on the lid in the shape of a double-sided female herm, are quite unusual. The vessel does not bear any hallmarks by a town guild or an individual master craftsman, as was not unusual for goldwork made for an aristocratic client. The carefully engraved varied ornaments on different parts of the vessel, above all the three clasps with female herms and faun mascarons, are evidence that the cup was made at the workshop of a master goldsmith. Similar clasps were used by Bartel Jamnitzer in Nuremberg and by Elias Geyer in Leipzig.

The unusually tall coconut goblet crowned by a leaping horse and with three heads of horses protruding from its shaft has a history, which can be traced back with a high degree of accuracy. In a receipt from May 1588 from the Dresden goldsmith Valentin Geitner it is referred to as a welcome cup for the Neuer Stall. In the previous year, Elector Christian I had laid the foundation stone for the stables to the east of the palace in Dresden. This was an almost palace-like building, which today houses the Johanneum. The state-of-the-art stables on the ground floor were intended for the Elector's large collection of precious horses that he brought to Dresden from the whole of Europe. The upper floor housed the armoury and other collections, and on the south side there were two suites of banqueting rooms. Each suite had a buffet in the shape of a matrix and was equipped with silver vessels. The coconut cup, for which Geitner had used an exceptionally large, almost completely spherical coconut as a cuppa, was the centrepiece of one of the parade buffets until 1718. It is one of the most splendid coconut cups that were made around 1600 and is a particularly well document-ed piece of late Renaissance goldwork.

DS

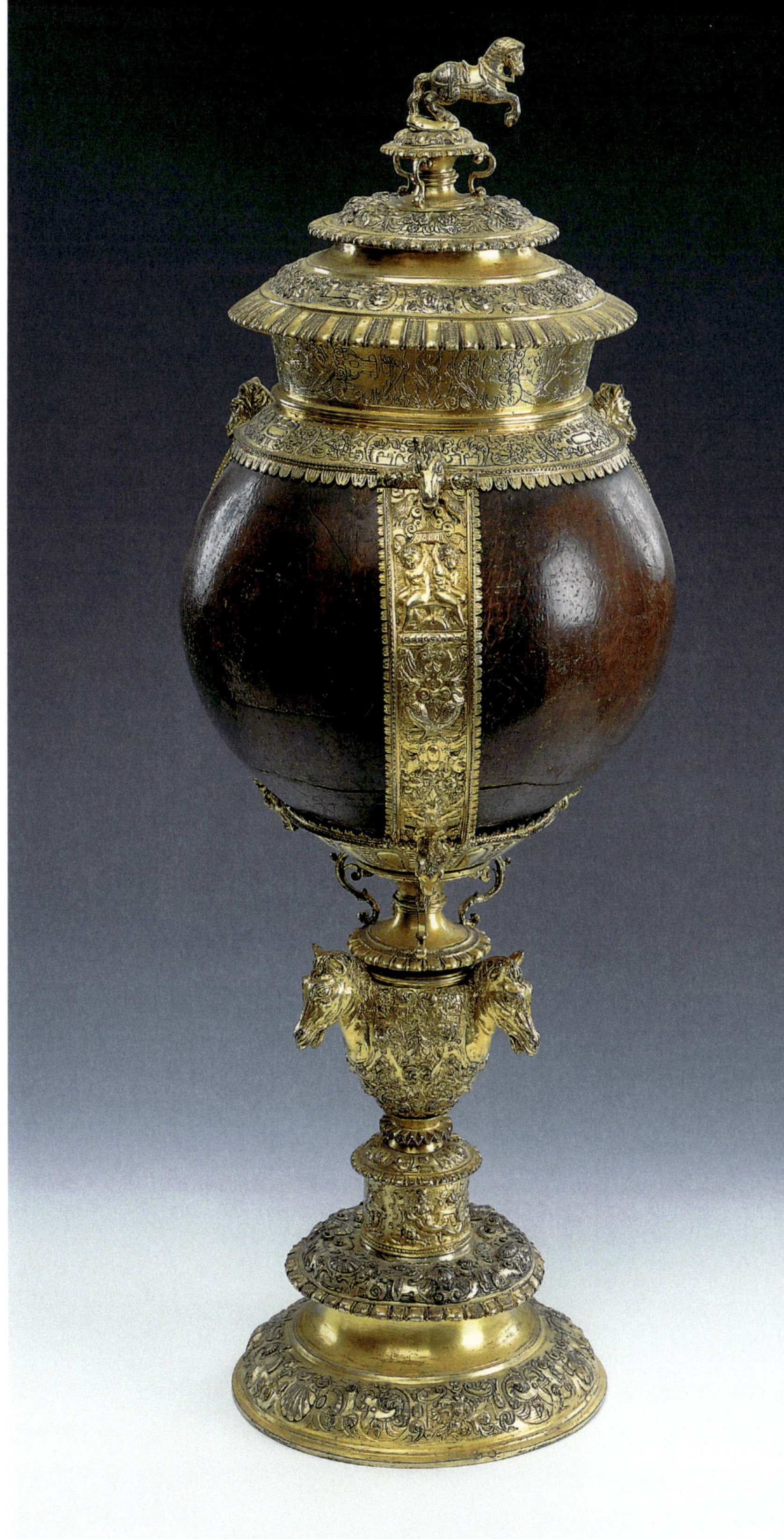

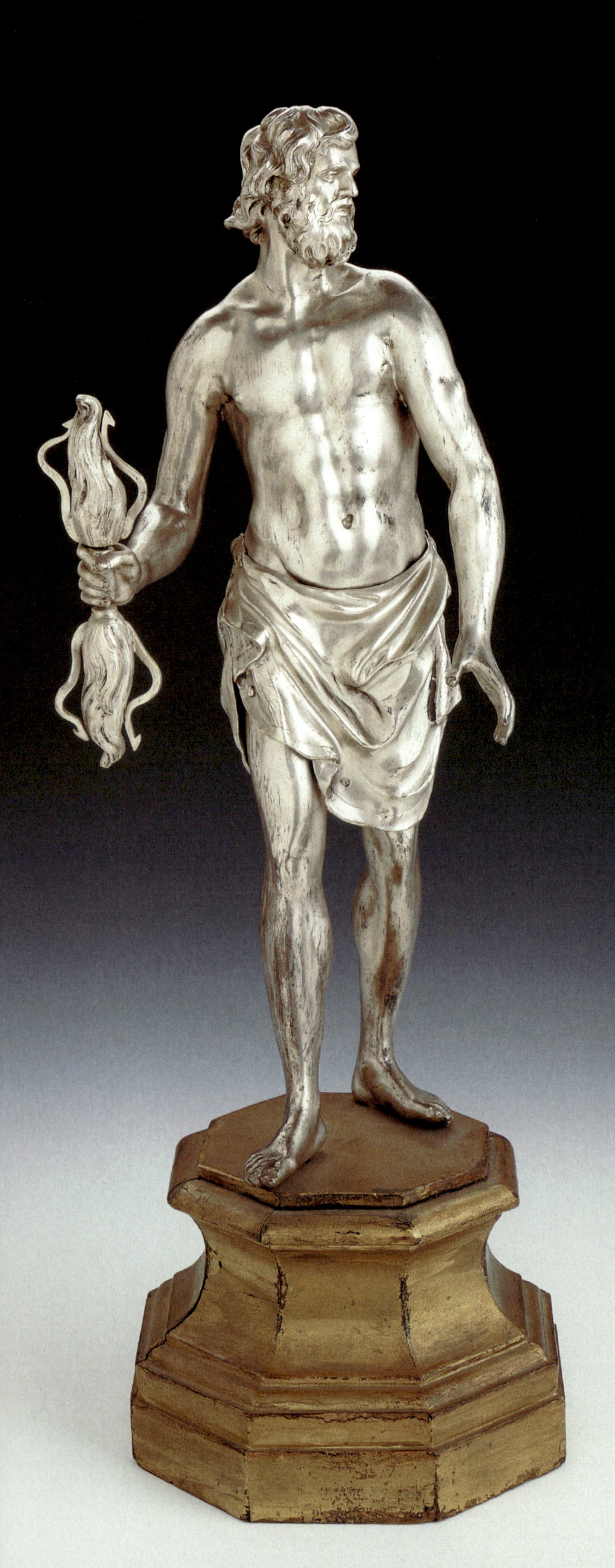

Statuettes of Jupiter and Pallas Athena

Silver, wooden pediment
Abraham I Drentwett
Augsburg, c. 1650 and end of 17th century
Pallas Athena: h. (with pediment) 52.1 cm, Inv. no. IV 305
Jupiter: h. (with pediment) 48 cm, Inv. no. IV 22

In 1772, the objects that had been part of the collection of the White Silver Room, established only forty years previously by Augustus the Strong, were melted down. Three statuettes, however, survived. The two silver figures of Pallas Athena and Jupiter by Abraham I Drentwett, and another figure of Athena made around 1670 by the goldsmith Philipp Küsel are the only objects from this room which have been preserved. They had been inherited by Augustus the Strong in 1717 from his mother, the Electress Anna Sophia, Princess of Denmark.

Large-scale silver statuettes consist of various different parts and were assembled by a goldsmith from carefully beaten silver sheets and cast parts. A number of goldsmiths from Augsburg specialised in the manufacture of such figures in the Baroque period. A relatively large number of figures of saints, which were displayed in Catholic churches, have been preserved. The same is true of figures representing rulers and kings. They often take the form of equestrian statues on ornamental silver plinths. Large-scale figures of deities from Classical Antiquity, by contrast, are very rare. As works of art in their own right, they were objects typically found in princely collections as the preciousness of the material and the difficulties involved in their production process made them very expensive. They were mostly exhibited in treasury collections of the high nobility.

The Augsburg goldsmiths used bronze statuettes or specially sculpted figures as models for their works. The identity of the model on which the figure of Athena was created remains obscure. It probably dated from the early 17th century as the dance-like, turning body movement of the goddess and the sweeping movement of her arms are still in the formal tradition of Mannerism. The gently flowing garments, the ornamental armour plate and the shape of the helmet are, however, more in line with the stylistic trends of the mid 17th century. In her raised left hand the bellicose goddess of wisdom probably held a spear, which has been preserved in the second silver statuette of Athena.

The model for the figure of Jupiter is well-known. It is the bronze statuette of Mars by Giambologna, which was popular with art collectors in the 17th century. The god of war, originally a nude figure, was equipped with a loincloth and an awesome bundle of thunderbolts, which he wields in his right hand. It is very likely that the figure of Jupiter was completed after the death of Abraham I Drentwett, whose hallmark is punched into the garment of the figure, in the workshop run by his wife and his two sons.

His younger son Abraham II, who became master craftsman in 1675, was held in high esteem in the last quarter of the 17th century by his aristocratic clients for his carefully crafted silver statuettes.

DS

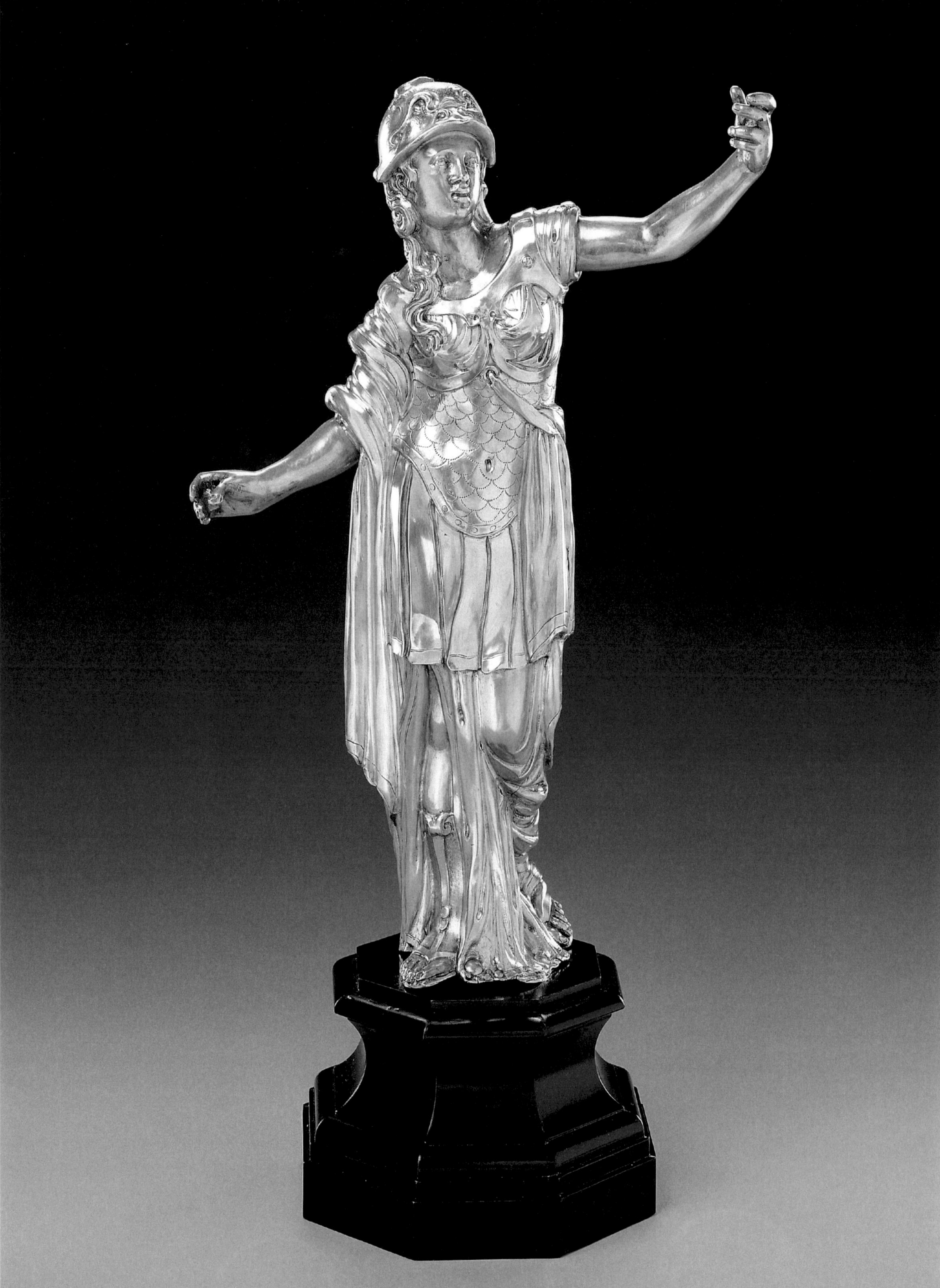

Astronomical Table Clock

Silver, copper-gilt, brass, steel, turquoises, amethysts, garnets
Clockwork: Jeremias Pfaff, Augsburg, end of 17 century
H. 29 cm, w. 31.3 cm, Inv. no. IV 247

Around 1600, table clocks with a horizontal display became aristocratic collectibles and were much in demand until the end of the 17 century. This type of clock is characterized by its square, almost box-like casing with sumptuously decorated walls. Unlike the table clocks from the late Renaissance period, this clock is a precision chronometer with clockwork and chimes that are controlled by a hidden pendulum. This clock, made around 1690 with clockwork signed by the Augsburg clockmaker Jeremias Pfaff, has five horizontal dials on the cover of the rectangular casing. It is an astronomical clock as, in addition to its large central dial indicating hours and minutes with a figure of Saturn as a pointer, it has four dials indicating the date, day of the week, month, and phase of the moon.

The function of table clocks of this type as chronometers was only theoretical as they were used primarily as highly decorative items. This is also true of the table clock illustrated here, first mentioned in the Kunstkammer inventory of 1732, and its decorative function is obvious when we look at it in its current position in the White Silver Room. Its representational character is emphasised by its four claw feet and ornamentation in ungilded silver. Four allegorical figures are affixed at the corners, and at the centre of each side a candelabra column supports the four smaller dials half-protruding beyond the edge of the cover. But above all, it is the rich ornamentation with large and small leaves in silver filigree and three filigree blooms with gemstone appliqués on each side that make this clock a collectible of outstanding splendour. In 1832, the astronomical table clock was given to the collection of the Grünes Gewölbe.

DS

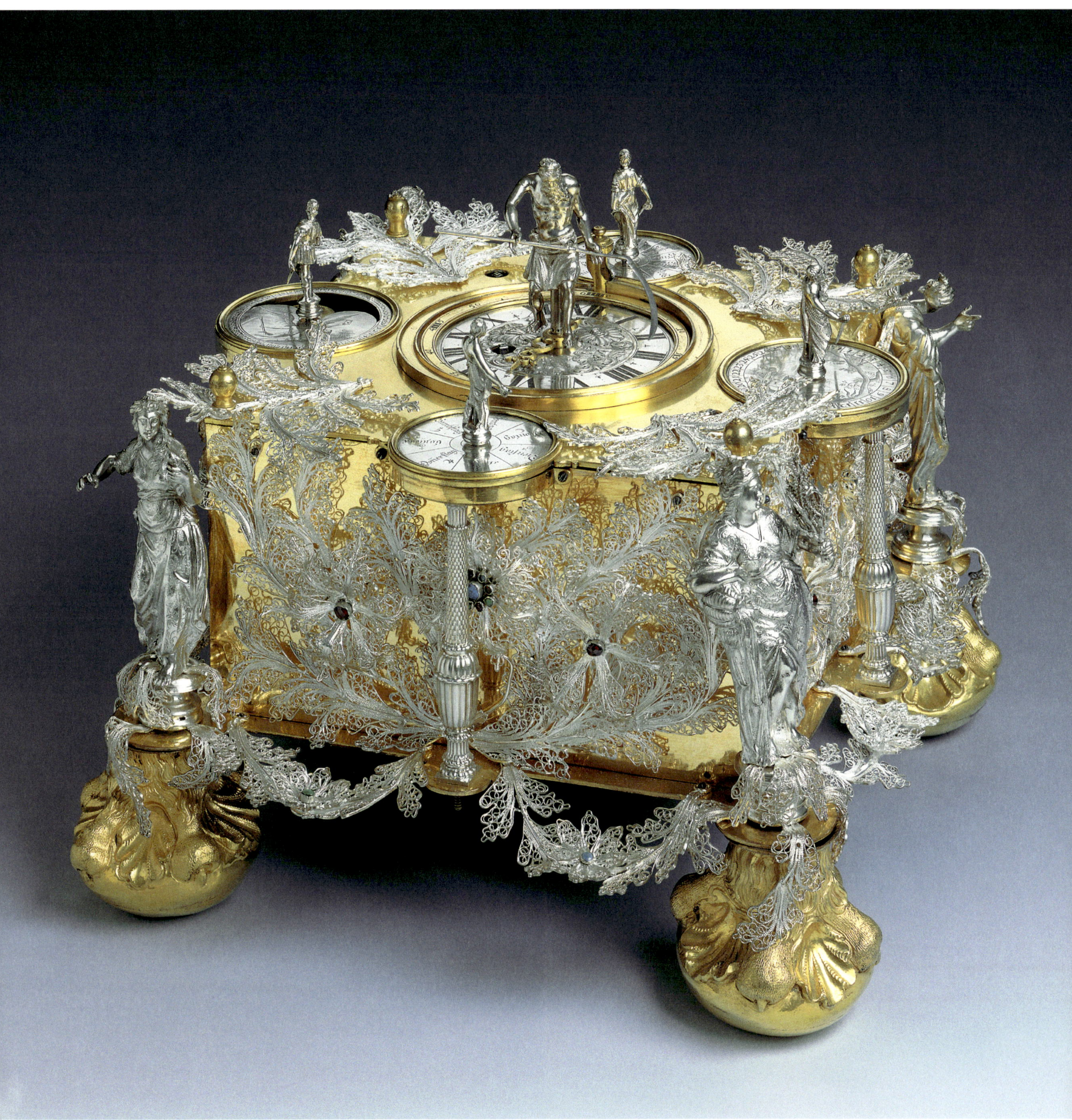

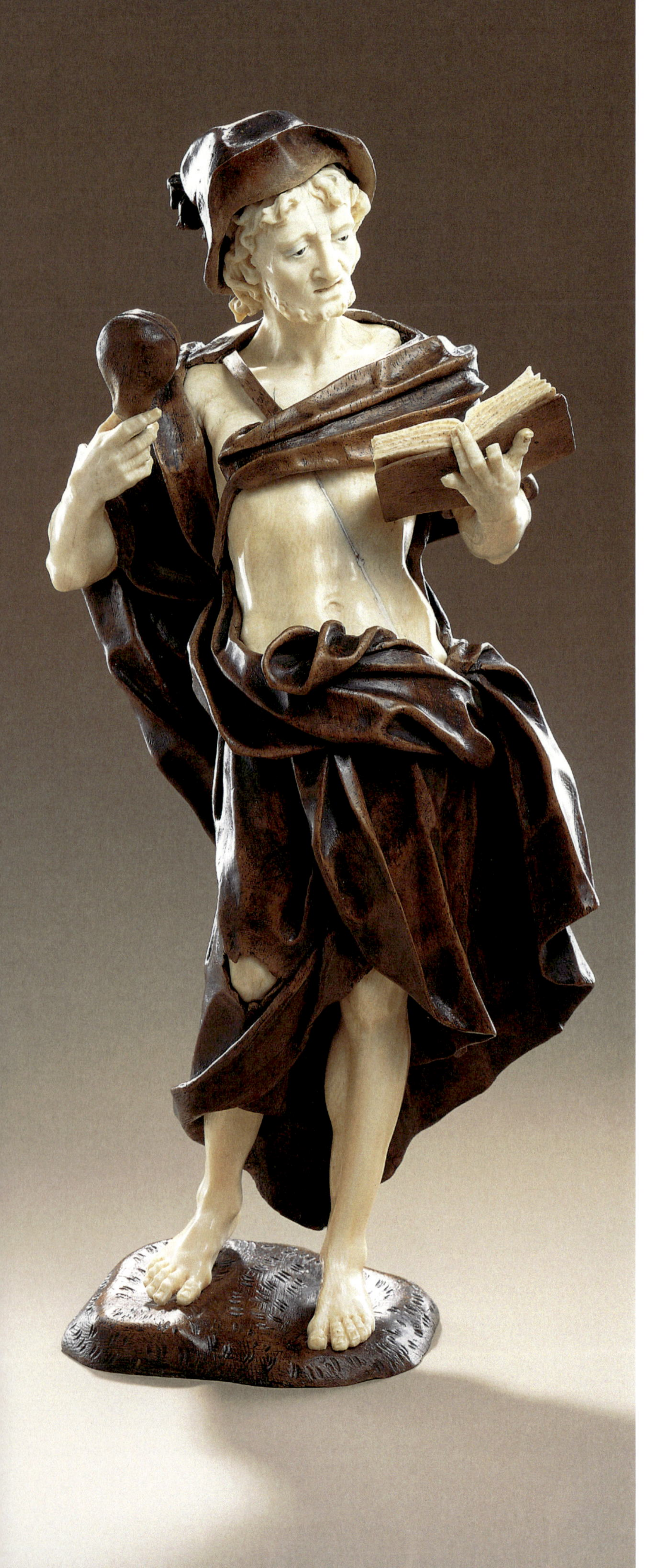

Beggar with Book

Ivory, wood
Matthias Kolb
c. 1730
H. 36.5 cm, Inv. no. II 217

Rape of Proserpina

Ivory, wood
Simon Troger
Before 1750
H. 102 cm, w. 92 cm, d. 50 cm, Inv. no. II 247

The combination of wood and ivory is a very attractive feature of the ›Kombinationsfiguren‹, a stylistically distinct group of ivory sculptures from the 18th century. They include statuettes of beggars, and large-scale groups with scenes from religion and mythology. The figures are composed of a large number of individual ivory parts that are skilfully assembled. The point at which arms and legs are attached to the body is concealed by the garments in wood or by narrow wooden straps. The eyes are made of glass and give the figures their poignant and compelling liveliness.

Simon Troger from eastern Tyrol is regarded as the most outstanding master of the ›Kombinationsstil‹. From c. 1732 onwards he had a workshop in Haidhausen near Munich. Two works exemplify his excellent skills as an ivory cutter and contributed to the esteem in which he was held even at the beginning of his career: the equestrian statuette of Augustus the Strong (St Petersburg, Hermitage) dated 1732, and the equestrian statue of King Frederik IV of Denmark which was acquired for the royal collection at Rosenborg castle in 1733.

Troger's workshop must have been highly efficient, strictly following the principle of division of labour. There is no other explanation for the large number of works produced in his workshop. Three statuettes of the Rape of Proserpina, only differing in small details, were manufactured at his workshop. Apart from the group at the Grünes Gewölbe – a gift from King Augustus III of Poland (reigned 1733/34 – 1763) to his daughter-in-law Maria Antonia of Bavaria (1724 – 1780) on the occasion of her saint's day on 5 May 1751 – there are two other statuettes that have been preserved in Munich (Bayerisches Nationalmuseum) and at the Hermitage in St. Petersburg. The statuette of the ›Beggar with Book‹, listed in the supplement to the inventory of the pretiosa of the Grünes Gewölbe (1725–1733), is in all probability also by Matthias Kolb.

JK

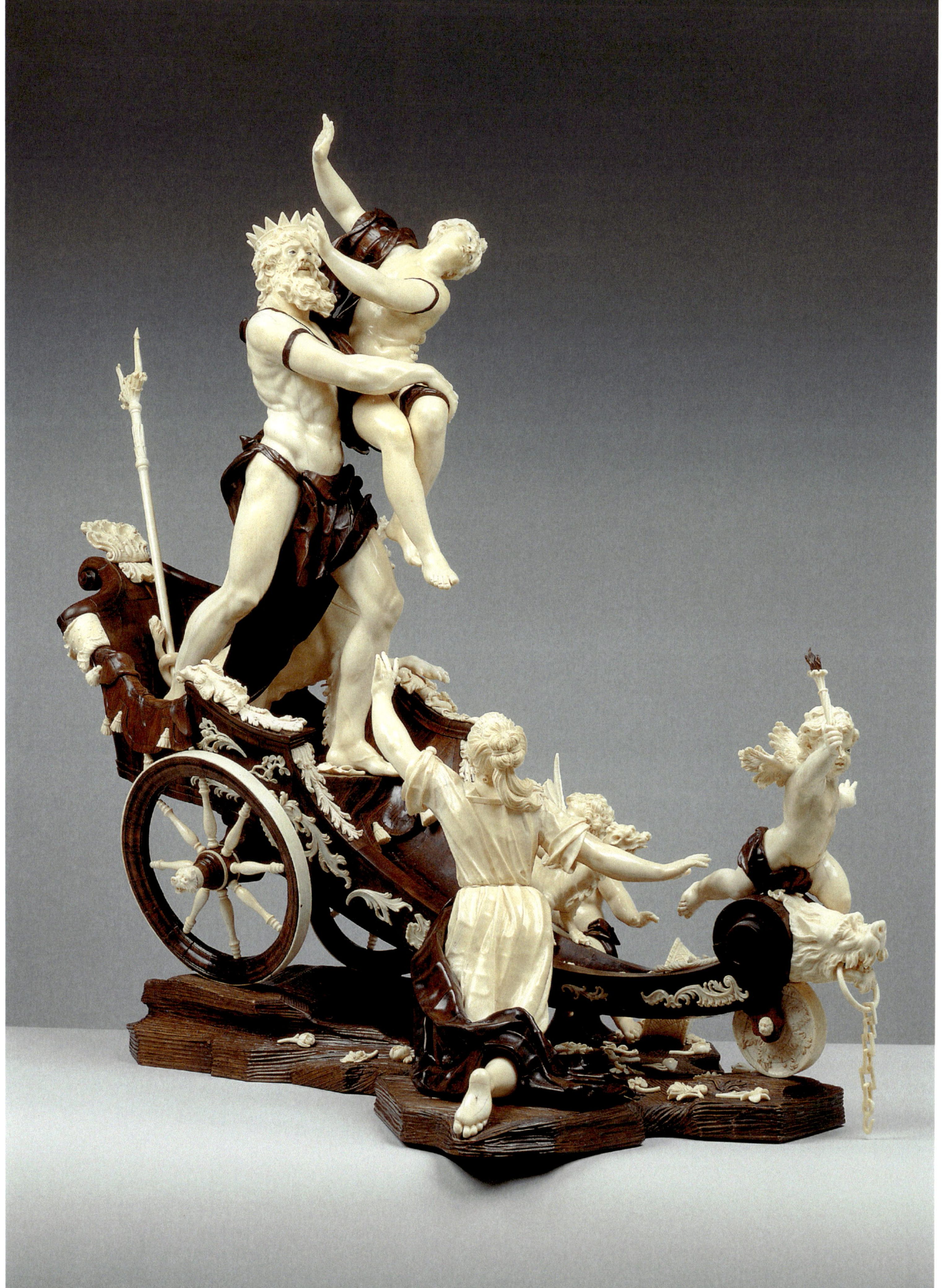

Silver Gilt Room

The Silver Gilt Room belongs to the original suite of rooms of the Grünes Gewölbe. After it was built in the middle of the 16th century this room, which opened on to the garden and the former Zwinger area in the Palace grounds via a door in the west wall and an outside staircase, was used for small functions until 1586. The stucco ornamentation of the original ceiling has been in part preserved. The door mountings of an internal spiral staircase in the south west corner of the room are still visible in he late Baroque interior. The spiral staircase enabled Augustus the Strong to gain access from his private apartments. After the Grünes Gewölbe had been transformed in its entirety into the state treasury, the room served as a »central« or »second« vault. At the end of the 17th century figurative and richly decorated silver works, which the Saxon electors used for representational purposes as befitted their status, were kept here in a number of cupboards.

When Augustus the Strong decided to transform the ›Geheime Verwahrung‹ into a publicly accessible collection of treasury art, the room was given interiors with a series of wooden wall panels with consoles and gilded ornamentation above a high oak dado. The original lime green paint was much less intense than it is now, which was true also of the mirrors fitted to the walls. In the first phase the Silver Room served as the entrance foyer to the collection. The door to the present White Silver Room did not yet exist and the first room of the treasury collection was entered from outside via the outside staircase. There were doors to the Hall of the Precious Objects and the present-day Coats of Arms Room – the latter is still visible in the present-day northeast wall panelling. In the second building phase between 1727 and 1729 the interiors were extensively refurbished and increased markedly in splendour. The Silver Gilt Room was integrated into the new room structure, the outside door was blocked off and the walls largely mirrored and re-painted. The bright wall paint, which only partly dates from this time was a mixture of verdigris and white lead.

An inventory of 1733 records the exhibits of the Silver Gilt Room as prescribed by Augustus the Strong. According to this there were roughly 300 goldsmith works on the more than 250 consoles, among them around 250 older works and about 50 late Baroque objects. A good two thirds were melted down in 1772 in the aftermath of the Seven Years' War and as a result of changing artistic tastes in the early neoclassical period. Among them was the greater part of the vessels in pure gold, which were displayed on gilded sculptors' consoles on the walls between the windows. Today, their place is occupied by vessels in gold ruby glass. The other consoles, usually made by carpenters, are filled with the surviving or later acquired collection of works in gilded silver. Apart from basin and ewer garnitures and parade vessels of the late Baroque period there is also the collection of figurative silver works and silver cups from the 16th and 17th centuries kept in the Grünes Gewölbe.

The Silver Gilt Room was heavily damaged in the night from the 13 to 14 February 1945. Fire penetrated this room from the Coats of Arms Room and destroyed and scorched the panelling. In the restoration and reconstruction replacement parts were integrated with parts of the original panelling which had been preserved thus recreating the condition of the panelling in 1733. Both the consoles that were empty from 1772 and the upper part of the walls between the windows damaged in 1945 illustrate the threats to its existence that the treasury museum has survived.

DS

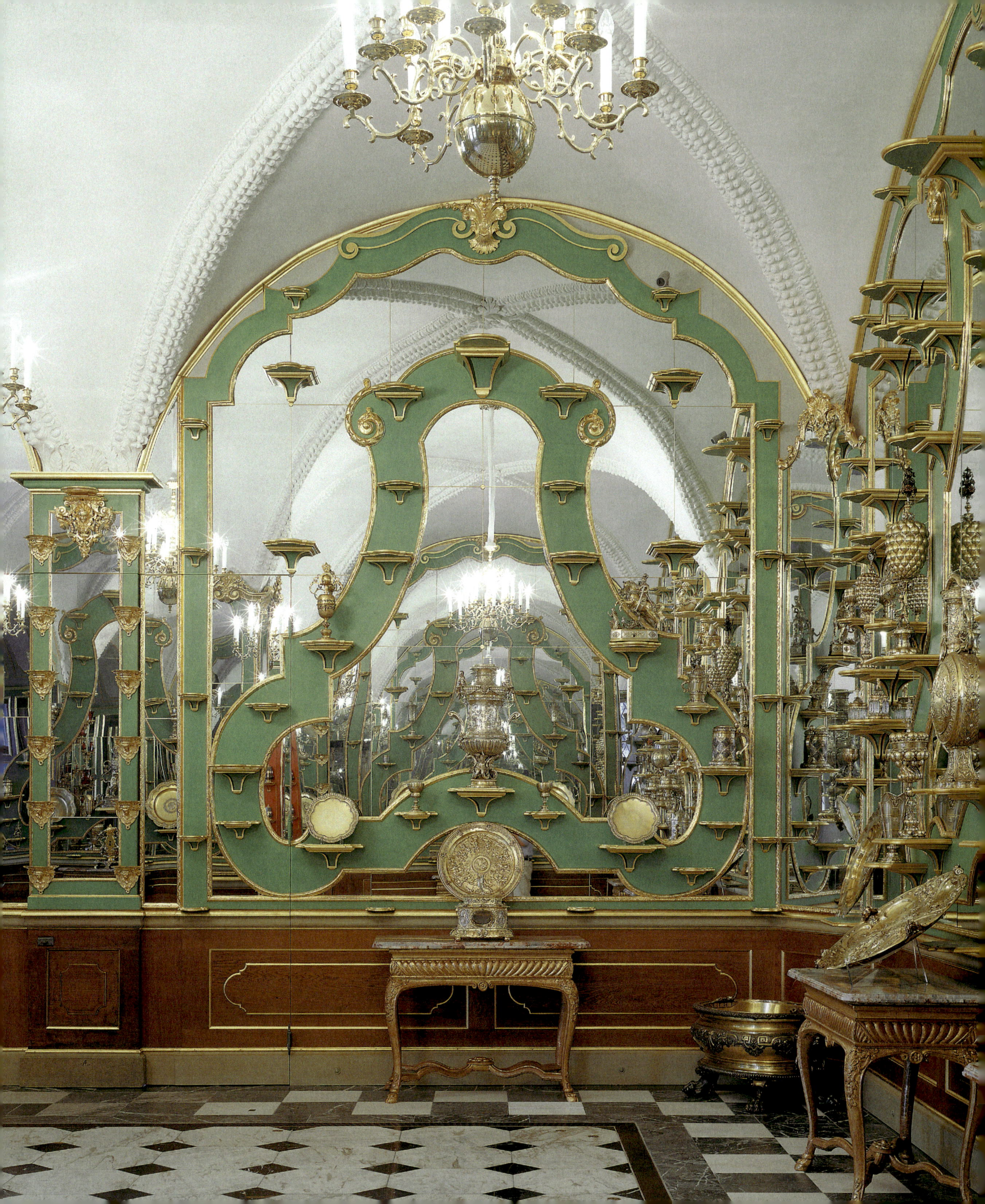

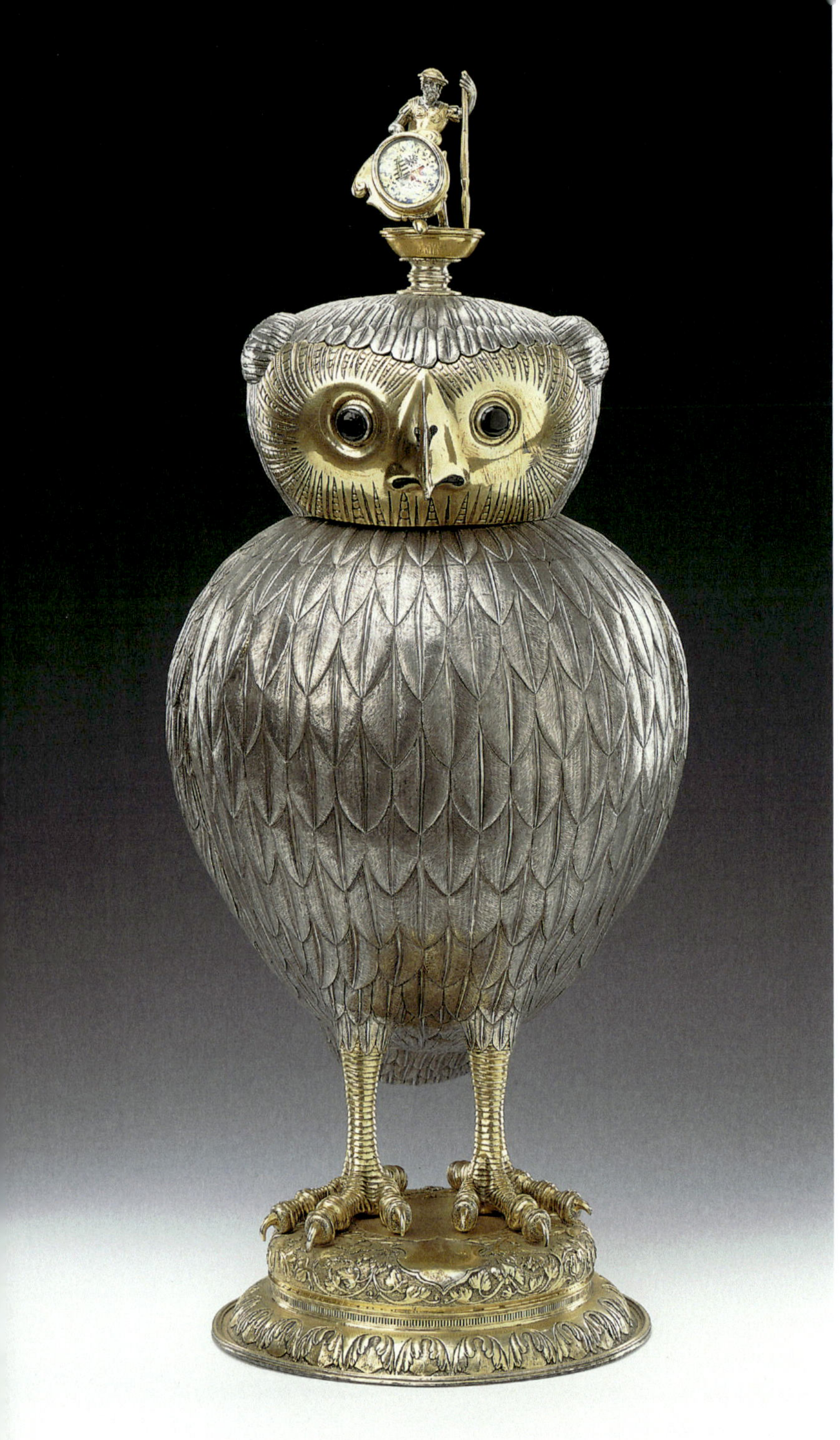

Owl as a Drinking Vessel

Silver, partly gilded, verre églomisé, enamel
Probably South Germany, c. 1540
H. 44.9 cm, w. 19.3, Inv. no. IV 302

This drinking vessel in the form of an owl is a rare piece of gold-smith work of princely rank. It not only exceeds the other owl vessels in size but is also one of the earliest examples of this genre. This also explains why the master who created this fascinating vessel remains anonymous as the stamping of silver objects with goldsmiths' marks was not done systematically at that time. The extremely finely chased plumage and the design of the foot with a subtle relief of foliage on a punched ground are of outstanding quality. Ornaments of this kind were extremely popular in the 1530s after they became well-known, partly as a result of engravings by Heinrich Aldegrever.

The owl cup did not come to the Grünes Gewölbe until the beginning of the 19th century. The fact that it was presented by the »Geheimes Finanz-Collegio« may suggest that up to that point it had been in one of the royal residences, for whose inventory this institution was responsible. In the inventory drawn up in 1587 of jewellery and silverware »1 silberne Eul mit einem kopf« (a silver owl with a head) is already listed, which might be the owl cup displayed. It is, however, uncertain for whom this vessel created in 1540 was originally made. The medallion in verre églomisé on the shield of the figure on the cover is a later addition. It shows the Alliance coat of arms of the Electorates of Saxony and Brandenburg and refers presumably to Elector Christian I and his consort Sophia of Brandenburg. The cartouche on the foot intended for the owner's coat of arms remained blank. Perhaps this part of the vessel was originally intended to be used elsewhere. The smooth surface on the upper side is also indicative of this, while the round form bears no relation to the owl standing on it.

The owl vessels, which were extremely popular in the 16th and 17th centuries, had many associations – many of them contradictory. The little bells frequently attached to the legs of the owl are reminiscent of its use as a decoy – and derived from this – its function as a symbol of temptation (to drink). But it was also an attribute of the goddess Minerva and a symbol of wisdom.

UW

Two Covered Goblets (originally a »Doppelscheuer«)

Silver-gilt, enamel
Hans Schebel
Augsburg, c. 1565 – 1571
H. 65.9 cm, Inv. no. IV 252; H. 55.3 cm, Inv. no. IV 254

Originally the two monumental cups formed a so-called Doppelscheuer, also called a »double-cup«, a two-piece drinking vessel popular in the Renaissance period. The two identical vessels could either be fitted together or when taken apart could be displayed as matching cups on a silver buffet. It was probably in this context that the two halves of the goblet were given the cover, which did not originally belong to them.

This double cup derives its vitality from the rhythmic contrast of its forms. Its silhouette is determined by an opposition between the convex and concave. The bulbous cuppa with a broad rim is supported by a high shaft in a number of different sections. Both the overall design and the details reveal the hand of a master who was familiar with numerous techniques and the latest ornamentation. The finely etched arabesques, the cold enamel in green – which in those days was much brighter – the violet and blue of the cylindrical shaft elements and the cast and finely embossed finial of fish-tailed herms enclosed in scrolls between three horned heads of Pan are of a particularly high quality. Three figures of goddesses between protruding female masks on the cuppa of each goblet are a quotation from classical mythology, while a scene from the Old Testament is concealed beneath the foot. A small medallion in relief portrays Lot and his daughters.

Hans Schebel who came from Hall in Tyrol made a name by creating important works for amongst others the Bavarian ducal family but his reputation was somewhat tarnished. After killing the father of his first wife, Petrina von Taxis, he had to leave Augsburg in 1560 but received permission to return in the same year. His masterly skills as a goldsmith may have been the reason for this leniency.

UW

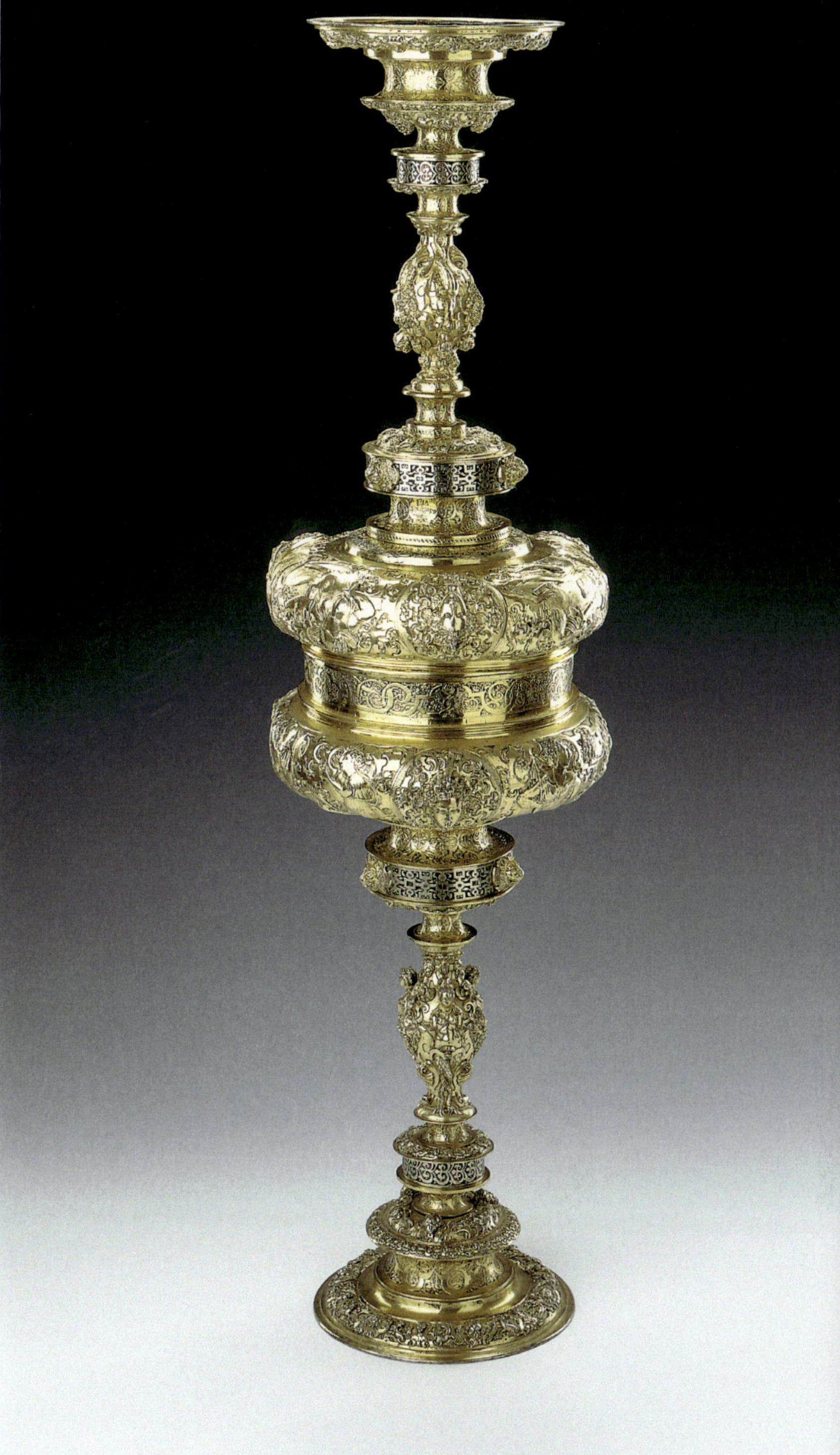

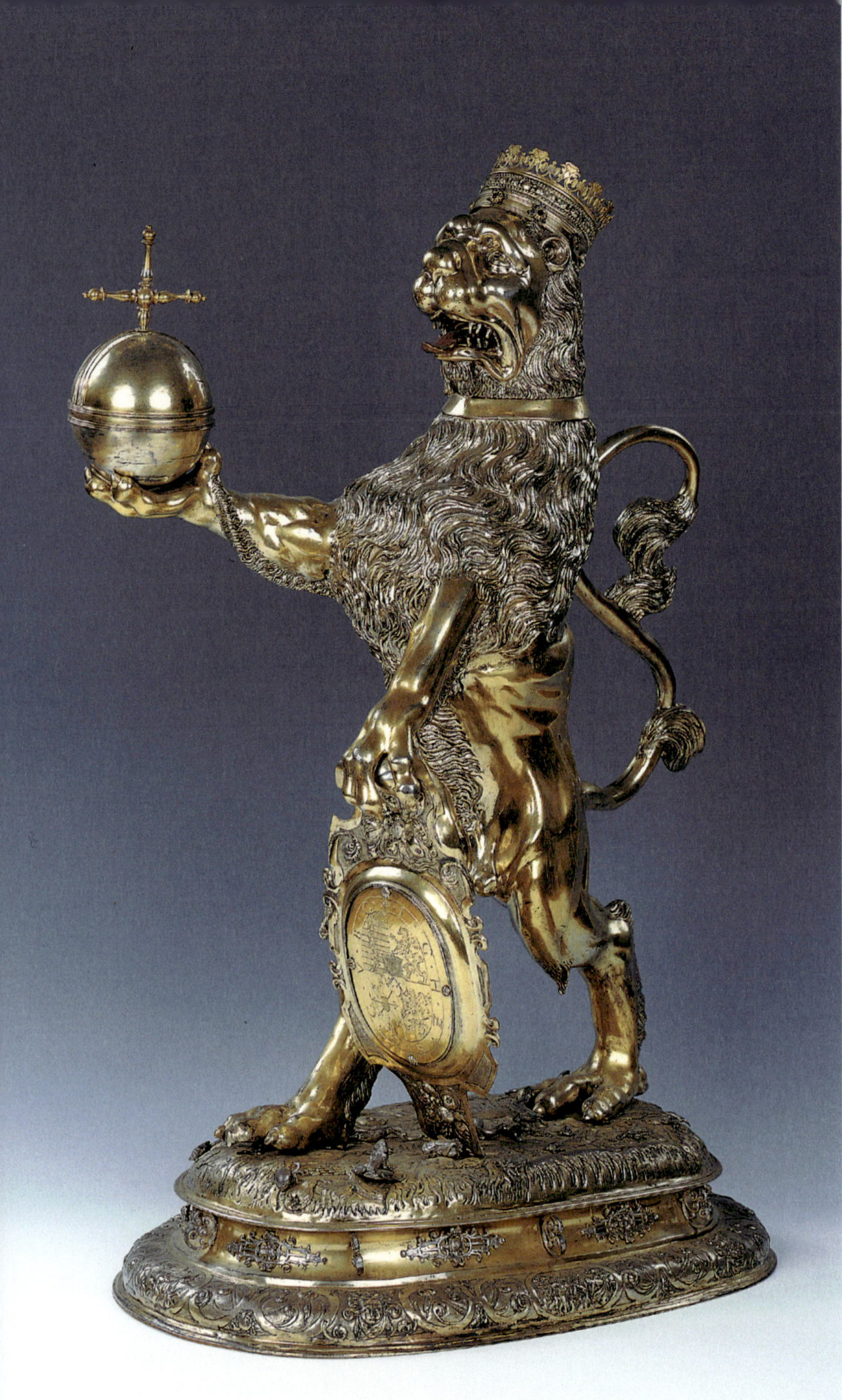

The silver inventory of 1723 lists under the heading »Allerhand Antique vergoldete Trinck Geschirre« (diverse antique silver-gilt drinking vessels) four figures of lions together with eagles, sirens, griffons, deer, and figures of St George. Among the lion figures there is this crowned lion holding an imperial orb in its right front paw, in its left a shield with a coat of arms of the Electorate of Saxony. It is highly unlikely that this monumental silver-gilt statue was actually used as a drinking vessel even though the head of the large animal is removable and the hollow body could be used as a container for liquids, it would have been almost impossible to employ the thin S-shaped tail as a handle for this vessel weighing roughly 9 kilograms. The proudly erect animal was displayed as part of representational buffets, which were arranged at the court in Dresden on festive occasions. These buffets that displayed zoomorphic goldsmith work together with goblets and double cups are evidence of the high quality of the collection and its rich traditions. In addition they had symbolical significance. This is also true of the lion illustrated here although the circumstances of its acquisition remain obscure. The motif of the crowned lion rampant presenting the imperial orb in its raised right paw resembles the coat of arms of the counts of the Palatinate near the Rhine and electors of the Holy Roman Empire. The silver-gilt statue may be a reference to the political relations between Christian I, who strove for a moderate Saxon position towards Calvinism, and the Pfalzgraf Johann Casimir. Together they tried to advance the unification of the Empire's protestant territories. This objective never materialised as a result of the death of the two monarchs in 1591 and 1592. The hypothesis that the lion may have been created in this context is contradicted by the preliminary dating of the hallmark to about 1593 – 98.

UW

Lion Rampant with Crown

Silver-gilt, vestiges of enamel, coloured stones
Urban Wolff
Nuremberg, c. 1585 – 1591 or: c. 1593 – 1598
H. 67 cm, Inv. no. IV 10

St George Slaying the Dragon

Silver-gilt, traces of cold enamelling
Hans Keller
Nuremberg, c. 1603 – 1609
H. 51.7 cm, w. 43.7 cm, Inv. no. IV 124

This goldsmith sculpture by the Nuremberg master Hans Keller portrays a moment of high drama. The highly dramatic scene shows St George fighting the dragon, as described in the Legenda Aurea, a collection of legends about the saints from the 13th century. St George clad in armour sitting high on his rearing horse has thrust his spear into the wide open mouth of the dangerous monster and is about to deal the death blow with his scimitar. By his heroic deed he rescued the Libyan princess from the monster who had demanded her death from the people as a sacrifice. After freeing her he converted the people to Christianity so that his portrayal as the slayer of the dragon soon became a symbol of victory over the heathens.

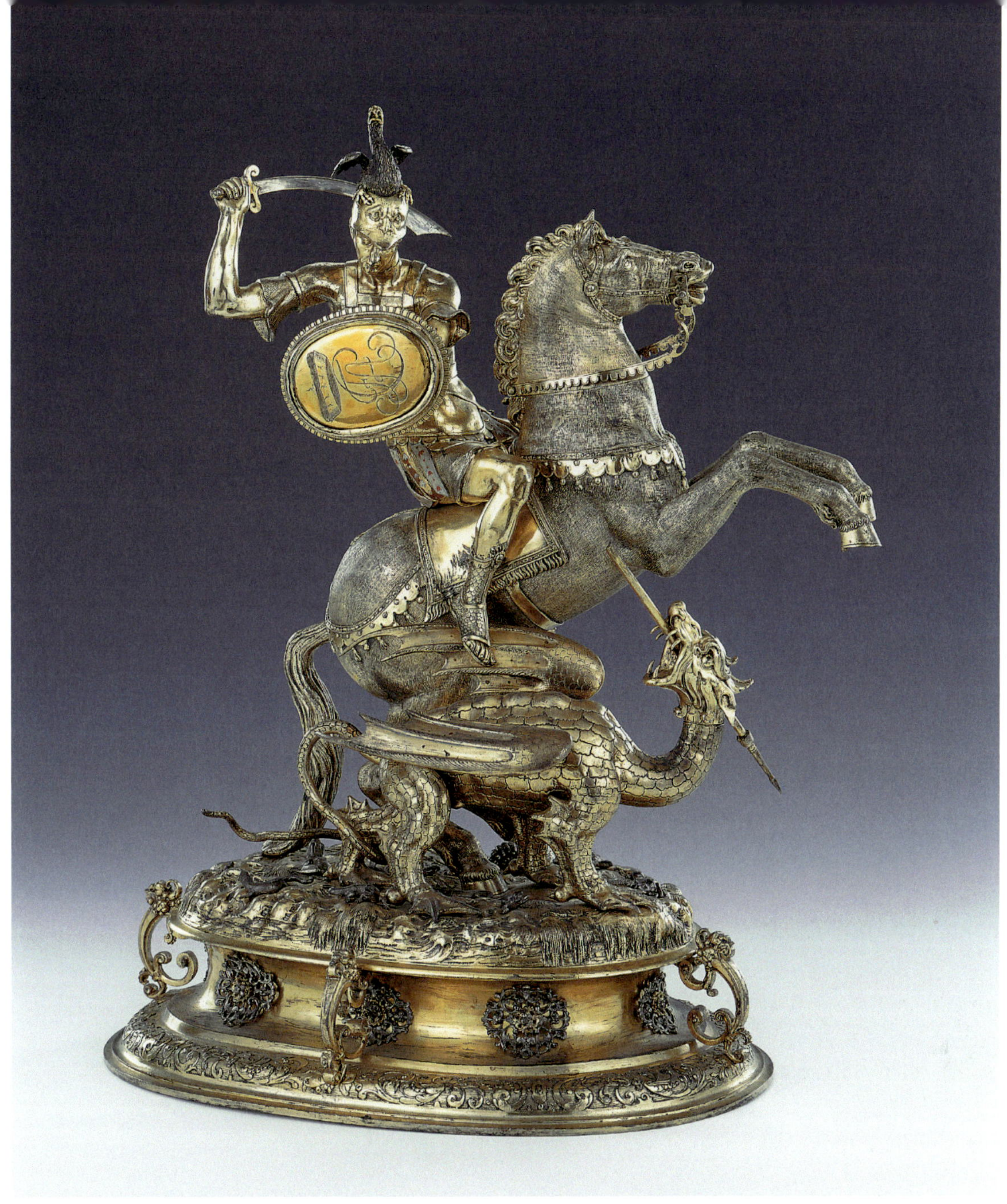

St George also had an important role as patron saint of the Order of the Garter, founded by Edward III in 1348. He embodied the virtues of the Christian knight and served both protestant and catholic rulers as a figure with which to identify – which explains his important role in goldsmiths' art. Reliquaries in the form of silver and gold statuettes were later followed by tableware and drinking games with the chivalrous saint as the slayer of the dragon. Usually – and this is also true of the Dresden St George group – the heads of the rider, horse and dragon can be removed and their bodies used as drinking vessels. It is, however, improbable that this often happened. At all events, works of this kind adorned the prestigious silver buffets that were arranged for official festivities. Thus, on 20 February 1683 there were three St George figures on the buffet in the »Eck-Gemach« (corner room) of the Dresden palace on the occasion of the carnival celebrations. As revealed by an entry in the Kunstkammer inventory of 1610, the opulent drinking vessel was a gift from Duke Johann Georg to his brother, Elector Christian II, whom he was to succeed as early as 1611. Originally the shield of the dragon slayer displayed the Saxon-Merseburg coat of arms alluding to the Duke who from 1592 was Administrator of Stift Merseburg (monastery) and bore the same name as the saint. The monogram »FAC« (Friedrich August Churfürst) which is still there, must have been engraved between 1694 and 1697 at the behest of Augustus the Strong, who in this way adorned himself with the virtues of the saint.

UW

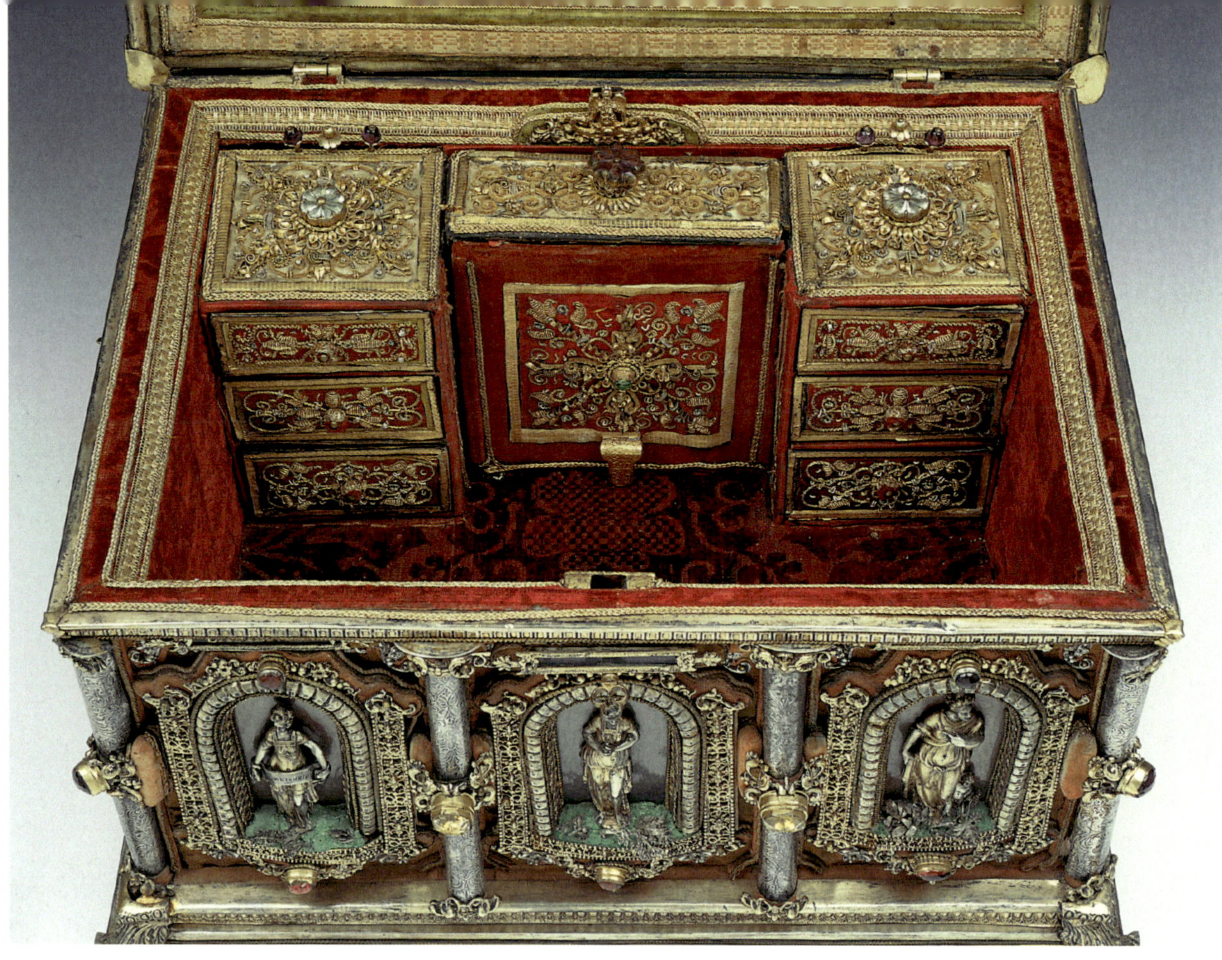

Parade Casket of Elector Christian I of Saxony

Wood, glass, silver, partly gilded, enamelled, shells, pearls,
precious stones, velvet, silk, gold braid, metal threads, cannetilles
Probably Nuremberg, c. 1589 – 1590
H. 42 cm, w. 49 cm, d. 36 cm, Inv. no. IV 145

Elector Christian I received this »Nöhe Lädtlein« (sewing box) on 28 February 1590 as a New Year's gift from his mother-in-law, Electress Elisabeth of Brandenburg. With the ten cast figures of Virtues arranged in the arcaded niches the precious gift may have been intended as a subtle reminder to the then 30 year-old of the moral principles and duties of a prince. Apart from this information on its provenance the Kunstkammer inventory of 1595 also gives a detailed description of the objects it contained. Numerous compartments and drawers were used to keep writing and sewing utensils, also two mirrors, three mother of pearl spoons and a »schlagend Uhrlein, so man am Halß tragen kann« (a small chiming clock such as can be worn round the neck). Even though these utensils have not been preserved, it is still worth looking into the inside of the parade casket with its perfectly preserved precious fittings. As they were protected from the light, the inside of the lid and system of drawers with their textile covering richly ornamented with precious stones and a wide variety of decorative devices appear in their original splendour.

The outside of the casket is also characterised by rich ornamentation whereby the somewhat unconventional combination of materials and techniques is striking. On the cloth-covered wooden core cast and stamped silver fittings alternate with friezes and gold braid. The four feet in the form of pomegranates consist of a putty-like mass. Upholstered cloth-covered wooden constructions enhance the plasticity, but reduce the stability of the heavy casket, which may have caused the clearly recognisable alterations on the outside.

In construction and imagery the casket resembles works from the workshop of the famous Nuremberg goldsmith Wenzel Jamnitzer whose parade caskets were highly coveted by princely collectors at that time. While the latter are, however, distinguished by their strictly structured architectural form, the individual architectural elements in the Dresden casket are simply placed one next to the other. The already mentioned ›ungoldsmith-like‹ use of pre-fabricated metal elements and the large amount of embroidery make the Dresden piece a curious but at the same time high-quality work of art.

UW

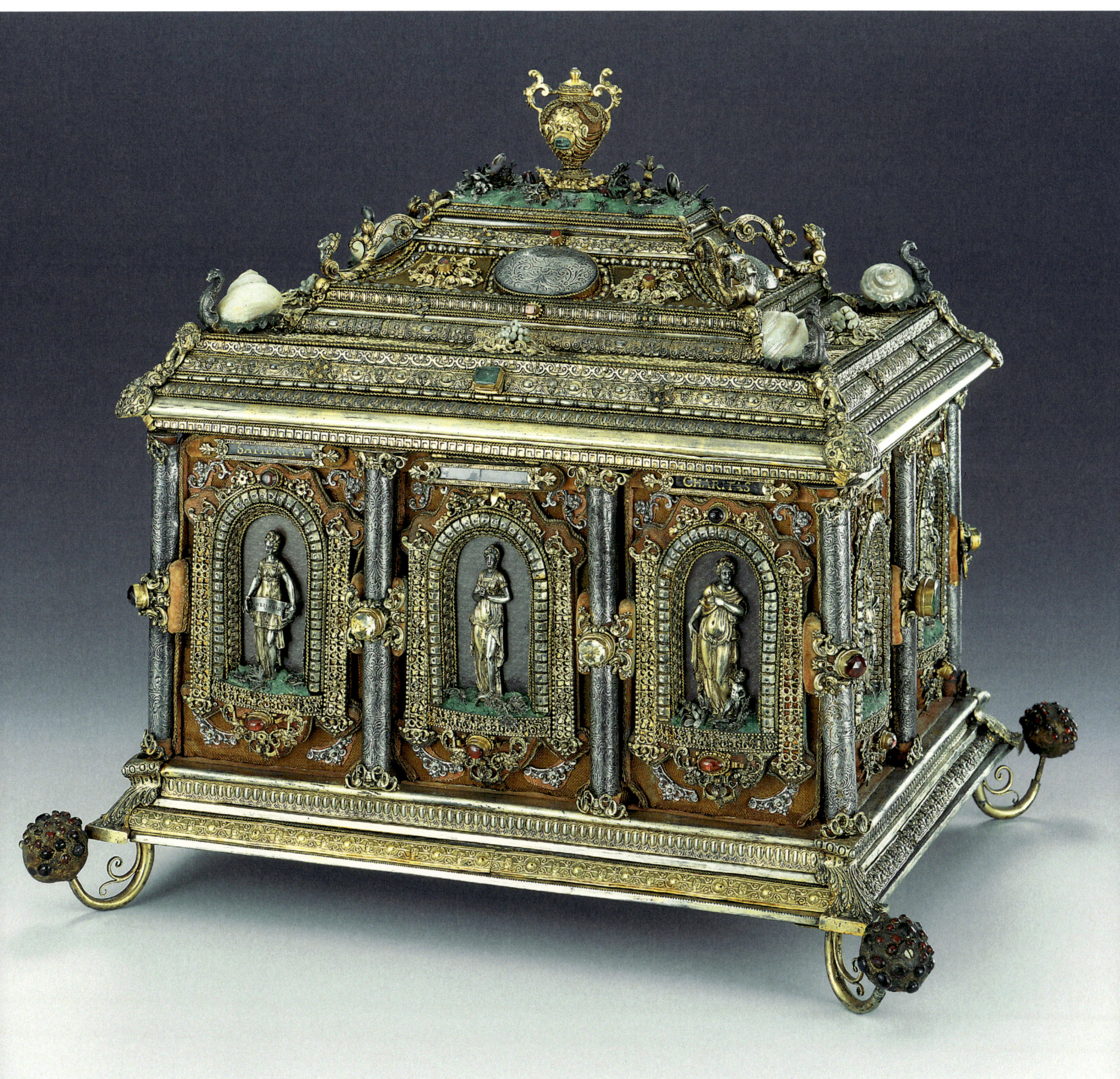

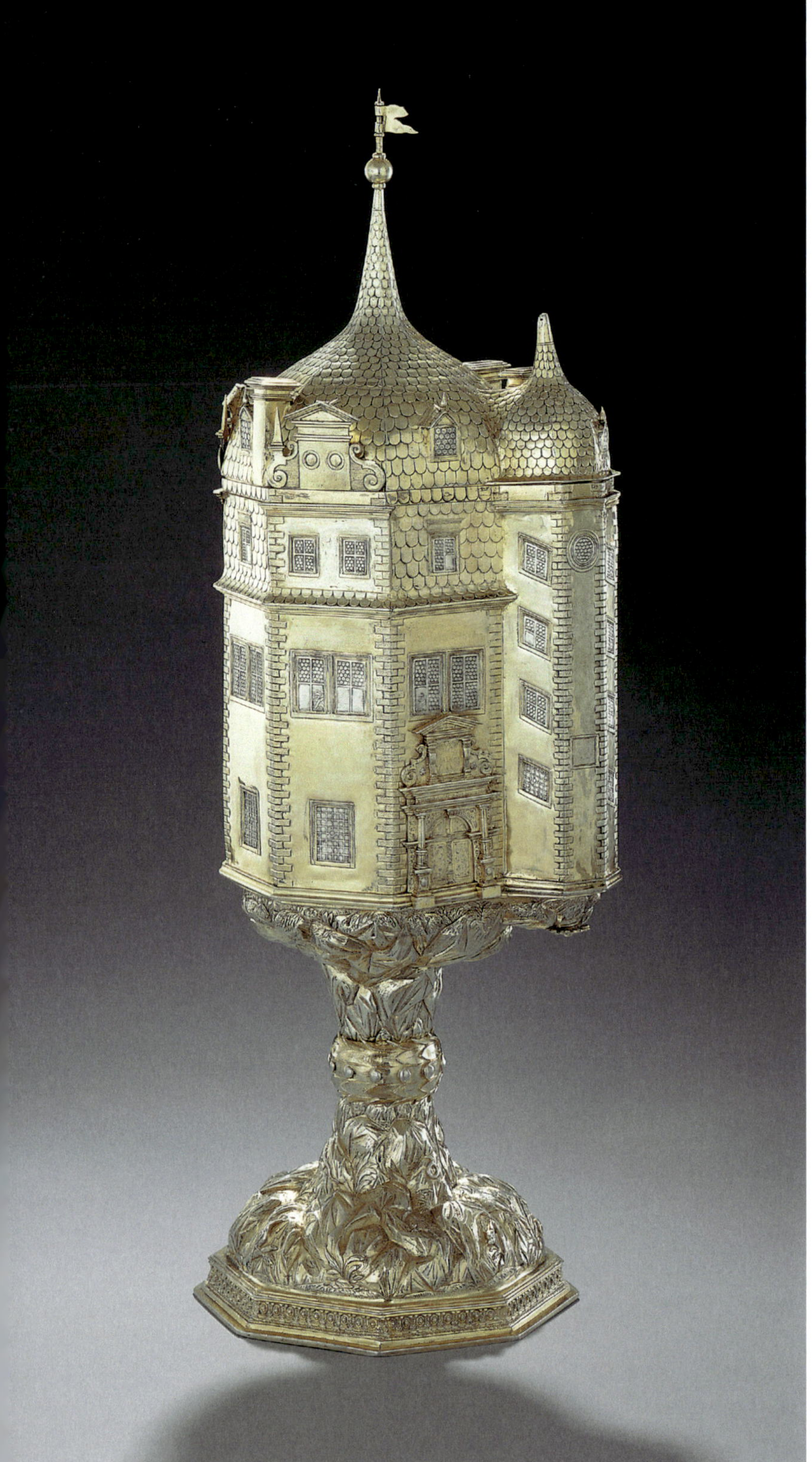

Covered Cup in the Form of a Small Castle

Silver-gilt
Georg Mond
Dresden, 1604 – 1606
H. 65.1 cm, w. 22.4 cm, d. 17.8 cm, Inv. no. IV 345

Elector Christian II commissioned this unusual cup from the Dresden goldsmith Georg Mond. It served as a welcoming cup in which guests were given their ceremonial welcoming drink. Although a device inside the huge vessel reduces its volume by approximately one third, it still has a capacity of 2.5 litres.

The shape of this prestigious drinking vessel mirrors that of the stately edifice for which it was intended. The cuppa is a detailed reproduction of the chateau de plaisance commissioned by Elector Christian II in 1604 to be erected on the Fortress of Sonnenstein at Pirna. The special architectural features were carefully copied and its location on top of a high rock is also evoked. Above the door there is the Saxon coat of arms and full title of the owner and on the tower enclosing the staircase the coat of arms of Rudolf von Bünau, from 1586 to 1615 head official at Sonnenstein, are displayed. Numerous details fill the small castle with life: behind the bull's eye panes the people living in there can be seen and on the rocky ground covered in luxuriant vegetation hares, squirrels and other animals abound.

The small castle was only available to the electoral court in Saxony for 35 years for hunting parties and social amusements. It was destroyed in the Thirty Years War, when a conflagration forced the Swedish army, which was entrenched there, to surrender. The cup itself survived the fire but its future was to be full of vicissitudes. First, it was taken to the Fortress of Königstein where it was displayed with other drinking vessels on the famous large wine vat. When the vat was removed in 1819 the cup was transferred to the Kunstkammer and after its dissolution in 1832 to the Rüstkammer (armoury). It was not until 1890 that the unusual »Willkomm« found its way into the Grünes Gewölbe.

UW

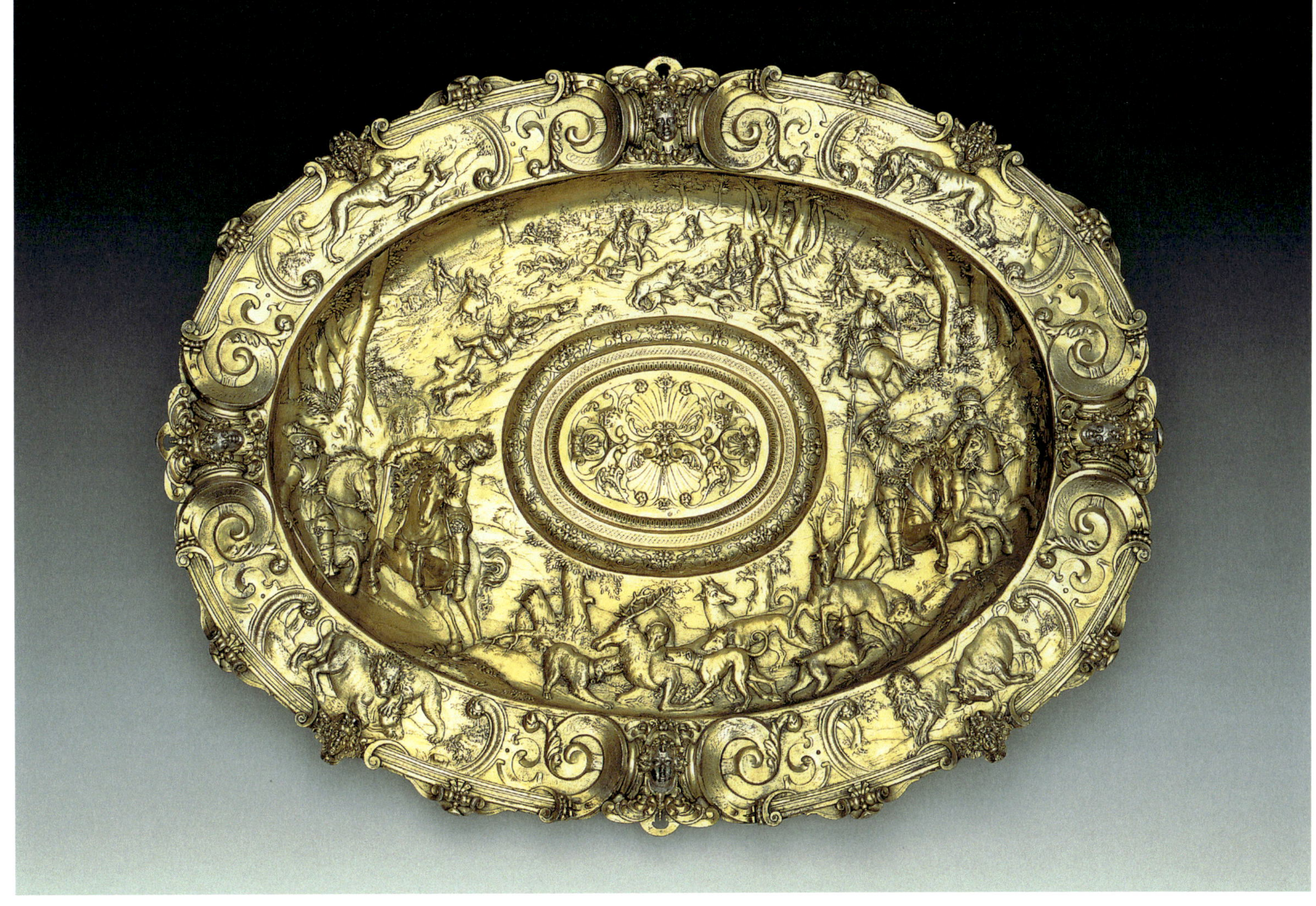

Oval Basin with Hunting Scenes

Silver-gilt
Elias Geyer
Leipzig, c. 1611 – 1613
L. 75 cm, w. 57 cm, Inv. no. IV 250

This splendid hunting basin by Elias Geyer, whose matching ewer was melted down in 1772, is recorded for the first time in the silver inventory of 1723. Under the heading »Antique vergoldte silberne Gieß Becken und Kannen« (antique silver gilt pouring vessels) parade vessels of the older electoral Saxon collections are listed, which Augustus the Strong a short time later displayed in the Silver Gilt Room together with newly acquired pieces. The pictorial area of this basin which can only be viewed from one angle and which is interrupted only by an oval reserve for the ewer, is predestined to be displayed against a wall. This type of design was in keeping with the heightened representational needs of the period and replaced the frieze arranged radially customary in the 16th century, which can only be viewed by turning the vessel.

The manufacture of a large-scale basin was one of the most challenging tasks for a goldsmith who was able to demonstrate his skills as a sculptor. Even though the basin does not come from the goldsmith cen-tre of Augsburg, which supplied luxury articles to princely European courts in the grand style, it does reflect the influence of the famous masters. Elias Geyer from Leipzig, one of the most innovative gold-smiths of his time, appears to have worked almost exclusively for the Dresden court. Roughly thirty of his works – and therefore by far the largest part of his oeuvre – are today in the possession of the Grünes Gewölbe. The hunting scenes portrayed on the vessel modelled on engravings by Antonio Tempesta, a copperplate engraver active in Rome, were transformed by Geyer with consummate skill into a relief which gives an impression of spatial depth. This he achieves with subtle gradations, which range from elements protruding from the surface to the finest transitions. Geyer went beyond the limits of the embossed relief by casting separately and attaching two sculpturally formed hors-es in the foreground. The accentuation of the four aristocratic horse-men on the left and right hand side of the basin consciously underlines the importance of hunting as a privilege of princes and as a courtly pursuit. It is no accident that they are stag hunting which – alongside hawking – is one of the most aristocratic and noble forms of hunting. The three examples of drinking vessels in the form of stags with antlers made of precious coral branches displayed in this room are evidence of the great prestige of hunting within the framework of princely court culture.

UW

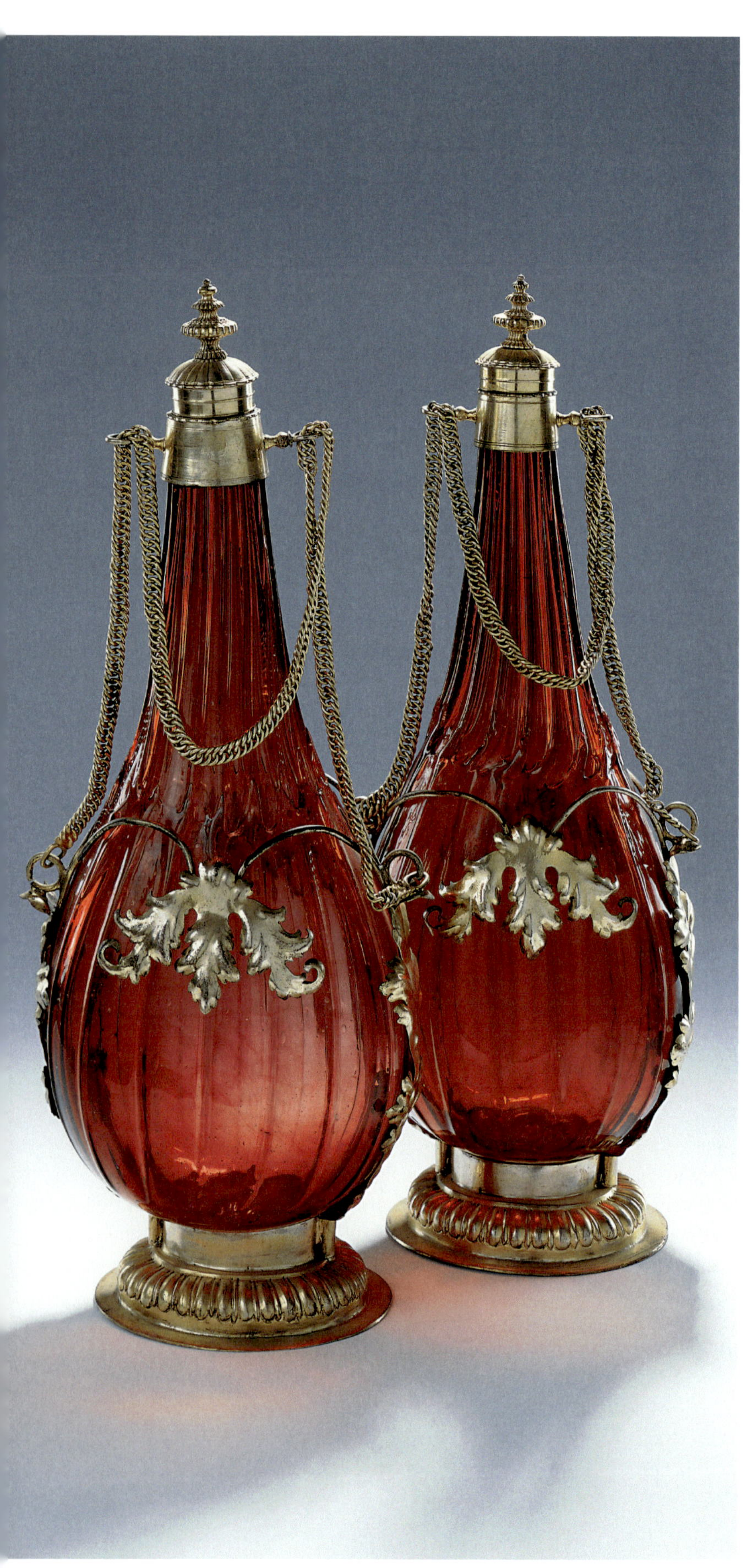

A Pair of Chain Bottles

Ruby glass, mount: silver gilt
Probably South Germany, c. 1700
Mount: Samuel Baur, Augsburg, c. 1700 – 1705
H. 36 cm, w. 14 cm, Inv. no. IV 219; H. 36.7 cm, w. 14 cm, Inv. no. IV 220

Two Salt Cellars

Ruby glass, mount: silver-gilt
Probably South Germany, c. 1700
Mount: probably Augsburg, c. 1700
H. 6 cm, w. 14.9 cm, Inv. no. IV 240; H. 5.8 cm, w. 14.7 cm, Inv. no. IV 241

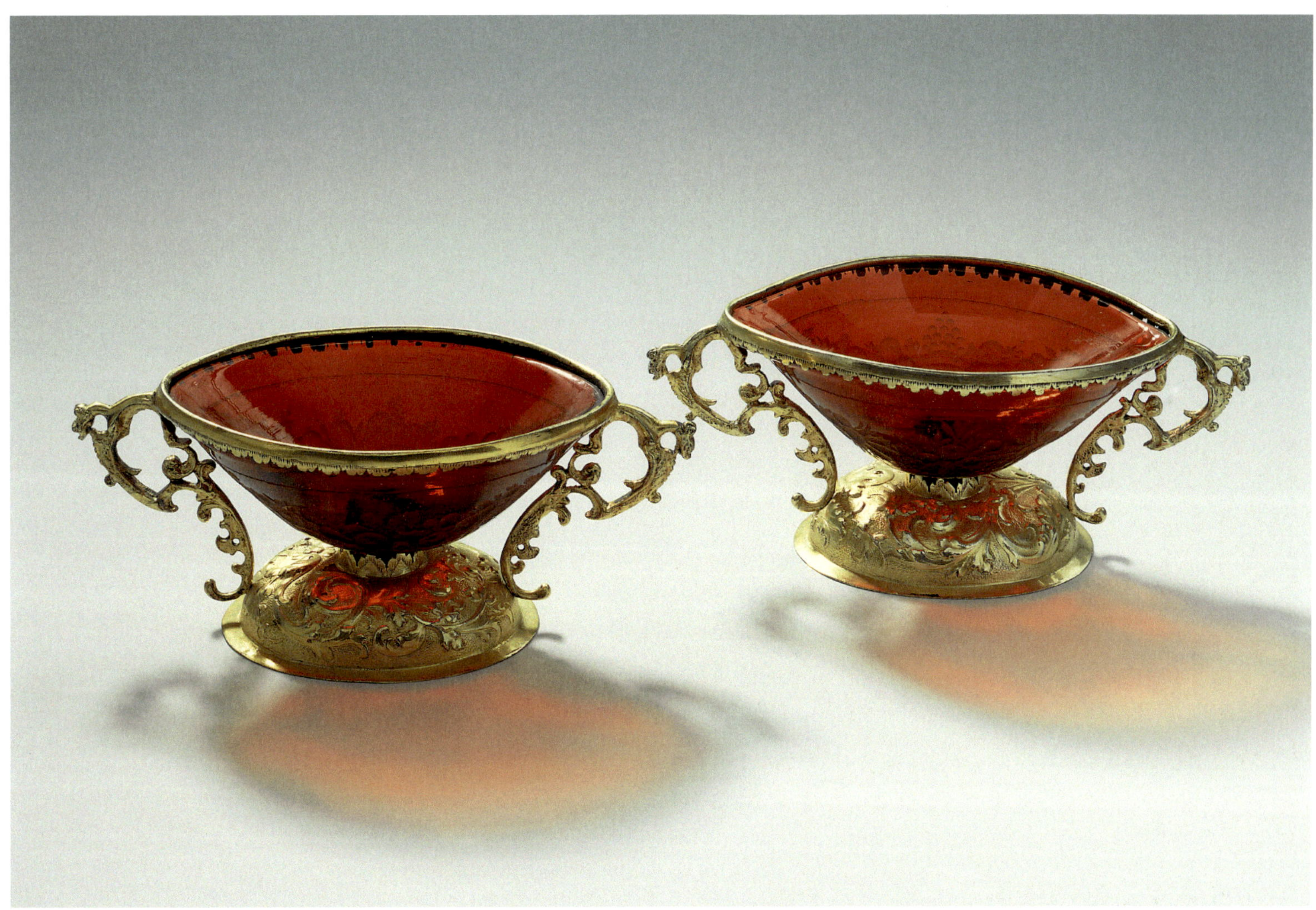

The model for the bright red, translucent glass and the stone it was named after was the ruby – a precious stone that was highly prized not only for its colour. It was said to have powers similar to those of the sun and was even able to glow in the dark (Albertus Magnus). The complex manufacturing technique is regarded as an invention of the famous alchemist and glassmaker Johannes Kunckel (1620 – 1703) who probably at the end of 1683 created »ins Glas gebrachten Rubin« (ruby introduced into glass) with the help of gold for the first time. The red colouring properties of gold were already known in Antiquity but only a single example exists of a vessel apparently created in this way. The process developed by Kunckel required great skill as the »Goldpurpur« (gold purple), the basic substance used in the process, was initially colourless. It was only by so-called »Tempern«, the re-heating of the glass that the desired red colouring appeared. Raising the temperature too high or maintaining it for too long led to brownish discolouration, maintaining it two briefly led to ugly streaks.

The vessels created in this way were often given a cut décor playing on the contrast between shiny polished and matt surfaces, which is for example to be seen in the two salt cellars decorated with festoons. Horizontal ribbing created an attractive iridescent effect of light and dark red. In keeping with the high esteem in which they were held ruby glass objects were often enhanced with a silver-gilt mount whose yellow shimmer harmonised perfectly with the warm tone of the glass. These mounts were generally commissioned in Augsburg where members of the goldsmith family Baur and other workshops had specialised in such work. The ribbed bottles with chains derive from pilgrims' bottles which could be suspended in water to cool the drinks they contained. The ruby glass bottles were naturally not intended for such practical use. The fact that they are usually in pairs seems to be due to the symmetrical arrangement on a prestigious parade buffet.

UW

A Pair of Ornamental Vases

Silver-gilt
Abraham II Drentwett
Augsburg, c. 1708 – 1710
Right: H. 65 cm, Ø 40 cm, Inv. no. IV 122;
Left: H. 63.5 cm, Ø 38.5 cm, Inv. no. IV 152

Each of the two large ornamental vases by the Augsburg goldsmith Abraham II Drentwett weighs almost eight kilograms. Augustus the Strong bought them almost ten years after they were made at the Leipzig Easter Fair of 1719, probably with the coming marriage of the Prince Elector to Maria Josepha, the emperor's daughter in mind. The splendid wedding festivities should put all similar events in the shade. Even if the pair of vases had not been expressly made for the wedding, the scenes on the friezes on the wall do bear some relation to the event. In both cases a sacrificial scene is combined with a scene from classical mythology. On one vase Venus, the goddess of love, leads a bride wearing a wreath of myrtle leaves to the wedding god Hymen while on the opposite side a sacrifice is brought to a fertility goddess (Astarte?) who holds a cow's horns in a sunburst. The pendant shows the Trojan hero Aeneas who is led by the Cumean Sybill into the underworld by means of a golden bough where he meets his ancestors. On the other side, a sacrifice is brought to Diana, the Huntress, a strict defender of virginity.

In 1733 the two vases flanked the door in the Hall of the Precious Objects leading to the Coats of Arms Room and were thus displayed in a prominent position. In the newly refurbished Grünes Gewölbe the two important pieces will be displayed in the Silver Gilt Room. They were already kept in this room, whose collection had been significantly reduced as a result of the number of objects melted down in 1772, after a reorganisation of the Grünes Gewölbe.

Abraham II Drentwett, whose symbol as a master craftsman was a squirrel, belonged to a famous and ramified Augsburg goldsmith dynasty. He worked as a wax embosser and engraver and was known for complex works usually with a rich sculptural décor.

UW

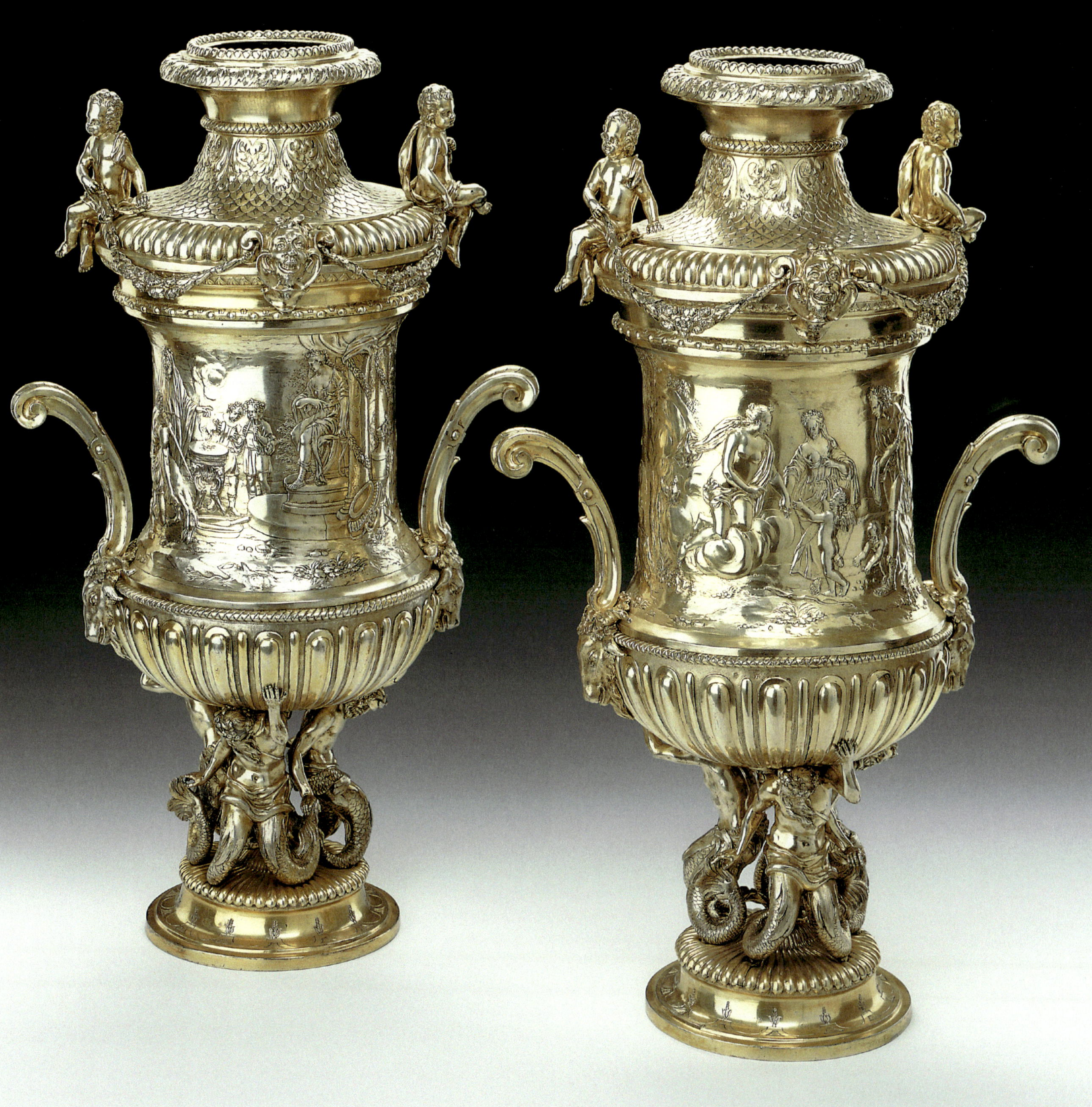

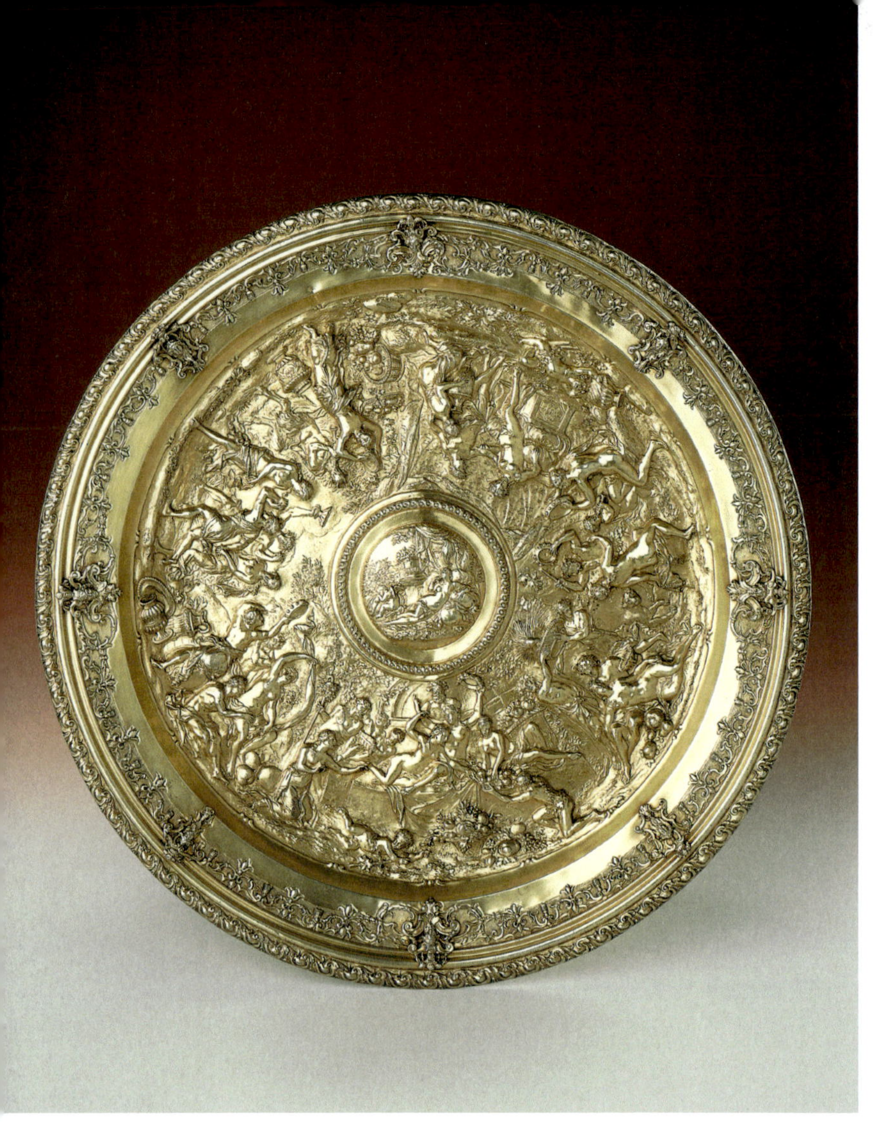

Allegorie« (inventions…with his knowledge of ancient history, fables, pagan gods and allegory) are also mentioned. Indeed, Thelott did have unusual creative skills, which he also exploited as a copperplate engraver. His sequence of etched illustrations on the wedding poem »Der reisende Cupido« (travelling Cupid), the playfully erotic theme of which is reflected in the small centre relief with Venus and Amor, became well-known. The scenes of the bacchanalia with its many figures round the basin can only be seen in their entirety by turning the vessel. Thelott – certainly quite consciously – takes up a Renaissance type of decoration which was later supplanted by basins to be viewed from one angle.

Thelott was able to realise his sculptural inventions impressively in three-dimensional goldsmith objects by means of embossing and chasing. Typical of his way of working is the use of relatively thin silver foil from which he models reliefs of considerable depth. While other master craftsmen used separately cast parts which were soldered on, Thelott succeeded in achieving this solely by means of his highly developed embossing technique. The thinness of the foil made it necessary to stabilise the basin by means of a smooth plate attached to the back. The basin does not have the customary goldsmith's marks, but was signed by Thelott – a procedure which manifests his considerable self-confidence as an artist.

UW

Parade Basin with a Bacchanalia

Silver-gilt
Johann Andreas Thelott
Augsburg 1714
H. 32. cm, Ø 47 cm, Inv. no. IV 5

As the silver inventory of 1723 shows, Augustus the Strong bought the basin at the Leipzig Fair in 1718, at which merchants from Augsburg offered the works from this goldsmith centre to a well-to-do public. The ewer which originally belonged to it, the wall of which was decorated in a décor of embossed river gods and naiads, fell victim to the melting down of many objects in 1772. The area where it stood can be seen in the middle of the basin.

Paul von Stetten, the chronicler of the Augsburg craftsmen, praised Johann Andreas Thelott in his history of art, crafts and guilds published in 1779 as »the most famous artist in embossed work« and mentions the ewer and basin garniture of the Grünes Gewölbe as one of the outstanding works. In addition, his »Erfindungen…mit Kenntnis der alten Geschichte, der Fabel, der heidnischen Götterlehre und der

Ewer and Basin

Silver-gilt
Johann Erhard Heuglin
Augsburg, c. 1717 – 1718
Ewer: H. 30.8 cm, Inv. no. IV 299; basin: Ø 54.1 cm, Inv. no. IV 282

The ewer and basin garnitures played an important role in the splendid effect of the Silver Gilt Room. In 1733 altogether 17 such ensembles were part of the collection displayed in a kind of permanent parade buffet in the largely mirrored room. Twelve of the garnitures distributed regularly over the individual surfaces of the walls were already listed in the silver inventory drawn up in 1723 under the heading »Modern vergoldtes Silber« (modern gilded silver). Most of them are acquisitions made by Augustus the Strong at the Leipzig Easter Fair in 1719 where the king bought a large number of the luxury articles from Augsburg, the goldsmith centre, which were highly fashionable at that time. These fine vessels, of which the ewer and basin garniture by Johann Erhard II Heuglin are an example, were to add festive splendour and glamour to the wedding of the Prince with Maria Josepha, the

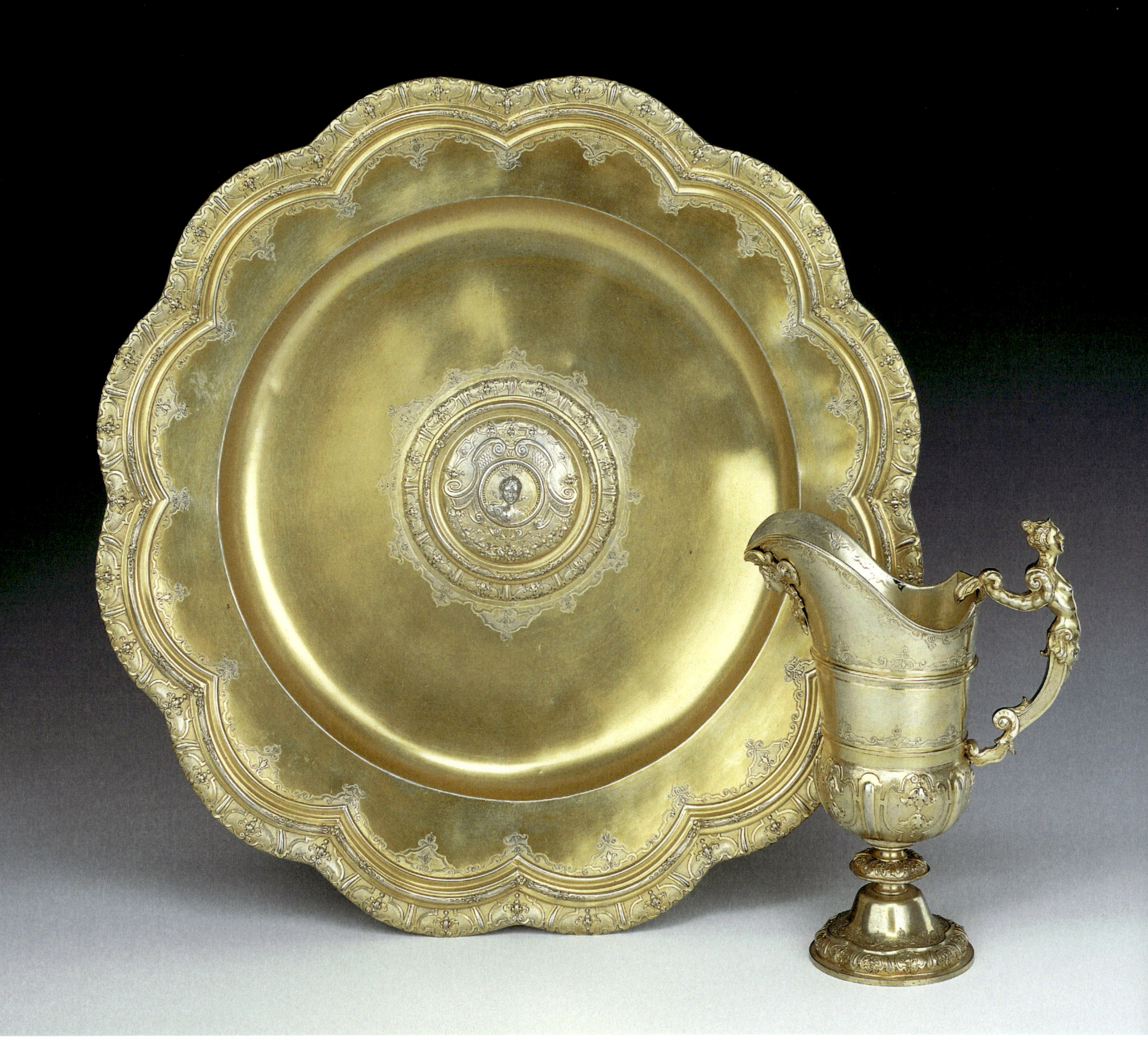

Emperor's daughter. The form of the basin with its rhythmic alternation of cut edges and soft, curving arches and the polygonal body of the ewer are characteristic of the ›Régence‹ style which rapidly spread from France to Germany. The décor of scrolls is in striking contrast to the polished surface of the body and the appliquéd medallions are also a typical decorative feature of these elegant garnitures. The two large chain flasks by the Augsburg goldsmith Georg Friebel are to be seen in the same context. They have a capacity of 3.4 litres each and were used to keep wine, or a mixture of water and wine, cool and fresh. During the meal they were put in an ice bowl and could be taken out easily by means of the chains (see p. 98).

UW

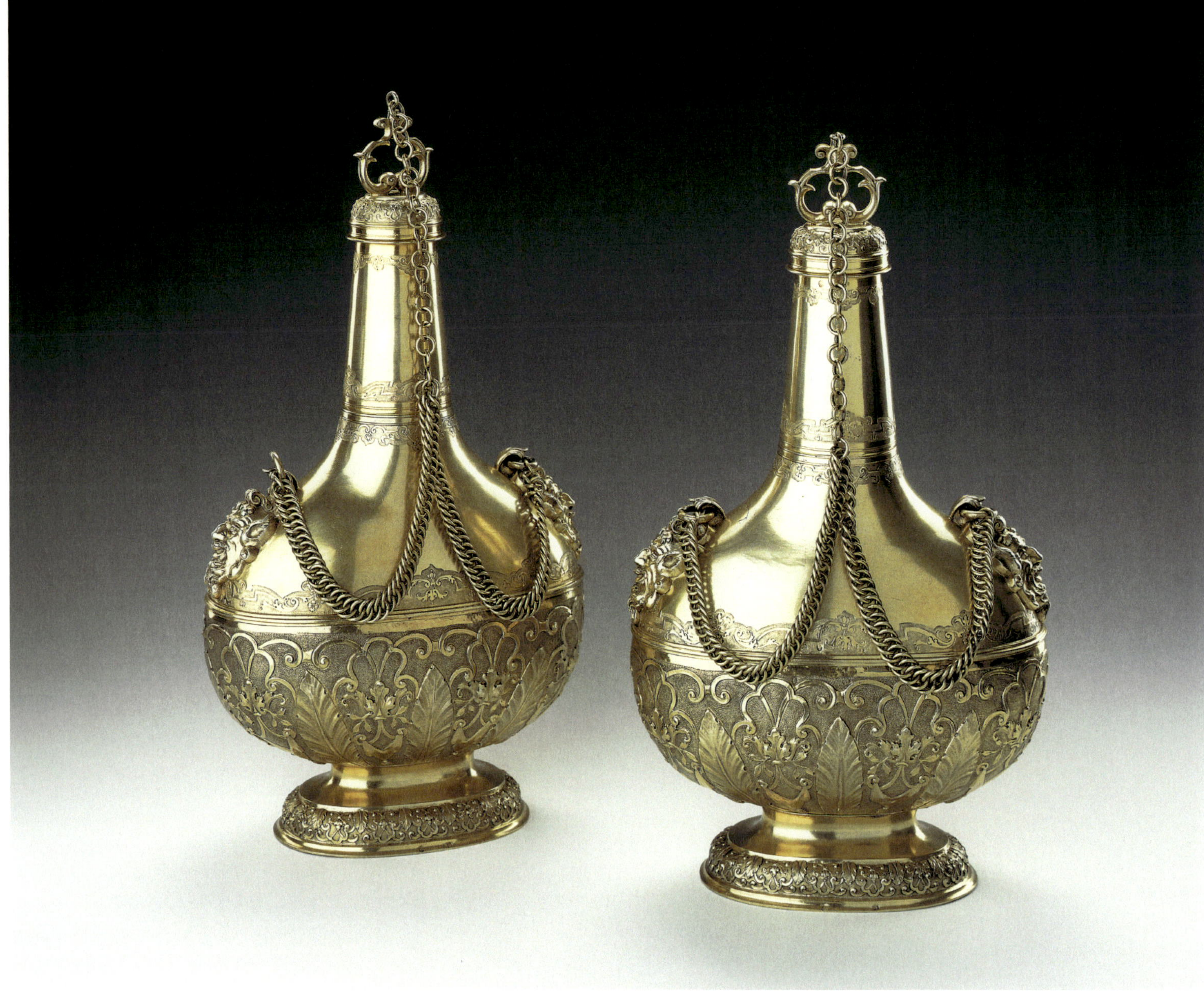

Two Chain Bottles

Silver-gilt
Georg Friebel
Augsburg, c 1712 – 1715
H. 41.6 cm, w. 24.2 cm, Inv. no. IV 258; H. 42.4 cm, w. 23.5 cm, Inv. no. IV 263

Coffee Pot with Réchaud and Tray

Silver-gilt
Johann Jakob Irminger
Dresden 1722
H. 47 cm, Inv. no. IV 251 and IV 200

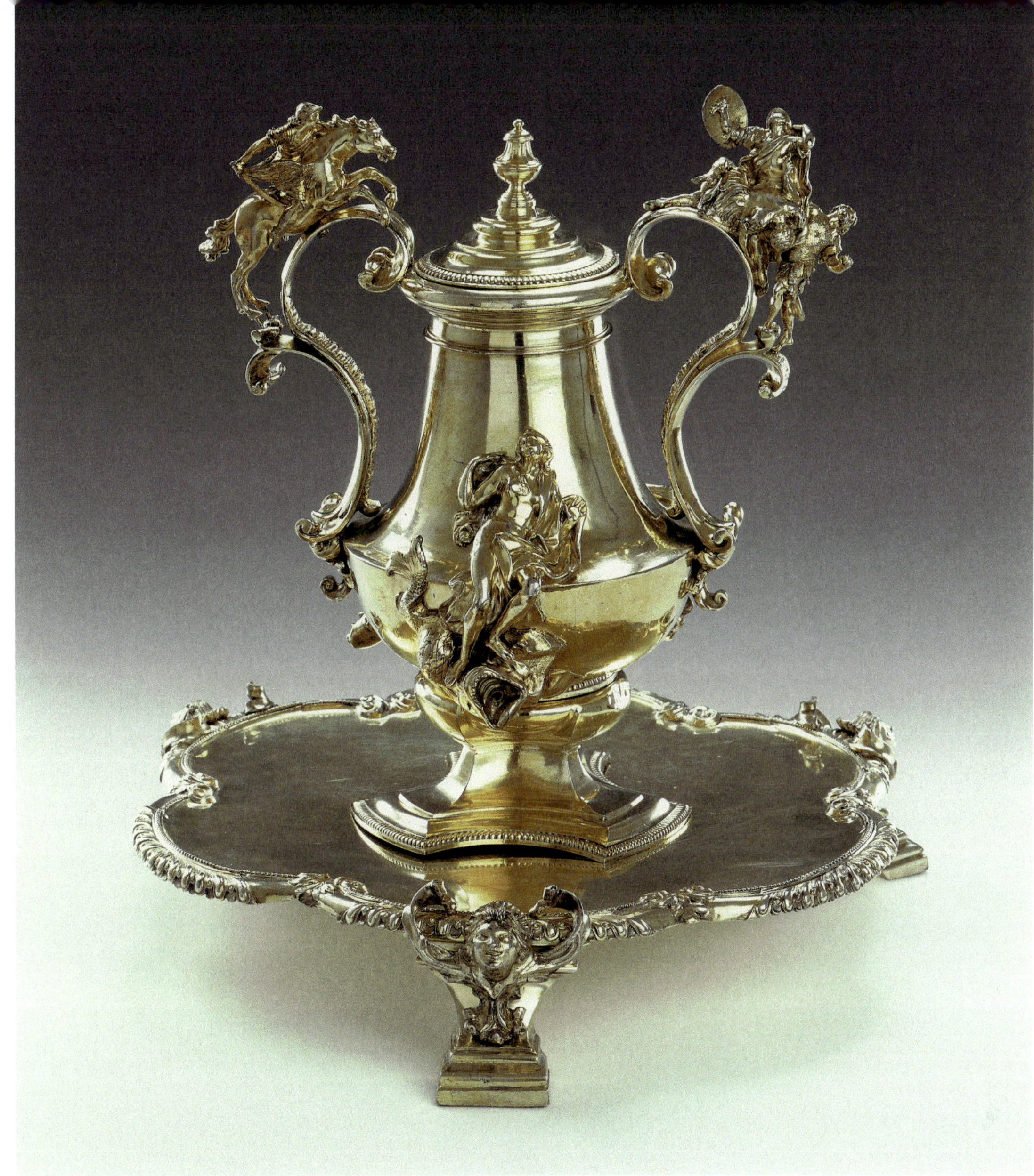

Two coffee pots created as a matching set are the only surviving evidence of the numerous tableware made for the Dresden court by Johann Jakob Irminger. The goldsmith, who fled to Dresden after a dispute in the Zurich guild hall, became a master craftsman in 1682 and was appointed court jeweller in 1687. Irminger played an important role from 1710 in the newly founded Meissen Manufactory, where he had a decisive influence on the design of early Böttger porcelain.

As a drawing, presumably by the goldsmith, shows, the two double-handled vessels both standing on trays belonged originally to a smoking service which Prince Friedrich August II (later King Augustus III of Poland) was given on his saint's day on 5 March, 1722 by his wife Princess Maria Josepha. This four-piece garniture has only been partly preserved. In the silver inventory of 1723 apart from the coffee pots only two sugar bowls and serving plates are mentioned, while the trays for smoking utensils, a liqueur service and drinking bowls pictured in the drawing are missing.

The powerful sculptural décor, the design of which is ascribed to the Saxon court sculptor Balthasar Permoser, contrasts effectively with the simple, well-proportioned basic forms of the two elegant coffee pots. The theme of the dramatic group of figures is in this example a legend passed down by Ovid according to which Perseus, a son of Jupiter, saved Andromeda, the daughter of a king, from a dangerous sea monster. On Pegasus his winged steed Perseus storms over the handle of the coffee-pot hurrying to save the princess portrayed on the belly of the pot with the monster. The sculptural group on the other handle relates the continuation of the story. The marriage of Perseus to Andromeda is disturbed by Phineas and his warriors, who demands the beautiful woman back, to whom he had been betrothed. The decoration shows how the intruders seeing the terrible head of the Gorgon held up by Perseus are turned to stone.

UW

Hall of the Precious Objects and Corner Cabinet

The Hall of the Precious Objects was the centre of the original room structure of the Grünes Gewölbe. At no other point in the palace is it possible to experience the original splendour of the interiors of this Renaissance palace so authentically as here. Conceived as a room for festivities and shortly afterwards embellished with a magnificent stuccoed ceiling by Italian artists in 1550, the room with its 191 square metres was from 1586 to 1719 the most secret room of the ›Geheime Verwahrung‹. Only the elector had a key to the ›back‹ or ›third‹ vault in which he kept his treasures. Many of the works in rock crystal and coloured precious stones, nautilus shells and turbo snail shells with gold and silver gilt mounts were already kept here.

The origin of the term Grünes Gewölbe was hidden after 1723 by the mirrored pillars of the room which hide marbled columns with verdigris capitals and bases. In 1709 Augustus the Strong not only had the large cabinet piece ›Throne of the Grand Mogul‹ bought from the court goldsmith Dinglinger displayed in this room but from 1719 to 1720 he also had a large glazed wall cupboard installed in which he intended to display his jewellery. In 1722 the ›Obeliscus Augustalis‹ followed which required a wall with mirrors for its presentation. These were fitted together with the Baroque interiors in 1723. Under the direction of the Oberlandbaumeister (minister of architecture) Matthäus Daniel Pöppelmann a festive display room was created with interiors which were inspired by the mirror gallery in Versailles, in which the collection of the French king was displayed, and the display rooms of the Prussian king in the palaces of Oranienbaum and Charlottenburg. The Hall of the Precious Objects and the rooms that were added until 1729 are, however, a unique Saxon ivention which – respecting older beautiful features such as the vaulted Renaissance ceiling – created something new.

In the first building phase between 1723 and 1724 the Hall of the Precious Objects was already a kind of mirror »Kabinett«. The interiors of the Corner Cabinet also date from this time but they were heavily renovated in 1890 to 1891. The tower room with an area of 16 square metres is an independent room separated from the Hall of the Precious Objects by a grille dating from the mid 16th century. With regard to the works of art displayed here the »Kabinett« was considered part of the Hall of the Precious Objects. The small treasury objects standing on green painted consoles of high sculptural quality are listed in the inventory of the Hall of the Precious Objects from 1733. Only a small part of the listed 478 objects in pearls, precious stones, gold and ivory are now in the Corner Cabinet and can be viewed through the wrought-iron screen. The greater part of this group of objects was almost completely preserved and they are now displayed in the New Grünes Gewölbe.

In the second building phase between 1727 and 1729 the Hall of the Precious Objects was given its present form. Above a high dado in oak the mirrored wall panels with appliquéd ornamentation in carefully worked gilded soft wood reach to the Renaissance ceiling. The court sculptor Benjamin Thomae was responsible for the sculptural ornamentation in the Hall of the Precious Objects and Corner Cabinet. He was helped by his pupil and employee Johann Gottlieb Kirchner, among others.

Although the interiors were preserved to a remarkable extent despite the Second World War and were restored, in the Hall of the Precious Objects two reconstruction measures were necessary. On the one hand this affected the fitted mirrors, which survived the bomb raid of 1945 but – like those in the White Silver Room and in the Silver Gilt Room – were largely lost after 1961. They were replaced in the last few years of the refurbishment of the Grünes Gewölbe by Stefan Noack. For this purpose the tin amalgam technique whereby the coating on the back of the mirror is applied by means of poisonous mercury, which had been forbidden in Germany since 1905, was revived. Thus the Grünes Gewölbe was given the optical effect characteristic of mirror »Kabinetts« in the 18th century. However, the ten paintings of the Saxon electors of the Albertine line of the Wettin dynasty from Moritz to Prince Friedrich August (II), which were removed together with their frames in 1942 and lost in the turmoil of war, were replaced by copies of existing paintings from the 16th to the 18th century. Both decisions in the process of reconstruction served the goal of making it possible to experience the original appearance of the Hall of the Precious Objects as nearly as possible.

With the same end in mind the form of presentation recorded in the inventory of 1733 was largely reconstructed. In this way the arrangement is again visible with which Augustus the Strong imposed order on the overwhelming abundance of objects he had acquired or inherited from his predecessors. The individual sections of the walls were systematically reserved for different materials. Two wall panels with almost 490 works in coloured precious stones were followed by a smaller central panel with works in amber and, framing the door to the Coats of Arms Room, a panel with turbo snail and nautilus shells in goldsmiths' mounts and a second with ostrich eggs with and without goldsmiths' mounts. Just as in 1733 the east wall, which is a good ten metres long, is covered in a large number of preciously mounted works in rock crystal. In 1723 they also framed the jewel cabinet. In the first plan of the second building phase this cabinet was to be replaced by the ›Obeliscus Augustalis‹ and on the left and right the ›Throne of the Grand Mogul‹ and the ›Golden Coffee Set‹ to form a magnificent climax. The gilded frames had already been fitted when it was decided – probably because of poor lighting – to place these highlights of Baroque treasury art in the Jewel Room. The architect Horst Witter has endeavoured in an unobtrusive manner befitting the character of the room to improve the lighting whose inadequacy has been bemoaned since the 18th century by indirect ceiling uplighters.

DS

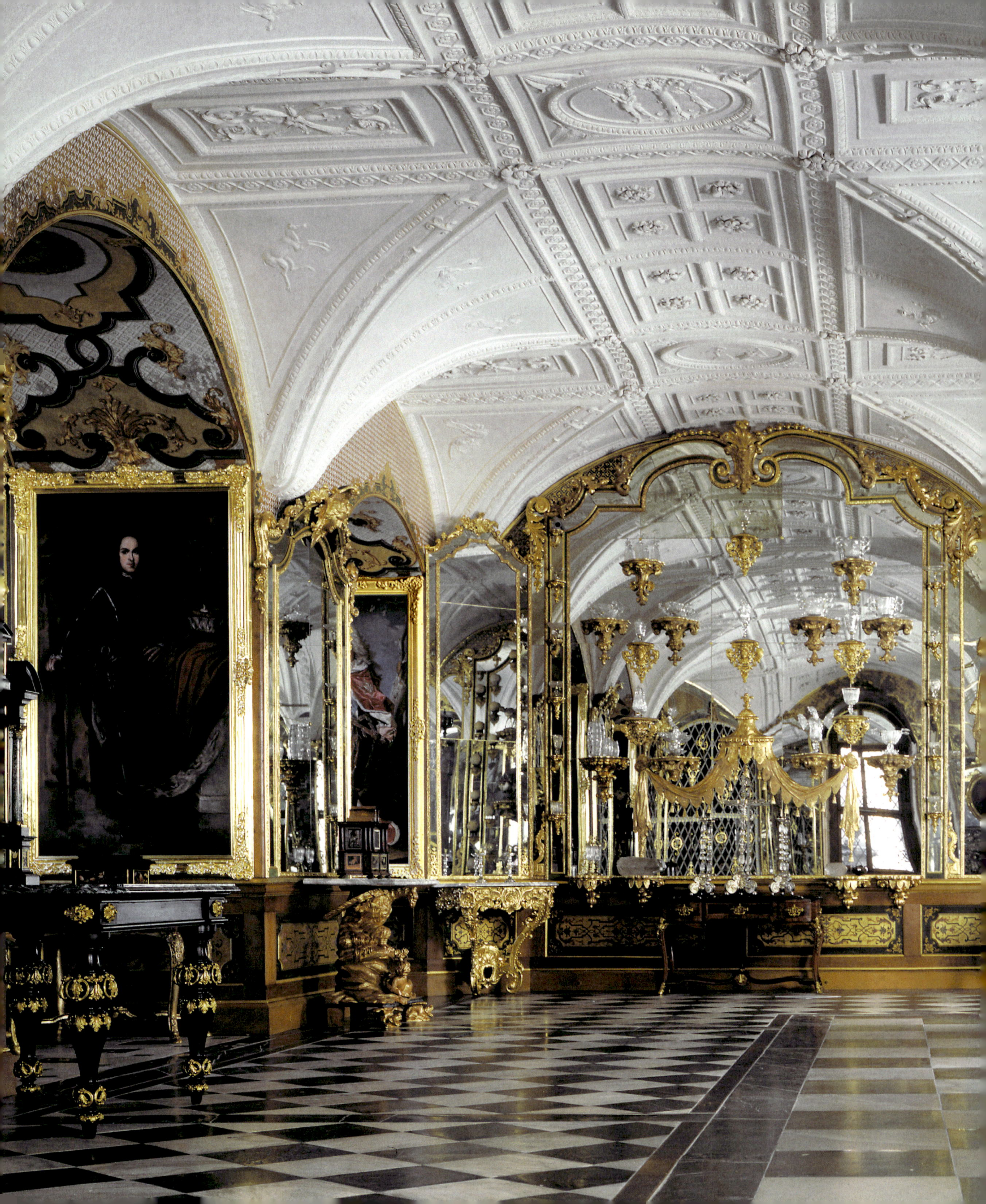

The Calvary

Silver-gilt, wood, shells, pearls, emeralds, turquoises, garnets
Elias Lencker
Nuremberg, marked 1577
H. 67 cm, w. 31 cm, Inv. no. III 187

The Cross of Christ rises above a large mount in precious pearls. It is a splendid devotional image and at the same time a unique work of treasury art. The Redeemer is crucified on a slender, tall cross consisting of a particularly rare and hard tropical wood. Above a plaque with an inscription from Genesis 3 there is the Serpent of Original Sin which was vanquished by the Passion of Christ. At the bottom of the cross the year 1577 has been inscribed.

The Calvary is composed of mother-of-pearl and irregular pearls which were taken to Europe in the late 16th century by Spanish and Portuguese traders from the Gulf of Mexico, the Persian Gulf and the Indian Ocean. From the 16th century onwards they were used in jewellery, but never in such abundance. In Christian iconography they stand for the permanent renewal of life on earth, the eternal life in God, divine purity and baptism. In medieval iconography, pearls were regarded as the result of divine conception. The iridescent shimmer of pearls and of mother-of-pearl was also regarded as the reflection of celestial light.

The splendour of the pearls was enhanced by a mount in massive gold, with appliqués in turquoise, emeralds and garnets. But there are also crickets, lizards, frogs and a small stork in the fashion of casts from nature that were popular in Nuremberg at that time as symbols of the transitory nature of life. Trees and shrubs made from silver wire complement the scene. The rock of Golgotha rests on a plinth made from ebony which includes six expressive scenes from the Passion of Christ made by the Nuremberg goldsmith Elias Lencker: the Mount of Olives, the Arrest of Jesus, Jesus before the High Priests, the Flagellation, Ecce Homo and the Bearing of the Cross. The four corners are adorned with eight personifications of virtues. The year 1577, indicated at the base of the cross, was of particular importance for Elector Augustus of Saxony. It was in that year that the concordat was drawn up in Dresden under his supervision, which separated Lutherism from Calvinism and gave the former an orthodox framework. In 1580, the Elector pushed through this tenet with the Lutheran estates of the Empire on the occasion of the 50th anniversary of the Augsburg Confession. The rock of Golgotha in pearls with the solitary figure of Christ Triumphant may have been regarded by the electoral couple as a triumph of their religion.

In 1733, at the behest of Augustus the Strong, this work of art was displayed on a table, the top of which was made of oriental marble and the frame of walnut, with hoofed feet and brass mountings, in front of the long south wall of the Hall of the Precious Objects. This is where this work is displayed today.

DS

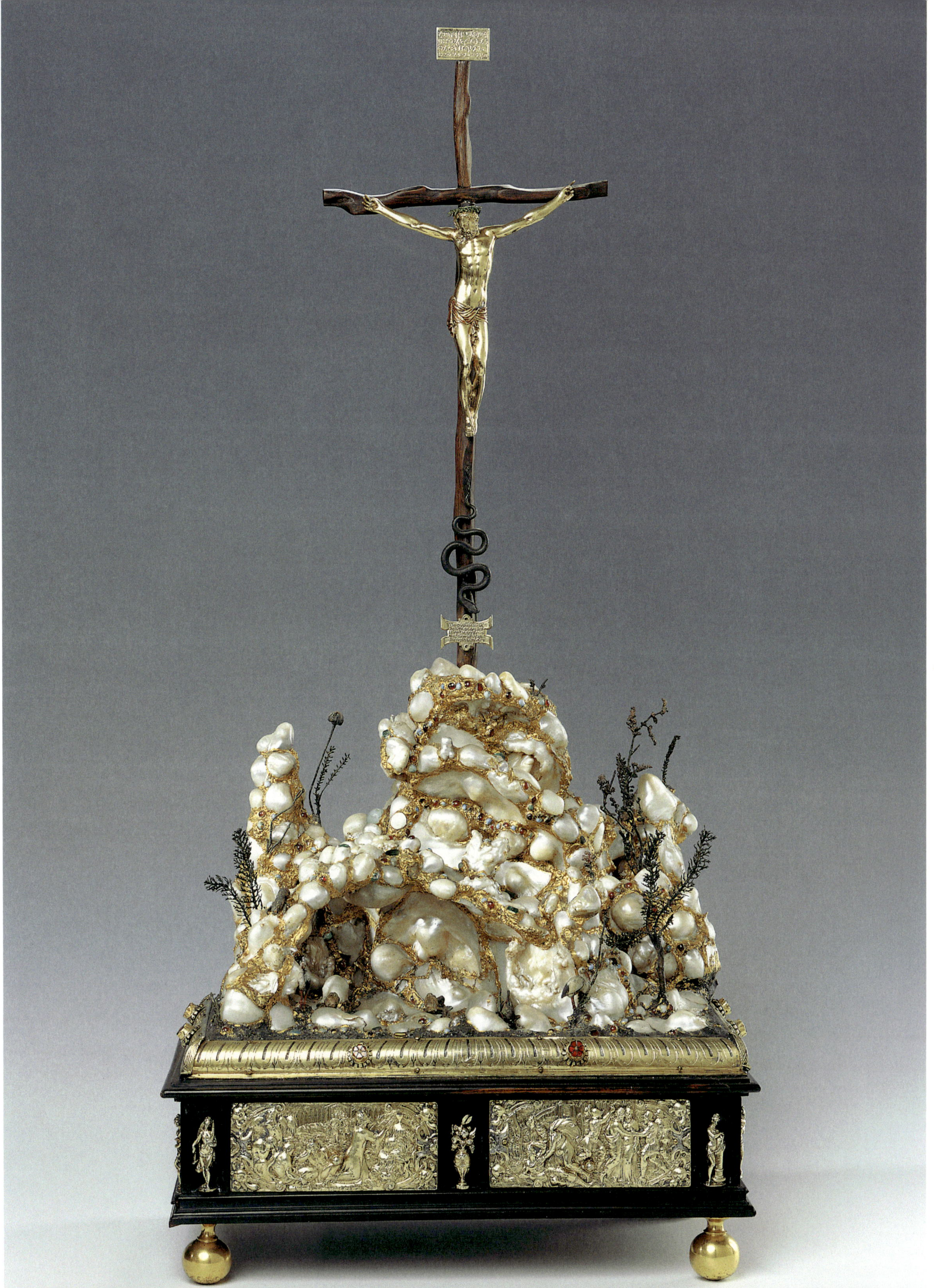

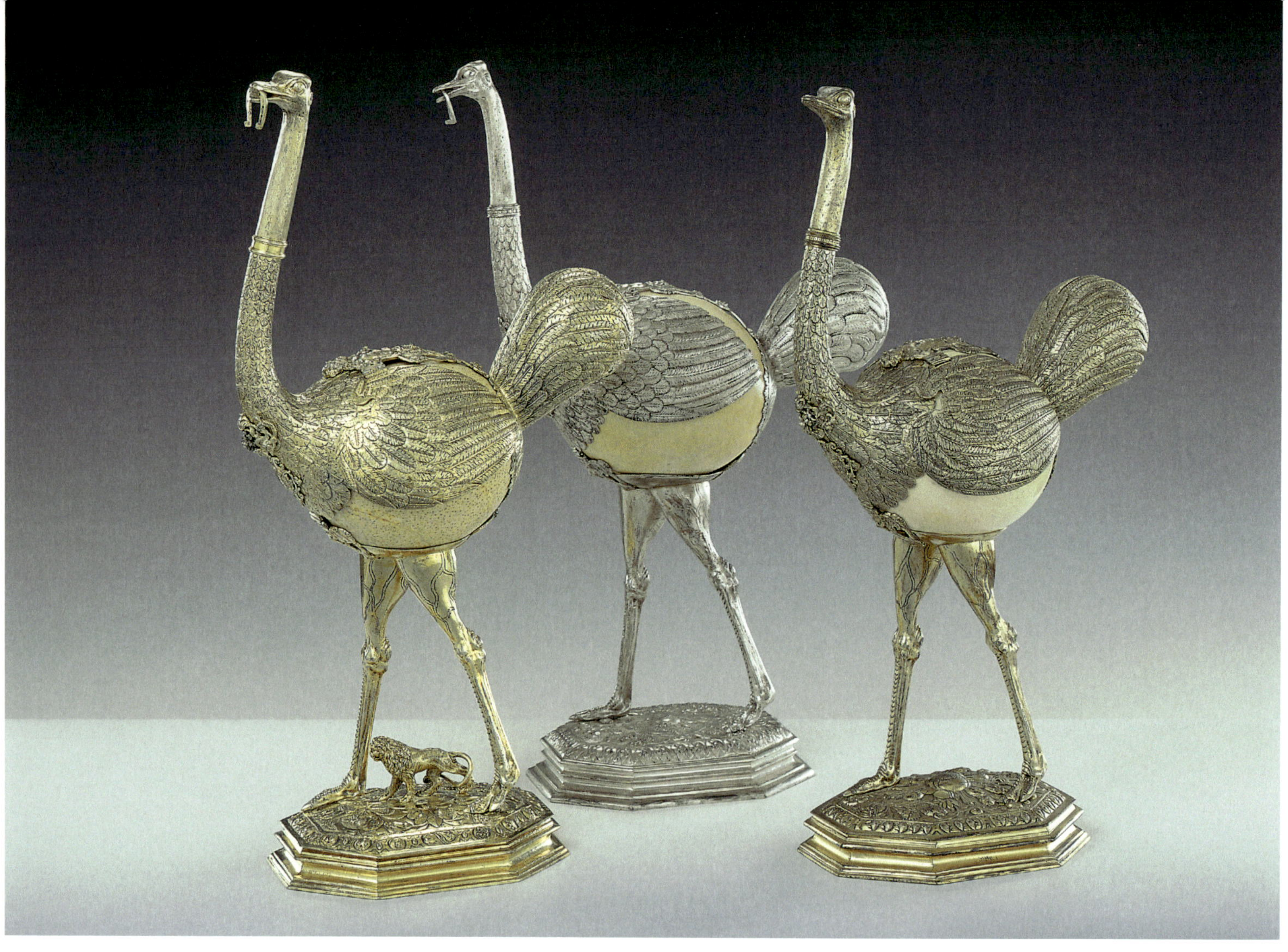

Three Ostrich-Egg Cups in the Shape of Ostriches

Ostrich egg, silver (III 115) and silver-gilt (III 227 and III 228)
Elias Geyer
Leipzig, c. 1589 – 1595
Left: h. 47.6 cm, w. 26 cm, Inv. no. III 228; centre: h. 46.3 cm, w. 36 cm,
Inv. no. III 115; right: h. 46.2 cm, w. 27 cm, Inv. no. III 227

More than two dozen works by Elias Geyer are part of the collection of the Grünes Gewölbe. Thus, almost the complete work of this eccentric artist which has been preserved is in Dresden. Geyer's goldwork is of high quality and is unique in the goldsmiths' art of Leipzig. It was obviously in keeping with the artistic taste of the electoral court. Veit Böttiger, a trader who was also from Leipzig, probably played an important role as an agent and many of the works by Geyer came to the Dresden Kunstkammer through him. These works are characterized by their preference for exotic materials and nephrite. Besides ostrich eggs, Geyer used conches, coconuts and mother-of-pearl. Another characteristic is a fantastic and grotesque element which manifests itself in

Geyer's sea shell vessels in the shape of hippocamps, gryphons and basilisks and in his tall ostrich-egg cups. Of the seven cups listed in the Kunstkammer inventory of 1595, five have been preserved. Arranged as a group, they form a unique and dynamic ensemble. It is not certain whether the tall birds, the heads of which can be removed, actually served as drinking vessels as the body of the cups were probably not watertight between the mount and the egg. It is typical of the bizarre sense of humour in those days that the wings of the bird flapped and hit the drinker's face when he lifted the vessel and that it was extremely difficult to drink from the vessel as the liquid came in short irregular bursts out of the narrow spout.

The different symbolical meanings attributed to the ostrich will have been familiar to an educated person. The bird, which allegedly fed on iron, was often depicted with a horseshoe in its beak and had been a symbol of the ability to benefit even from great adversity from classical antiquity onwards. In Christian iconography the ostrich was regarded as a symbol of the ›immaculate conception‹ as the bird has its eggs, which it buries in the sand, apparently hatched by the sun.

UW

Drinking Vessel in the Shape of a Partridge

Silver-gilt, mother-of-pearl plaques, emeralds, garnets
Friedrich Hillebrand
Nuremberg, c. 1593 – 1602
H. 27.8 cm, w. at top 16 cm, Inv. no. III 150

Drinking Vessel in the Shape of a Parrot

Silver-gilt, mother-of-pearl plaques, emeralds,
rubies, enamel, vestiges of paint
Hans I Rappolt
Nuremberg, c. 1593 – 1602
H. 32.5 cm, w. at top 19 cm, Inv. no. III 151

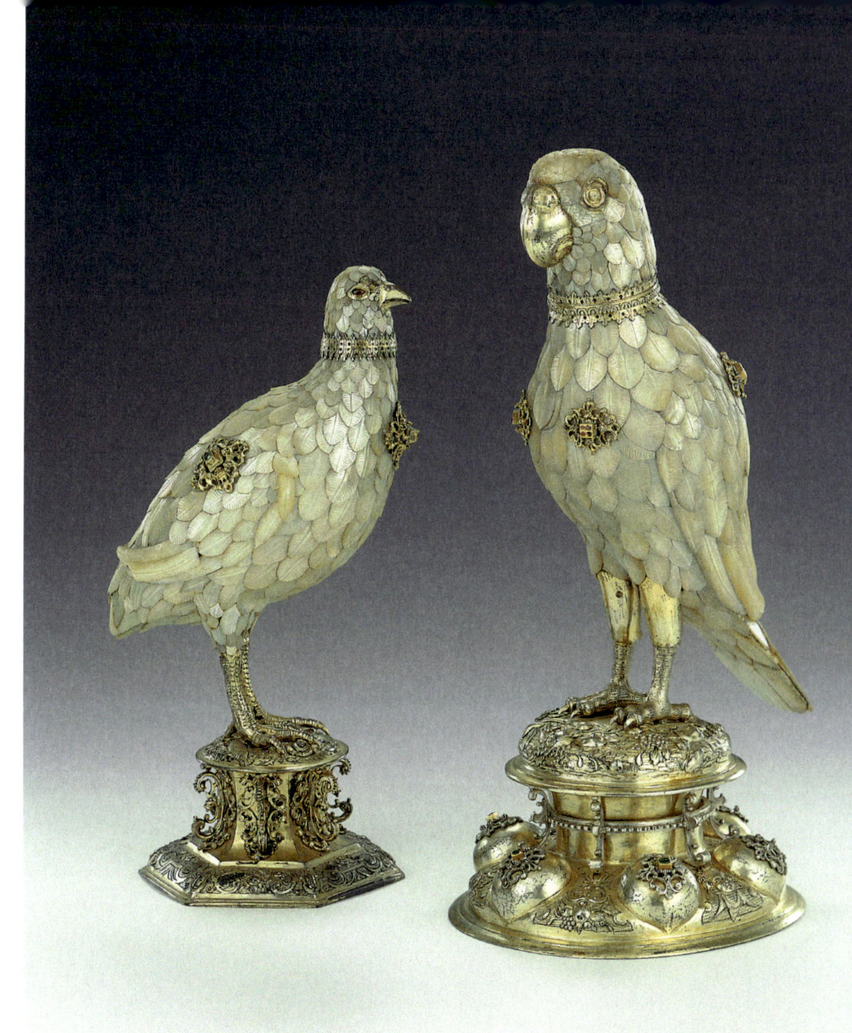

Zoomorphic drinking vessels were made in the 16th and 17th centuries in all shapes and forms. The parrot and partridge cups, however, have a prominent position. Mother-of-pearl was made from sea shells and was an expensive exotic material. Its soft shimmer made the vessels highly coveted collector's items. That is why the few pieces which have been preserved are mainly found in princely collections.

The mother-of-pearl plumage of the birds was given particular attention by the artist. The delicate engravings on the feathers, which are arranged in a roof-tile pattern on the body, give the birds a very naturalistic appearance. This naturalism, however, is in contrast to the gemstone appliqués on the breast and back of the birds. The Kunstkammer inventory of 1640 refers to these ornamentations as »Rößlein« (rosettes). They were originally combined with enamels, which will have strongly influenced the overall appearance of the objects. Vestiges of cold enamels are still discernible on these vessels, as on many other goldsmith's works in the Grünes Gewölbe.

As representational goldsmith's works, they were first displayed in the Kunstkammer. It was only on special occasions that these vessels were used as welcome cups for guests. Their heads can be removed so that liquid could be poured into the vessels. This may be the reason why the delicate, fragile mother-of-pearl has been damaged. Records as early as 1640 mention that several mother-of-pearl feathers beneath the tail of the parrot are missing. When Augustus the Strong furnished his treasury museum, he removed numerous works from the Kunstkammer and had them repaired between 24 November 1723 and 25 August 1724 by Johann Heinrich Köhler. Besides the parrot, which received ten new feathers, the court jeweller restored 154 other works to make them worthy for the splendour of the newly established magnificent rooms of the collection.

UW

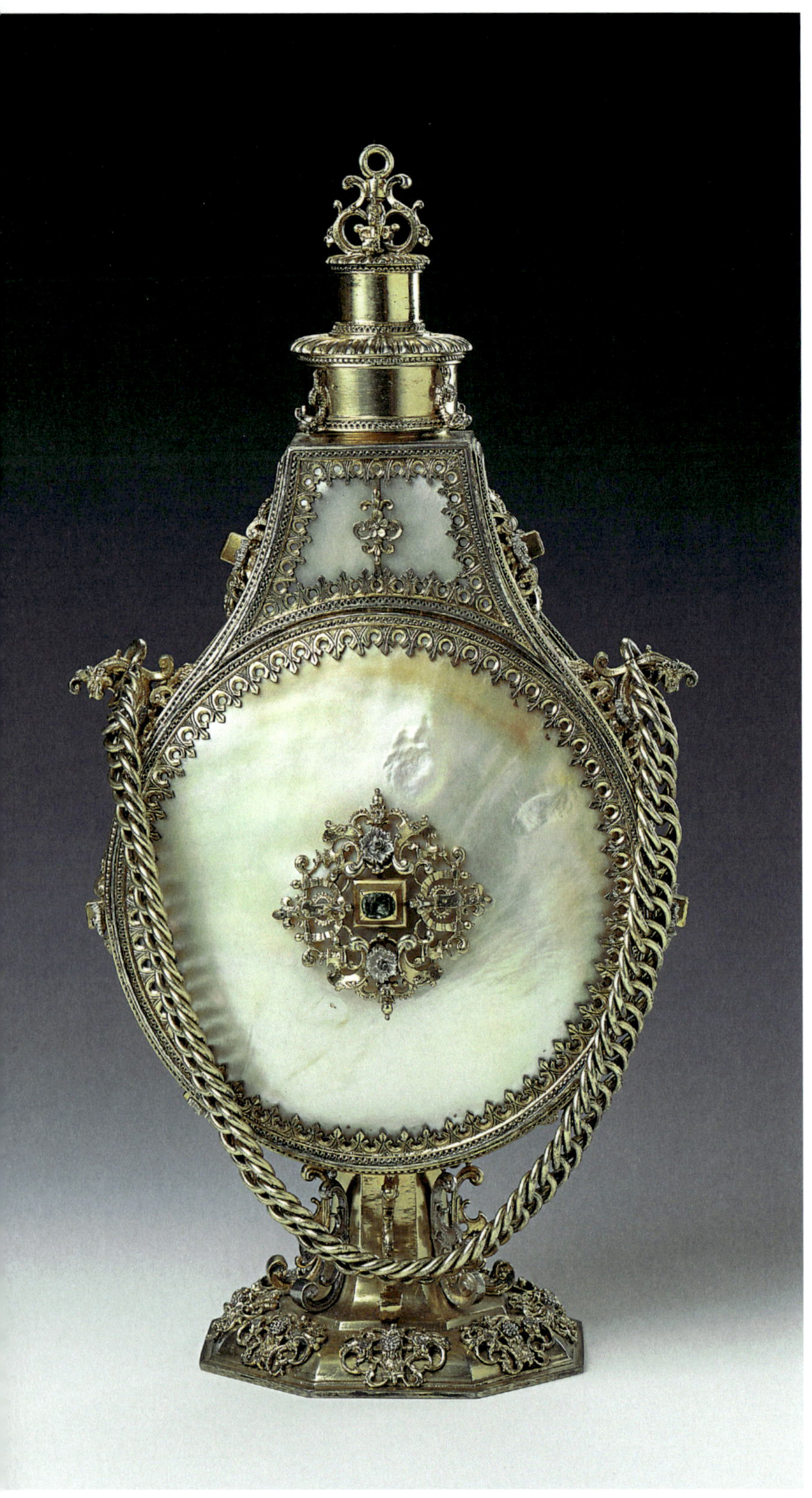

Chain Flask

Silver-gilt, mother-of-pearl plaques, emeralds
Joerg (Georg) Ruel
Nuremberg, c. 1598 – 1602
H. 27.4 cm, w. 14.9 cm, d. 9.6 cm, Inv. no. III 192

The elegant chain flask bears witness to the creativity and technical skill of its creator. It is characterised by unusually large mother-of-pearl plaques covering the front and back of the wall. The exotic naturalia are framed by finely indented frames. Their centre is accentuated by a gemstone appliqué. There are three similar appliqués on the narrow sides of the flask. The Kunstkammer inventory of 1640 describes these ornamentations, which were very popular at that time, in great detail and mentions eight roses in openwork fashioned like jewellery, each adorned with an emerald and embellished with two small white rosettes. This type of chain flask, or pilgrim's flask, which was used by travellers to cool drinks by putting the flask into cold water, was thus reinterpreted as a precious Kunstkammer object in which the iridescent shimmer of the material used competes with the ingenuity of artistic creativity. Joerg Ruel had a very productive workshop in the goldsmith centre of Nuremberg and manufactured mainly figural drinking vessels. According to the records, there is evidence of more than thirty works by Ruel, two of which are at the Grünes Gewölbe. His comprehensive work shows that he was a versatile artist specialising in pieces using conches and ostrich eggs.

UW

Sailing Ship

Nautilus shell, silver-gilt
Joerg (Georg) Ruel
Nuremberg, early 17th century
H. 59.5 cm, Inv. no. III 152

Augustus the Strong had almost an entire wall panel in the Hall of the Precious Objects covered with exhibits made from the iridescent mother-of-pearl of sea shells, and above all nautilus shells. Almost all these exhibits mentioned in the inventory of 1733 of this room have been preserved. Thus, it has been possible to largely reconstruct the original arrangement of this room. The sheer number of objects displayed on the consoles, which are part of the interior decoration of the room, is amazing.

The Grünes Gewölbe has one of the largest collection of nautilus vessels from the 16th and 17th centuries. Most of the shells used in the manufacture of the exhibits are from ›Nautilus pompilius‹, an ancient type of squid or cephalopod that lives in the Indian Ocean and the South Pacific at a depth of between 50 and 500 metres. It hardly ever comes to the surface.

The stylised man-of-war, created by the Nuremberg goldsmith Joerg Ruel shortly after 1600 is part of a group of four ships at the Grünes Gewölbe whose hulls are made from nautilus shells. The small vessel, its sails billowing and its crew ready to fight, is transported on the back of the kneeling sea god Neptune. The dragon-shaped spout at the bow and the delicate handle at the stern suggest that it may have served as a drinking vessel. It may, however, be assumed that due to the fragility of the shell and the silver-gilt rigging, the vessel was only used as a precious collector's item alluding to the maritime origin of the valuable natural material from distant, perilous climes. This assumption is supported by the high railing of the ship engraved with a series of fighting sea gods which invites the viewer to study the depictions at close range. Vessels of this kind are also a visualisation of the myth, handed down by authors of classical antiquity, that the bizarre sea creatures were able to glide over the waves with their shells turned upside down and a sail-like organ stretched out between their tentacles. This is the reason why the nautilus shells were referred to as ›pearl boat‹ or ›small skipper‹. This old theory may seem bizarre, but it is based on the observation that after the death of the animal its hard shell detaches itself from the soft parts of the body and – owing to the fact that the inner chambers of the shell are filled with air – floats on the surface of the water until it is washed ashore.

DS

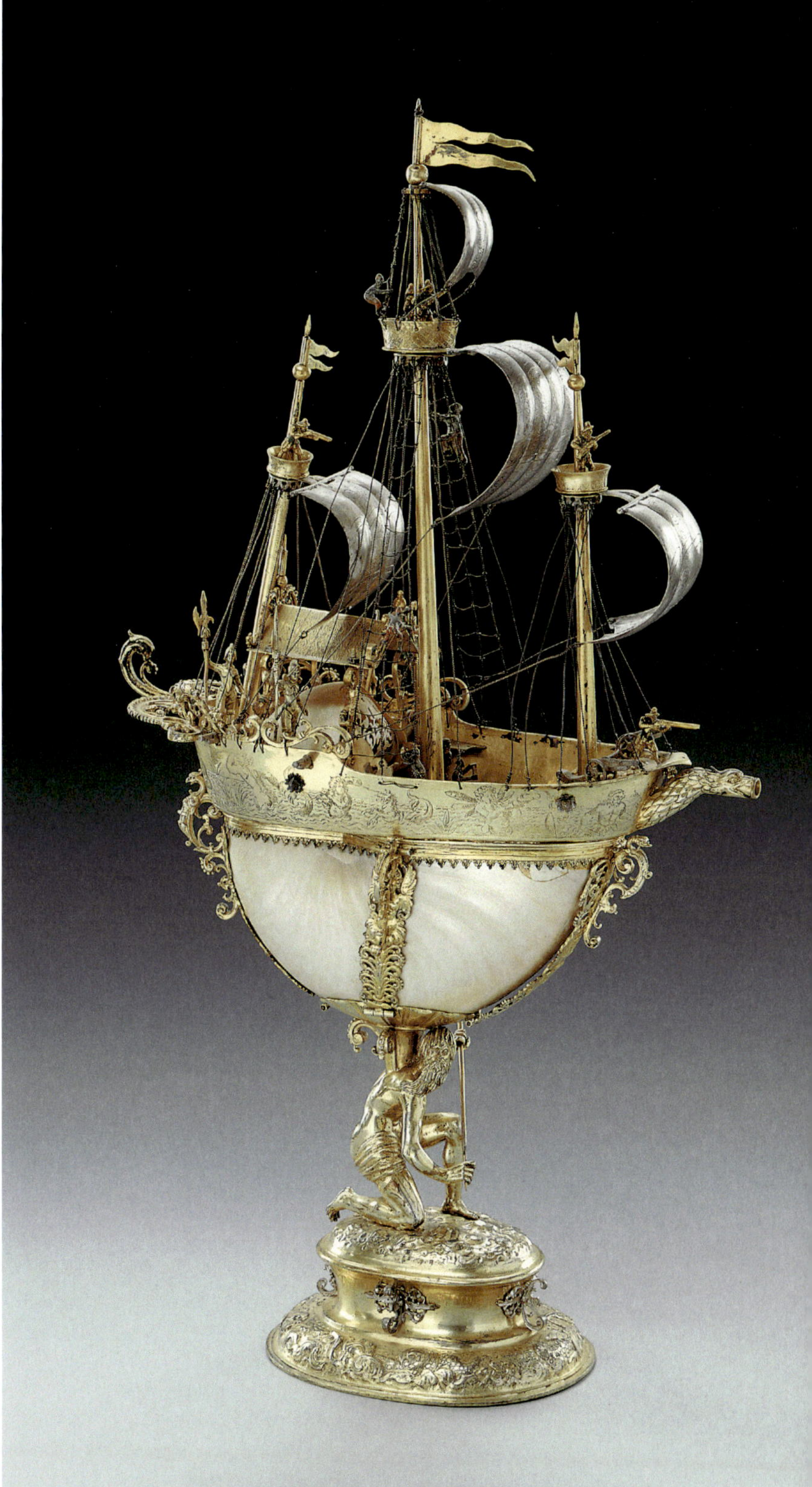

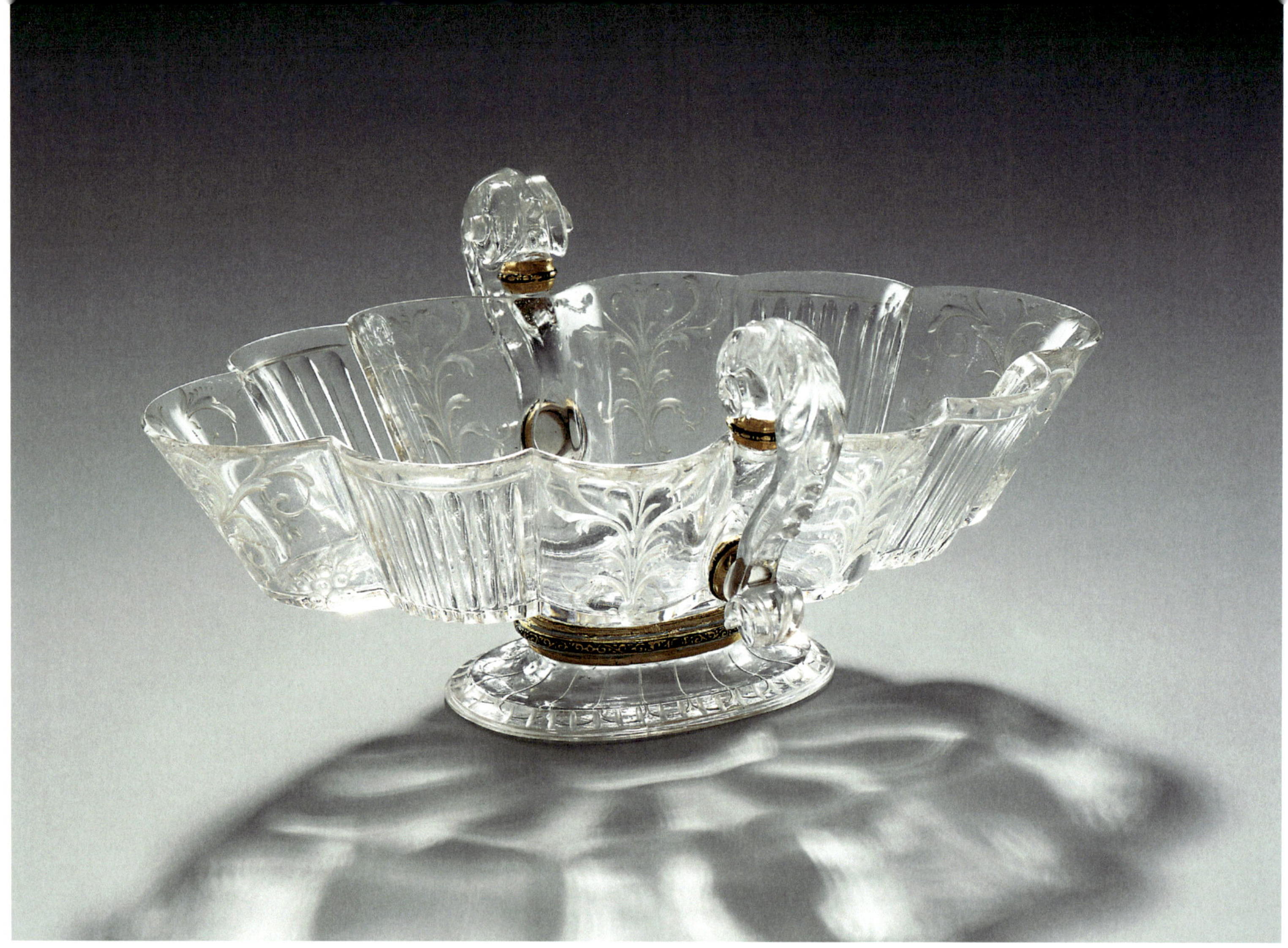

Shallow Bowl with two Handles

Rock crystal, gold, enamel
Workshop of Gasparo Miseroni
Milan, c. 1550
H. 8.9 cm, Inv. no. V 345

Small Bowl on a Dolphin

Rock crystal, gold, enamel
Ottavio Miseroni
Prague, c. 1605 – 1610
H. 13 cm, Inv. no. V 310

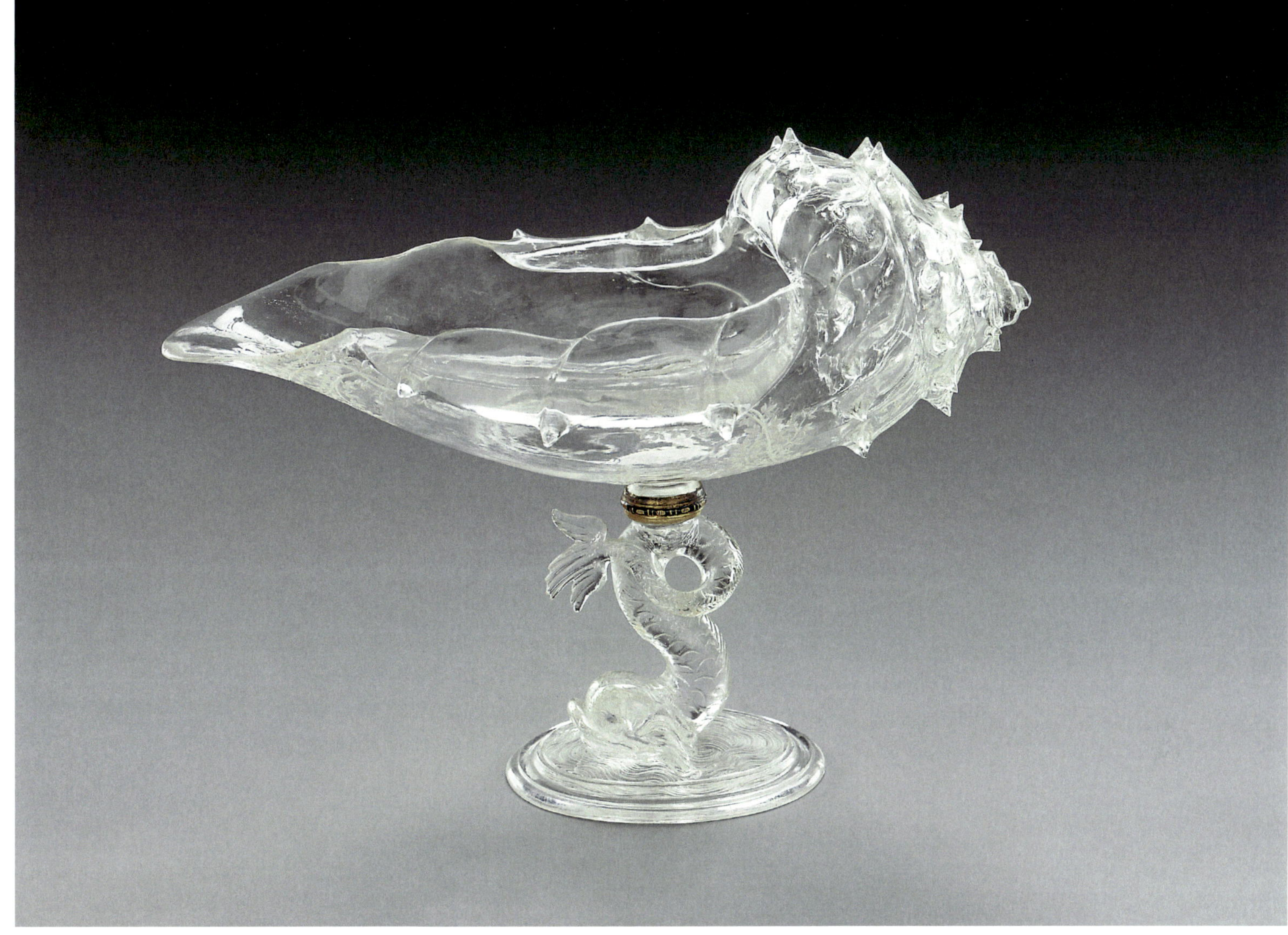

This shallow ten-lobed bowl with handles can be attributed to the Milan workshop of Gasparo Miseroni because of its perfectly cut shape, the precision of the intaglio work and the excellent quality of the enamelled gold mount between foot and body of the vessel. Gasparo Miseroni founded the reputation of the workshop that became the leading manufacturer of cut vessels and attracted illustrious customers such as Cosimo I de Medici, Caterina de Medici, the Queen of France and Emperor Maximilian II (reigned 1564 – 1576).

Exotic seashells served as a model for this delicate rock crystal bowl. The inventory of the pretiosa of 1725 refers to it as a crystal shell with a spiny snail shell at one end, decorated with an ivy ornamentation engraved in the well. The crystal foot is in the shape of a dolphin, its head and tail turned towards the front of the vessel. To be able to manufacture a vessel of such high artistic quality required outstanding skills. The bowl creates the illusion of having been effortlessly moulded from wax. In truth, it was created in a process involving complicated and laborious cutting techniques. Vessels of this type are typical of the ›soft style‹, which characterised Ottavio Miseroni's work between 1600 and 1612. The artist from Milan was active from 1588 onwards at the court of Emperor Rudolf II (reigned 1575/76 – 1612) in Prague and created above all vessels in jasper, agate, nephrite, and heliotrope. These ›arte grossa‹ – stone cutting – masterpieces were his strength. His rock-crystal production was not nearly as extensive as that of the Miseroni working in Milan. Thus, this extremely light and delicate bowl in rock crystal that has been preserved in the Grünes Gewölbe is a particularly rare and precious example of Ottavio Miseroni's art. The bowl may be one of the three rock crystal vessels which Christian II of Saxony (reigned 1601 – 1611) bought from Ottavio Miseroni and for which there is proof of payment in July 1610.

JK

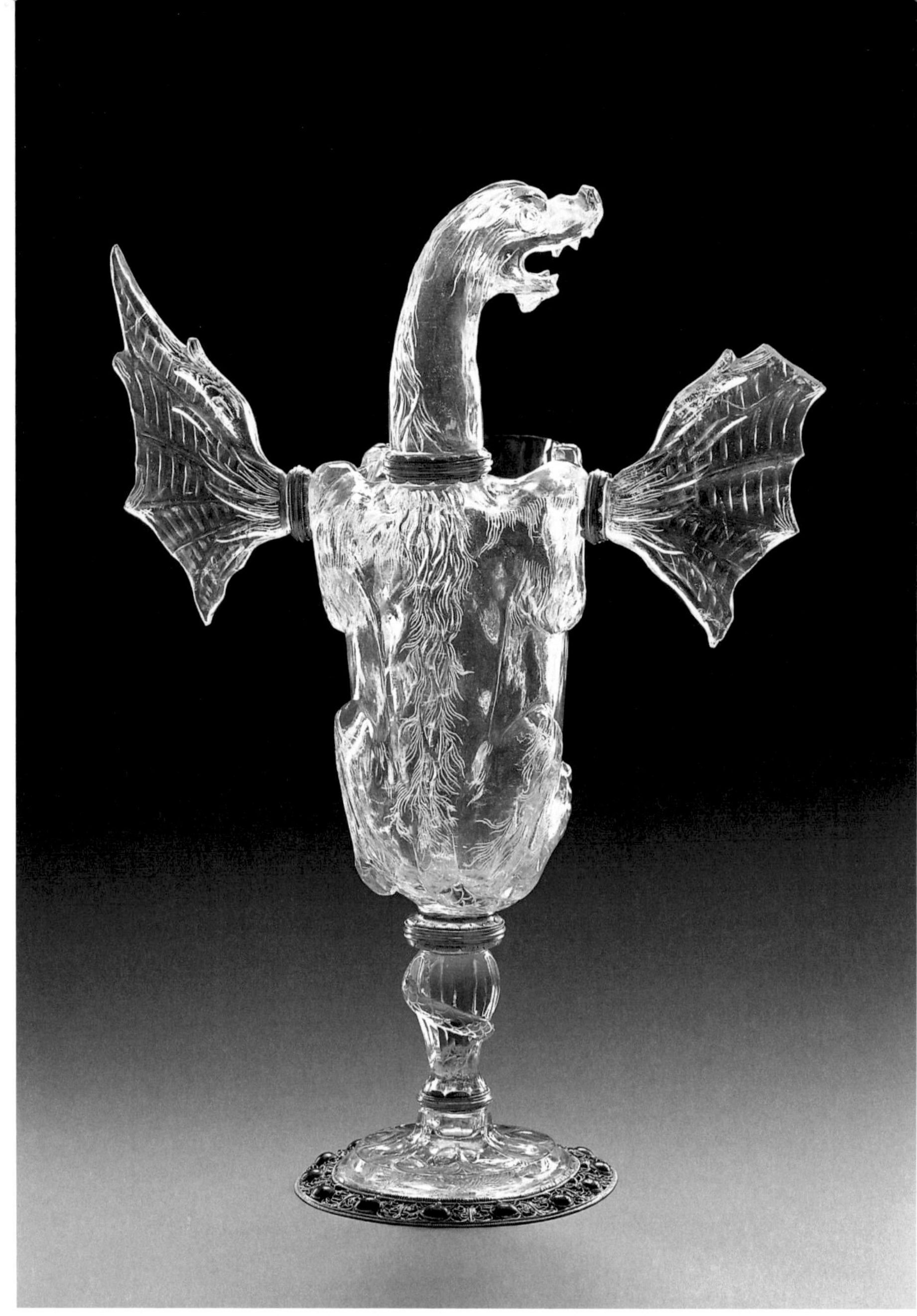

Cup in the Shape of a Winged Dragon

Rock crystal, silver-gilt, lapis lazuli
Giovanni Battista Metellino
Milan, 1715/16
H. 39.1 cm, Inv. no. V 315

Shell-shaped Parade Bowl with two Dolphins

Rock crystal, silver-gilt, lapis lazuli
Giovanni Battista Metellino
Milan, c. 1720
H. 21.5 cm, Inv. no. V 249

The rock crystal vessels by Giovanni Battista Metellino are characterised by their imposing size, excellent cut, sculptural dolphins or dragons and silver-gilt mounts with small appliqués in lapis lazuli. Among the eminent customers of the Milan artist were Louis XIV of France, the French Dauphin and Augustus the Strong. It is thanks to the Elector that the Grünes Gewölbe houses the worldwide best collection of works by Metellino.

In 1715 Augustus the Strong commissioned a »Drago« (dragon) in rock crystal. More than a year later he settled the bill for 200 ducats as is recorded in a statement. The vast sum and the description of the object suggest that they refer to the vessel illustrated here. The reverse of the cup is decorated with the magnificently cut back of a crouching drag-

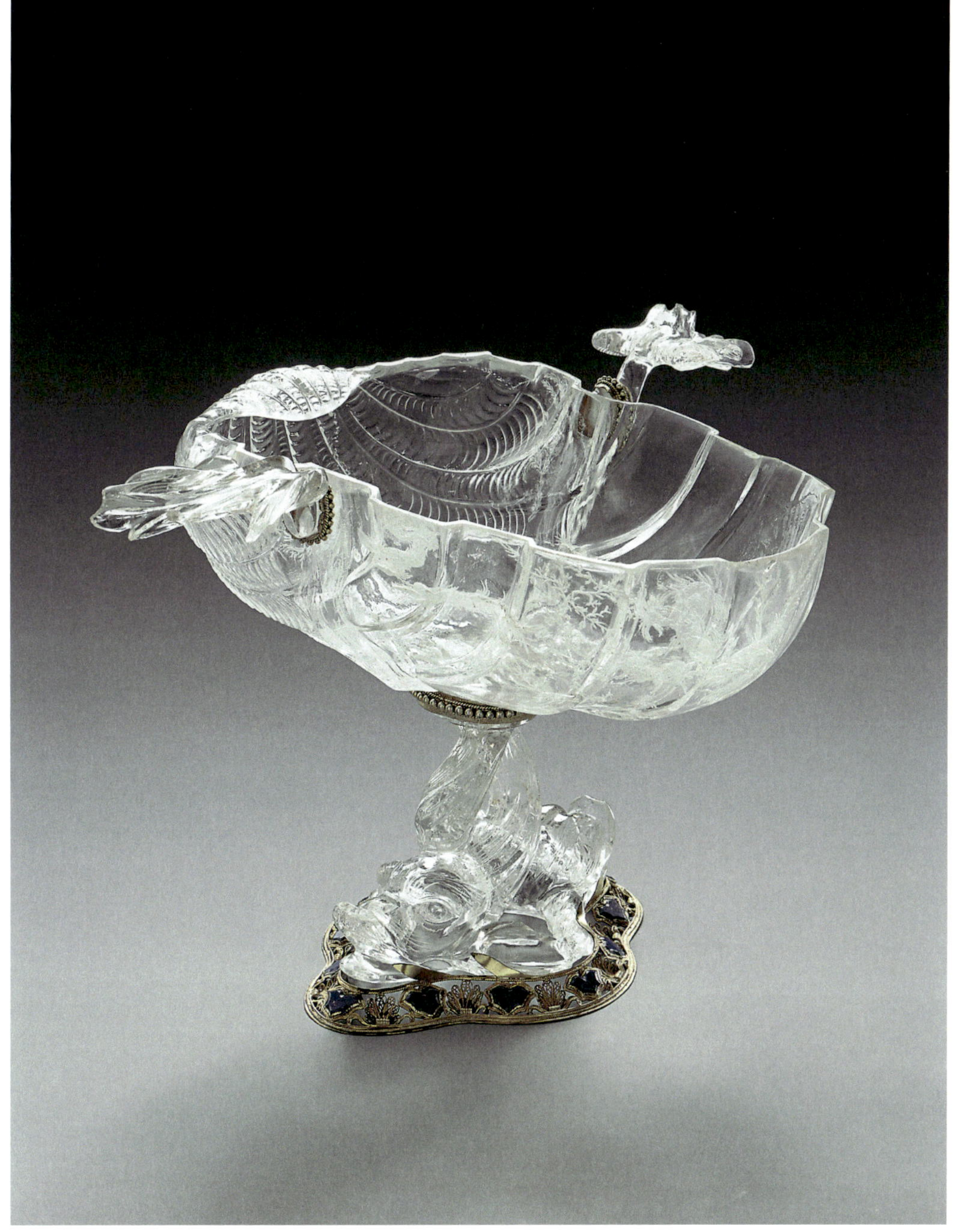

on. The head of the monster, its mouth wide open, rises above the rim of the vessel. The dragon's two wings add to the elegance of this eccentric composition and turn it into a splendid showpiece. The archives show that Augustus the Strong's important business transactions with Italy, and above all with Metellino, were mainly conducted between 1713 and 1718 by the privy finance counsellor Alphonso, an Andalusian who lived in Dresden. Alphonso died in 1722, shortly before Metellino. Thus, the recommendations for the acquisition of crystal vessels from the estate of Metellino, which were first offered as drawings in 1724 (Dresden, Kupferstich-Kabinett), were not written by the experienced privy counsellor who had been on very friendly terms with Metellino, but by Leplat, the King's art director.

The second bowl is also quite clearly a work by Giovanni Battista Metellino, as even small details show. The cut was deliberately executed in a slightly wavy fashion in order to give the surface of this shell-shaped vessel its soft shimmer, the result of light reflections. Delicate sprigs of flowers and herbs – like those on Metellino's shell-shaped bowl with a dolphin at the Prado in Madrid, recorded as early as 1689 in the Inventory of the Grand Dauphin – along with tiny insects and other animals seem to float in the clear crystal as if they were weightless. The foot of the bowl is formed of two closely intertwined dolphins. Their long tails wind upwards along the sides of the bowl to form two extremely decorative, if not very practical, handles.

JK

Rock Crystal Cabinet

Ebony, rock crystal, glass, copper plaques, partly gilded, silk
Presumably Italy, mid 17th century
H. 116 cm, w. 73 cm, d. 43 cm, Inv. no. V 232

The narrow east wall of the Hall of the Precious Objects had been occupied from 1719 by a wide display cabinet with glass doors where Augustus the Strong kept his jewellery. In 1723/24 the display wall was refurbished with mirror glass and skilfully carved and gilded consoles. The display cabinet remained in place. The consoles were used to display the most precious objects from the collection of pretiosa – works in rock crystal. In the course of the second building phase between 1727 and 1729, the jewellery cabinet was removed and the design of the wall was changed. This arrangement has remained until the present day. The three panels of the east wall were decorated with gilded festoons in wood beneath which the large cabinet pieces by Johann Melchior Dinglinger were to be displayed – in the centre the ›Obeliscus Augustalis‹ flanked by the ›Golden Coffee Set‹ and the ›Throne of the Grand Mogul‹. During the building works, however, a decision was taken to display these unique works of art in the Jewel Room of the newly extended Grünes Gewölbe where they could be shown to their best advantage. According to the inventory of 1733, the central wall panel

was occupied by a marble cross with the coat of arms of the King of Poland and Lithuania, which is, however, no longer extant.

This prominent position in the Hall of the Precious Objects is today occupied by a remarkable piece of furniture: a small cabinet in ebony in the shape of a temple with a domed top at the centre. This top is crowned by a large glass vase. The transparent walls of this small cabinet are made of facetted rock crystal plaques, as are the barley-sugar columns, the rail and the feet. The balustrades are adorned with flower vases in rock crystal. Through the clear crystal plaques the observer can see the shelves in gilded copper inside the cabinet. These are ornamented with engraved tendrils. The cabinet is used to keep collectibles, yet the objects are not visible at first glance because they are in drawers hidden behind the horizontal architecture of the ebony frame. This unusual piece of furniture was probably referred to as early as 1679 in the Weck'sche Chronik according to which there was an elaborate cabinet in the Dresden Kunstkammer, made from rock crystal, transparent on all four sides, with doors that could be opened. It was only in 1815 that this unique cabinet for collectibles, which was probably made in Italy in the mid 17th century, was mentioned again when it was moved from the private apartments of the Saxon King Friedrich Augustus I to the Kunstkammer from which it was eventually taken to the Grünes Gewölbe.

DS

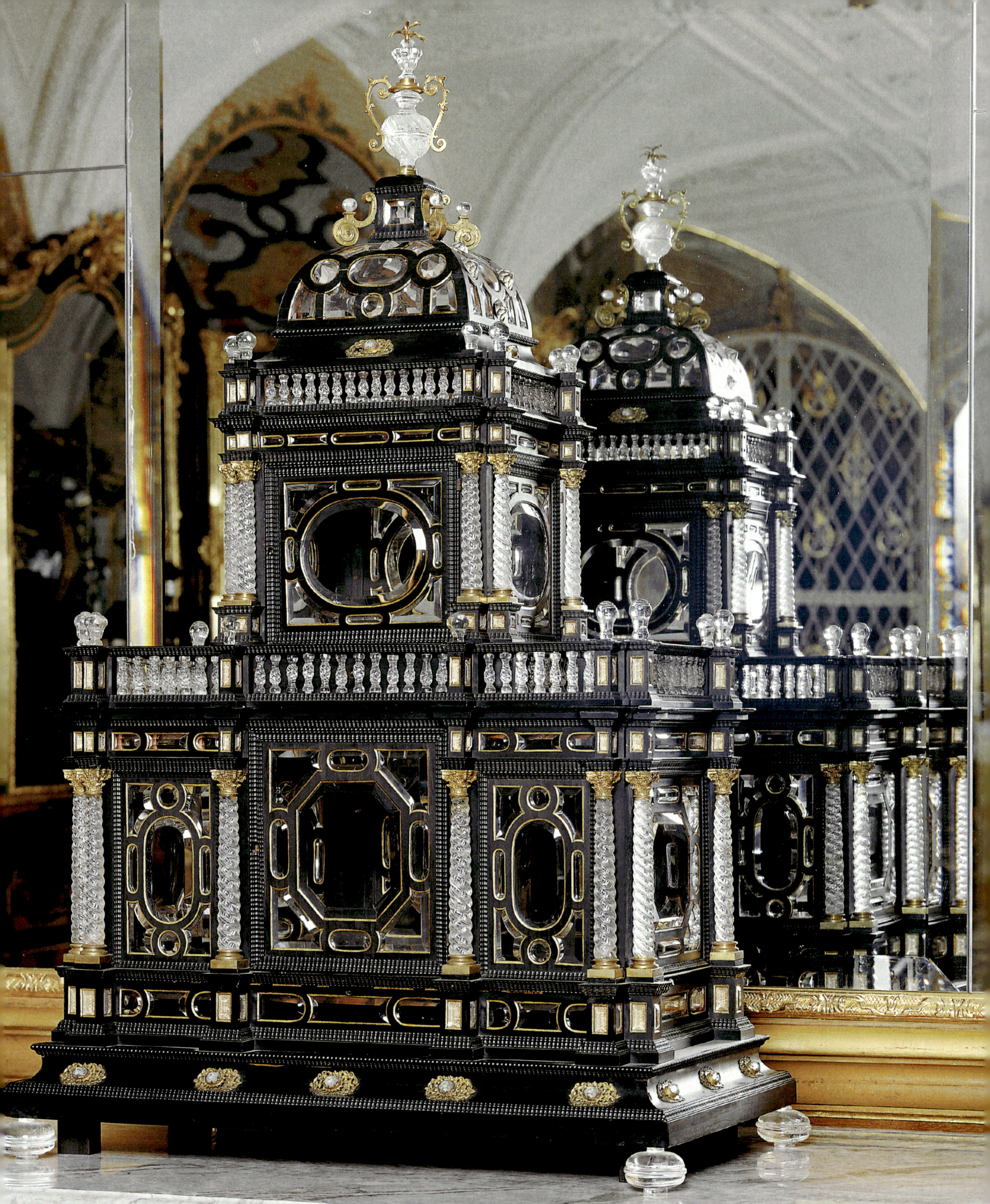

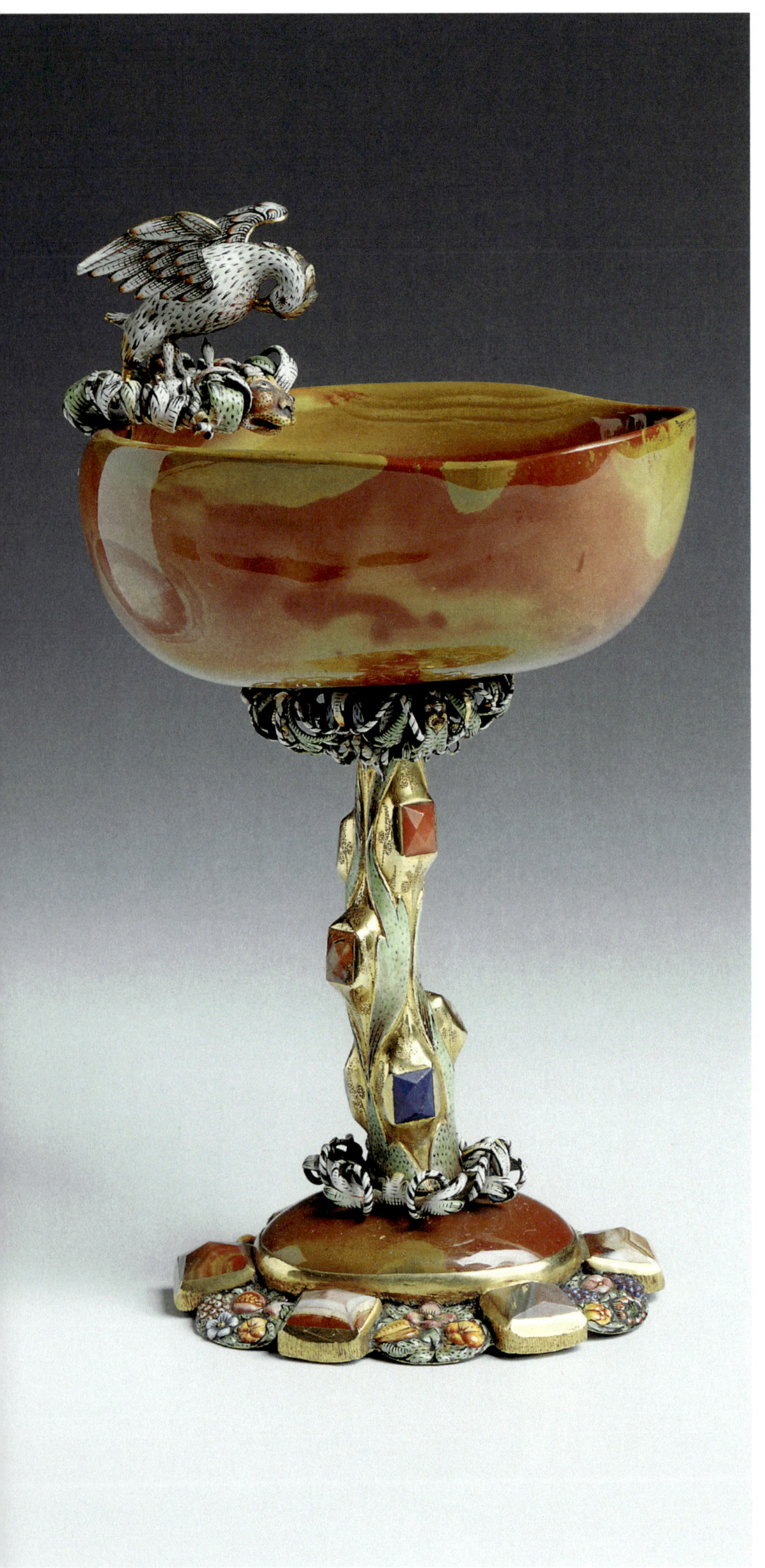

Oval Bowl, Crowned by a Pelican with its Young

Red Egyptian jasper, agate, gold, enamel
Presumably Germany, early 17th century
H. 17.5 cm, Inv. no. V 33

Covered Bowl with Shaft in the Shape of two Tree Trunks

Oriental jasper, speckled with green and white, rock crystal, gold, enamel
Presumably Italy, 2nd half of 17th century
H. 17.7 cm, Inv. no. V 36

In 1733, the walls of the Hall of the Precious Objects to the left and right of the door leading to the Silver Gilt Room displayed an abundance of exhibits – all in all there were 490 objects ranging from vessels, parts of cutlery services, boxes, caskets, figures and other pretiosa made from cut gemstones such as jasper, carnelian, nephrite, garnet, lapis lazuli, agate, chalcedony, onyx, serpentine, marble and alabaster. Among these objects, there were more than 130 gemstone bowls with a mount in gold or silver-gilt and additional decoration with enamel and precious stones. Most of the exhibits mentioned in the inventory are still extant. The present-day display is largely a reconstruction of the original presentation, although there is now a stronger emphasis on the stable and secure presentation of the objects and on aspects of conservation. Under Augustus the Strong, gemstone bowls with particularly precious mounts were displayed on the gilded wall-consoles with their ornamental carvings between the two west windows of the Hall of the Precious Objects. Almost two-thirds of these gemstone vessels are today again displayed on these consoles.

Among them is an oval bowl in red jasper resting on a tree trunk made from solid gold with enamelled foliage. Its foot is richly decorated with agates, jaspers and coral in a box mount. The rim of the bowl is embellished with an enamelled pelican in gold feeding its young on the blood from a wound in its breast which it has pecked open. This is a Christian symbol of Christ's self-sacrifice. Another gemstone bowl, which according to the inventory of 1733 was exhibited on one of the larger display walls, today replaces a parade vessel which, for reasons of conservation, is today exhibited in the New Grünes Gewölbe. The particularly attractive gemstone vessel has a jasper cover speckled green and white. The shaft is worked in the shape of the intertwining tree trunks in rock crystal in a gold mount with turquoise appliqués. This parade bowl, the origin of which has not yet been determined, is an example of the high quality of Augustus the Strong's collection of pretiosa.

DS

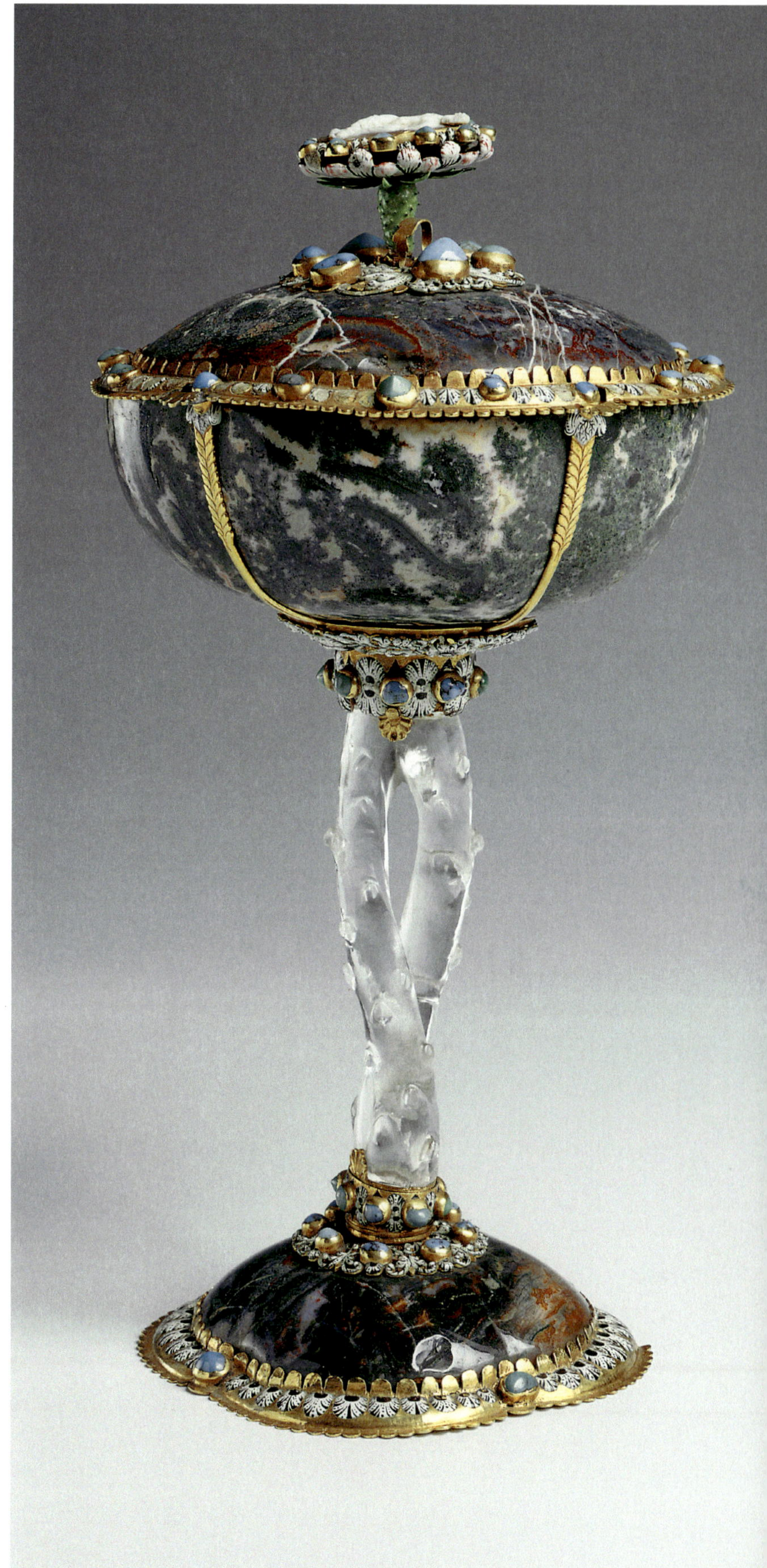

Covered Cup with Cameo Appliqués

Silver-gilt, rock crystal, cameos
Abraham Pratsch
Augsburg, c. 1717/18
H. 50.8 cm, Inv. no. V 10

From the mid 17th century onwards, vessels were adorned with contemporary or older cameos in order to present a glyptic collection in the framework of a pretiosa »cabinet«. The large covered cup, manufactured by the goldsmith Abraham Pratsch follows this tradition.

The cup, made around 1717, is first mentioned in the inventory of the pretiosa of 1725 where it mentions that it was acquired from Nessler. Johann Christoph Nessler was a goldsmith from Freiberg in Saxony who was active in Dresden. Besides this large parade cup, he supplied at least nine more works for the pretiosa »cabinet« of Augustus the Strong, among them small, painted ivory objects, most of them with a goldsmith's mount. In the case of this cameo cup, Nessler, who had business contacts with Augsburg, only acted as a trader.

This large silver-gilt cup is in the tradition of a type of vessel that was used in the early 18th century for large ceremonial cups in silver or glass. The inset conical beaker in silver-gilt would have made its practical use as a drinking vessel theoretically possible. Instead, it found its way into the Grünes Gewölbe where it was exhibited as a parade cup. The rock crystal bust of the goddess Athena as a finial underlines the function of the vessel as a precious display object. The goddess of wisdom was carved by an unknown gemstone cutter and is a delicate and sensitive work of art. Those parts of the bust representing the naked skin of the goddess have a matt sheen, while hair, garment and pupils are highly polished. The same is true of the helmet to which a plume in silver-gilt was affixed. The heads depicted on the seven large and four smaller cameos on the cuppa of the vessel are treated in the same way. The body of the cup – decorated with delicate ornaments – is designed in such a way that the cameos of varying size fit into the depressions. Four small cameos adorn the foot, and four the cover of the cup. Abraham Pratsch designed the foot with particular care and gave it an almost fragile lightness by adding four volutes. The rock crystal embedded in the shaft underlines this lightness and almost gives the impression that this heavy parade cup defies gravity.

A few years after Augustus the Strong had bought the cup from Nessler, he commissioned his court jeweller Johann Heinrich Köhler to manufacture two other cameo cups, even more sumptuously decorated with 168 and 176 cameo appliqués. This colourful group of three parade cups with their glyptic collection now dominates the wall panel in the Hall of the Precious Objects to the right of the entrance from the Silver Gilt Room. In all probability, the cups are now displayed on the same consoles as in 1733.

DS

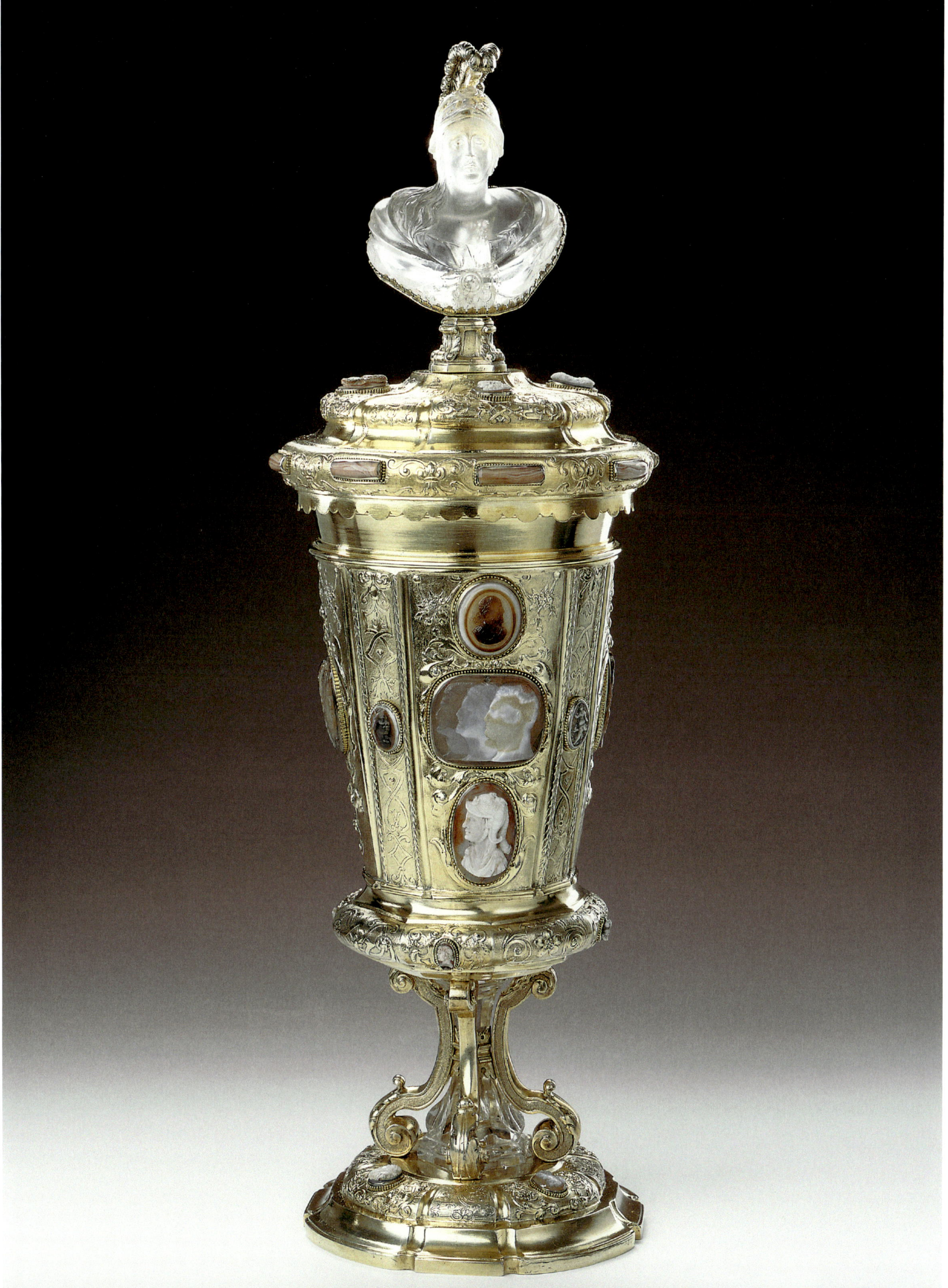

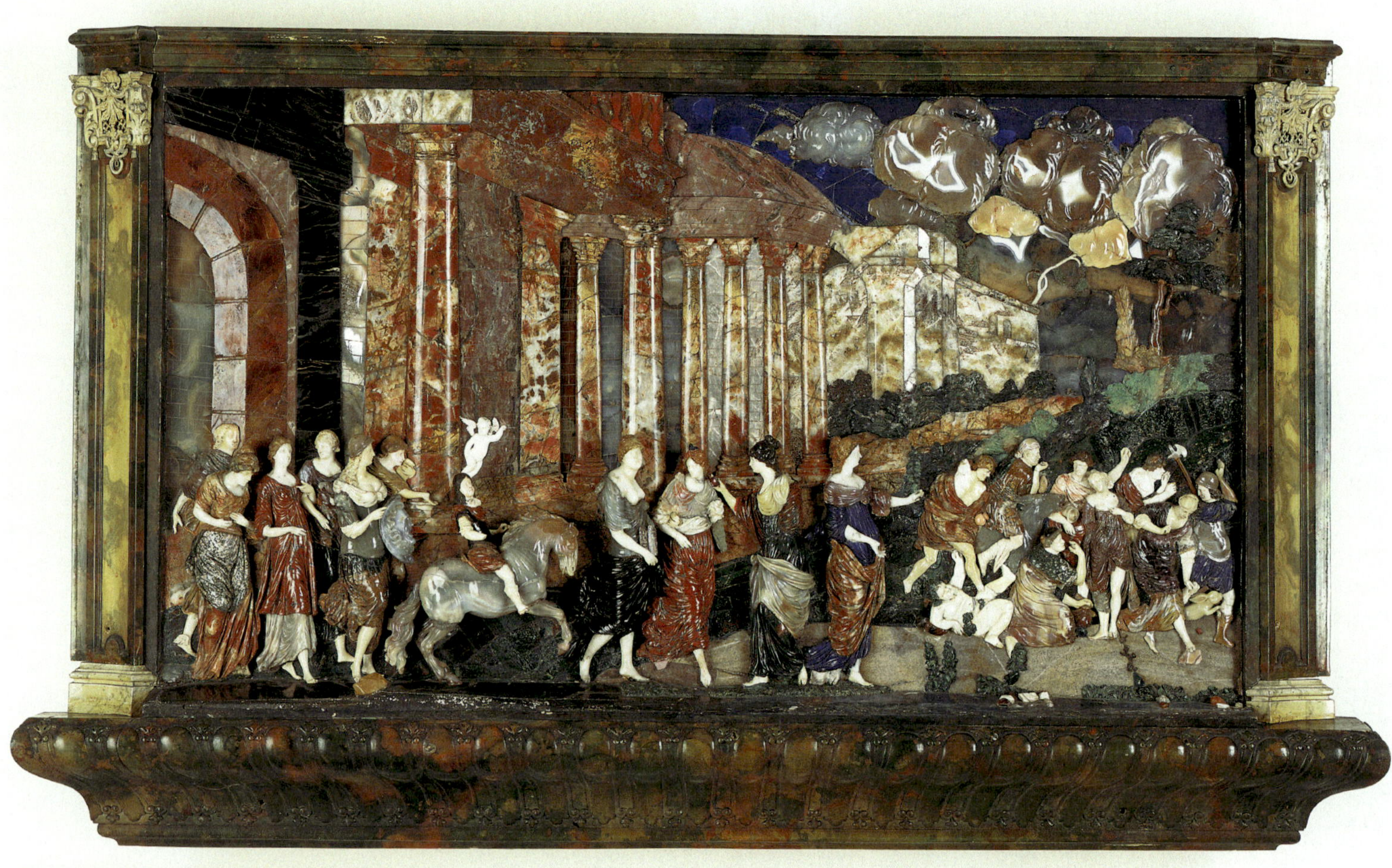

Chimney Piece

Different varieties of gemstones, frame in marbled wood
Stonecut: Christoph Labhardt
Idstein, between 1671 and 1679
Frame (later addition): Dresden 1729
H. 79 cm, w. 142 cm, Inv. no. V 146

The tableau composed of various different gemstones, some cut in relief, some fully sculptural, is one of the major works of German gemstone cutting. Its genesis had long been obscure and it was only in 1997 that some revealing information was found in the archives. According to these records, the precious stone tableau originally adorned the fireplace in the ›Emperor's Room‹ at Idstein Castle – a long way away from Dresden. Count Johannes von Nassau-Idstein (reigned 1629–1677) had it manufactured for the moral instruction of his son Georg August Samuel (1665–1721). In a detailed Memorandum, the count gave a meticulous description of the pictorial programme he had in mind to teach a young gentleman what he ought to do and what to avoid. It

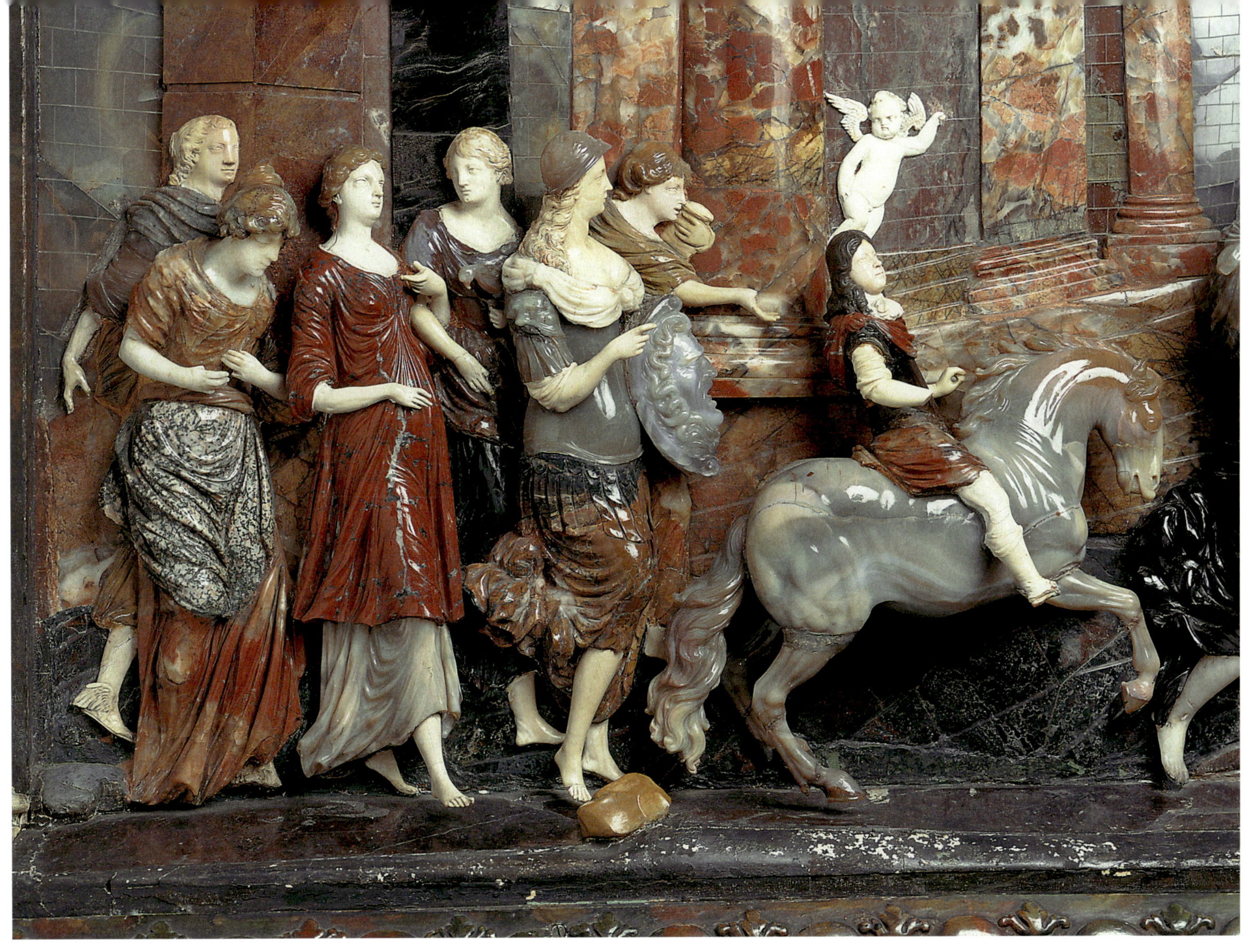

took the stonecutter Christoph Labhardt almost eight years to complete the work and adhered, by and large, to the instructions of this client. Georg August Samuel is depicted as a youth on horseback. Minerva, wearing a helmet and holding a shield, and the personifications of Prudentia, Temperentia, Justitia, Pietas, Liberalitas, Spes, Historia, Ars and Diligentia accompany the horseman. They drive the representations of the vices away to protect the rider. These flee from the strong hero Hercules. The message was quite obvious. The future regent was to shun the vices of inebriation, sloth, wastefulness, avarice, licence, godlessness and desperation. The figure of timidity, accompanied by a hare, admonishes the young man not to be a cowardly ›Hasenfuss‹ (lit. ›hare's foot‹ = coward). Christoph Labhardt succeeded in creating a magnificent work of art that clearly showed his excellent skill as a craftsman and paved the way for an appointment as stonecutter at the court in Kassel in 1680.

Labhardt's stone tableau remained at Idstein Castle as part of the chimneypiece until the death of Henriette Dorothea, widow of Georg August Samuel, in 1728. Her daughter Henriette Charlotte, married to Duke Moritz Wilhelm of Saxony-Merseburg, inherited the work and had it taken to Merseburg. Shortly afterwards, it was acquired by Augustus the Strong and displayed on a pillar on the west wall of the Hall of the Precious Objects at the Grünes Gewölbe.

JK

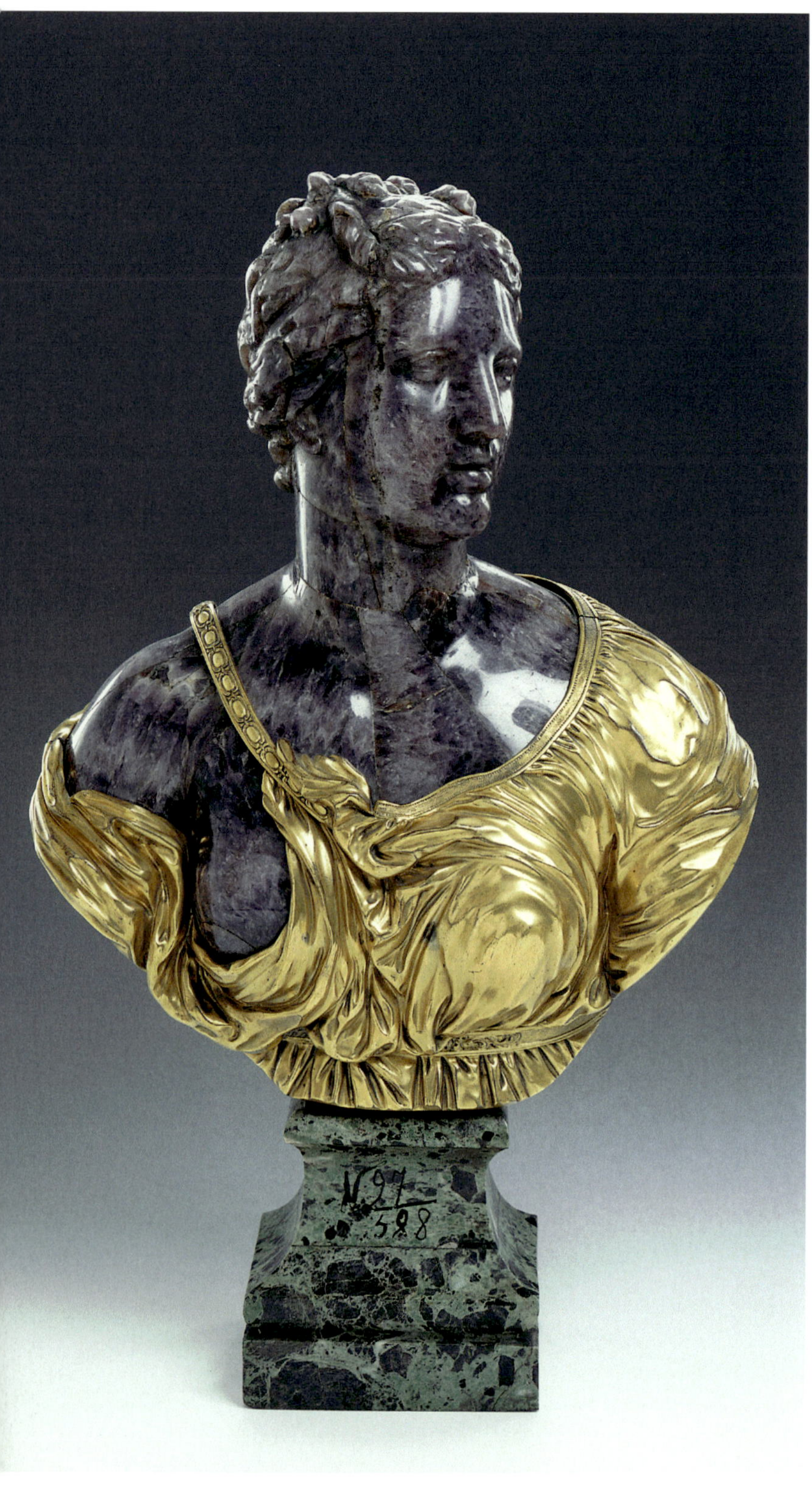

Bust of a Female Figure

Bust: amethyst on tuff, iron plug, garment: bronze-gilt,
plinth: verde antico (serpentine breccia)
Design: Paul Heermann
Stone cutting: possibly Johann Christoph Hübner
Dresden, between 1725 and 1730
H. 55.5 cm, Inv. no. V 592

Particularly beautiful pieces of amethyst with a pronounced crystalline structure were used for this bust. This purple quartz variety was found and quarried in the area around Dresden, in Schlottwitz near Glashütte. The first records of deposits in that area date back to 1721.

In order to be able to create a bust of this size and sculptural quality, particularly large pieces of crystal were required. Although the Schlottwitz quarry yielded a good supply of amethyst, it was rare to find a lump big enough to sculpt a bust from just one piece. Consequently, a number of ›tricks‹, hidden from the observer, were used in the manufacture. It is only when the bust is ›disrobed‹, i.e. when the skilfully cast parts of the garment are removed, as was done in 1990 in the course of restoration work, that the breast part, cut from tuff, becomes visible. This material was used up to the base of the neck. Those parts not covered by the garment were appliquéd with smoothly polished, relatively thin amethyst segments. They were cut to fit and affixed with cement. The neck and head – except the right half of the face, which is composed of several smaller pieces of amethyst – was cut from one large piece of crystal and connected to the body using a solid iron plug.

This bust in the collection of the Grünes Gewölbe is an outstanding example of Saxon sculpting and stonecutting. The design and also partly the manufacture of the breast part in tuff were almost certainly executed by the Dresden court sculptor and restorer of antiques, Paul Heermann. This is supported by the similarity of this bust to his ›Venus Resting‹ (c. 1720) at the Dresden Skulpturensammlung, which is also designed ›all'antica‹. Only a stonecutter of great skill would have been able to master the difficulties involved in working pieces of amethyst. In the period around 1725 there was no better craftsman in that field than Johann Christoph Hübner whose outstanding talent above all in the manufacture of cameos was highly appreciated by the famous Dresden court jeweller Johann Melchior Dinglinger.

JK

Large Enamel Portrait of the Virgin Mary

Copper, enamel
Signed by Georg Friedrich Dinglinger
Dresden, dated 1712
W. 68 cm, h. 90 cm, Inv. no. V 152

Georg Friedrich Dinglinger proudly noted on the reverse of his large enamel portrait of the Mater Dolorosa that this was his first attempt at creating an enamel work on a large scale. Even as late as the 1780s there are records that this portrait was the largest and most beautiful work in enamel that had been created so far. Shortly after 1710 Dinglinger began experimenting with formats that went beyond the usual scale. This was an attempt to compete with painting in the ›grand style‹. The technical problems involved in that process were, however, enormous. One of the dangers was that the long firing process, which such large-scale pieces required, would overheat the plate so that the enamels changed in colour or sank into the enamelling ground. Another risk were cracks as a result of the difference in expansion between the metal support and the enamel layers. Dinglinger managed to avoid the danger of discolouration by limiting the palette to only a few colours covering large areas.

An anecdote from 1786 relates that the creation of this masterpiece of enamelling was the result of a contest between Dinglinger and the Copenhagen oil and miniature painter Ismael Mengs (1688 – 1764). According to Carl Heinrich von Heinecken, Mengs copied a life-size oil painting of the Mater Dolorosa by the court painter Adám Mányoki (1673 – 1757) in enamel. As a result, the King felt compelled to commission Georg Friedrich Dinglinger with the production of another copy in enamel, which, however, only succeeded after several unsuccessful attempts. It is uncertain whether this anecdote is actually true as Adám Mányoki only came to Dresden in 1713 and Ismael Mengs in 1714 – i.e. after the large enamel work was created – where they were appointed court painter and court miniature painter respectively.

In 1714 the portrait of the Virgin was acquired by Augustus the Strong for 1,500 thalers. The portrait, also referred to as ›Wunderstück‹, was given a prominent place on the west wall of the Hall of the Precious Objects where the visitors’ eyes were drawn to this magnificent work in its carved and gilded frame.

UW

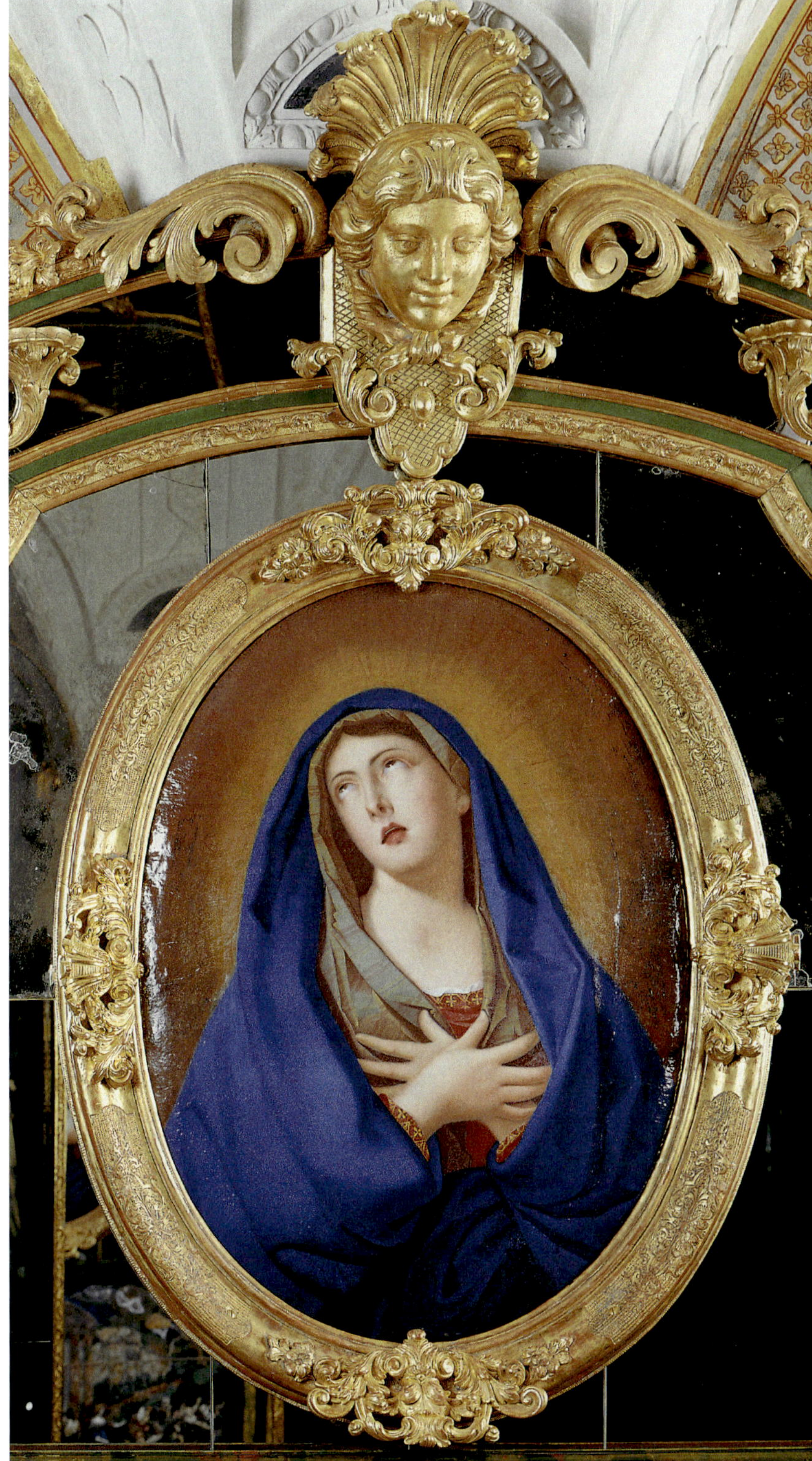

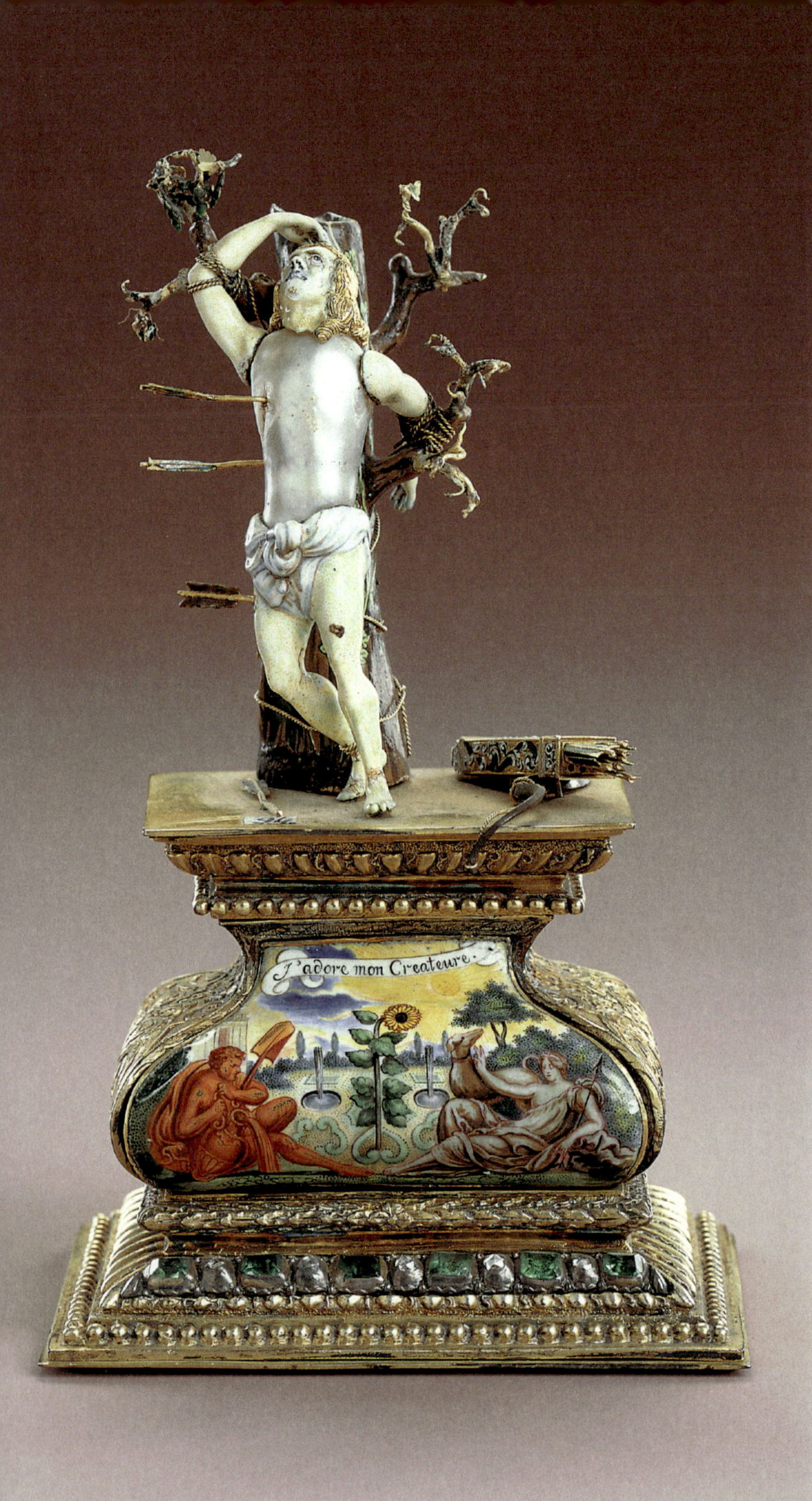

Saint Sebastian

Barocco pearl, gold, enamel, silver-gilt, diamonds, emeralds
Acquired from Guillaume Verbecq
Frankfurt, before 1706
H. 12.5 cm, Inv. no. VI 106

Two Busts of Roman Emperors

Presumably Germany, 2nd half of 17th century
Chalcedony, wood, h. 15.4 cm, Inv. no. VI 151
Heliotrope, wood, h. 16.2 cm, Inv. no. VI 143

A large elongated pearl forms the body of the martyr St Sebastian who is pierced by arrows. This Roman army officer stood steadfastly by his Christian belief and was consequently tortured. The gaze of the saint, who is tied to a tree trunk covered with vine shoots, is directed towards heaven. His passion was impressively translated into the formal canon of barocco pearl pretiosa. The scene is mounted on a magnificent pedestal, the front of which is decorated with an enamel painting, which serves as an interpretation of St Sebastian's Christian compassion in the symbolical formal language of Baroque. The pearl figure was part of Augustus the Strong's first collection of pretiosa which was mortgaged in 1706.

The work has now returned to the Corner Cabinet that the Elector-King had built between 1723 and 1724 as the last in a series of collection cabinets and rooms where he kept over a period of almost 40 years his continuously growing collection, which eventually became the largest collection of pretiosa of that period. The inventory of the pretiosa of 1733 lists 464 objects. 14 other objects were added later. Among these works were 47 figures in gold enamel for the manufacture of which barocco pearls were used. As the small Corner Cabinet, which only measures 16 square metres, is no longer accessible to visitors, most of the precious objects originally exhibited there were incorporated into the presentation of the New Grünes Gewölbe. More than 170 small-scale pretiosa are still displayed on the 102 consoles, skilfully carved in the shape of expressive masks of fauns, dragons or female figures. The overwhelming wealth of small-scale fashionable articles, accessories and delicate vessels, of figures in gold enamel, gemstones, pearls, ivory and ebony, of enamel medallions and large parade bowls by Dinglinger and Döring must have turned the Corner Cabinet into an incredibly sumptuous collection room.

Today, it accommodates a large number of unmounted gemstone bowls that were originally displayed on the consoles of the two wall panels to the left and right of the door leading to the Silver Gilt Room and most of the 37 busts and heads cut in gemstone that were originally displayed in that room. Most of these are busts of Roman emperors, mounted on wooden plinths. Augustus the Strong seems to have loved these masterpieces of Baroque glyptic art. They crown the silver cup with cameo appliqués by Abraham Pratsch and the ›Obeliscus Augustalis‹. Johann Melchior Dinglinger obviously supplied these large, finely worked heads of Roman emperors, which, at a price of 300 to 400 thalers, were quite valuable objects. The two heads illustrated here – manufactured by an unknown, possibly German stonecutter – are characterised by their delicately worked surface and sensitive portrayal of the emperors' physiognomy. They are part of a group of four busts of emperors mounted on identical pedestals.

DS

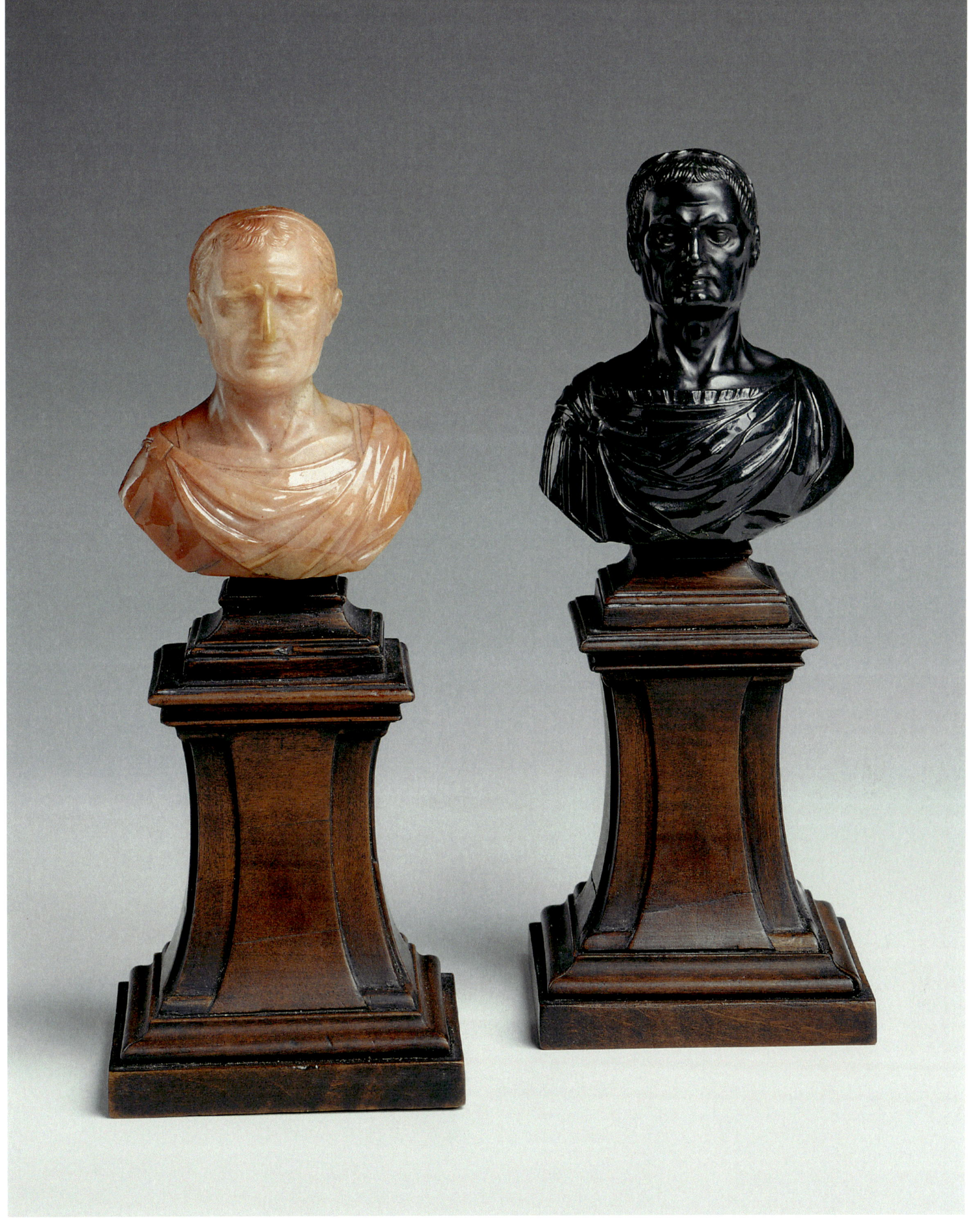

Coats of Arms Room

Since the mid-16th century, the room devoted to coats of arms has been part of the group of interiors that later came down in history as the »Grünes Gewölbe«. It was directly linked via the northwest circular stone staircase to the Great Courtyard of the palace. This door still exists and is hidden behind the wall panelling to the left next to the window. Before the suite of rooms of the treasury had been extended, the Coats of Arms Room possibly served as a kind of banqueting room. Subsequently, the room became the ›first‹ Grünes Gewölbe (green vault). At that time there was only one other entrance to the later Silver Gilt Room, the ›second‹ or ›central‹ Grünes Gewölbe apart from the entrance via the Great Courtyard of the palace. Until the 1720s the Coats of Arms Room in conjunction with the ›Geheime Verwahrung‹ was used as an »Expedition«, a kind of mail room, in which valuable objects which arrived at the palace were kept until they were taken to the place where they were to be used. Files were also kept securely in the cupboards.

When Augustus the Strong decreed in 1723 that the Grünes Gewölbe should be converted into a publicly accessible treasury, the Coats of Arms Room was initially not included and appears to have retained its original functions. Between 1724 and 1727 it was given new fittings on the three windowless sides in the form of built in cupboards in stained oak. In the extended plan of the second building phase the room became the Coats of Arms of the Provinces Room and thus part of the tour of this museum-like institution. Thus, the plan sketched by Augustus the Strong shows that doors were to be created to the Hall of the Precious Objects and the future Jewel Room. In a letter written at almost the same time in spring 1727, in which the Elector-King explained his expansion plans to Dresden officials, there are also instructions with regard to the interiors. He decreed that they should »look in the Royal wardrobe to see how many province coats of arms there were fixed to the cupboards and to check whether they could be used on the cupboard doors in the first Grünes Gewölbe and they should make a sketch to scale of such cupboards, how large, wide and deep they are and send it here as soon as possible«. This cloakroom was seemingly in what was then the south wing of the palace (now the intermediate north wing) and in the last few years of the 17th century had been given a decorative interior with coats of arms of Saxon provinces and shields with the ornamentally elaborated initials of the elector. 27 of these large beaten copper shields were then mounted in pairs one above the other in the door panels of the Coats of Arms Room of the Grünes Gewölbe. In order to fill the walls and also to do justice to the changes in the power structure Augustus the Strong had 17 further coats of arms and initial shields made. Thus now there are not only the initials of Johann Georg IV but also those of the electoral predecessors of Augustus the Strong, his own as elector and as king, and the coats of arms of the parts of the Holy Roman Empire ruled and claimed by him, united with the coats of arms of Poland and Lithuania. The gold glittering shields with coats of arms arranged closely one above and next to the other determined the effect made by the room.

The question of the function of the built-in cupboards remained undecided. The inventory of 1733 lists a large number of works in gold ruby glass and serpentine, which can only have been kept in the cupboards, but the possibilities of the room were not fully exploited. Later travel writers reported that the coronation robes of Augustus the Strong and Augustus III and the robes of the great European orders to which both monarchs had been admitted, were to be kept here. Outside the cupboards there were only a few works of art displayed on two tables in front of mirrors and on a small number of consoles. In the middle of the room Augustus the Strong had had an ›Oraculum‹ placed which could move its eyes and utter indeterminate sounds. In 1738 he had this strange automaton removed.

In the night of 13 to 14 February 1945 the Coats of Arms Room burnt down. Numerous remains of the shields were salvaged from the rubble. They had almost all lost their original hot-dip gilding but 36 were sufficiently well-preserved to be restored. A number of shields were very badly damaged or had melted down to the central part. From 1977 the coats of arms were restored as far as possible and gilded where justified. The aim was to preserve as much of the originals as possible, not to recreate the old shields without a trace of damage. Today all the preserved coats of arms are affixed to the doors on which they originally hung. The Coats of Arms Room can thus again be experienced as the expression of the royal and dynastic thinking of the late Baroque period. At the same time the damage to the coats of arms and the Maxen marble floor caused by war can still be seen. The coats of arms encourage the visitor to reflect on the transience of princely power – an effect Augustus the Strong wished to achieve with his ›Oraculum‹.

DS

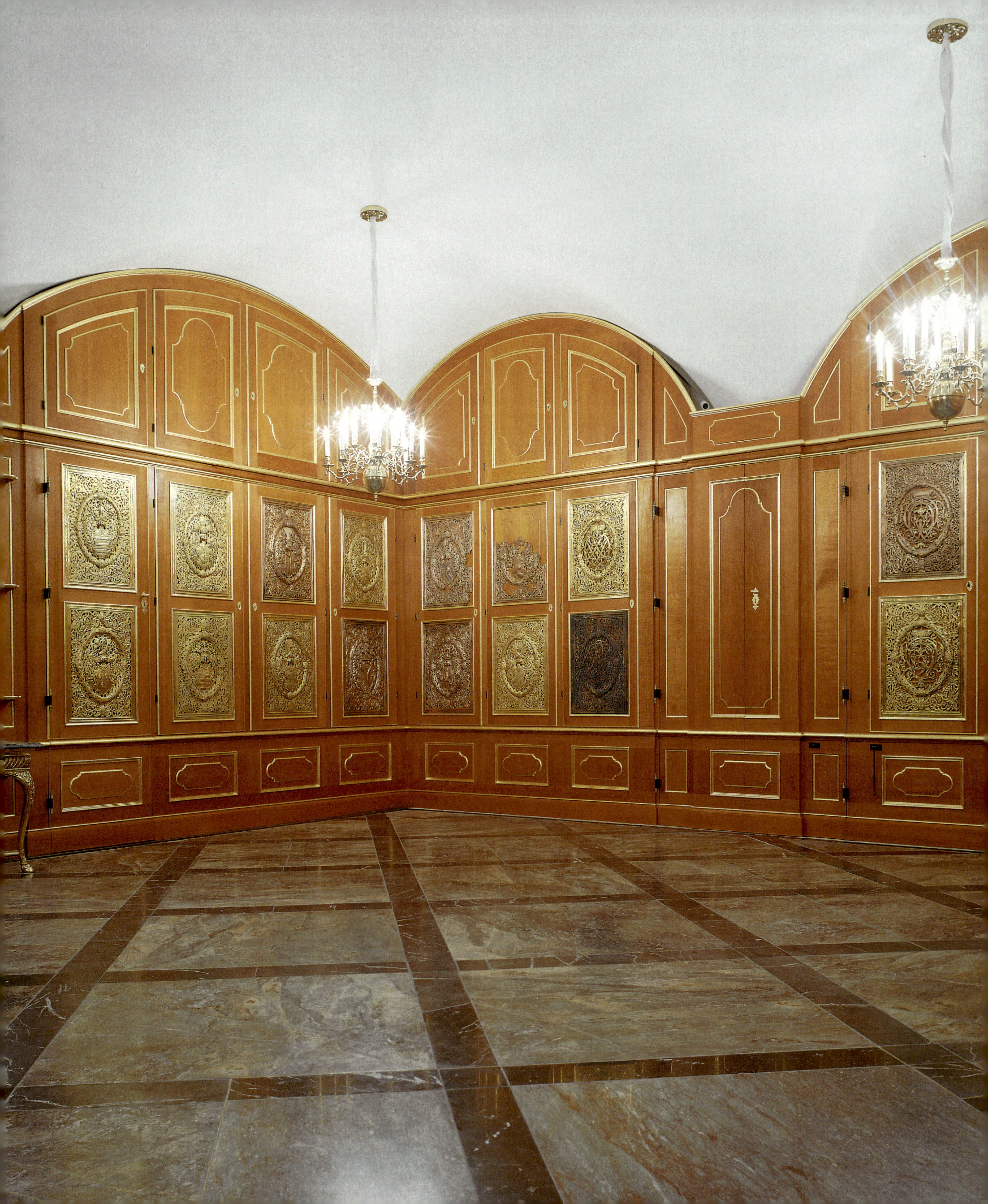

Coat of Arms of the Kingdom of Poland (escutcheon)

Copper, re-gilded
Christian Friedrich Holland
Dresden, 1727 to 1728
H. 80 cm, Inv. no. VII 290

In summer 1697 Augustus the Strong was elected King of Poland and Grand Duke of Lithuania by the Polish and Lithuanian nobility in a complicated and controversial vote. The personal union thus created, in which the monarch ruled the Electorate of Saxony to which he had succeeded as Friedrich August I and the Kingdom of Poland and Lithuania to which he had been elected as King Augustus II, is reflected at various points in the Grünes Gewölbe by the Polish-Lithuanian state coat of arms. However, nowhere in the Grünes Gewölbe was the long-term claim which Augustus the Strong laid to the Polish crown for the Wettin dynasty so frankly proclaimed as in the Coats of Arms Room. On the south wall directly next to the window the armorial escutcheons of the aristocratic republic of Poland and the Grand Duchy of Lithuania begin the series of 33 coats of arms of the territories and provinces to which the Saxon elector laid claim. Two escutcheons or two monograms of the monarch are fitted one above each other in the door panels of the cabinets.

They were made in two stages: 27 of the beaten copper escutcheons were made in the penultimate decade of the 17th century.

Another 17 were added between 1727 and 1729. On closer examination it is apparent that some of the escutcheons vary in size considerably. This can be explained by the fact that they were being used for the second time in the Coats of Arms Room. The older coats of arms and escutcheons with initials made for the electoral wardrobe of Johann Georg III or IV also differ in their finish from the additional ones commissioned by Augustus the Strong. They have a more carefully designed surface and flat ornamentation of acanthus leaves, while the later ones have more vigorous foliage forms and armorial field and have a more summary treatment of the coats of arms. Otherwise the design of the older and the more recent copper escutcheons is identical. The acanthus foliage so popular towards the close of the 17th century surrounds a tall oval central field, in which either the coat of arms or the monogram of a Saxon elector ›distorted‹ in the Baroque fashion is inserted. The more recent coats of arms came from the Dresden goldsmiths Christian Friedrich Holland and Johann Siegmund Weniger and the coppersmith Thiermann. It is no longer known who created the older coats of arms.

DS

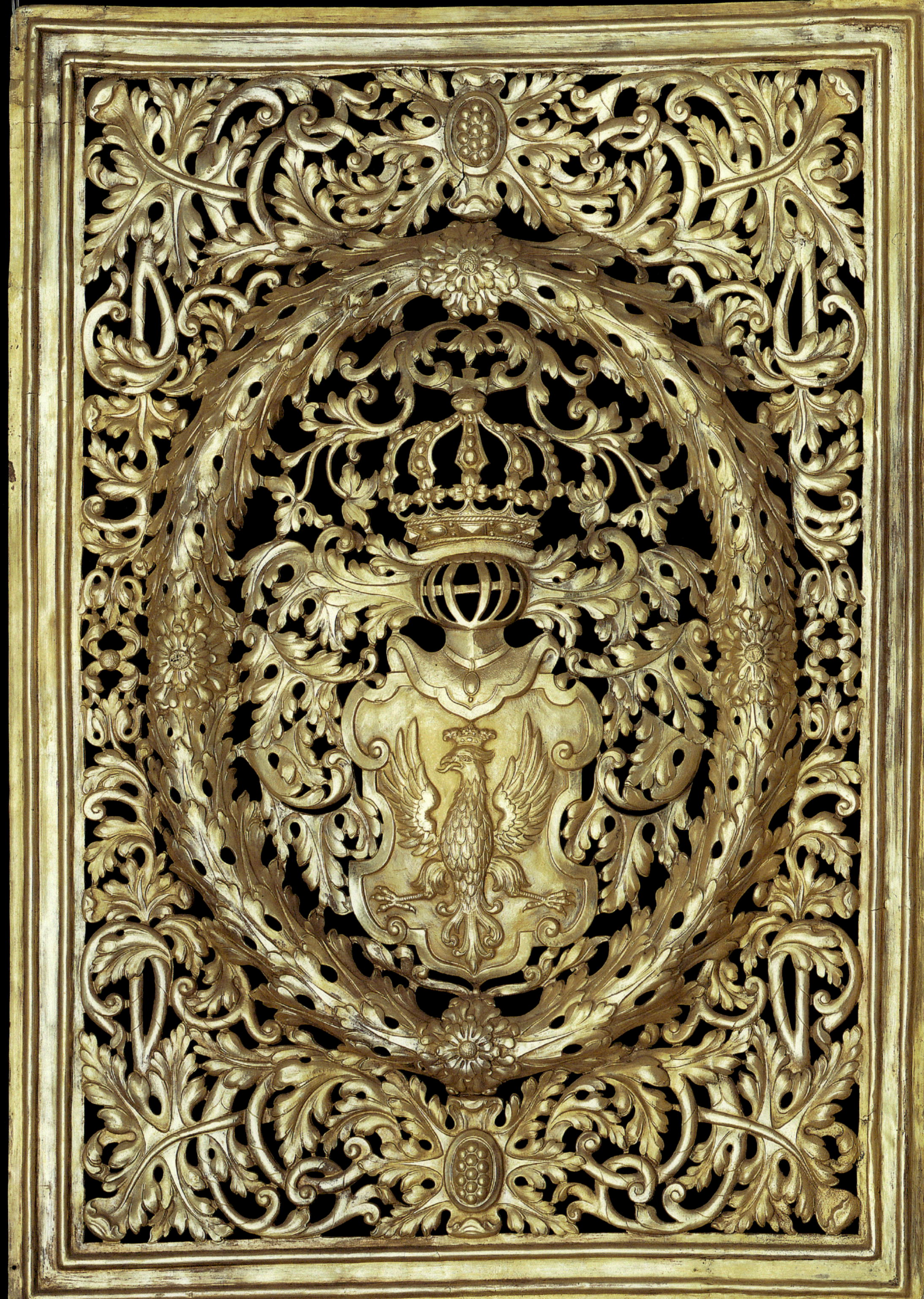

Two Astronomical Table Clocks

Brass cast, gilded, steel, enamel, silver
Augsburg, probably last quarter of 16th century
Left: h. 41 cm, pediment: w. 20.2 cm, d. 14.8 cm, Inv no. IV 283
Right: h. 41.3 cm, pediment: w. 25.4, d. 19 cm, Inv. no. IV 285

In 1733 the two table clocks made at the end of the 16th century could already be viewed in the Coats of Arms Room. For the late Baroque observer the complex astronomical clocks had above all a decorative function. As instruments for the precise measurement of time – like most other spring-driven astronomical clocks of the late 16th century – they were inadequate. Nevertheless, in the late Renaissance they were regarded as perfect examples of human creation, as they could be used to calculate the movements of the heavenly bodies. Around 1600 the latter were thought to reflect divine order and harmony.

The two clocks belong to a type of astronomical measuring instrument indigenous to Augsburg. Free-standing clock casings in the shape of small towers were made from the last quarter of the 16th century. The strictly architectural casings with their restrained ornamentation enclose several clockwork units, which are reflected on the outside in various gauges. The measuring instruments, which were made independently of each other, have largely the same system of dials. The centre of each of the two display sides sports an astrolabe. The second side is devoted to a calendar and the measurement of time. The main dial is framed by four smaller dials, which make possible special adjustments to regulate the instruments and take a variety of readings. Two additional dials for control functions involving the chimes and quarter-hourly chimes are to be found on the end sides.

The two astronomical parade instruments come from the electoral Saxon Kunstkammer. Augustus the Strong allocated especially beautiful and materially valuable clocks to his treasury on the occasion of the expansion of the Grünes Gewölbe between 1727 and 1729. After the dissolution of the Kunstkammer in the year 1832 further clocks came from this collection to the Grünes Gewölbe. The largest part, however, was integrated in the Mathematisch-Physikalischer Salon founded by Augustus the Strong.

DS

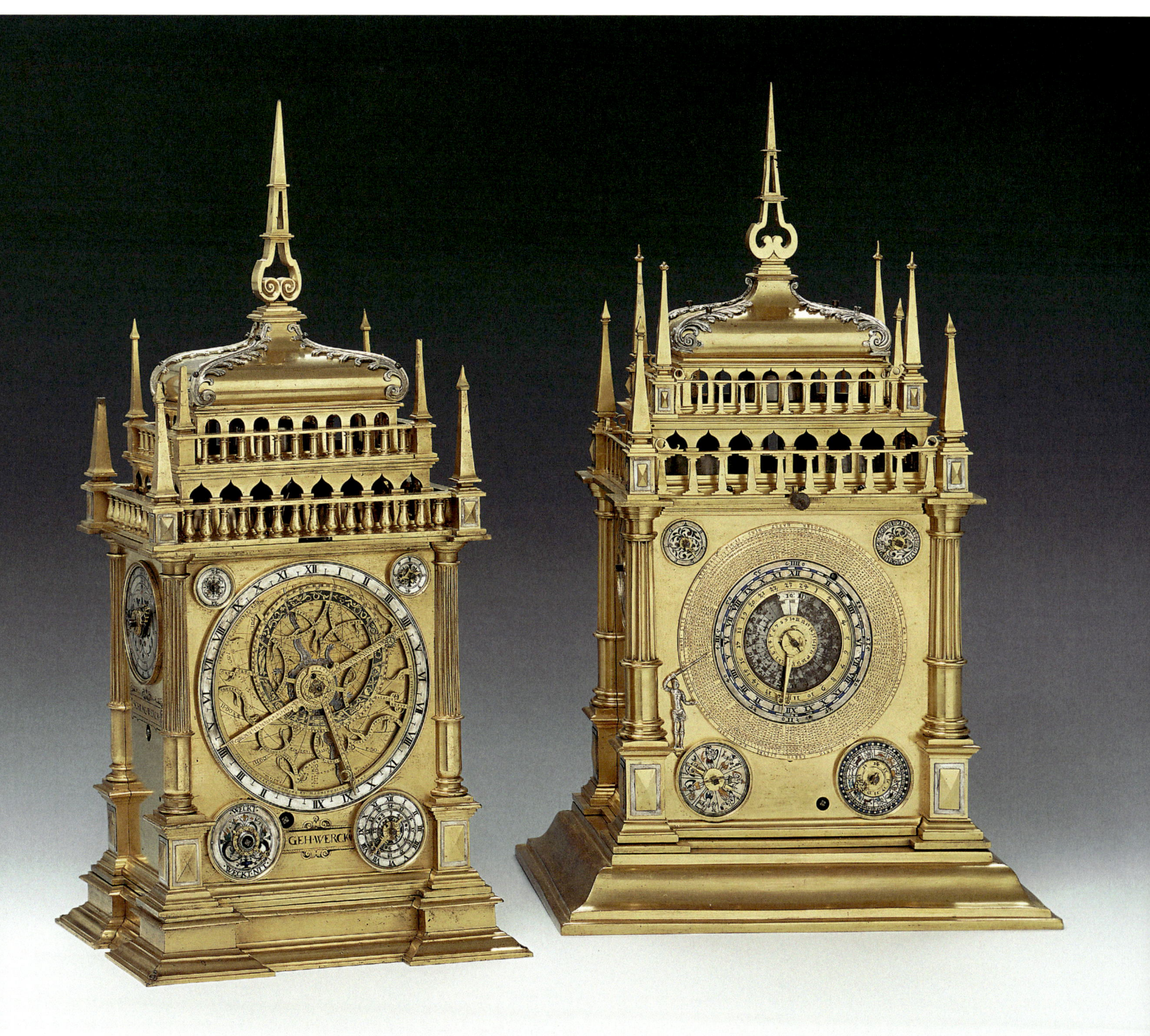

Jewel Room

Between spring 1727 and autumn 1729 in the second phase of expansion the most magnificent room of the treasury museum, the »Jewel Vault«, was created. This room is an architectural treasure whose painstakingly executed interiors befit the inestimable material value of the jewellery garnitures displayed. The verre églomisé painting, which was executed by Isaak August Wiwield as ornamental gold etchings, and which were backed by Christian Reinow in colour, were in this concentration unique in Europe.

The Jewel Room burnt out completely on 13 and 14 February 1945. Later a part of the vault collapsed. Only shards of the precious ornamented mirrors were preserved. Thanks to black and white photographs and one coloured gouache it was possible to reconstruct the room between 2002 and 2006. The reconstruction is a remarkable joint enterprise of many artists and craftsmen. Special mention should be made of Almuth and Henner Frank, who created the gold-etched mirrors, and Rosi Schwabe who directed the restoration of the carved works.

Augustus the Strong not only had the most precious objects of his treasury collection displayed, he used the mirrors with the etchings in the verre églomisé technique to demonstrate the majesty of his royal rank. For this reason the middle of each wall pillar is embellished not only with fashionable ornamentation in the shape of foliage and scrolls but also with the Polish-Lithuanian state coat of arms with the Saxon centre shield. The badge of the Polish White Eagle Order was engraved above and the star below. Beneath the gilded crowning ornament of the central pillar, embellished on all sides by the monogram of Augustus the Strong beneath the royal crown, there are the symbols of the noble orders of which the monarch was a member: the Order of the Golden Fleece, the Polish White Eagle Order, which Augustus the Strong himself founded, the Russian Order of St Andrew and the Danish Elephant Order. The room is also dominated by the large supraportas of gilded acanthus leaves. On that of the door leading to the Coats of Arms Room there is the decorative monogram of the king »FAR« (for Friedrich August Rex) beneath the royal crown and sceptre. Above the door to the Bronze Room, also on a red cushion, the electoral cap and sword with the monogram »CFA« (for Churfürst (elector) Friedrich August) are to be seen.

The unique state treasure of the Elector-Kings is now kept in the four large built-in display cabinets of the Jewel Room as it was in the past. Today there are ten more or less extensive ensembles, of which Keyssler in his famous description noted: »Hierauf folget eine ganze Garniture von Diamanten, worunter die Knöpfe des Kleides, der Ritter=Orden, der Stern, die Schnallen, das Degen=Gefäß und der Stock=Knopf begriffen sind. Gegen über siehet man mit Verwunderung eine dergleichen Garniture Carniol, die gar hoch geschäzet wird, eine andere von Smaragden, eine Garniture von Saphyren, eine von Rubinen, eine von Rauten=Diamanten, und noch eine von Brillants. In dem goldenen Vließe, so zur lezt gedachten Garniture gehöret, pranget ein Diamant, welchen der König erst vor etlichen Jahren mit zwey hundert tausend Thalern bezahlet hat.« (Here follows a whole garniture of diamonds, including the cloak buttons, the insignia of the order, the star, the buckles, the rapier sheath and the walking-stick finial. Opposite one is amazed to see a similar garniture in carnelian, which is highly prized, another of emeralds, a garniture of sapphires, one of rubies, one of lozenge-shaped diamonds and one in brilliant cut. In the Golden Fleece, to which the last garniture belongs, a diamond gleams which the king bought only a few years ago for two hundred thousand thalers). In 1733 the cabinet on the north wall to the Coats of Arms Room accommodated four garnitures on six shelves. Apart from the silver and the gold garniture, which no longer exist, there was the largely lost agate garniture and the tortoiseshell garniture. The jewellery ensembles were exhibited alongside splendid sabres, daggers, swords and rapiers and walking sticks. On the opposite south wall, again on 6 shelves, the garnitures in carnelians, emeralds, sapphires, rubies diamonds in a rose cut and diamonds in brilliant cut were displayed. This cabinet also contained the long staff of the Lord Chamberlain. On the west wall to the left of the ›Obeliscus Augustalis‹ in the glass cabinet 15 rapiers and daggers, a sword and the large electoral sword as a symbol of the power of the ruling dynasty were displayed. To the right of the obelisk there was the miner's outfit, eight daggers and smaller hunting knives, ten large gold chains, 66 buttonhole mounts with diamond roses, a walking stick, a pair of spurs and a hunting knife with a four-part rapier belt.

Parts of these pieces of jewellery were altered in the ensuing decades, but most of the precious stones displayed at that time in the Jewel Room have been preserved in new jewellery. The splendid swords, rapiers, hunting knives and daggers are now to be found in the Rüstkammer (armoury). Their place is taken up by walking sticks set with precious stones. Pretiosa such as the insignia of the Golden Fleece, which in 1733 were the private possessions of the king, are also on display. The presentation of the jewellery garnitures at that time was much more crowded; the jewellery that has been preserved has been given much more space in the re-arrangement of the display.

The most precious and artistic works were displayed on the tables of the Jewel Room. In addition to the ›Obeliscus Augustalis‹, the two ›Blackamoors‹ with the emerald and local stone cluster and the ingenious cabinet pieces with the ›Phases of Life's Pleasures‹, the ›Golden Coffee Set‹ and the ›Throne of the Grand Mogul‹ were originally also displayed in the Jewel Room. The parade bowl with ›Diana bathing‹, the bowl with Hercules fighting, the bowl with Hercules seated and the ›The cabinet piece with the cameo of a Roman emperor‹ were also displayed on column tables. Some of these are now again to be seen in the Jewel Room.

DS

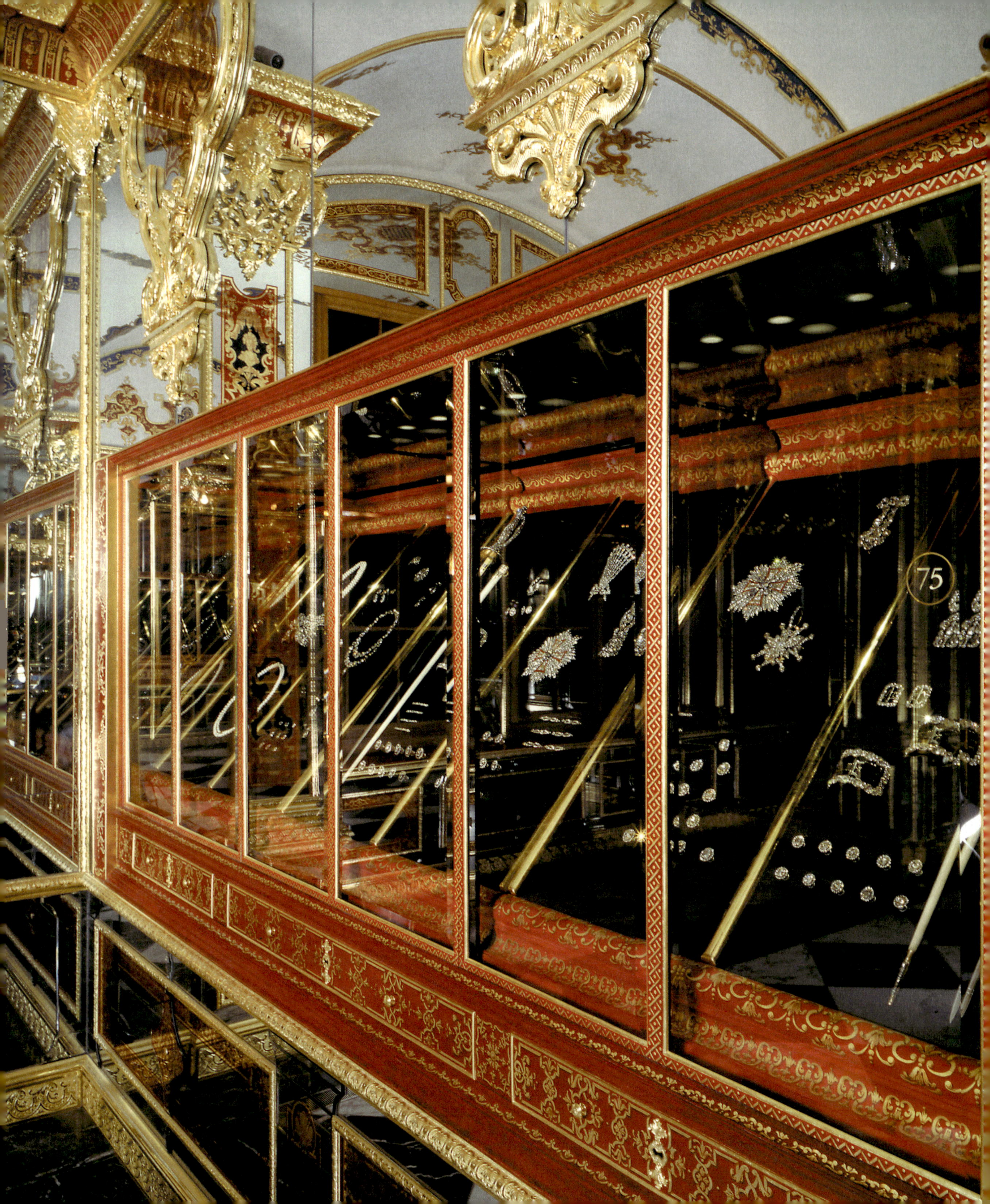

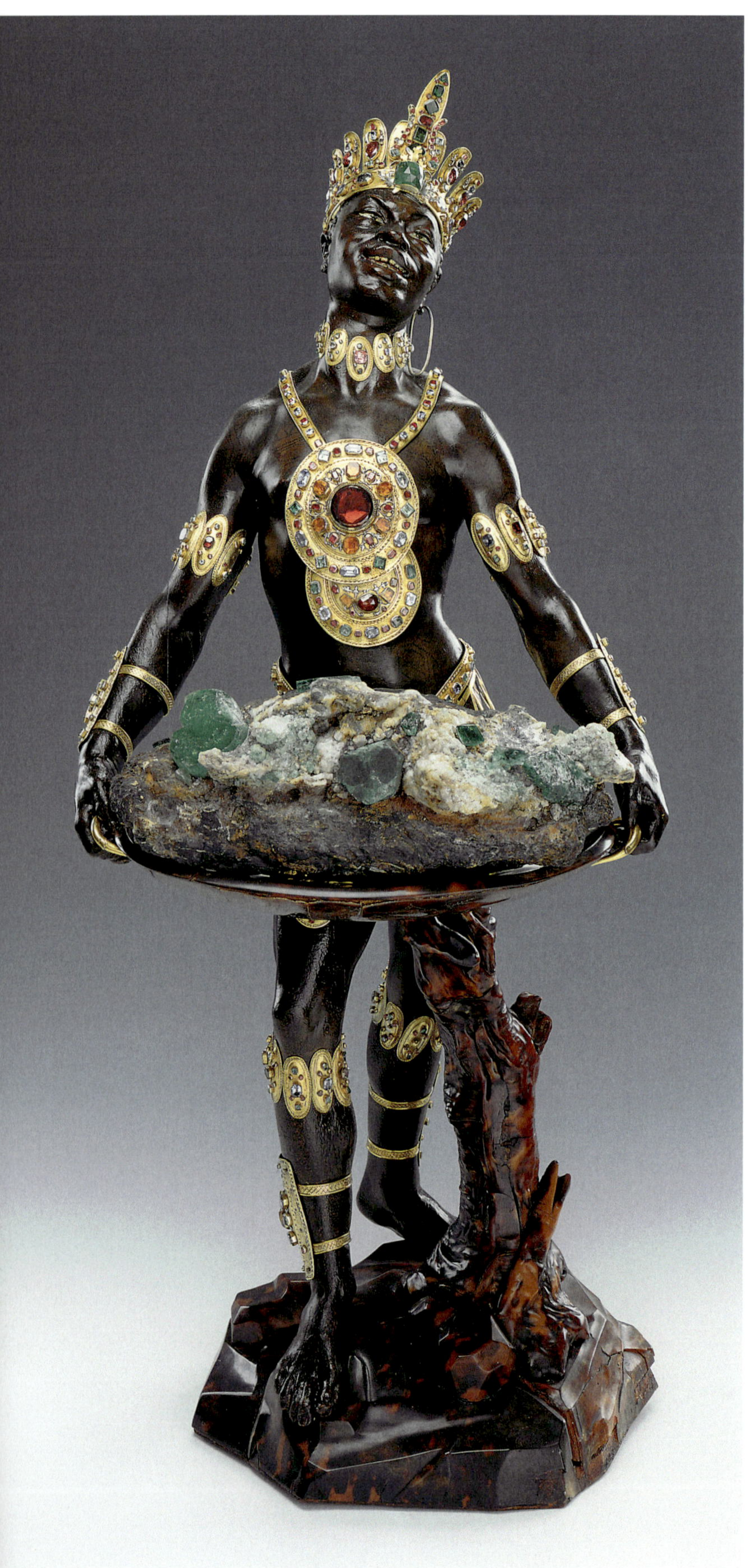

Moor with Emerald Cluster

Pear wood, lacquered, silver-gilt, large emerald cluster, emeralds,
rubies, sapphires, topazes, garnets, almandine, tortoiseshell
Sculpture: Balthasar Permoser
Mount: Dinglinger workshop
Tortoiseshell veneer: Wilhelm Krüger
Lacquer work: presumably Martin Schnell
Dresden, probably 1724
H. 63.8 cm, Inv. no. VIII 303

Blackamoor with an artificial Saxon Cluster

Lacquered wood, silver ore matrix with Saxon gemstones
(carnelian, amethyst, smoky quartz)
Copper-gilt, brass, various gemstones
Sculpture: unknown Dresden sculptor (Permoser workshop)
Mount: Johann Heinrich Köhler
Dresden 1724
H. 67 cm, Inv. no. V 165

It is very rare that the accoutrements of an exhibit surpass the precious object itself as far as its artistic value is concerned. This is clearly the case with this exhibit, the blackamoor with an emerald cluster, probably manufactured by Balthasar Permoser in 1724. Without the redecoration of the Grünes Gewölbe in the baroque style, this statuette would not have been manufactured at all. It was created because Augustus the Strong wanted to exhibit a precious object from his Kunstkammer in the new treasury museum. The object is mounted on a large piece of limonite, studded with 16 emeralds, some of which are extremely large. This stone was a gift from Emperor Rudolf II to Elector Augustus in 1581. The dark green emeralds were quarried at a mine in Chivor-Somondoco (Colombia), opened only a few years earlier. At the behest of the elector, this ›miracle of nature‹ was to be preserved at the electoral palace as a commemorative exhibit. The Conquistadores presented the emerald cluster as evidence of the wealth of this newly conquered part of South America.

The young, athletic man in dark brown pear wood, striding along in an elegant and lithe fashion, presents the Colombian emerald cluster on a tray in tortoiseshell. Yet, he is not a ›blackamoor‹, but judging from his garments and jewellery, a South American Indian. His tattoos as well as his precious necklaces, bracelets, breastplate, feather crown, loincloth and footwear clearly show that he is a native South American. These were manufactured after a copperplate engraving in Dinglinger's workshop. The second figure of a ›blackamoor‹ presents an artificial Saxon cluster symbolizing Saxony's wealth in silver and precious stone deposits. An invoice made out in 1724 by the court goldsmith Johann Heinrich Köhler for this figure has been preserved.

The two impressive ›blackamoors‹ are neither servants nor slaves, but appear to be of royal blood. The way they present their riches expresses power and freedom. The sculptures presenting the clusters have been part of the collection of the Jewel Room since 1729. Permoser's exotic work may have been inspired by two »Amerikanische königliche Prinzen« (American royal princes) who, from 1722, lived in Dresden as the »property« of an English captain where they were presented to the amazed public. The king took the two natives into his royal household. They were baptized as Lutherans and eventually ›passed on‹ to the Tsarina of Russia.

DS

›Obeliscus Augustalis‹

Jasper, carnelian, marble, Kelheim stone, Böttger stoneware,
gold, silver, partly gilded, enamel, ivory, gemstones, cameos
Design and goldwork: Johann Melchior Dinglinger
Stonecutting: Johann Christoph Hübner
Stone sculpting: Gottlieb Kirchner
Dresden, before 1722
H. 228 cm, w. 122 cm, Inv. no. VIII 350

The ›Obeliscus Augustalis‹ is a chef d'œuvre of late Baroque treasury art. The unusual monument to a king is one of the three works by Johann Melchior Dinglinger – alongside his ›Golden Coffee Set‹ and the ›Throne of the Grand Mogul‹ – which gave character and profile to a particular room. It was acquired by Augustus the Strong direct from Dinglinger's workshop. At the same time, it is the first cabinet piece in Dinglinger's œuvre of a pronounced architectural character. This cabinet piece, conceived as an indoor monument, dominates in an impressive fashion the architecture of any interior by its sheer size, and also by its material splendour and majestic form. Quite obviously, the display in this room is of necessity subordinated to the obelisk as it is designed in such a way that it requires a mirror wall, reflecting its ›missing‹ parts, in order to appear as a three-dimensional entity. While the previous large-scale cabinet pieces by Dinglinger and his parade bowls were intimate works of art tailor-made for the king as a collector, the ›Obeliscus Augustalis‹ addresses a larger public. It is a representational showpiece, which encourages the viewer to study its details, but it is also seen to advantage from a distance. Augustus the Strong himself is at the centre of this monument. The portrait of the Elector-King, skilfully executed in enamels in the style of a cameo ›all'antica‹ dominates the plinth of the obelisk. It depicts Augustus with the electoral cap, the crown of Poland-Lithuania and the traditional emblems of a sovereign with a fighting spirit. He is not represented as a contemporary ruler, but as a king revered by peoples from classical antiquity. Four soldiers in historic armour rest on the forecourt while representatives of various classical cultures are seen admiring the monument. The obelisk is a direct reference to the Elector-King, but there is also an allusion to the marriage of Maria Josepha, the Emperor's daughter, to the Saxon Prince Friedrich Augustus in 1719. The cameos on the shaft of the obelisk, skilfully cut by Johann Christoph Hübner, depict famous men and women from Antiquity and symbolize the virtues of the future royal couple.

Around the year 1728, six years after the ›Obeliscus Augustalis‹ had been acquired by Augustus the Strong, he had this cabinet piece exhibited as a focal point in the Jewel Room. It is surrounded by display cabinets filled with the both aesthetically and materially impressive crown jewels of the Saxon-Polish dynasty, and by other major works by Dinglinger. This gemstone monument is a well-balanced combination of elements of late Baroque treasury art and contemporary emblems of royal power.

DS

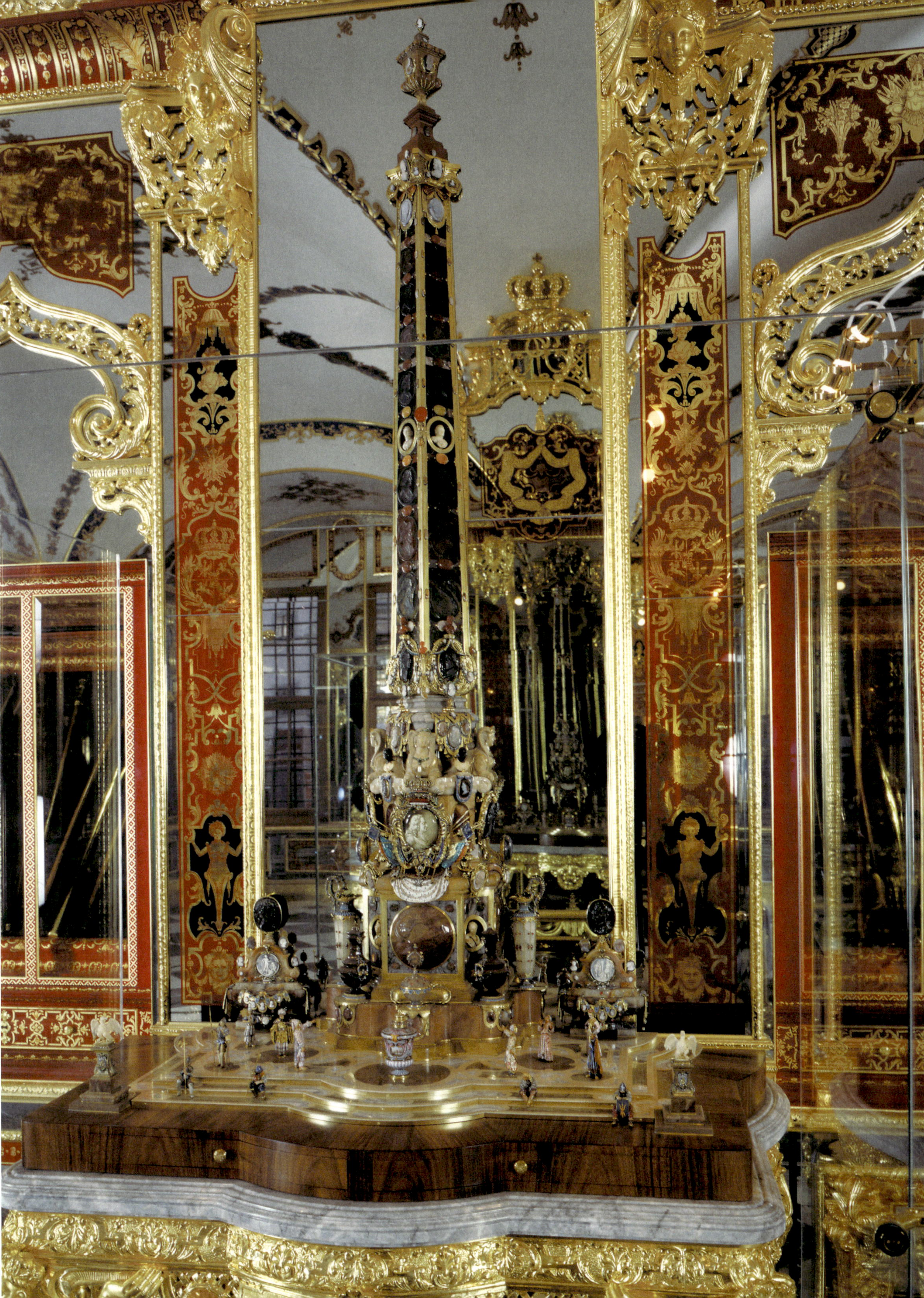

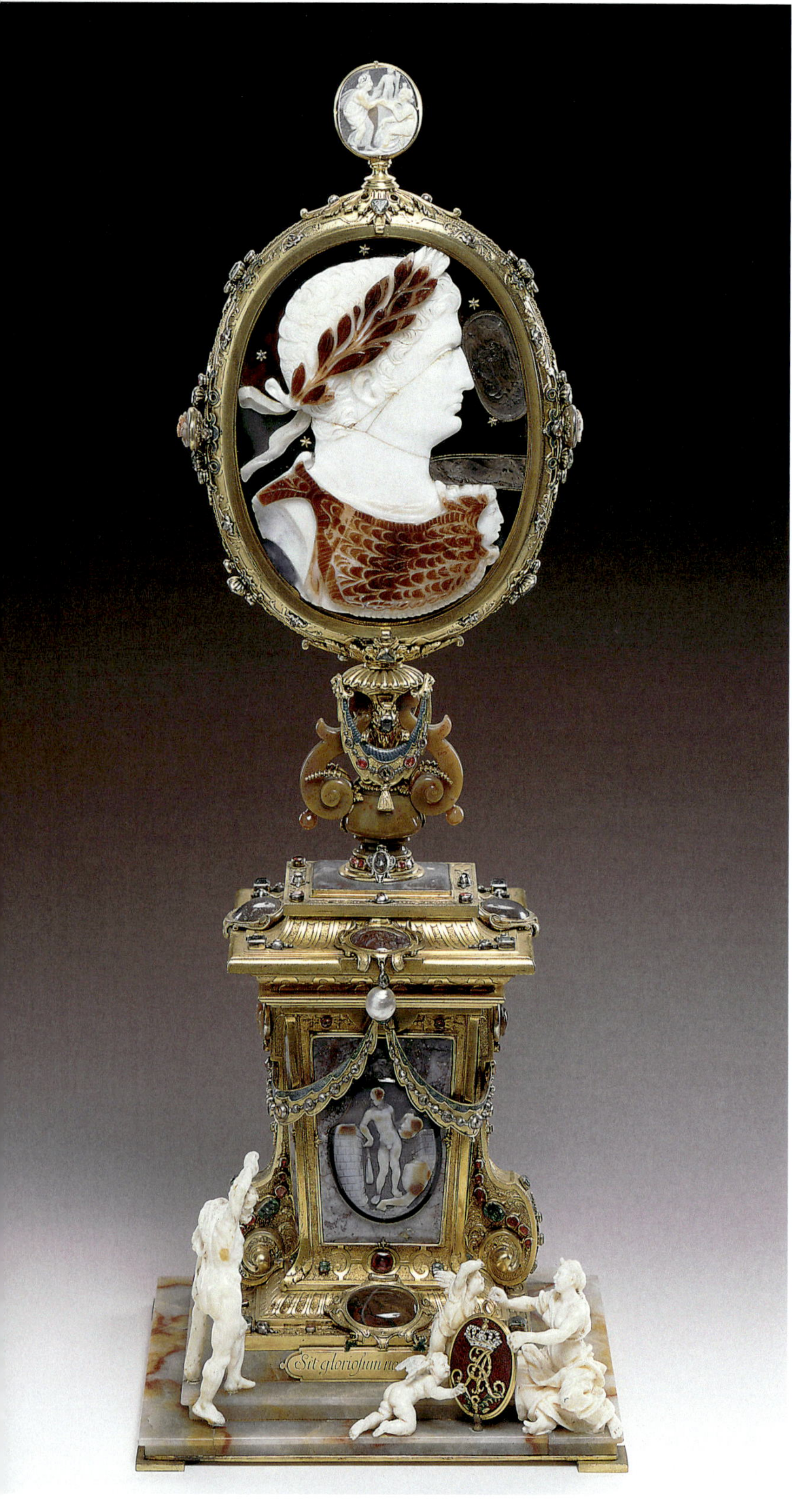

Cabinet Piece with the Cameo of a Roman Emperor

Cameo in onyx, ivory, cameos, gemstones, pearls,
agate, jasper, gold, silver-gilt, enamel
Cameo: Roman, probably 41 AD
Goldwork and design: Johann Melchior Dinglinger
Ivory sculptures: Balthasar Permoser
Dresden, before 1722
H. 44 cm, Inv. no. V 1

The centre of this cabinet piece is the 13 centimetres high and 10 centimetres wide onyx cameo with the portrait of Emperor Claudius. This rare example of antique stonecutting was interpreted in the early 18th century as a likeness of Emperor Augustus and thus associated in this cabinet piece with Augustus the Strong. For this reason, Dinglinger had two intaglios inserted into the surface of the portrait, which is executed in alto rilievo. They represent a dolphin and a ›goat fish‹ – or Capricorn in the zodiac. These are the birth signs of Emperor Augustus. The golden stars inserted into the surface of the classical cameos are also Baroque additions. The gold frame around the classical portrait was crowned by Johann Melchior Dinglinger by a small cameo with the representation of two women making a sacrificial offering before an idol.

The symbolical cabinet piece with its agate plinth is decorated in sumptuous fashion with 106 diamonds, 77 rubies, 58 emeralds and 2 pearls. The magnificent, relatively high pedestal makes this work of classical antiquity appear like a secular reliquary or monument. Groups of dramatic figures in the grand style, ascribed to Balthasar Permoser, are loosely arranged around the pedestal. According to the description of 1722 a female figure on the right represents Eternity, holding a shield with the name AR in her left hand, pointing with her right hand to the name, thus immortalizing it. The same description mentions various different genii venerating the king with the words ›sit gloriosum nomen tuum‹. The figure of Hercules with his club and lion's head points upwards with his right hand to the portrait of Augustus in a gesture of veneration of the values of classical antiquity.

Augustus the Strong acquired the cabinet piece in 1722 for 12,000 thalers, well aware of the fact that the veneration of his Roman namesake entailed the veneration of his own glory as ruler and patron of the arts. The cabinet piece is one of Dinglinger's late works, characterised by classical stylistic severity, monumentality and the incorporation of stonecuts.

DS

Parade Bowl with Hercules resting

Chalcedony, gold, enamel, pearls, gemstones
Signed: Johann Melchior Dinglinger
Dresden, dated 1713
H. 34.5 cm, Inv. no. VIII 302

Within a period of a good ten years a number of outstanding parade vessels were manufactured at the workshop of Johann Melchior Dinglinger. Like the first vessel of this type, the bowl with ›Diana Bathing‹ completed in 1704, their elaborately designed mounts in precious materials all feature meaningful figurative representations with an intellectually sophisticated topic.

In October 1715 Augustus the Strong acquired three extravagant cabinet pieces from Dinglinger's workshop for a total of 21,000 thalers, among them the ›Bowl with a Billy Goat‹, also referred to as ›Children's Bacchanalia‹, which was created in 1711 and cost 9,000 thalers. The ›Pocal von Renoceros mit dem Neptuno‹ was sold for 2,000 thalers. Both cabinet pieces are now part of the collection of the Grünes Gewölbe. The most expensive object from the convolute was the ›Parade Bowl with Hercules‹ for 10,000 thalers. The depiction of this parade bowl shows the demigod resting after his glorious battles. At the time of its acquisition it was of political relevance for Augustus the Strong as he had only a few years previously regained the Polish crown and reached the pinnacle of his power in 1711 as incumbent Reichsvikar (acting representative of the Emperor).

The chalcedony bowl ›all'antica‹ with a golden spout is crowned by a figure of Hercules sitting on an elaborately worked seat. The figure is made from barocco pearls, gold and enamel. The demigod leans on his club while a dragon can be seen above him with its tongue darting out. His back support is formed of the weapons given to him by the gods. The elaborate shaft in openwork is formed of objects alluding to Hercules' heroic feats. The foot of the bowl is inscribed with the artist's full signature. This vessel with Hercules and his lion skin, created and made by Dinglinger himself, is a reference to Augustus the Strong's identification with the Greek hero and his superhuman deeds. Unlike Hercules, however, Augustus did had no opportunity to rest from his heroic deeds, as in autumn 1715, shortly after he had bought the bowl, he had to travel post haste to Poland to quell civil unrest.

The parade bowl was so important to Augustus the Strong that he had it displayed on a gilded column table against the long west wall of the Jewel Room in 1729. Today, the precious object is exhibited together with the ›Cabinet Piece with the Cameo of a Roman Emperor‹ on the large table in front of the window shaft in the Jewel Room. These two important examples of Baroque treasury art highlight the artistic development of Dinglinger between 1713 and 1722 and are very vivid representations of the Saxon-Polish Elector-King's models from classical antiquity – Hercules and the Roman Emperor Augustus.

DS

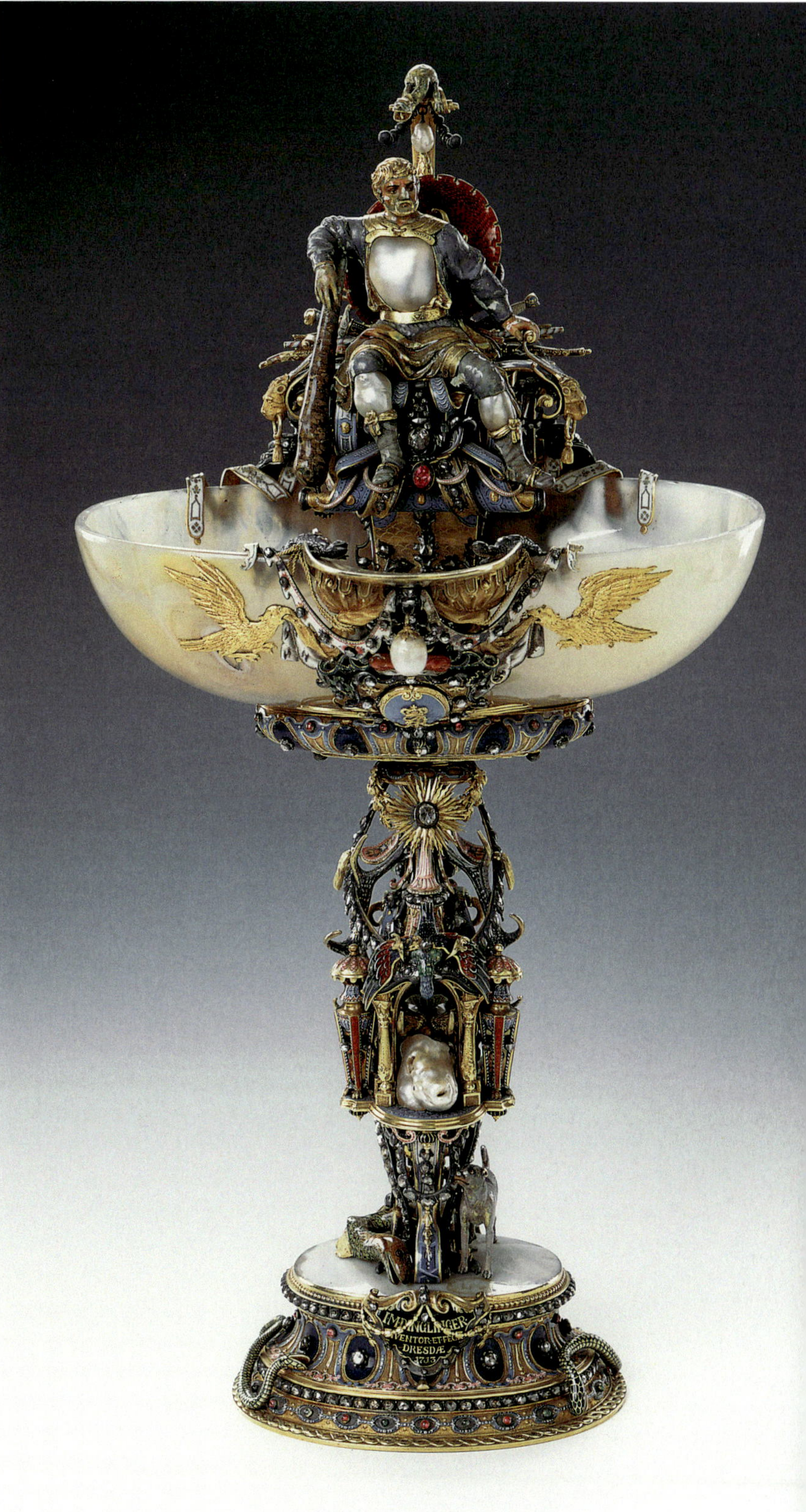

Cabinet Piece ›The Greatest Joys in Life‹

Sardonyx, agate, Kelheim stone, horn, gold, silver-gilt,
enamel, cameos, pearls, diamonds, sapphires, topazes,
rubies, emeralds and other precious stones
Goldwork: Johann Melchior and Georg Christoph Dinglinger
Sculpture: Christian Kirchner
Stonecutting: Johann Christoph Hübner
Dresden, dated 1728
H. 139 cm, Inv. no. VIII 379

Three unusually large and eccentrically shaped cabinet pieces by Johann Melchior Dinglinger are closely connected with the furnishing of the Grünes Gewölbe. Two of them were created as pendants. The supplement to the inventory of the pretiosa of spring 1733 refers to them as ›origin and outburst‹ and ›consequence and end‹ of human happiness. One of the objects shows a sculpture at its foot representing Bacchus as a child with the goddess Ceres, and on a large agate panel a depiction in relief of the sacrifices to the god of wine and the goddess of agriculture. The other object includes representations of Pluto and Proserpina and a depiction in relief of the shades of the dead crossing the Styx, the river of the underworld. Thus, both cabinet pieces deal with the jux-taposition of the rich abundance of life and almighty death. When Johann Georg Keyssler visited the Grünes Gewölbe in October 1730, the two objects were already displayed against the mirrored central pillar of the Jewel Room.

The third cabinet piece, the ›Baccanalia‹, which is characterized by its sumptuous splendour, was inspected by this urbane and sophisticated writer of travelogues when it was still at Dinglinger's workshop. Keyssler refers to him as the most skilful artist in Dresden who had made a name for himself with a number of excellent works in the col-

lection of the Grünes Gewölbe. He describes the »Baccanalia« as a work showing at its centre the triumphant entry of Bacchus on a sardonyx, with women wearing masques, harlequins and other amusing depictions on the sides. A few years later, possibly after Dinglinger's death in 1731, the work was moved to the third side of the central pillar thus redefining the other two works as a late Baroque representation of the joys of life and a ›memento mori‹.

This central cabinet piece is, with regard to the size and elaborateness of its artistic design, the climax of the trilogy. At the centre of the overall composition is a cameo in oriental agate. With a width of 28 centimetres and a height of 16 centimetres this cameo is unusually large. It shows the triumphal procession of Bacchus as the height of joie de vivre. The imaginative mount with its many figural elements and its intertwined bands in silver-gilt and enamel with mascaron appliqués is decorated with a large number of precious stones. These three large cabinet pieces are an aesthetically very pleasing comment on the riches assembled in the Jewel Room. Surrounded by the most precious objects in the collection of the Saxon-Polish Elector-Kings, these cabinet pieces are a playful, yet unmistakable comment on the futility and vanity of human life, but also on the attendant joys.

DS

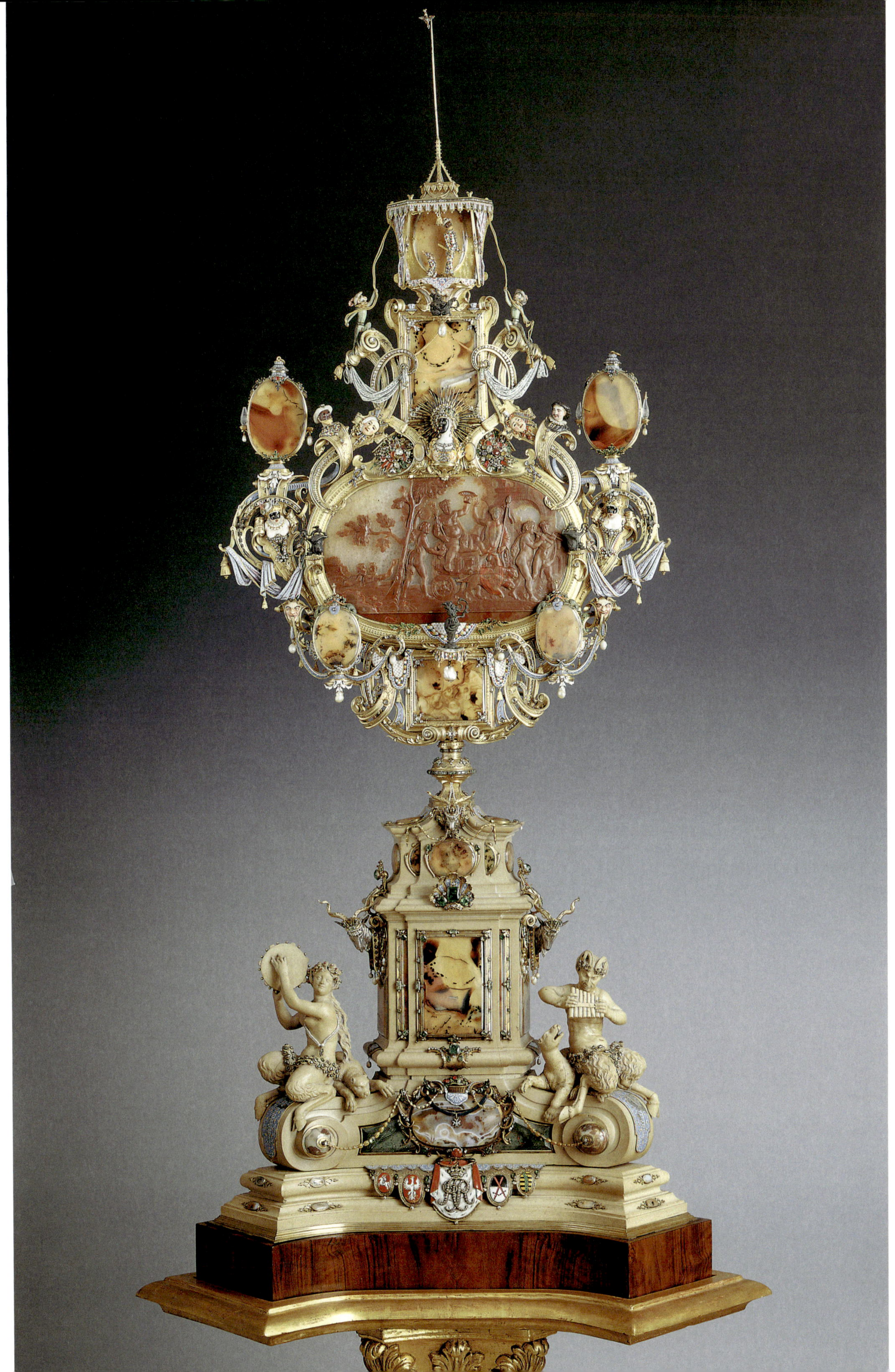

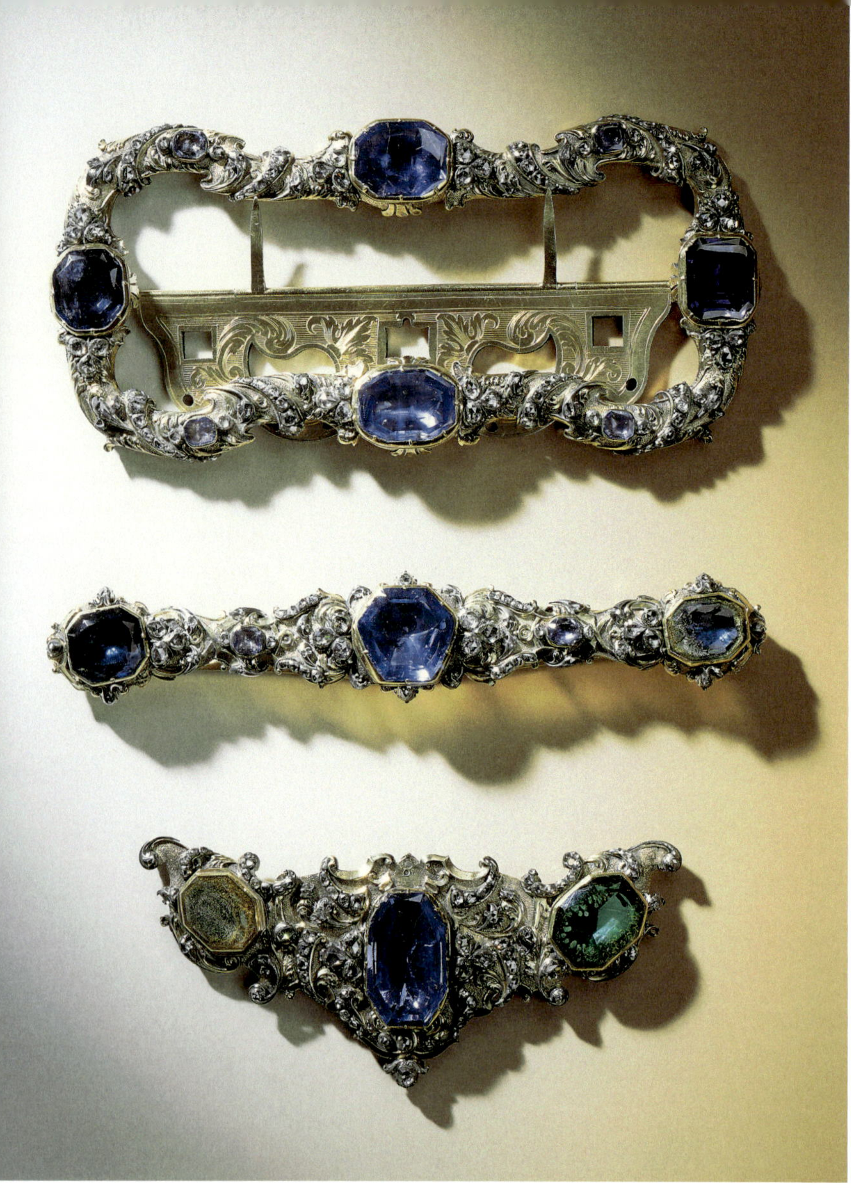

Large Buckle, Loop and pointed Clasp of the 10-piece Parade Rapier Belt from the Sapphire Garniture

Johann Melchior Dinglinger
Dresden, c. 1710, alterations 1719 – 1721
Large buckle: 8 sapphires, 116 diamond roses, gold, silver
L. 18.5 cm, h. 8.5 cm, Inv. no. VIII 159
Loop: 5 sapphires, 56 diamond roses, gold, silver
L. 18.5 cm, h. 3.2 cm, Inv. no. VIII 158
Clasp: 3 sapphires, 80 diamond roses, gold, silver
L. 14.1 cm, h. 5.9 cm, Inv. no. VIII 157

The sapphire garniture is not the oldest of Augustus the Strong's jewellery ensembles, but it contains some of his oldest pieces of jewellery. Among them the badge of the Polish Order of the White Eagle created around 1710, and, above all, the 10-piece, fully preserved rapier belt – a historical rarity of the highest order. Around the year 1700, the rapier was worn on a wide belt around the right shoulder fastened in the middle of the breast. The buckles and loops served to secure the belt and were at the same time particularly representational pieces of jewellery adorning the garments of the king.

The parade belt consists of three buckles, three loops and four pointed clasps. The largest buckle with loop and clasp illustrated here were affixed to the king's breast as a sparkling set of jewellery. The two slightly smaller buckles with loops and clasps were connected with the belt, widening towards the bottom and separating into two parts. They concealed the holder on the left hip in which an ornamental rapier or hunting knife was worn. The remaining ornamental clasp round off the rich jewellery ensemble at the bottom. Only a few jewellery garnitures in the possession of Augustus the Strong contained such a »Leib Gehencke« (rapier belt). The Jewel Inventory of 1719 records similar sets for the emerald, diamond rose and diamond garnitures. A fifth set consisting of nine pieces was part of the ruby garniture. The carnelian garniture from 1719 includes a smaller set consisting of a large buckle and seven trimmings. It is probably a more modern version of princely jewellery as the large parade belt sets consisting of several pieces started to go out of fashion at that time.

The elegant ornamentation of the pieces consisting of rocailles in countermovement and acanthus leaves gives us a hint of the time when the work was created. It suggests a time shortly after 1700. The first version of the sapphire garniture was probably also made in that period. In 1719 the parade belt was estimated at 22,000 thalers in the Jewel Inventory. It was thus by far the single most expensive item from the still incomplete garniture which was valued at 73,390 thalers. In spring 1721 Augustus the Strong increased the value of his sapphire garniture considerably by having a richer decoration with diamond roses added. The pieces that were part of the parade belt, initially decorated with large sapphires only, were also studded with hundreds of small diamond roses in Dinglinger's workshop. Although the pieces are adorned with very rare and large sapphires of excellent quality, they were neither remodelled nor broken up during the 18th and early 19th century.

DS

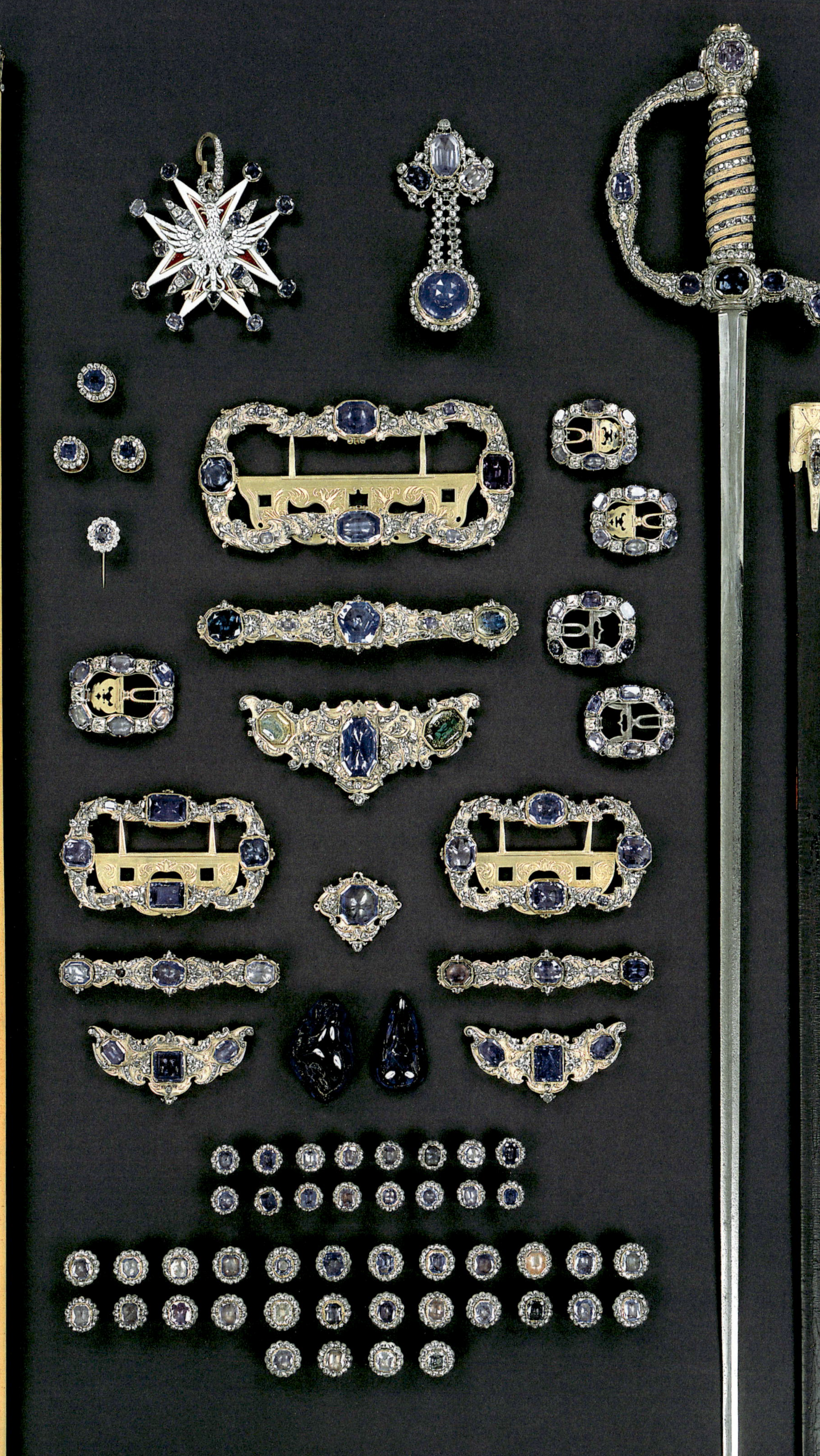

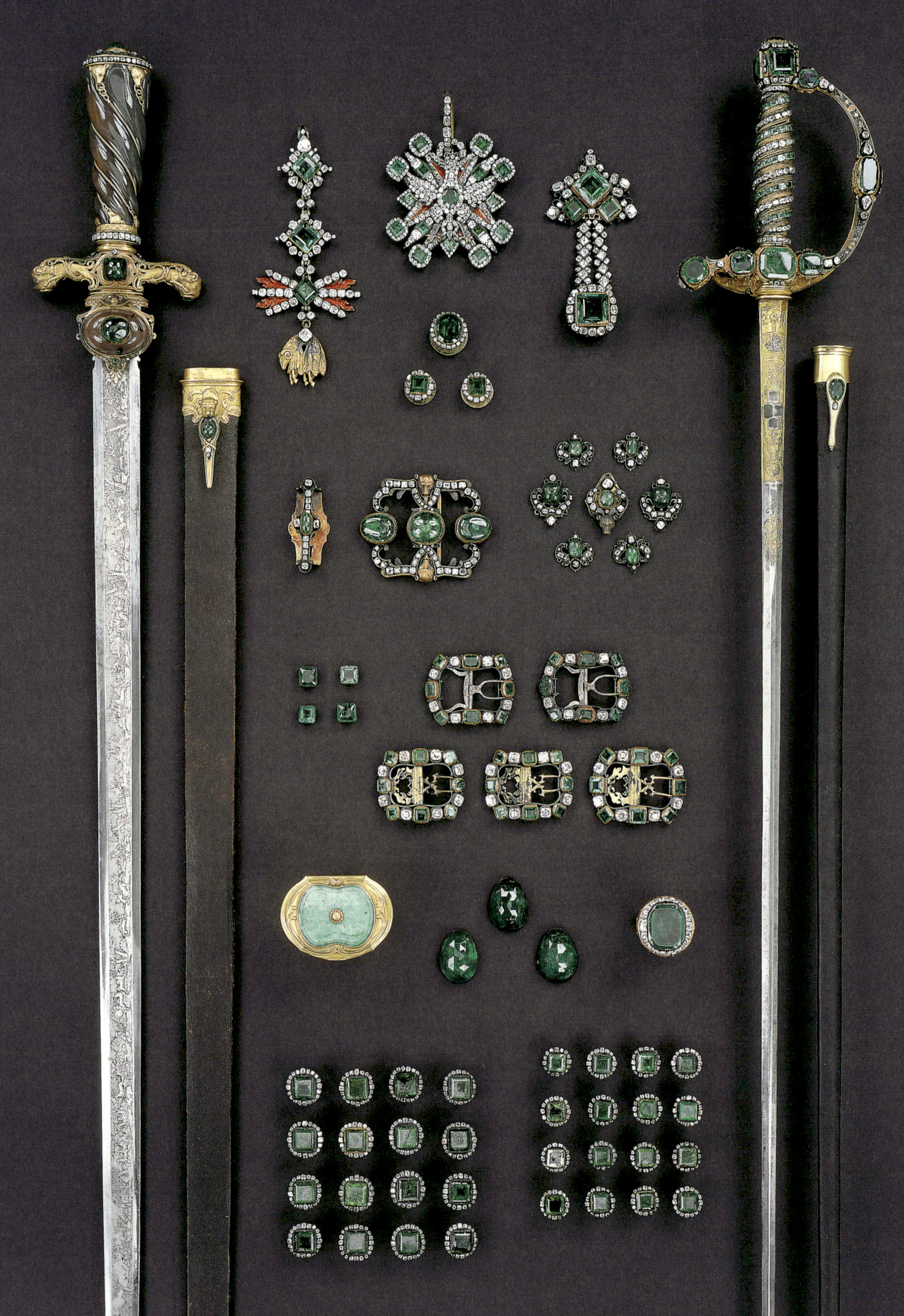

Hunting Knife with Scabbard from the Emerald Garniture

9 emeralds, 78 diamonds, agate, gold, silver, silver-gilt, steel, leather
Johann Melchior Dinglinger
Dresden, before 1719
L. 80 cm, Inv. no. VIII 144

At the time of Augustus the Strong, the emerald garniture was even more extravagant and artistically more impressive than today. Almost all the larger pieces of this ensemble, including the dress rapier and the hunting whip, are decorated with figural hunting motifs. Only the rapier-like hunting knife has been preserved. Stabbing weapons of this kind had the central function of a parade weapon in hunting garnitures. This representational hunting weapon, which was only worn on the occasion of hunting festivities, is derived from 17th and 18th century stabbing knives that were used by hunters to deliver the coup de grâce to the wounded animal. An enthusiastic huntsman, Augustus the Strong possessed several hunting garnitures and four hunting knives have been preserved in his jewellery ensembles. In the carnelian garniture it was the only parade weapon.

The blade of the hunting knife from the emerald garniture is sharpened on both sides and thus fulfils the functional requirements of a proper hunting weapon. Above all, it is an extremely magnificent ornamental object. Its compact hilt is made of light-brown agate with a spiral pattern of incised grooves with twisted gold cords embedded in them – a typical feature of the ceremonial weapons from Dinglinger's workshop. With this hunting knife, Dinglinger created an ornamental weapon of outstanding quality with carefully designed details. It is one of the most attractive objects in the jewellery collection of Augustus the Strong. Hunting motifs in different variations adorn the protective guard cast in gold and the fastener for the gold cords attached to the hilt. The ornamental motifs consist of heads of exotic lions cast in gold and carefully designed depictions of indigenous game. These motifs also adorn the opening of the sheath and the shell-shaped ornament in agate at the base of the blade. The steel blade is decorated on both sides with engraved representations of hunting scenes. The game include red deer, bears, wild boar, foxes and hares. The engravings were executed by the Dresden court copperplate engraver Moritz Bodenehr who was also responsible for the decoration of the hunting knife from the carnelian garniture. The skilfully crafted hunting knife from the emerald garniture originally formed an integrated whole, together with the parade rapier, which was broken up in 1737, and the hunting whip. This ornamental garniture established a link between courtly hunting and treasury art with its focus on detail.

DS

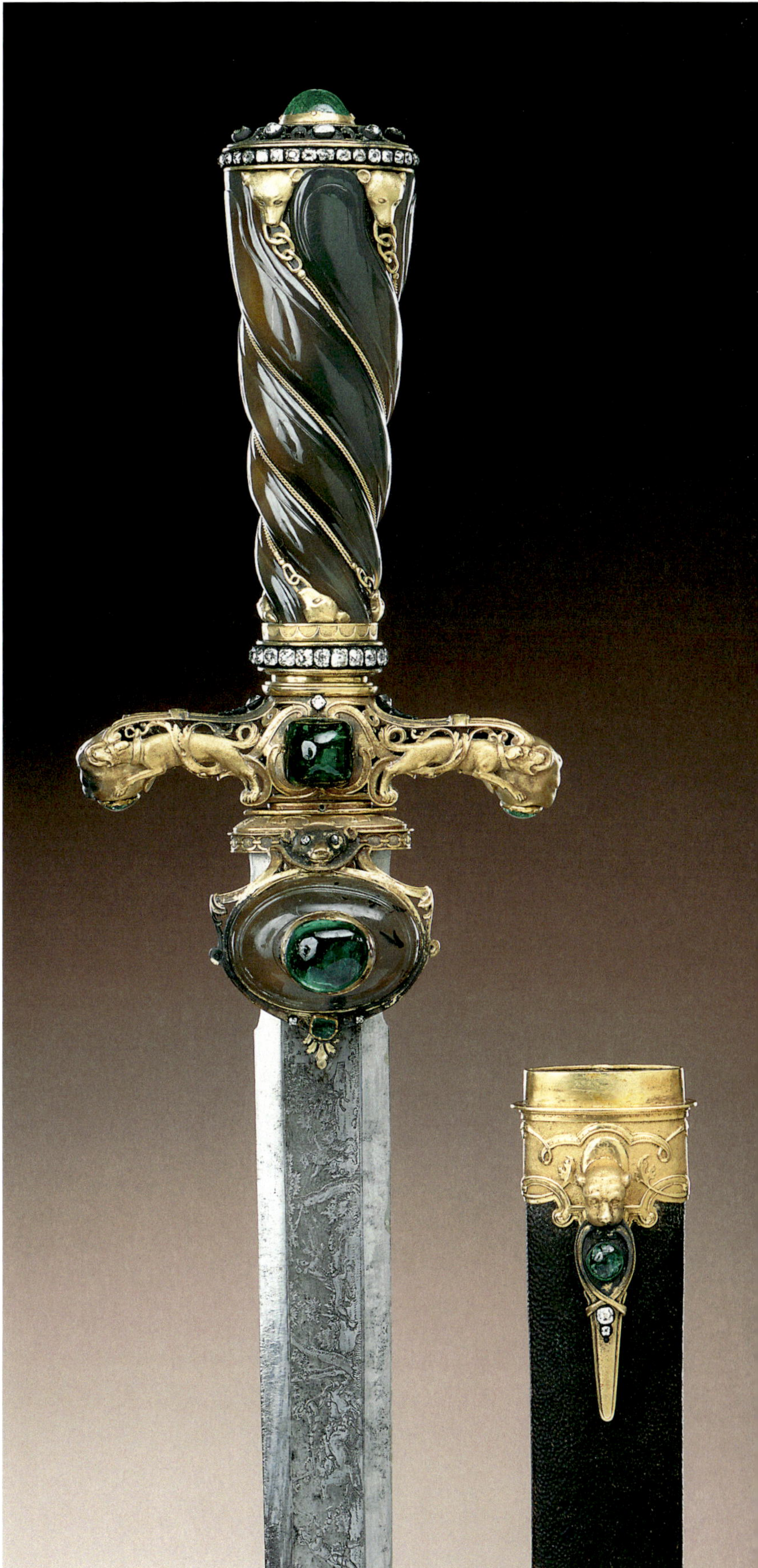

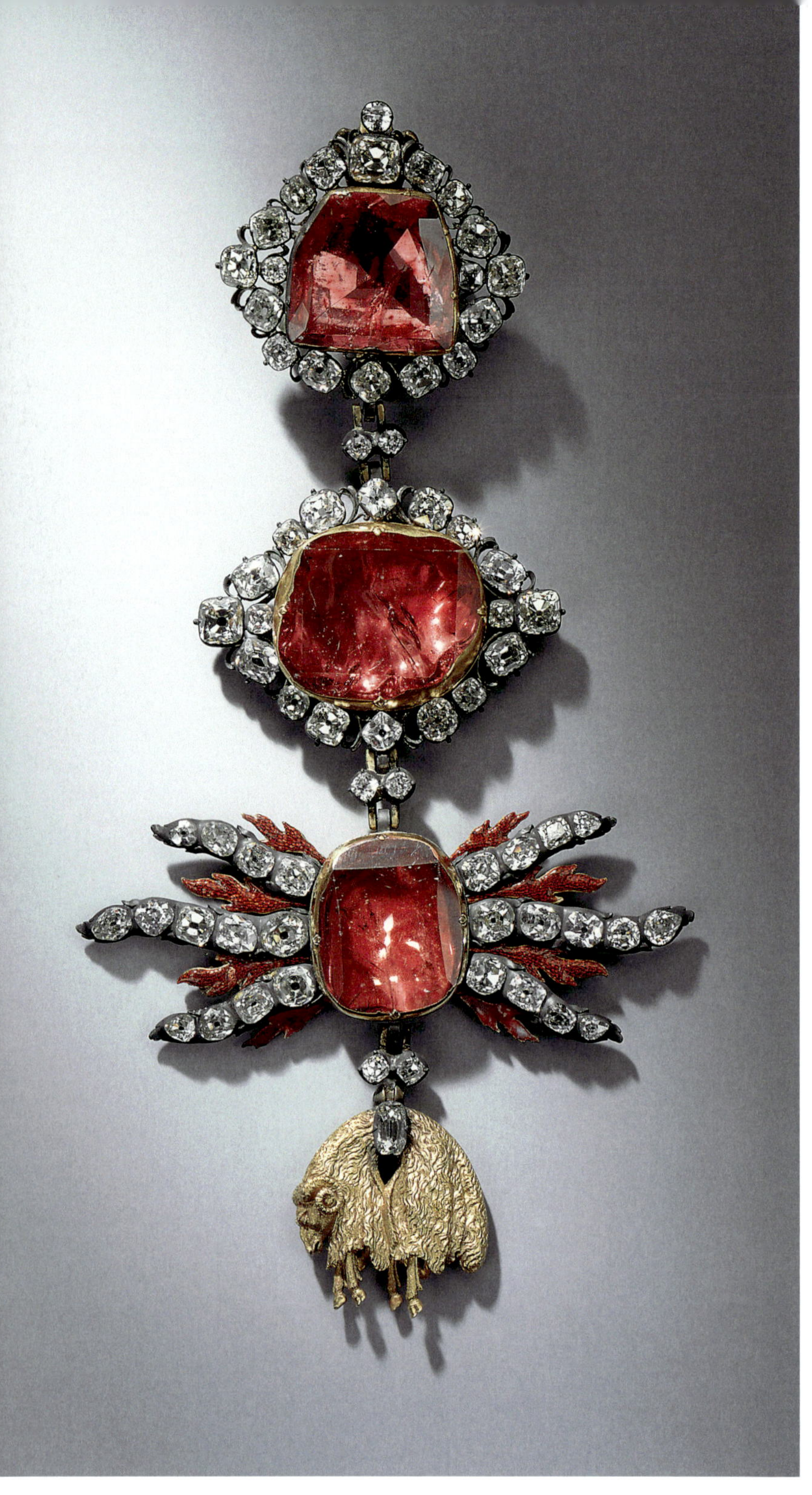

Of all Augustus the Strong's jewellery garnitures, the ruby garniture has the greatest political symbolic significance. The red colour of the rubies and spinels and the white colour of the diamonds represent the national colours of Poland. But even before he was elected King of Poland-Lithuania, Augustus owned a garniture of ruby jewellery studded with diamonds as precious ruby garnitures were extremely fashionable princely accessories in the last few decades of the 17th century.

The badge of the Golden Fleece from the ruby garniture was entered in the inventory on 29 June 1722. It is thus one of the first garnitures Augustus had had made for himself. A few weeks previously, he had officially been admitted to the highest Catholic order of knights. Badges of secular orders of knights were the most exclusive jewellery items adorning the garments of princes. The Order of the Golden Fleece was founded as ›Toison d'Or‹ by Duke Philip the Good of Burgundy in 1430 and from the early 16th century onwards it was the highest decoration of the Hapsburg dynasty which had inherited Burgundy and thus the sovereignty over the order. The insignia awarded to a knight had to be returned to the chambers of the order after his death. It consisted of a gold badge in the shape of a fleece worn around the neck on a collar. This collar consisted of alternating links in the form of whetting steel and flaming flintstone. The fleece, like the fire symbols, are a reference to the Greek myth of the Argonauts which tells the story of the capture of the famous golden fleece by a group of intrepid heroes.

After the death of the last King of Spain from the Hapsburg dynasty who held the office of the sovereign of the order, the rightful succession to the office was controversial. After the end of the Spanish War of Succession (1701 – 1713/14), the new King of Spain, a Bourbon, and the Hapsburg Emperor held the office jointly. Augustus the Strong was listed from 1697, the year he was elected King of Poland, as the second Wettin prince, after Duke George the Bearded (1531), as knight of the order. But it was only in 1722 that he was officially awarded, together with his son, the insignia at the behest of Emperor Karl VI. The Emperor granted them the unusual privilege of being knights of the Order of the Golden Fleece and at the same time sovereigns of their own Polish Order of the White Eagle. Besides they were permitted to have parade versions of the insignia made for their personal use. Thus, after 1722, a large number of badges decorated with precious stones were created, eleven of which have been preserved in the Grünes Gewölbe.

For the badge from the ruby garniture Dinglinger used three unusually large spinel rubies. They have preserved their original table cut with irregular outline which was executed in India. This triad became the ideal of a parade badge for the Order of the Golden Fleece. In order not to detract from the unusual size of the gemstones, Dinglinger refrained from using other symbols and ornamentations – apart from the inevitable flames and fleece.

DS

**Badge of the Order of the Golden Fleece
from the Ruby Garniture**

3 large spinel rubies, 70 diamonds, gold, silver, silver-gilt, enamel
Workshop of Johann Melchior Dinglinger
Dresden 1722
L. 17.9 cm, w. 9.5 cm, Inv. no. VIII 122

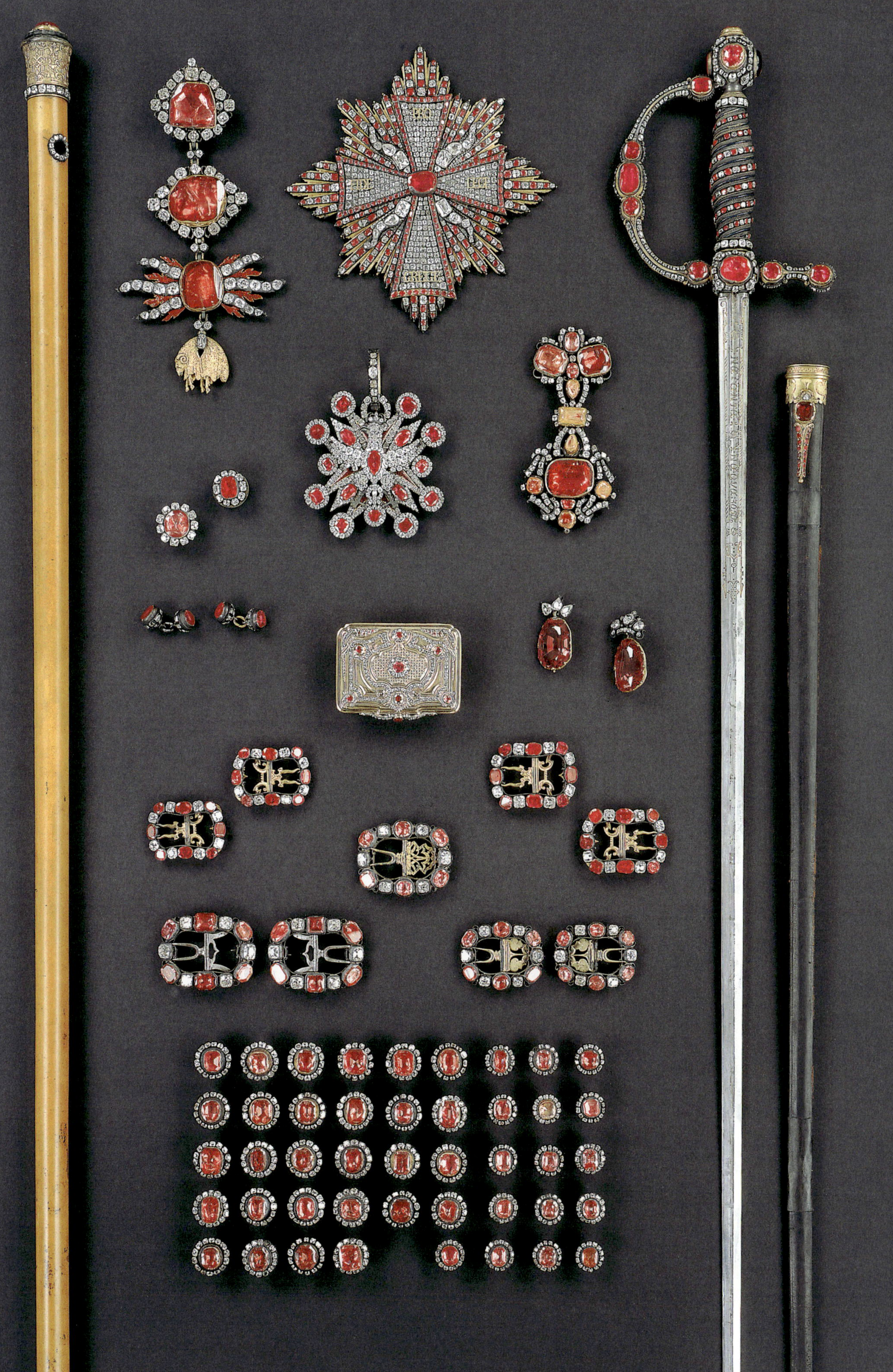

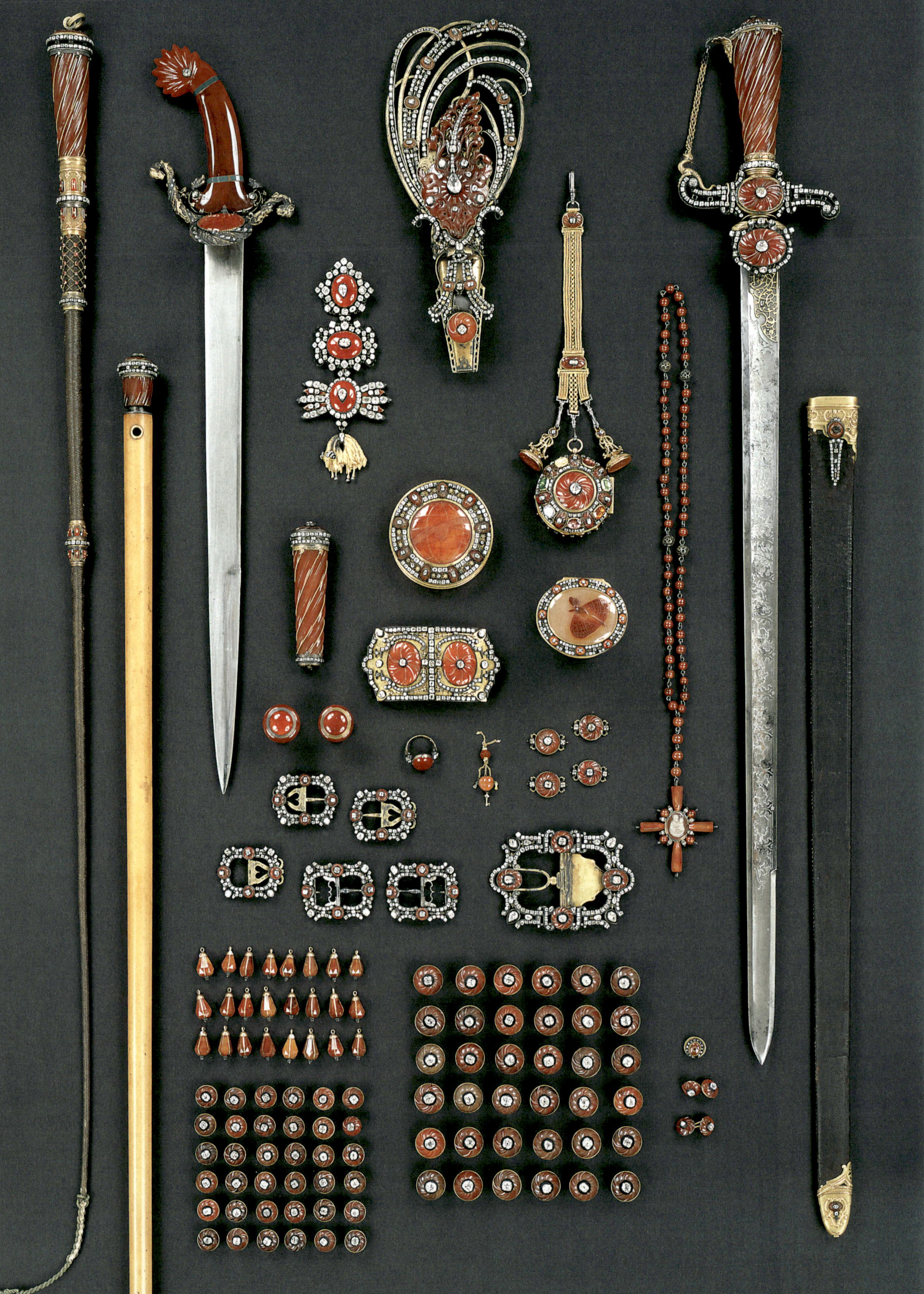

Hat Aigrette from the Carnelian Garniture

Carnelian plaque, 10 round carnelians, 1 (orig. 3)
diamond drops (ca. 3.39 ct.), 408 (orig. 418) brilliant cut diamonds, gold, silver
Johann Melchior Dinglinger
Stonecutting: Johann Christoph Hübner
Dresden, before 1719
H. 26 cm, h. of carnelian plaque 10.6 cm, Inv. no. VIII 233

Augustus the Strong acquired most parts of his carnelian garniture from the court jeweller Johann Melchior Dinglinger on the occasion of the wedding of his son to the Hapsburg Archduchess and daughter of the Emperor, Maria Josepha. Apart from the tortoiseshell garniture, which was made a short time later, this is the largest of Augustus the Strong's jewellery ensembles – in addition, it is a creative work of jeweller's art of the highest rank.

The most conspicuous element of this carnelian hunting garniture, studded with large and small diamonds is the aigrette – a type of headdress which was popular in Germany from the late Renaissance. The centre of the aigrette is dominated by a large carnelian plaque cut in relief. It has the shape of a symmetrical rose flower with naturalistically arranged stamens and small ornamental leaves at the top. The sensitive, naturalistic depiction of the rose derives its dynamism from a panicle with small leaves and buds, which emerges above the flower and bends slightly to the right. Both stonecutting and jeweller's work were made in Dresden. Johann Melchior Dinglinger probably collaborated with the stonecutter Johann Christoph Hübner and contributed the design and the jeweller's work. The asymmetrical silver-gilt feathers emerging from the sides of the carnelian rose complement the excellent stonecutting work. Slender engraved feathers alternate with broader feathers studded densely with diamonds. The plate at the bottom of the aigrette from which the crowning rose and feather arrangement emerges is decorated with the letter »A«, the monogram of Augustus II, composed of numerous diamonds. It hides the cartridge used to hold a plume of egret's feathers. A large carnelian rosette with a spiral décor is affixed below the plate and served as a button to fix the aigrette to the turned up brim of the hat. Smaller carnelian rosettes adorn the monogram and are also appliquéd to the silver feathers at the top of the aigrette. The two diamond pendants that were suspended from loops and framed the monogram of the king are no longer extant.

The aigrette crowned with its floral ornamentation and asymmetrical, waving silver feathers is a sparkling fireworks display of courtly elegance, a unique late Baroque jewellery work, and an impressive demonstration of Johann Melchior Dinglinger's unsurpassed artistic skill and ingenious sense of form.

DS

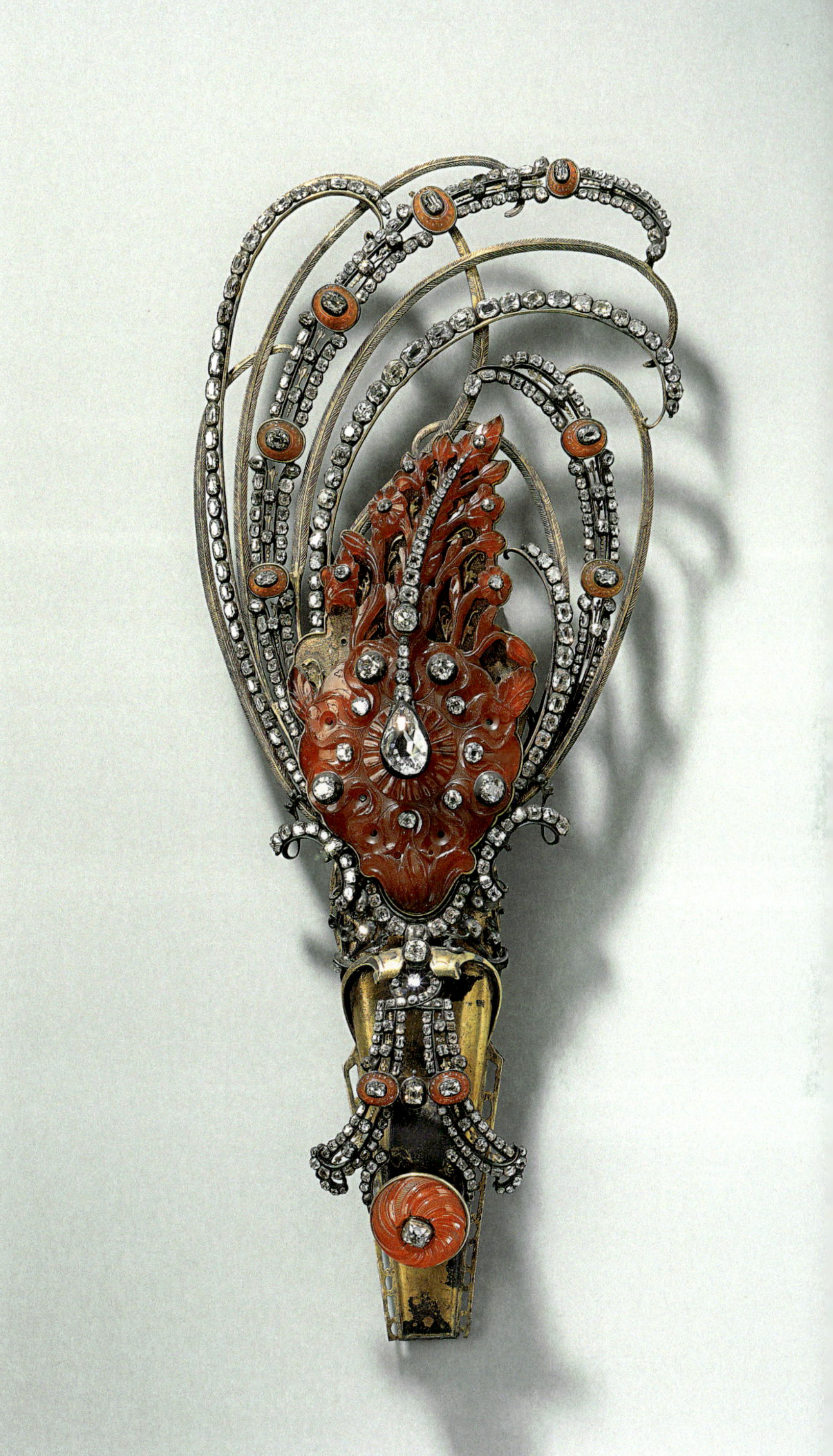

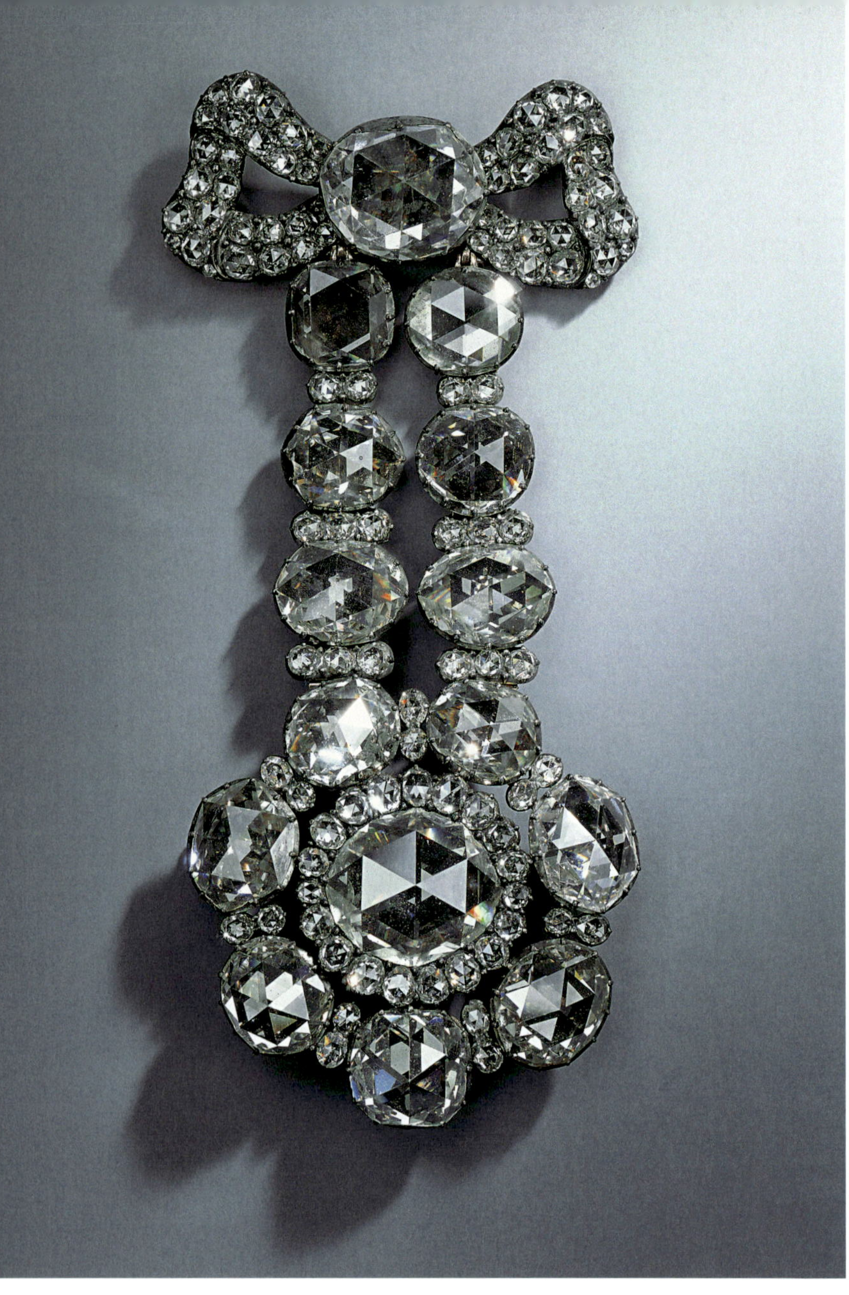

Hat Brim Ornament from the Diamond Rose Garniture

15 large and 103 small diamonds, silver, gold
Christian August and August Gotthelf Globig
Dresden, 1782 – 1789
L. 13.5 cm, w. 6.5 cm, Inv. no. VIII 10

Louis XIV, the French ›sun king‹ and passionate collector of diamonds, did not differentiate between his impressively large diamonds in rose cut and the mostly smaller, but highly sparkling ones in brilliant cut. The diamonds used for rose cut were relatively flat with a dome-shaped top formed of triangular facets that met in the centre. This cut made the diamonds appear very large, but was at the expense of the stone's brilliance which was less pronounced than in stones with the 58-facet brilliant cut.

Augustus the Strong may have been the first European king to have a complete garniture in brilliant cut and an even larger one in rose cut made for ceremonial occasions. The large diamond roses, whose sheer size suggested wealth, went out of fashion in the first few decades after 1700. Yet, the two Saxon-Polish Elector-Kings remained faithful to this impressive jewellery. Elector Friedrich Augustus III, after 1806 King Friedrich Augustus I of Saxony, had a new parade garniture manufactured between 1782 and 1789 by Christian August Globig and his son August Gotthelf using his grandfather's diamond rose jewellery which was broken up in 1749. This new garniture is still extant. Among the pieces of this ensemble is the ornament for a hat brim, which takes up the traditional French form of princely Baroque hat ornamentation.

The main button, which was sewed on to the brim of the hat, was in such a conspicuous and important position that was given a very striking design. At its centre is a 16.015-carat diamond. Although it is not the heaviest stone incorporated into the ornament, it is one of the largest. It is wreathed by an inner circle of 19 smaller diamonds and a second circle of seven large diamonds. Together, they form a magnificent rosette of select gemstones. The two bands and the second button at the top have a design resembling that of the shoulder piece of the garniture so that the epaulette and hat brim ornament correlate with each other to form a stylistic unity. At the centre of the diamond-studded bow at the top of the ornament is a very tall, 24.984 carat diamond rose. It could be affixed to the felt of the tricorn hat using a screw fastener which is no longer extant. The opulence of this hat ornament – the larger diamonds alone have a total weight of 135.5 carats – is still in the tradition of the jewellery garnitures from the first half of the 18th century. Its largest stone, the tall diamond rose, had already been used in the hat brim ornament from the diamond rose garniture of 1719. But that ornament did not meet the requirements of a fashion-conscious elector in the late 18th century. Thus, four braids were made, each almost seven centimetres long, densely studded with twelve diamond roses each. It is not quite clear how they were affixed to the tricorn, a hat fashionable at that time.

DS

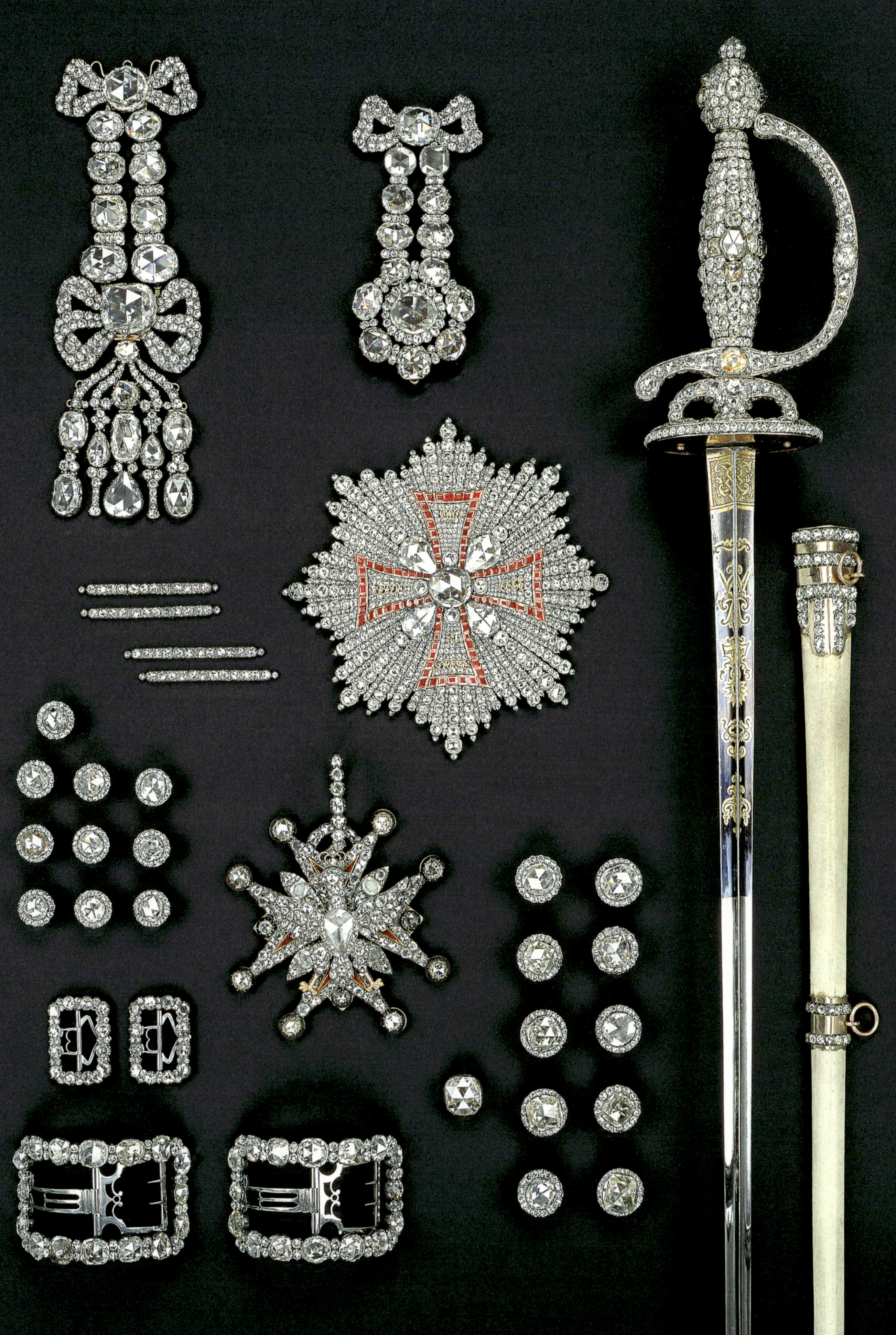

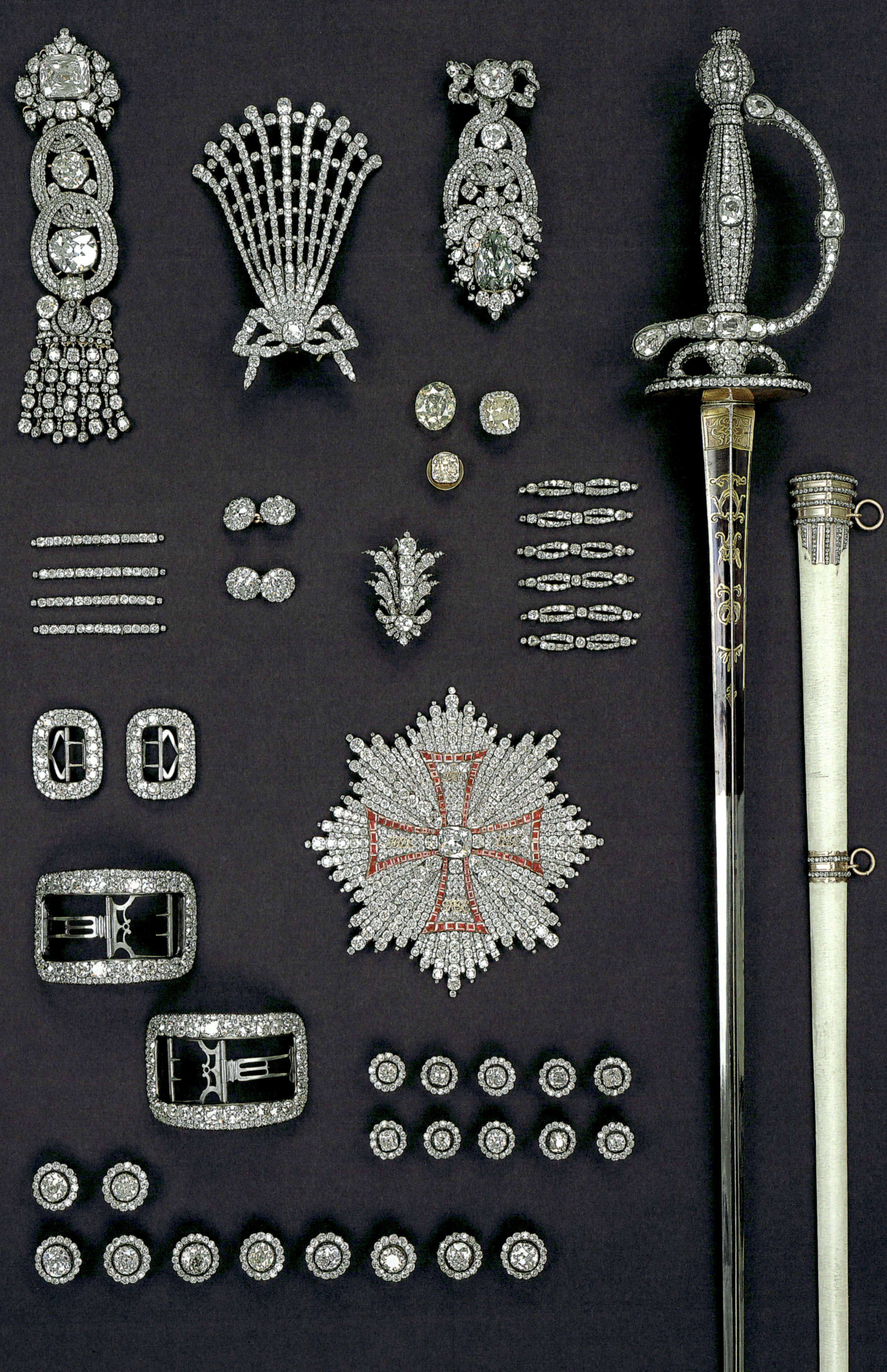

Epaulette from the Brilliant Cut Diamond Garniture

Large white diamond in brilliant cut (›Saxon White‹), 49.84 ct.,
two large diamonds in brilliant cut (39.53 and 21.01 ct.),
medium-sized and small diamonds, silver, partly gilded
Christian August Globig
Dresden, between 1782 and 1789
Parts of the epaulette by Franz Michael Diespach, Dresden/Prague 1769
and of a badge of the Order of the Golden Fleece by Jean Jacques Pallard,
Vienna/Geneva 1746 – 1749
L. 20.4 cm, Inv. no. VIII 25

The by far most precious jewellery garniture at the Grünes
Gewölbe is the diamond garniture with stones in 58 facet brilliant cut.
It was at the centre of courtly representation and, like no other garniture, was altered, improved and modernised several times. When in
1768/69 Franz Michael Diespach made a small brilliant cut diamond
garniture for Elector Friedrich Augustus III, who had just come of age,
the most important elements of the epaulette from the diamond garniture in its present form were also made. This ornamental shoulder
piece was intended as a representational complement to the hat brim
ornament with the ›Dresdner Grüne‹ diamond. It was worn on the
shoulder with the lower parts hanging down loosely. The two bows,
densely studded with small diamonds, which resemble the bows of the
hat ornament, are from the epaulette. Almost twenty years later, the
epaulette from the diamond garniture was given its present form.
Christian August Globig added the ›Sächsische Weisse‹ (Saxon White),
with 49.84 carats the largest diamond in brilliant cut in the possession
of the Wettin dynasty. Like no other piece of jewellery from the Saxon
garnitures, this epaulette documents the passion for particularly large
and beautiful gemstones that held three generation of rulers in thrall.

 The ›Saxon White‹ was acquired by Augustus the Strong on 1 February 1728 for 200,000 thalers, or two tons of gold, from the Hamburg
jeweller Moses Abraham. Together with this crown diamond of the first
Elector-King, he also acquired a diamond of 19.28 carats for 20,000
thalers. Today, it adorns the upper part of the hat ornament with the
›Dresdner Grüne‹. In addition, Augustus paid 120,000 and 162,000
thalers respectively for two other, not identified, diamonds supplied in
1726 by Moses Meyer Comp. in Amsterdam. Of the two other large,
round diamonds in the epaulette, only the price of the larger 39.53-
carat stone is known. It was bought in Vienna in 1742 for 80,000
thalers. For the contemporaries of Friedrich Augustus III, the value of
the epaulette from the diamond garniture was stupendous. The diamonds incorporated in the epaulette cost more than all the cabinet
pieces of Johann Melchior Dinglinger taken together.

DS

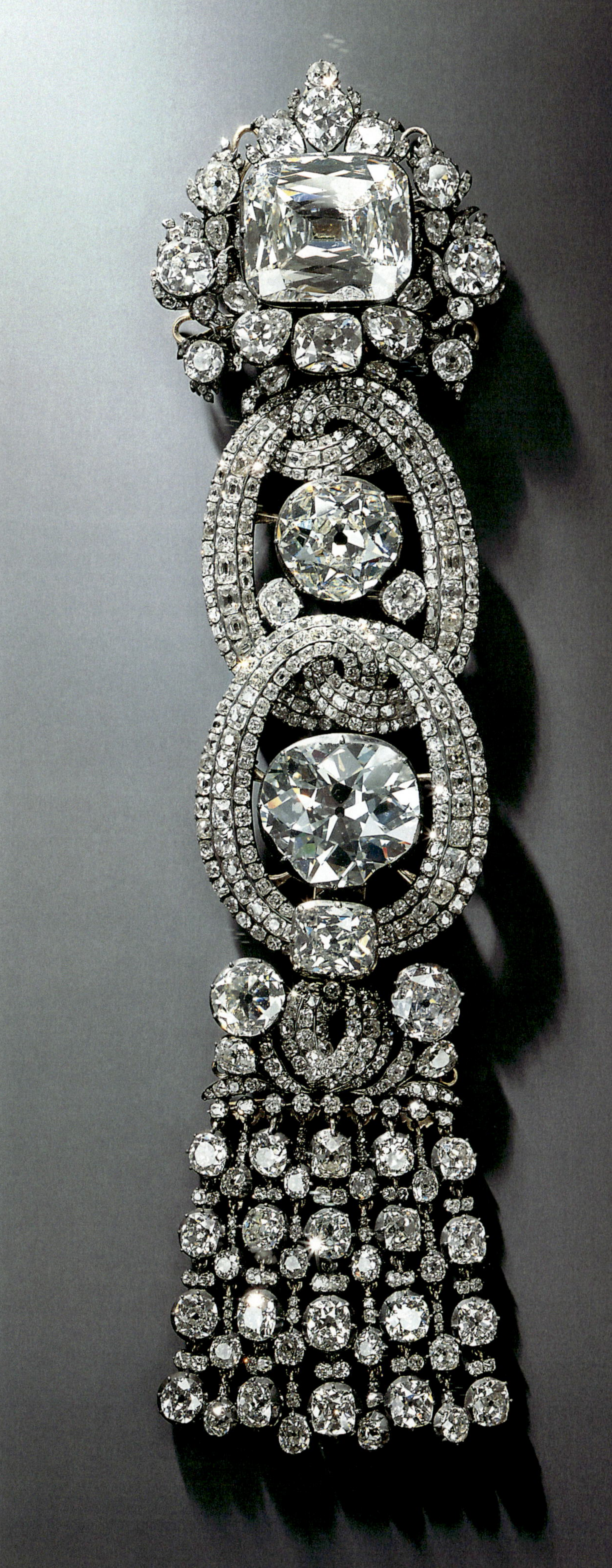

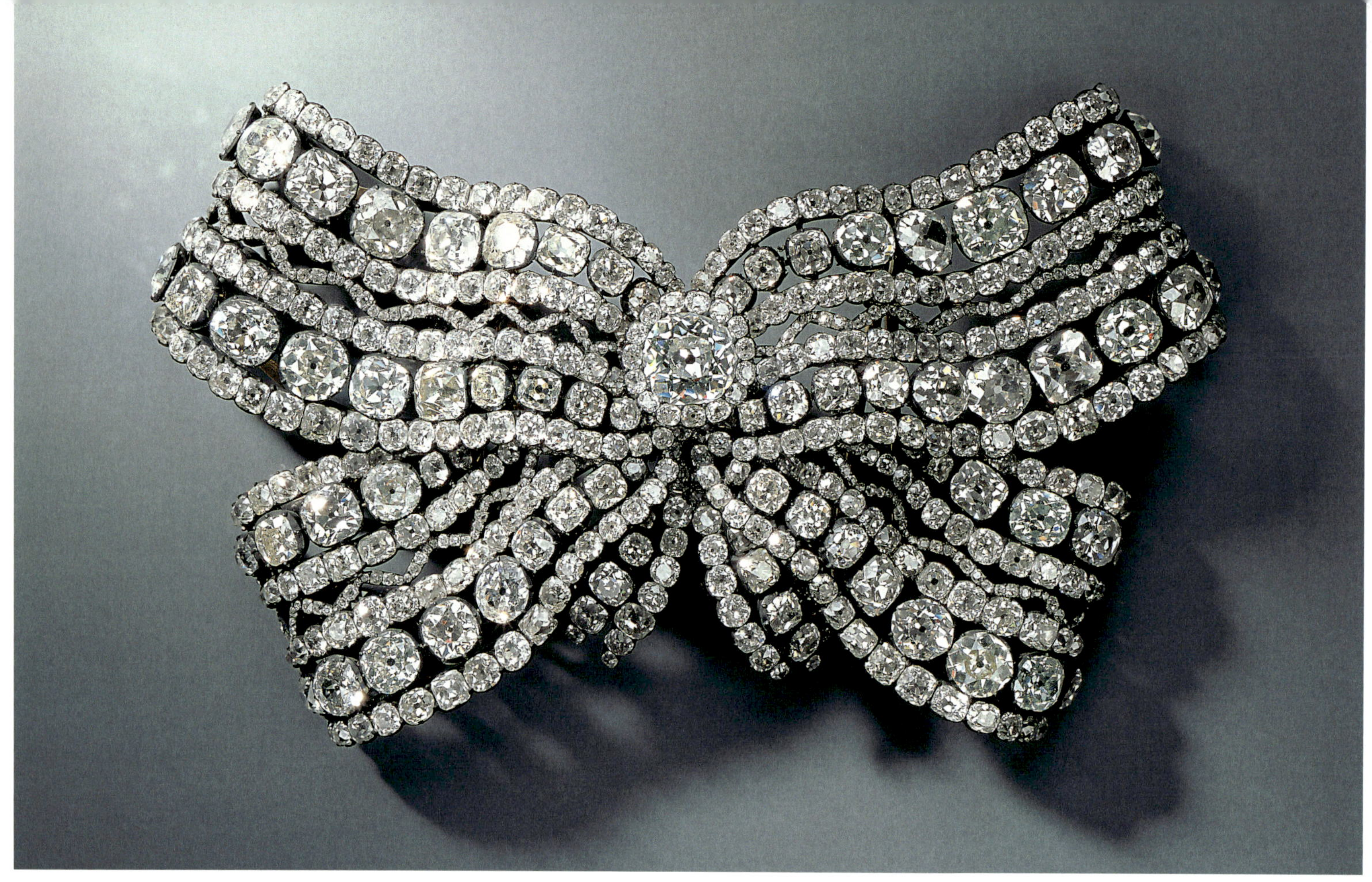

Large Bow-shaped Brooch from the Queens' Jewellery

Brilliant cut diamonds, silver, gold
Christian August Globig
Dresden 1782
H. 12.5 cm, w. 21.4 cm, Inv. no. VIII 36

The by far largest part of the pieces of jewellery displayed in the Jewel Room is ceremonial jewellery for the male members of the Saxon dynasty in the 18th century, although their consorts were also very extravagant in their jewellery, which was their private property and to be used as they wished. It was only around the middle of the 18th century that a piece of jewellery for a woman, the diamond collar of Queen Maria Josepha, was recorded in the state treasury of the Grünes Gewölbe. The collar has been preserved, with alterations, in the large diamond collar from the ensemble of diamond and pearl jewellery of the queens. Around the year 1820, the items of jewellery manufactured after that time were combined in a jewellery garniture. The most splendid and precious pieces from the garniture were created – or modified in their present form – between 1782 and 1824 for Amalie Auguste, the first Saxon Queen. Besides the above-mentioned collar with its 38 large

diamonds, the garniture comprises two ear pendants, two small brooches, three aigrettes in the shape of a sun, a rising sun and a crescent moon, and the large brooch in the shape of a bow. These ornamental bows were worn below the neck and were a popular item of court jewellery for women until around 1800. In 1782 Elector Friedrich Augustus III had this splendid bow with its unusually rich diamond decoration made for his consort Amalie Auguste. The gift, probably on the occasion of the birth of their first child, was assigned to the official ceremonial jewellery of the Wettin dynasty and thus became part of the collection of the Grünes Gewölbe. It was manufactured using diamonds from 27 coat buttons, 12 waistcoat buttons and other pieces of jewellery from the older diamond garniture.

The bow is shaped like a gathered ribbon with its ends hanging down. At the centre of this wide piece of jewellery is the shirt button from the diamond garniture preserved in its original box mount. The brooch is studded with 51 large and 611 medium-sized to small diamonds. The total weight of the diamonds used is c. 614 carats. The weight of the brooch, including the mount, is 556 grams, which will have made this piece of jewellery rather uncomfortable to wear. Yet, it was still worn on the occasion of some court ceremonies by Queen Carola of Saxony in the 1870s and 80s.

DS

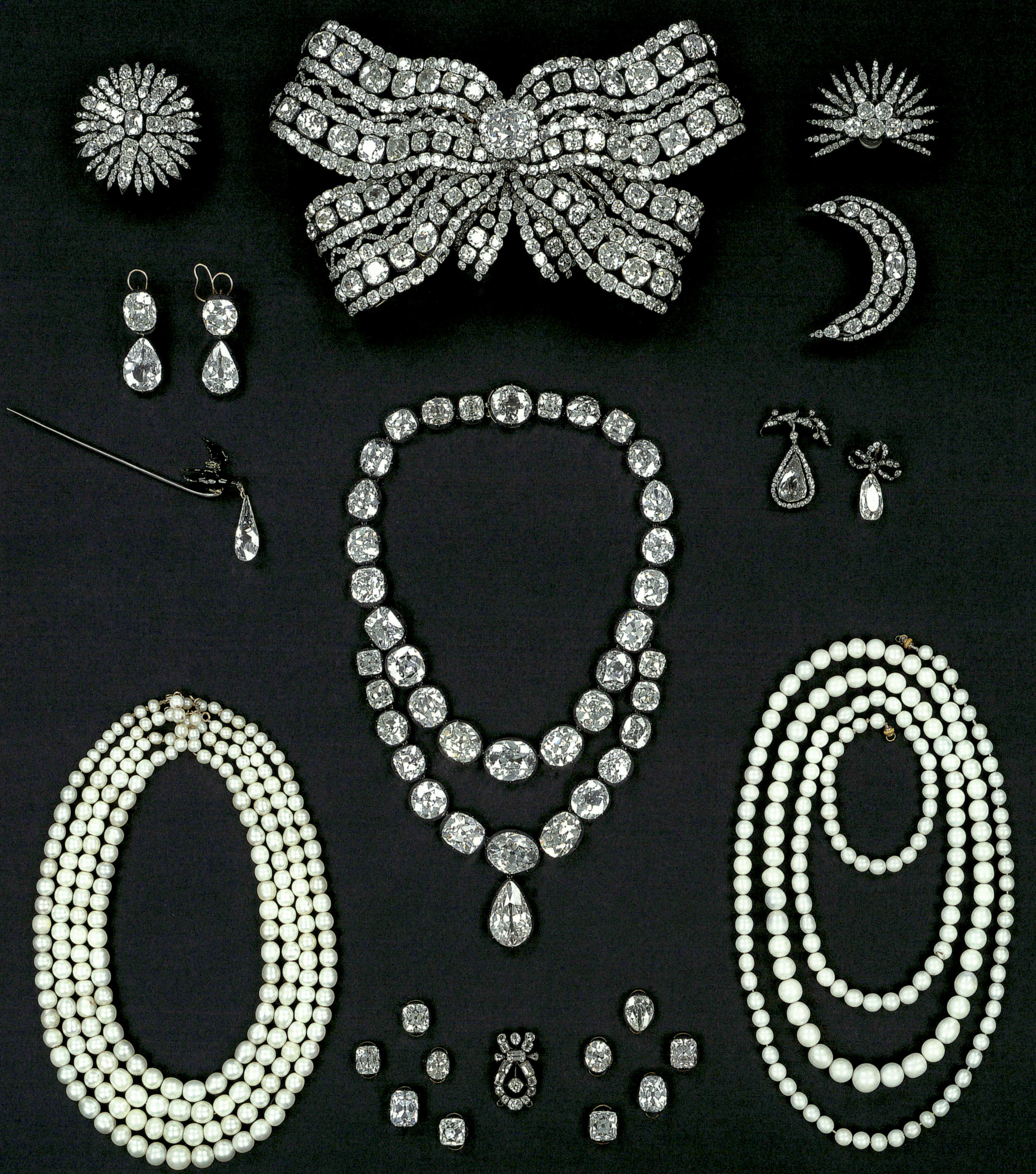

Room of Bronzes

In the context of the structure of the Baroque collection conceived by Augustus the Strong the Room of Bronzes served visitors in the 18th century both as an entrance and as an exit. The »Kabinett«-like room with an area of roughly 40 square metres was presumably intended to form a contrast to the display rooms both in size and in the growing splendour of their exhibits. 103 bronze statuettes, some of which were of considerable size, and two English long-case clocks with chimes stood against a festive but unobtrusive backdrop of oak profiled panelling. Most of them were small copies of famous sculptures from Antiquity or well-known marble sculptures of French courtly art under Louis XIV, which were displayed on consoles arranged one above the other and on the shelf running round the room, as in the Ivory Room. Ten larger bronze groups stood on boulle pediments, some of which had been bought with the sculptures in Paris. The two large bronze statuettes, which portrayed Augustus the Strong on horseback, attracted special attention. One was bought with a superb pediment in Paris and can be attributed to the workshop of François Girardon. The other is by Jean-Joseph Vinache who was active in Dresden and shows the type of equestrian statue that the Elector-King wished to erect, portraying him as a larger-than-life ›Golden Horseman‹. Vinache's portrayal of Augustus the Strong on a rearing horse is now in the New Grünes Gewölbe.

Starting from two historic photographs and technical surveys of the building the Room of Bronzes that was burnt out in February 1945 in bomb raids was faithfully reconstructed after the original. It was restored to its original dimensions, which it had lost in Jean Louis Sponsel's extension of the Grünes Gewölbe in 1913/14. At that time, like the Ivory Room, its original area had been extended to the south and at the same time the external wooden vaulted arches were removed to let in more light. The copper medallions with the portraits of Augustus the Strong, his son, Prince Friedrich August and his wife Maria Josepha and the portraits of the Brandenburg-Prussian royal couple, King Friedrich Wilhelm I and Queen Sophia Dorothea who made a state visit to Dresden in 1729, which are also part of the exhibits in the room, were preserved as a result of wartime safety measures. Of the precious boulle pediments only four returned to Dresden after the war. The missing three have been reconstructed.

The artistic magnificence, which Augustus the Strong assembled in the Room of Bronzes, can now be experienced without any barriers. Almost all the statuettes mentioned in the bronze inventory of 1733 have been preserved. Only a few were sold or transferred to the Sculpture Collection. Nine masterpieces of Renaissance art which at the time of Augustus the Strong made the well-stocked dado shelf even fuller are now to be seen in the Room of Renaissance Bronzes. The large white eagle in wood, which Augustus the Strong hung between the chandeliers as a symbol of his royal power, has been lost.

DS

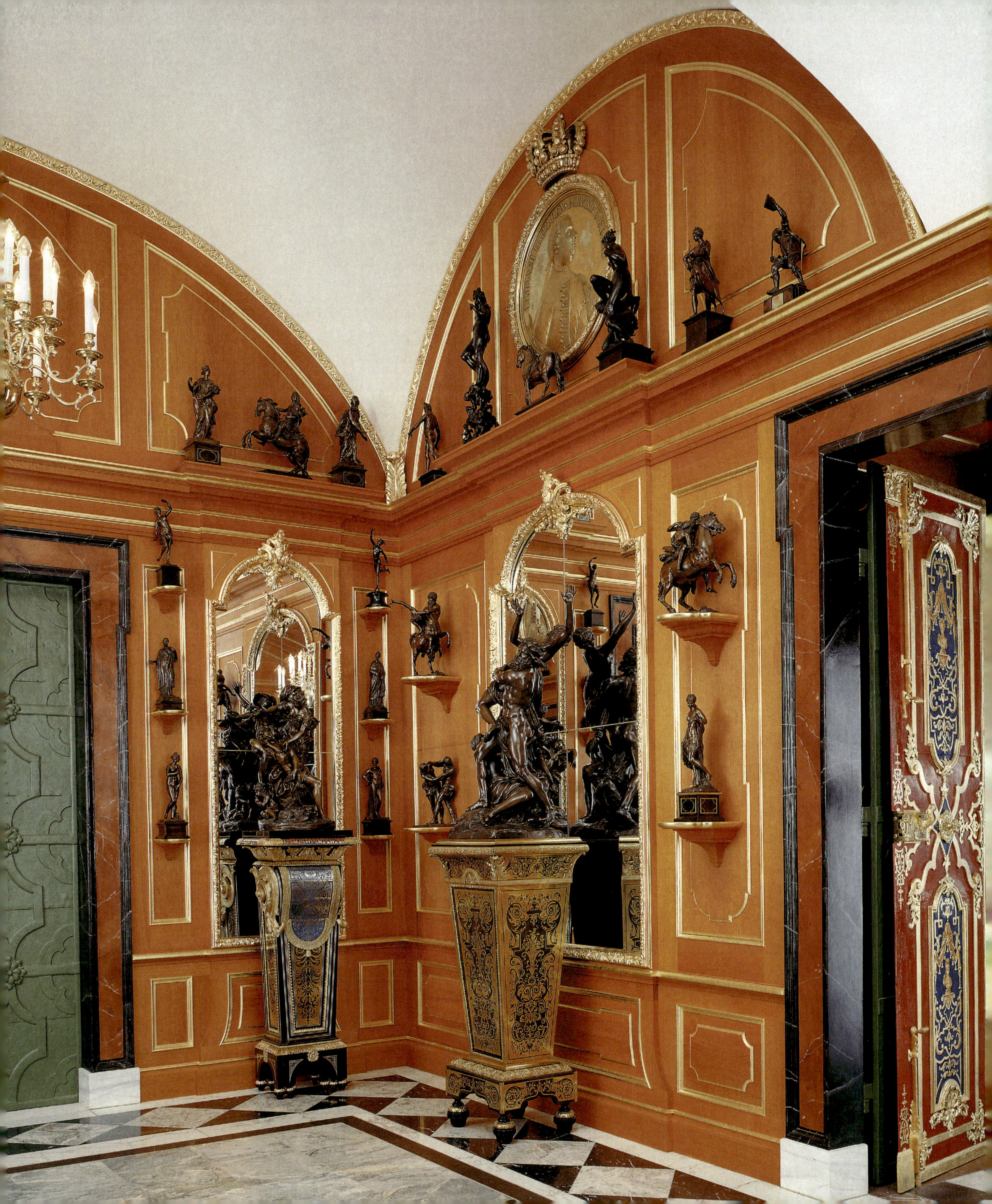

Selene and Endymion

Bronze
Model: Cornelis van Cleve
France, c. 1700
H. 76 cm, Inv. no. IX 24

This group of figures representing Selene and Endymion came into the possession of Augustus the Strong in 1715 as part of the convolute bought in Paris. It was one of the largest bronzes of this convolute and was acquired for 690 Saxon thalers. It was displayed on a magnificent pedestal by Boulle in the Room of Bronzes as the pendant of the similarly proportioned group with Hercules and Antaeus.

The motif relates to a story from classical mythology, which was particularly popular during the Baroque period. Endymion, a shepherd or hunter of great beauty, was granted the wish of eternal youth and eternal sleep. The moon goddess Selene, enchanted by his beauty, visited the youth every night in his cave near Mount Lathmos in Caria to kiss him clandestinely.

The dynamism of this helical group is the result of the contrast between Endymion resting on a rock and the moon goddess who approaches from above, her garments billowing. With a gentle hand, Selene lifts the cloth covering the sleeping youth to contemplate his face. The scene takes place in complete silence as even the sheepdog lying at its master's feet is not disturbed. The viewer takes on the role of a hidden observer witnessing an intimate scene full of tenderness and grace. The figure of Cupid, sitting on the back of the rock, holds his index finger to his lips in a gesture admonishing the viewer to silence.

Cornelis van Cleve, an artist of Flemish extraction, was an extremely productive sculptor who worked for the church and the court at Versailles and was elected a member of the French Academy in 1681. In 1704 he exhibited ›Selene and Endymion‹ on the occasion of the ›Salon‹ in Paris. He created a complex group of figures full of sensual appeal. The figure of the sleeping Endymion was undoubtedly inspired by the ›Barbarinian Faun‹ (Munich, Glyptothek), a Hellenistic marble sculpture which became one of the most popular classical works after its discovery in the first half of the 17th century.

UW

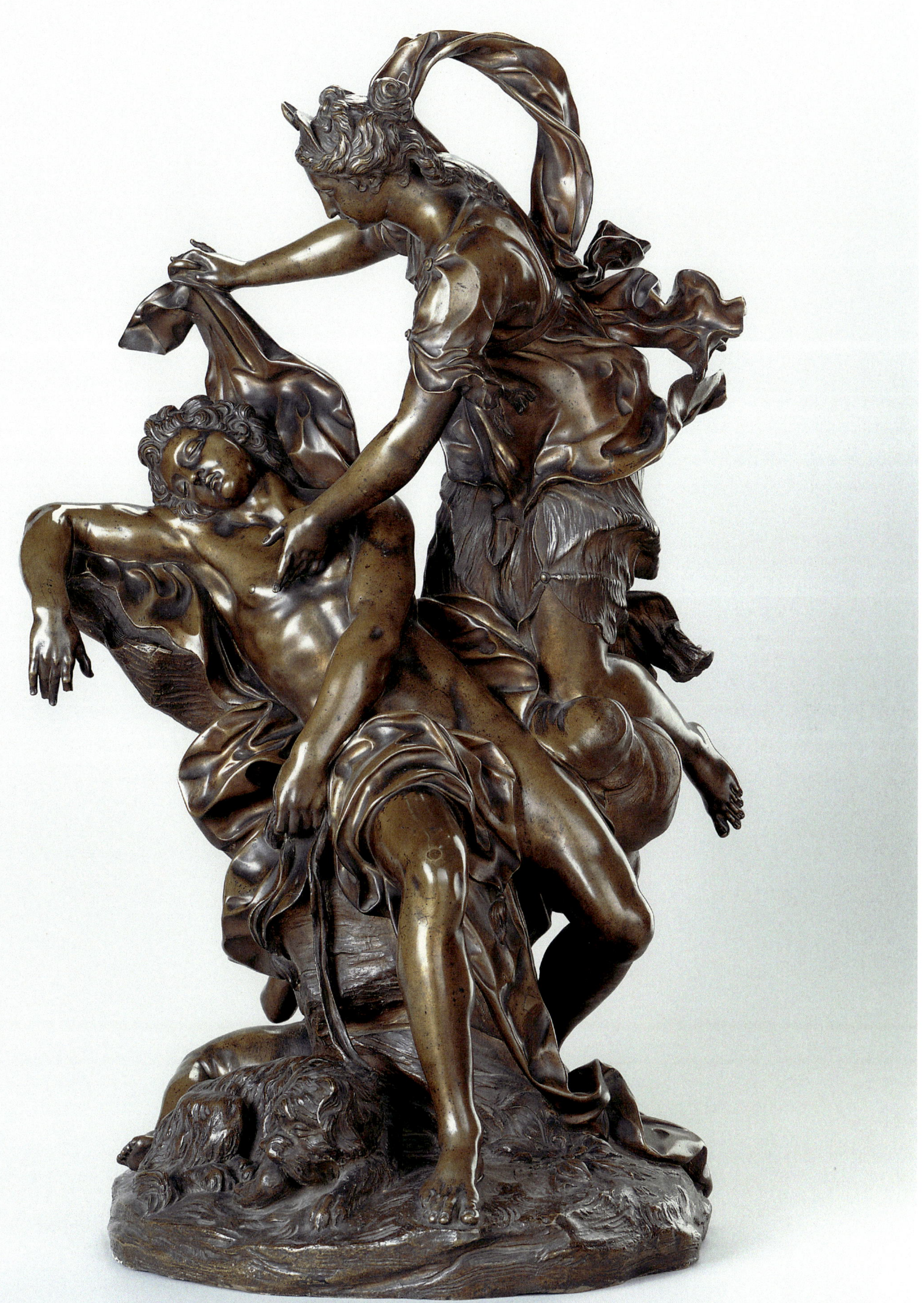

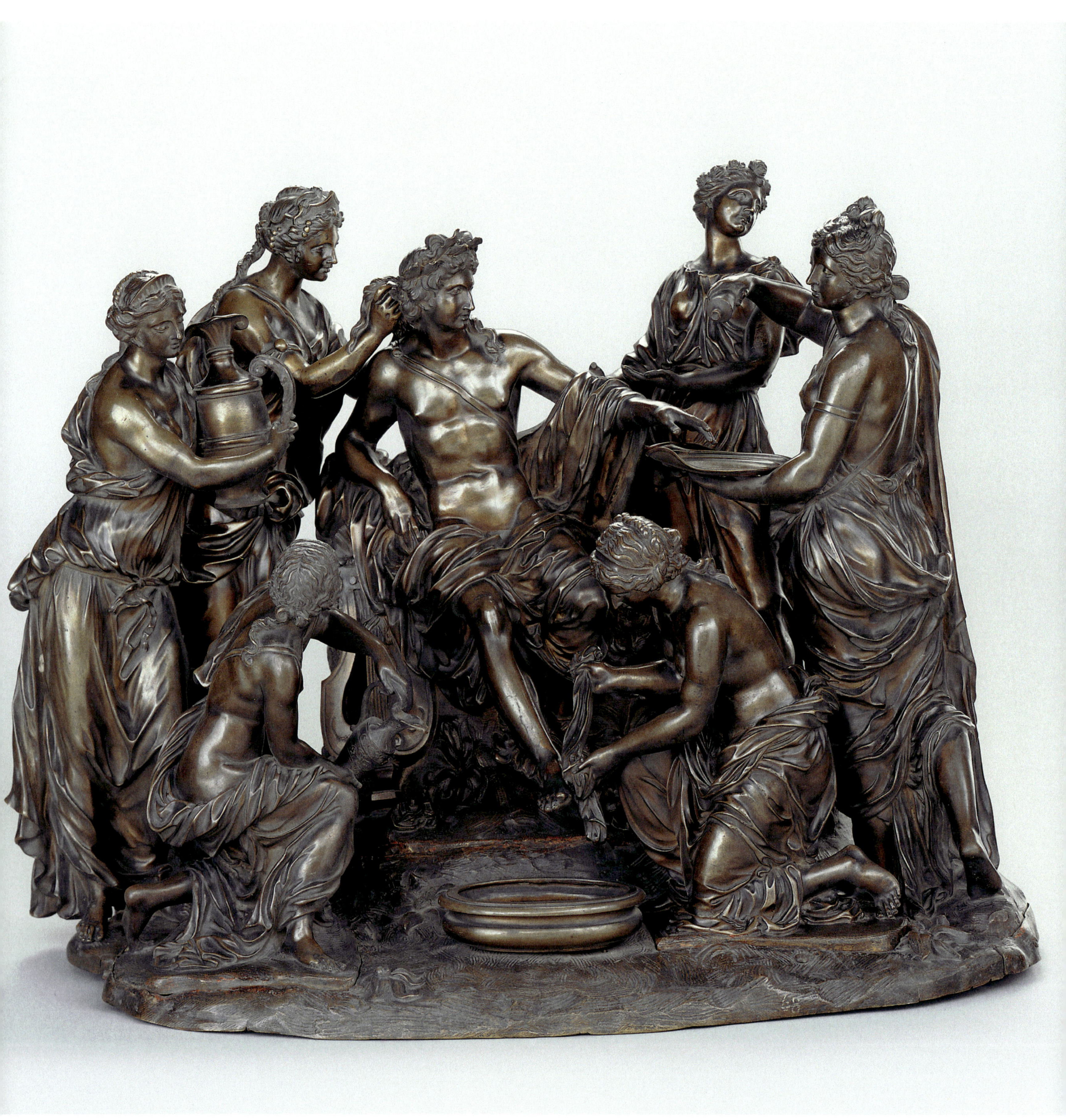

Apollo Bathing

Bronze
After the marble group by François Girardon
and Thomas Regnaudin
Design: Charles LeBrun
France, before 1715
H. 59.5 cm, w. 78 cm, d. 53 cm, Inv. no. IX 23

This bronze group weighing more than 70 kilograms is among the best-known acquisitions by Raymond Leplat on behalf of Augustus the Strong. It was bought in 1715 and was the second convolute – after the large-scale acquisition in 1699 – that the art agent managed to secure for Augustus. It comprised 38 small bronzes for the decoration of the royal apartments. A list which has been preserved records that the Saxon-Polish Elector-King paid 1,650 Saxon thalers for the ›Bathing Apollo‹. The price included a pedestal sumptuously decorated with tortoiseshell, brass and bronze-gilt from the workshop of the famous ébéniste André Charles Boulle in Paris. ›Apollo Bathing‹ was, after the equestrian statue of Augustus the Strong, the second most expensive bronze of this remarkable convolute.

This bronze group is a copy of a marble sculpture – on a reduced scale – by François Girardon and Thomas Regnaudin after designs by Charles LeBrun. The group, created between 1666 and 1675, was originally intended for the Thetis grotto – a folly embellished with shells and stalactites in the park of Versailles – where it was placed in the central conch in a set of three. It was flanked by two sun horses on either side, which were watered by Tritons. These figures were created by Marsy and Gilles Guérin. The figure of a river god was placed in the lunette above the group. The grotto symbolizes the palace of the sea goddess Thetis beneath the water where Apollo, the sun god, was wont to rest from his day's work. Thetis, recognisable by her diadem, washes her guest's hair and is thus very close to him. Apollo was associated with Louis XIV of France who referred to himself as ›roi soleil‹ (sun king). Seen in this context, the group may have symbolized rest after the exhausting task of reigning.

The ›Thetis grotto‹ was demolished in 1684, and it is only thanks to an engraving by J. Lepautre from 1676 that we know what it originally looked like. The reduced-scale bronze version of ›Apollo Bathing‹ at the Grünes Gewölbe is the only sculpture showing the original composition of the marble group, which in the course of its history has often been rearranged.

UW

Bacchus

Bronze
After Louis Garnier
France, model and cast before 1699
H. 37 cm, Inv. no. IX 38

Amphitrite

Bronze
After Michel Anguier
France, model 1652, cast before 1699
H. 37 cm, Inv. no. IX 62

In 1699, Baron Raymond Leplat, who was active as an agent in Paris for Augustus the Strong, successfully acquired his first batch of works of art. A convolute consisting of furniture, Chinese porcelain and small bronzes were taken to Warsaw via Frankfurt, Leipzig and Wroclaw. The objects were to be part of the magnificent furnishing and decoration of the royal palace. However, as early as 1702 some of the items, among them 44 bronze figures were sent to Dresden, presumably in response to the increasingly critical situation in Warsaw as a result of the Nordic War, which had been raging since 1700.

Leplat's list of acquisitions from 1699 records the two bronzes illustrated here as »Bacchus et Amphitrite antique«, despite the fact that they are French works from the second half of the 17th century. Yet, Louis Garnier and Michel Anguier had indeed been directly inspired by classical models. The beautiful sea nymph is Amphitrite, Poseidon's consort. She is accompanied by a dolphin swimming at her feet. When she fled the sea god's amorous pursuits, he sent the dolphin after her.

The animal managed to find her and get her to marry Poseidon. For Anguier, the bronze figure had an additional meaning. It was part of a series of seven deities each representing a different emotional state. Anguier emphasised the statue's »beautiful, elegant proportions« and characterized it as »fresh, exquisite, clear and transparent« – qualities that he associated with »serenity«.

Although the figure of Bacchus was originally not created as a counterpart to Amphitrite, it does form a perfectly matching pendant. The slightly inclined head of the god of wine with its wreath of grapes and vine leaves, the position of his arms and his elegantly casual counter-posture can be seen as a response to the beautiful nymph. The two bronze figures, which are roughly the same size, are therefore recorded in two further instances as matching pieces. Augustus the Strong bought several figures or groups of figures that relate to each other and that were particularly suitable for display on the console walls with their baroque symmetry.

UW

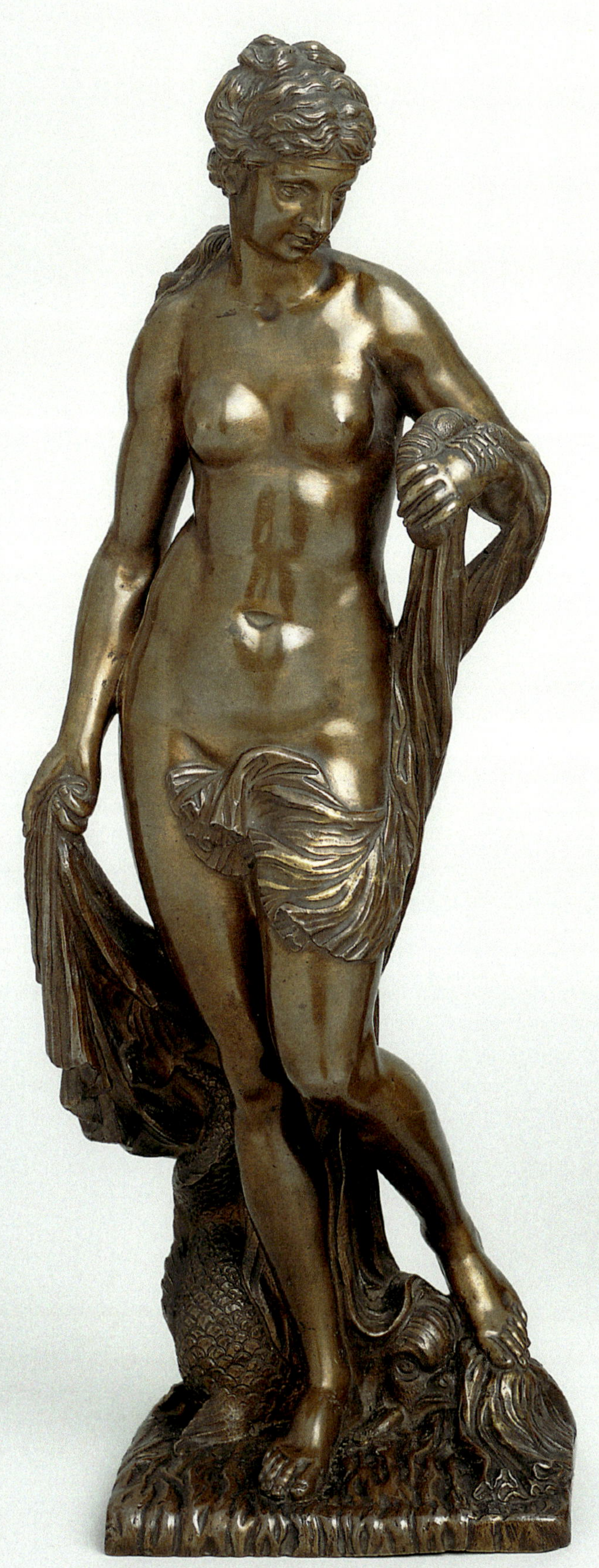
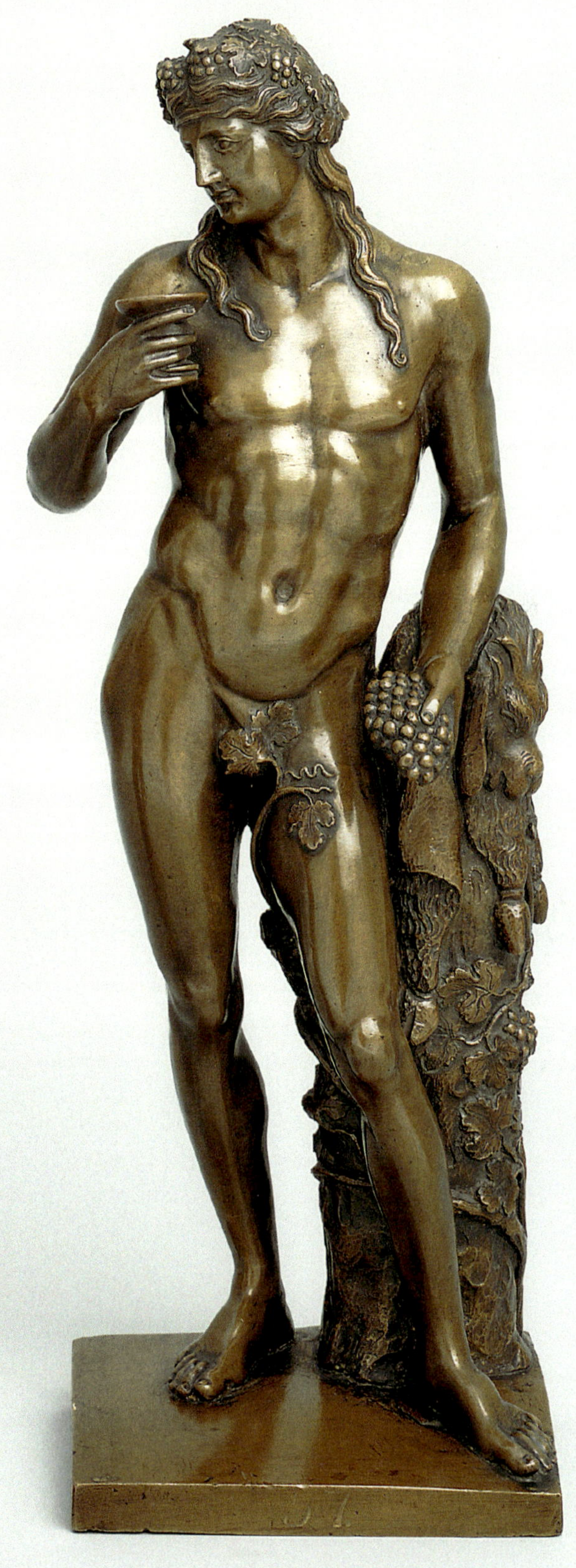

Equestrian Statue of Augustus the Strong

Bronze, pedestal: wood with mirror glass, marble, bronze-gilt, enamel
Circle of François Girardon
Paris, before 1715
Statuette: h. 105 cm, pedestal: h. 260 cm, Inv. no. IX 67

This monumental bronze figure represents Augustus the Strong as a Roman emperor in a majestic pose on a striding horse. The work, commissioned by Raymond Leplat in Paris, cost 5,300 thalers and was thus the most expensive item of the convolute acquired in 1715. It was also the most prominent work, intended as a central monument for a large room (»pour mettre dans le millieux d'un salon«). Years later, it was transferred to the Grünes Gewölbe where it constitutes a magnificent highlight, along with another equestrian statue of Augustus the Strong which was made in Dresden after a model by Jean-Joseph Vinache. The bronze statue illustrates in an impressive way to what extent Augustus the Strong was influenced by the court of the ›roi soleil‹ in his self-presentation as an absolutist monarch. It is closely modelled on the six-metre high monumental equestrian statue of Louis XIV by François Girardon. This colossal statue was unveiled in Place Louis-le-Grand (now: Place Vendôme), Paris, in a festive ceremony on 13 August 1699. In 1792, during the French Revolution, it was destroyed, but numerous bronze versions on a reduced scale (e.g. Lou-vre, Paris, Windsor Castle and Hermitage, St Petersburg) as well as a great number of graphic reproductions have made this monument famous far beyond France.

Augustus the Strong had himself represented as a victorious commander and peacemaker with an imperious gesture of his right hand and a laurel wreath upon his head. The representational pedestal contributes to this glorious image of the Saxon-Polish Elector-King. Two bronze plaques in relief, originally affixed to the long side of the plinth, show Augustus the Strong receiving ambassadors in Warsaw, and a scene from the victorious battle near Kalisz in which the Polish army delivered a devastating blow to the Swedes on 29 October 1706. Both plaques, together with the original plinth, were destroyed by fire in 1945. Only the four figures of slaves, the two coats of arms and four brackets in bronze for the marble plinth have been preserved. They were incorporated into the reconstructed pedestal in 1986/87 so that the viewer can form an idea of the original appearance of the ensemble.

UW

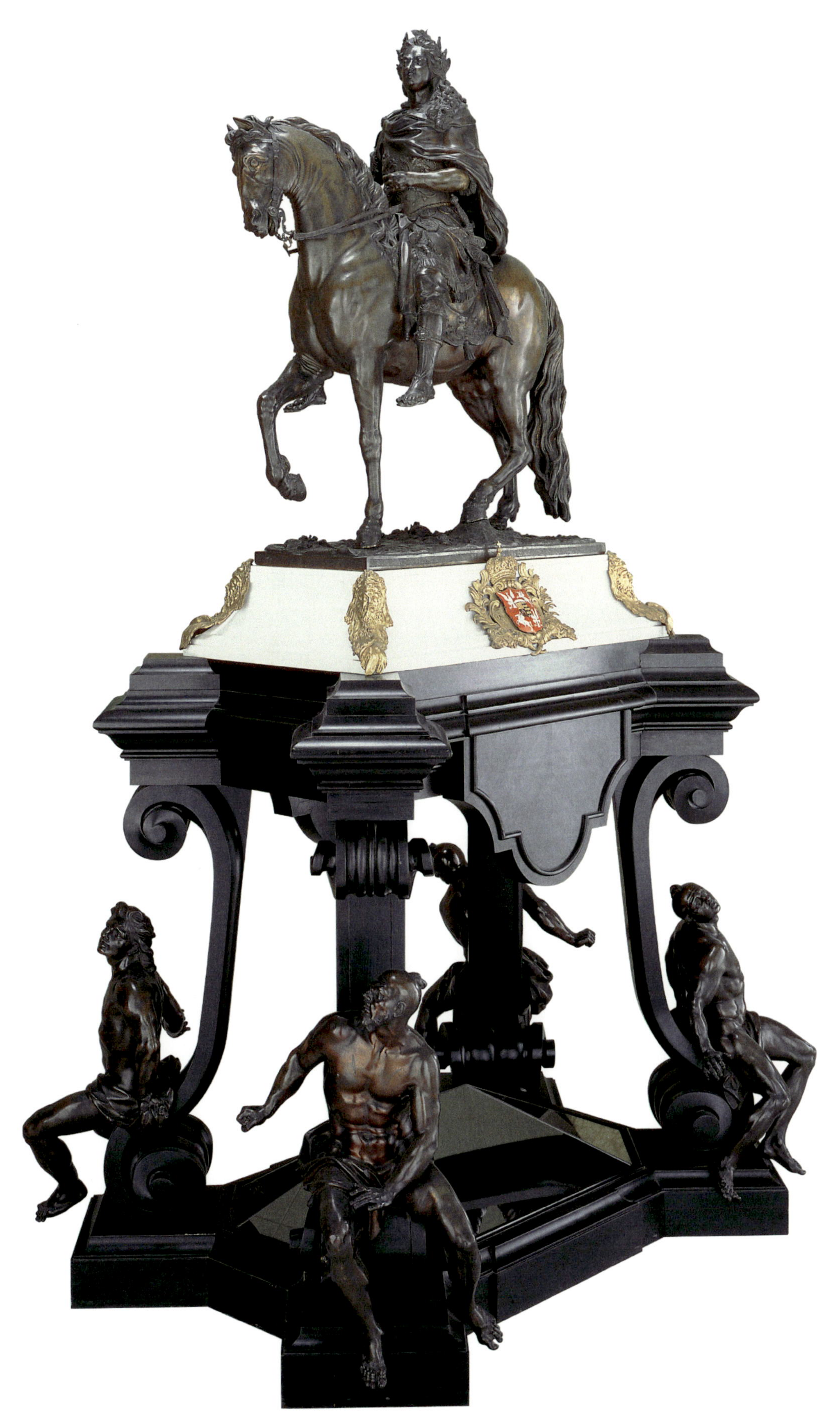

Room of Renaissance Bronzes

Like the Room of Bronzes the present Room of Renaissance Bronzes was one of the suite of smaller rooms in which the administrative office of the »Geheimes Kabinett« was housed until 1727. This important institution of government was moved at the behest of Augustus the Strong. The new room, which was one window section wide, thenceforth served as a foyer in which visitors could be received by the duty inspector before the tour. Here, as the travel writer Georg Keyssler describes in 1730 »[…] den Fremden die Schuhe genau abgekehret, damit destoweniger Staub hineingetragen werde […]« (the visitors' shoes were brushed clean so that they brought in less dust), and in this room noblemen deposited their swords. Today, the erstwhile entrance has become the exit. Like the adjacent Amber Cabinet to the west the Room of Renaissance Bronzes serves at the same time as a bridge between the modern exhibition of the collection of the Grünes Gewölbe and the sequence of rooms to be experienced emotionally as a Baroque »Gesamtkunstwerk«, through which the visitor has just passed.

Nine important bronzes from the decades around 1600 are presented against an architecturally more restrained backdrop. Among them are works by Giambologna and his workshop and by Adriaen de Vries, which are among the outstanding achievements of mannerist art in Europe. Standing free in the room without obtrusive glass panels they can be experienced as the artist wished to present them to the collectors of his time. In this way the Room of Renaissance Bronzes adumbrates the display form, which awaits the visitor in the Vorgewölbe and in the New Grünes Gewölbe.

DS

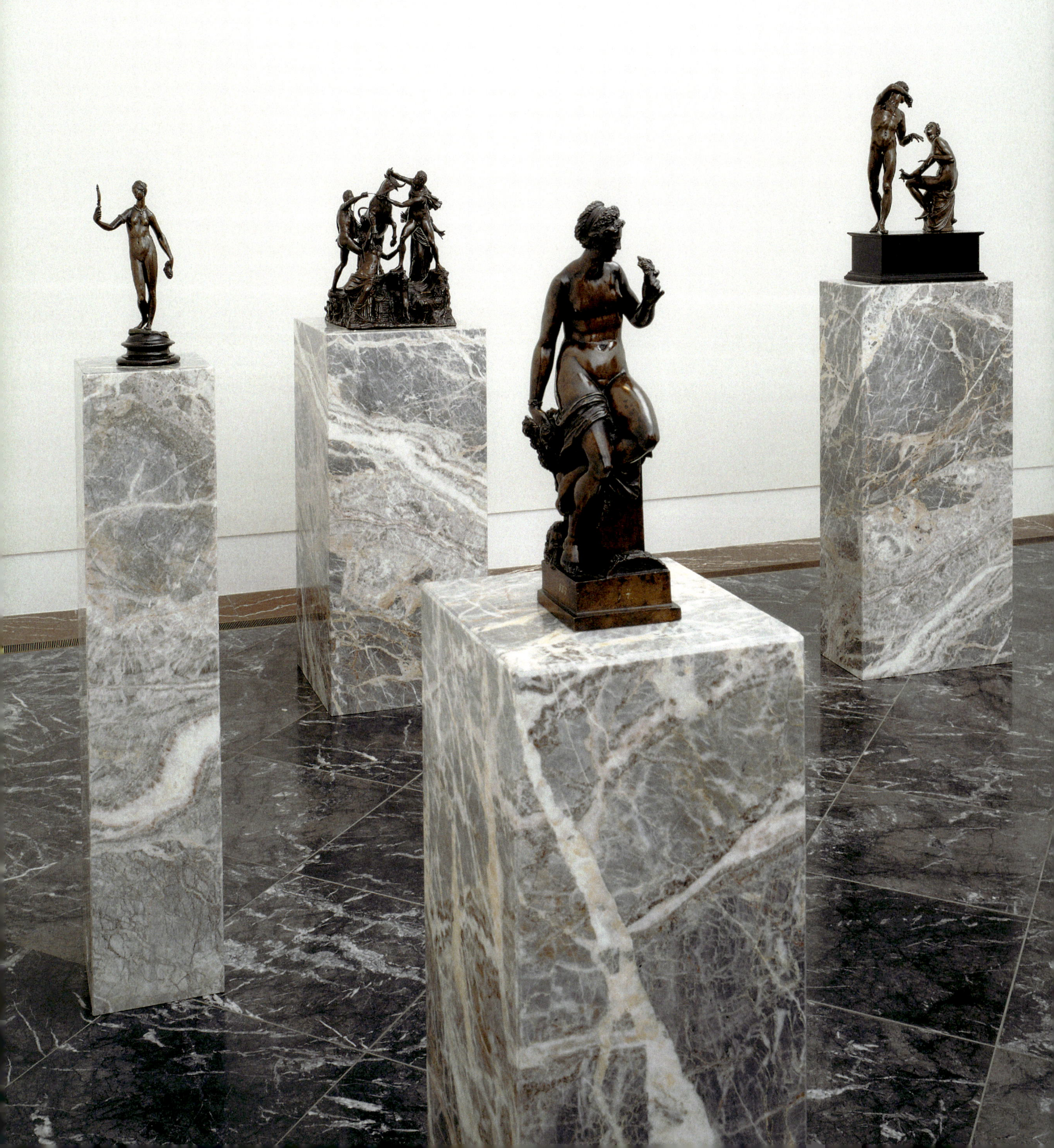

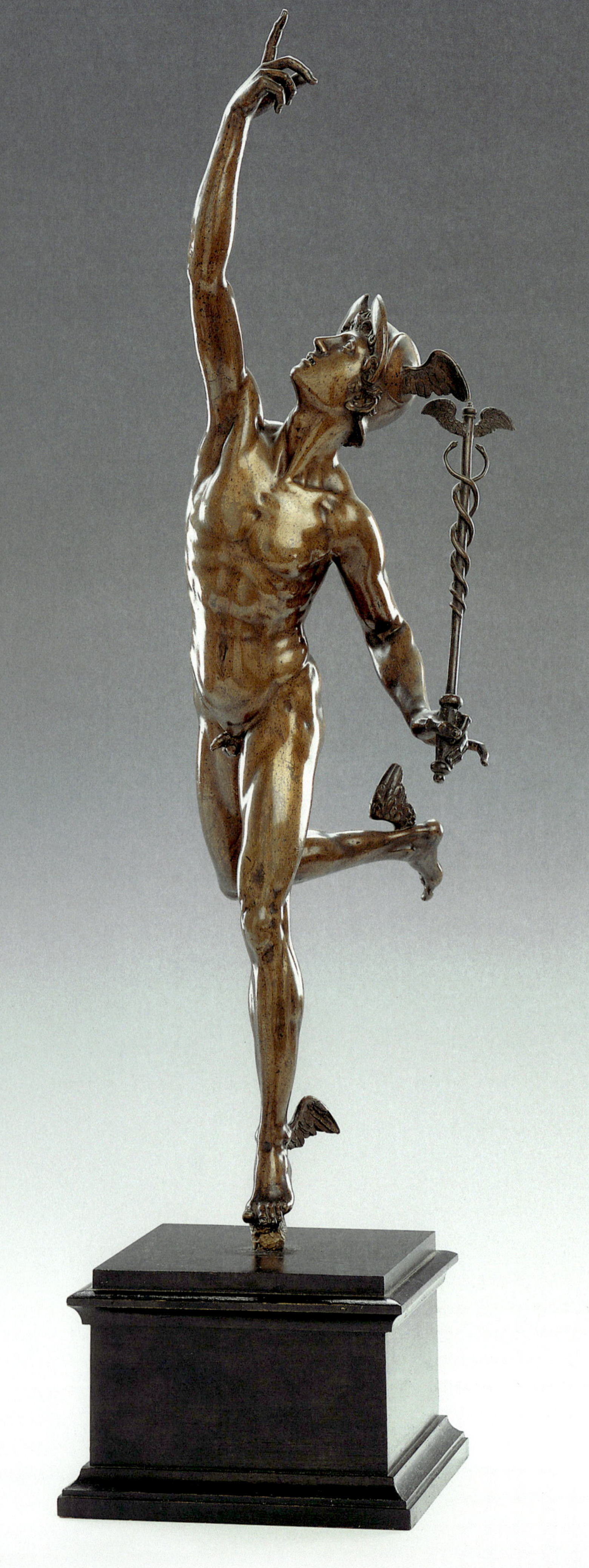

Mercury

Bronze
Giambologna
Before 1587
H. (without plinth) 61.8 cm, H. (incl. plinth) 73.4 cm, Inv. no. IX 94

With only the tip of his left foot touching the ground, Mercury is about to soar heavenwards. His raised arm, elongated index finger and gaze directed towards the sky all point to the realm into which he is about to disappear. The jaunty lightness of the slender, elegant body that seems to wind its way upwards around an invisible axis makes the viewer almost forget the heaviness of the material. It is not for nothing that this masterpiece, which appears to surmount with playful ease the technical difficulties involved in creating such a challenging composition, is regarded as one of Giambologna's most outstanding works. Numerous copies of this masterly crafted figure have been made to the present day.

As early as 1597, the figure of Mercury and two other small bronze sculptures came to the Dresden Kunstkammer as a gift from Francesco I de Medici to Elector Christian I who had begun his rule in the previous year. The young elector would have considered this gift from the Grand Duke of Tuscany as a token of high esteem. At that time, Mercury was regarded as a complex allegorical figure. The youthful god with his winged hat and feet carrying a herald's staff was not only regarded as messenger of the gods and executor of the divine will, but was also interpreted as the god of eloquence and trade. Besides, he was seen as the embodiment of ›industria‹ (diligence) and ›felicitas‹ (here: fame, success) and thus symbolized, as a diplomatic gift from another ruler, ›good governance‹. The figure was exhibited in the Grünes Gewölbe high up on a ledge together with its counterpart, which has been lost, and another, much smaller version.

As the sources are not quite clear, the identification of the figures is only partially possible, and it cannot be said with absolute certainty that the bronze at the Grünes Gewölbe is indeed the gift from the Grand Duke.

UW

Sleeping Nymph with Satyr

Bronze
Nymph: Giambologna
Satyr: Antonio Susini, probably after a model by Adriaen de Vries
Before 1587
H. (incl. plinth) 31.4 cm, l. 34 cm, Inv. no. IX 34

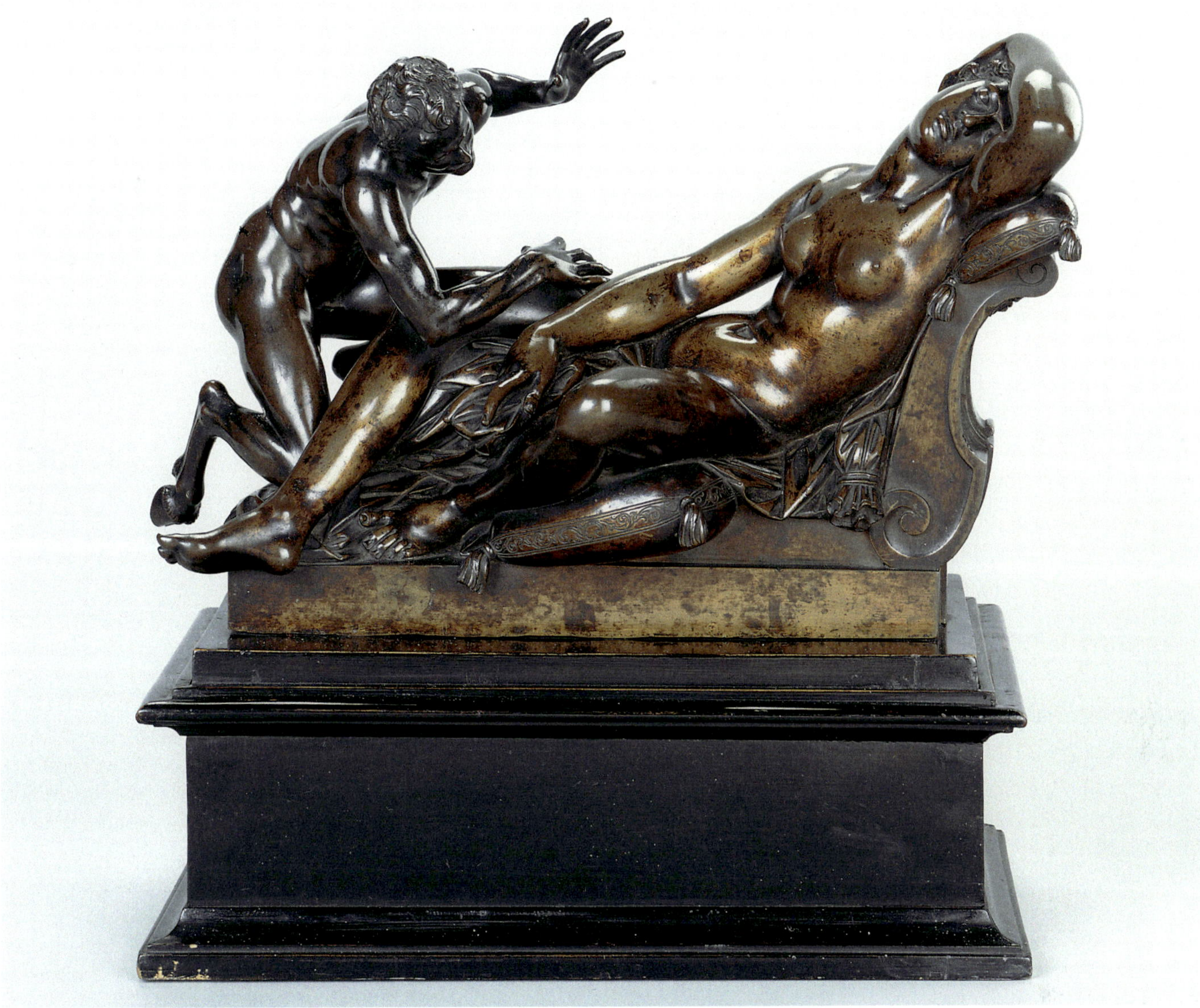

The nymph is depicted reclining on a divan with cushions. Her left arm is placed over her forehead, while with her other hand she reaches into the cloth on which she reclines. In the original version, her sleep remained undisturbed as the inquisitive satyr approaching her from the foot of the bed is a later addition. A closer look reveals that the faun is smaller and his patina is slightly darker than that of the sleeping beauty by the Florentine artist Giambologna. The figure of the satyr is now generally ascribed to Adriaen de Vries, a pupil of Giambologna. The latter obviously appreciated the figure so much that he added it to his nymph, probably using a later cast by Antonio Susini.

The sleeping nymph in the Grünes Gewölbe, later interpreted as a representation of Venus, is mentioned as early as 1587 in the first inventory of the Kunstkammer. It may thus be considered the oldest version of this much-reproduced sculpture and the only one documented during the lifetime of the artist. It is very likely that Giambologna himself put the finishing touches to this group. It was presented, together with the figures of ›Mercury‹ (see page 166) and ›Nessus and Dejanira‹ (now: Dresden, Skulpturensammlung), to Elector Christian I of Saxony by Francesco I de Medici. Giambologna, who had closely studied Roman sculpture, was regarded – not only at the court in Dresden – as the best sculptor in Europe. An educated princely collector will have been aware that Giambologna's work was based on his excellent knowledge of classical sculpture. Christian I will most certainly have been familiar with the most famous statue of classical antiquity at that time – the figure of ›Sleeping Ariadne‹, on which Giambologna's reclining nymph is quite obviously modelled. Gabriel Kaltemarckt, the art advisor to the Saxon Elector, even remarked that the works from Florence surpassed those from classical antiquity in their artistic quality. The gift from Florence was thus a conversation piece, which lent itself particularly well to a discussion about artistic quality and references to historical models.

UW

Striding Horse

Bronze, plinth: wood, jasper and agate variations
After Giambologna
Model/cast: presumbaly Antonio Susini, Florence, c. 1605
Plinth: presumably Castrucci workshop, Prague, c. 1610
H. (incl. plinth) 38.7 cm, w. 28 cm, plinth: 25 x 14.2 cm, Inv. no. IX 33

The bronze figure of a striding horse is modelled on a design by Giambologna for an equestrian statue of Cosimo I de Medici. This monumental sculpture was completed in 1593 and erected in 1594 in the Piazza della Signoria in Florence. It was succeeded by numerous bronze reductions, which differed in detail. Many of them were manufactured at the workshop of Antonio Susini, a pupil of Giambologna, who had also made the models and casting moulds for the equestrian statue. There are a number of replicas without riders. The bridle bit, visible at the side of the mouth, and the wrapped tail indicate that this bronze figure is modelled after the equestrian monument.

Giambologna's model was inspired by the equestrian statue of Marc Aurel at the Capitol in Rome. He surpasses the classical model as far as the well-balanced proportions and the complete harmony of the animal's movement is concerned. He created the ideal type of a noble horse. The animal ambles, its head bent downward in an elegant pose and its right foreleg lifted.

The Dresden version is remarkable in many respects. Not only is it of excellent quality, it also differs from other versions in that it is mounted on a plinth decorated with precious pietra dura plaques. The complicated technique of ›commesso di pietre dure‹ first emerged in the Castrucci workshops that were active for the Medici. Hard stones (›pietre dure‹) were cut into thin plaques, polished and arranged to form tableaux in such a way that the grain and colour of the different stones enabled the artists to create complex compositions. When the Florentine master craftsmen Cosimo and Giovanni Castrucci arrived in Prague around 1600, a second centre of pietra-dura technique evolved at the court of Rudolf II. It was there that the plinth for the Dresden horse was made, as stylistic comparisons suggest. At the court of the Emperor – an art connoisseur – the combination of bronzes with pietra-dura work was regarded as particularly precious and exuberant. It can be assumed that the sculpture came to Dresden via Prague, where it was mounted on the sumptuously decorated plinth. It is conceivable that the horse came to Dresden as an imperial gift to the Saxon Elector, although there is so far no clear evidence for this assumption.

UW

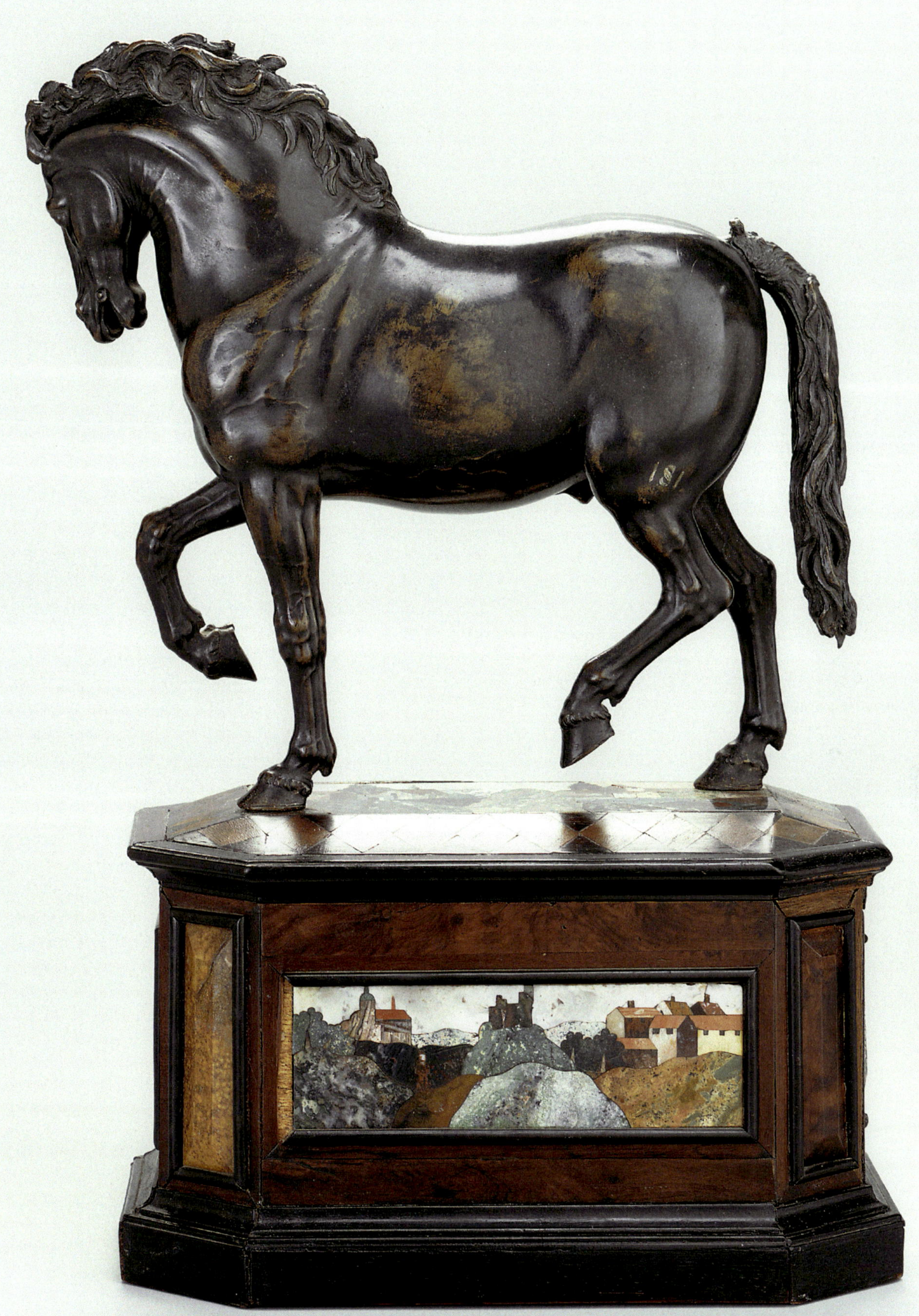

Faun and Nymph

Bronze
Adriaen de Vries
c. 1580/90
Faun: h. (without plinth) 48.1 cm, Inv. no. IX 36
Nymph: h. 34.6 cm, Inv. no. IX 20
Plinth: h. 15.1 cm, w. 39.7 cm, d. 22 cm

The dynamism of this group is generated by the posture of the bodies, as well as gestures and eye contact. The faun, who turns to the nymph seated on a draped rock, makes an obscene gesture directed at the beautiful woman. She looks at him while pointing towards her mirror image – originally, the nymph with her neatly arranged hair held a mirror in her right hand. The twisting motion of the two figures invites the viewer to look at the group from different angles to fully appreciate the different aspects of the scene: the lithe movement of the faun, his body turned to the left, striding dance-like past the nymph, his unequivocal gesture and the expression of surprise on the face of the nymph with her mouth slightly open. The interpretation of this group, in the early 17th century referred to as ›Venus and Adonis‹, remains ambiguous. The latest interpretation is that it is a representation of virtue and vice.

Like his teacher Giambologna, Adriaen de Vries trained his artistic skill by studying the works of classical sculptors, which according to his biographer Joachim von Sandrart, he intended to examine as thoroughly as possible. Among his sources of inspiration was probably the Hellenistic marble sculpture of a faun turning round in a dance as if to catch his own tail. Adriaen de Vries developed this composition to create an independent work. The revolving figure, also known as ›figura serpentinata‹, was regarded as the ideal of Mannerist sculpture at that time. De Vries mastered this technique in a remarkable fashion and his sculpture of the faun – beautiful from all angles – perfectly meets the artistic requirements of Mannerism. The elegant group, together with two other versions, came to the elector's Kunstkammer in 1622 from the estate of Giovanni Maria Nosseni, art director and universal artist who worked for the court in Dresden from 1575. Two of the bronzes were unchased raw casts, which were completed by a goldsmith in Dresden. This suggests that Nosseni received them from Adriaen de Vries in 1588 on the occasion of a journey to Italy, as an artist might have given an unfinished work to an artist colleague, but not to a collector.

UW

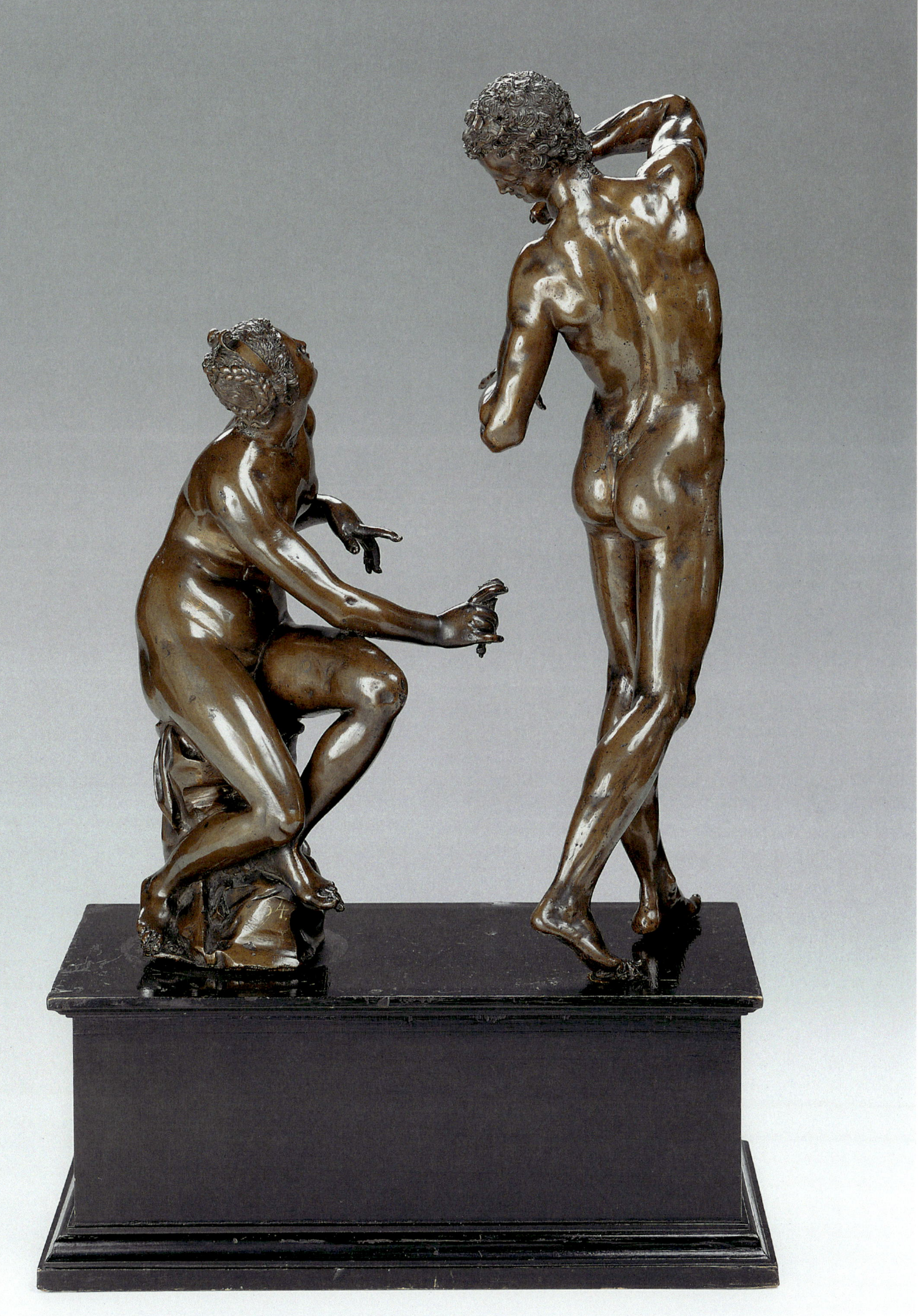

List of artists with dates

Artists who are only mentioned are given in italics

A

Aldegrever, Heinrich (1502 – between 1555 and 1561) 84
Anguier, Michel (1612 – 1686) 160

B

Barthel, Melchior (1625 – 1672) 64, 65
Baur, Samuel (c. 1649 – 1705) 92
Beham, Hans Sebald (1500 – 1550) 60
Bodenehr, Moritz (1665 – 1748) 142
Boulle, André-Charles (1642 – 1732) 158
Borisch, Martin (1583 – 1649) 60

C

Cleve, Cornelis van (1646 – 1732) 156
Collaert Adriaen (1560 – 1618) 41
Courteys, Martial (first mentioned 1579 – 1592) 36

D

Diespach, Franz Michael (according to the records
    Dresden 1763 – 1799) 19, 150
Dinglinger, Georg Christoph (1668 – 1746) *15*, 138
Dinglinger, Georg Friedrich (1666 – 1720) 10, 11, *15*,
    121
Dinglinger, Johann Melchior (1664 – 1731) 10, 11, 15,
    16, 18, *19*, *112*, *120*, *122*, 134, 136, 137, 138, 140, 142,
    144, 146, *159*
Dinglinger, Johann Melchior (workshop) 11, 132, 144
Dobbermann, Jacob (1682 – 1745) 49
Döbel the Younger, Michael (1635 – 1702) 65
Döring, Gottfried (1686 – 1718) 15
Drentwett, Abraham I (1614 – 1666) 76
Drentwett, Abraham II (c. 1647 – 1729) 76, 94
Dürer, Albrecht (1471 – 1528) 37
Duquesnoy (Du Quesnoy), François (1597 – 1643) 65

F

Flötner, Peter (c. 1485 – 1546) 35
Fra Bartolomeo (mentioned c. 1472/74) 13
Friebel, Georg (first mentioned 1696 – 1730) 97
Friedel, Georg (active 1610 – 1640) 58, 59

G

Garnier, Louis (c. 1639 – 1728) 160
Geitner, Valentin (1551 – 1593/1612,
    master craftsman 1580) 74, 75
Gerhardt, Hubert (between 1540 and 1550 – 1620) 37
Geyer, Elias (c. 1560 – 1634) 75, 91, 104,
Giambologna (Giovanni Bologna, 1524/1529 – 1608)
    37, 65, *76*, 164, 166, 167, 168, 170
Girardon, François (1628 – 1715) 154, 158, 162
Globig, Christian August (1762 – 1798) 148, 150, 152
Globig, August Gotthelf (first mentioned 1769, last
    mentioned 1819, master craftsman 1781) 148
Goltzius, Hendrik (1558 – 1616) 63
Grießmann, Balthasar (1620 – 1706) 62

H

Heermann, Paul (1673 – 1732) 10, 15, 120
Heiden, Marcus (1597/98 – still active 1664) 58, 59
Heise, Jacob (active 1654 – 1667) 45
Heuglin, Johann Erhard II (before 1687 – 1757) 97, 98
Hillebrand, Friedrich (first mentioned 1580 – 1608)
    105
Holland, Christian Friedrich (1724 – 1773) 126
Hübner, Johann Christoph (1665 – 1739) 120, 134,
    138, 146

I

Irminger, Johann Jakob (first mentioned 1682 –
    after 1721/1724) 98, 99

J

Jamnitzer, Wenzel (c. 1507/0 – 1585) 71, 88
Jamnitzer, Bartel (first mentioned 1548/4 – 1596) 75

K

Keller (Kellner), Hans (first mentioned 1582 –
    last mentioned 1617) 86
Kern, Johann Georg (1622 – 1698) 61
Kern, Leonhard (1588 – 1662) 60, 61
Kern, Leonhard (workshop) 60
Kirchner, Christian (1691 – 1732) 138
Kirchner, (Johann) Gottlieb (1706 – 1732) 134
Köhler, Johann Heinrich (1669 – 1736) 5, 42, 43, 51,
    105, 116, 132, 133
Kolb, Matthias (active in the first half
    of the 18th century) 80
Krüger, Wilhelm (1680 – 1756) 132
Küsel, Philipp (before 1643 – 1700) 76

L

Labhardt, Christoph (1644 – 1695) 118, 119
LeBrun, Charles (1619 – 1690) 158
Lencker, Christoph (first mentioned 1596 – 1613) 37
Lencker, Hans   (1523 – 1585) 55
Lencker, Elias (first mentioned 1526, died 1591) 102
Lobenigk, Egidius (died 1595) 54, 55, 57

M

Mair, Hans Jakob (c. 1641 – 1719) 72
Mányoki, Adám (1673 – 1757) 121
Maucher, Christoph (1642 – 1706/07) 49
Maucher, Johann Michael (1645 – 1701) 62, 63
Mengs, Ismael (1688 – 1767) 121
Metellino, Giovanni Battista (active in the last quarter
    of the 17th century – 1722/23) *16*, 110, 111
Miseroni, Gasparo (c. 1518 – 1576) 108, 109
Miseroni, Ottavio (c. 1568 – 1624) 108, 109
Mond, Georg (first mentioned 1599 – after 1623) 90

N

Neuber, Johann Christian (1736 – 1808) 66
Nosseni, Giovanni Maria (1544 – 1620) 68, 69, *170*

P

Pallard, Jean Jacques (1701 – 1776) 19, 150
Parmigianino (Francesco Mazzola, 1503 – 1540) 65
Permoser, Balthasar (1651 – 1732) *15*, 65, 99, 132, 136
Permoser, Balthasar (workshop) 132
Pfaff, Jeremias (mentioned 1651/1700) 78
Pfaff, Nicolaus (1556? – before 1612) 72, 73
Pfründt, Georg (1603 – 1663) 73
Pöppelmann, Matthäus Daniel (1662 – 1736) 5, 7
Pöppelmann, Carl Friedrich (1696/97 – 1736) 7
Pratsch, Abraham (c. 1686 – 1731) 116, 122

R

Rafael (Raffaelo Santi, 1483 – 1520) 13
Rappolt, Hans I (first mentioned 1580 – 1625) 105
Redlin, Michel (according to the records c. 1688) 46
Regnaudin, Thomas 158
Reinow, Chistian (1685 – 1749) 52, 130
Ruel, Joerg (Georg) (first mentioned 1598 – 1625)
    106, 107

S

Sandrart, Joachim von (1606 – 1688) 65, *170*
Sarto, Andrea del (1486 – 1530) 13
Schebel, Hans (first mentioned 1555 – 1571) 85
Schmidt, Nikolaus (first mentioned 1582 – 1609)
    70, 71
Schnell, Martin (c. 1675 – before 1740) 132
Schneeweiß, Urban (1536 – 1600) 68, 69
Schreiber, Georg (according to the records active
    in 1614 – 1643) 40, 42, 43,
Strauss, Bernhard (c. 1640 – after 1681) 61
Susini, Antonio (active 1572 – 1624) 65, 166, 168
Susini, Giovanni Francesco (1529 – 1608) 65

T

Thelott, Johann Andreas (1655 – 1734) 96
*Thiermann, Johann Gottfried (first mentioned 1709 –
    last mentioned 1754)* 126
Thomae, Benjamin (1682 – 1751) 100
Troger, Simon (1683 – 1768) 80
*Turau (Turow), Nicolaus (according to the records
    1670 – 1681)* 46, 49

V

Vinache, Jean-Joseph (c. 1696 – 1754) 154, 162
Visscher, Cornelis (c. 1520 – 1586) 46
Vos, Marten de (1532 – 1603) 41
Vries, Adriaen de (1556 – 1626) 164, *166*, 167, 170

W

Wecker, Georg (c. 1550 – after 1626) 54, *55*, *57*
*Weniger, Johann Siegmund (first mentioned 1726 –
    last mentioned 1748)* 126
Wickert, Andreas I (1600 – 1661) 61
Wolff, Urban (Meister 1585 – 1598) 86

Z

Zeller, Jacob (um 1581 – 1620) 59

Literature

Catalogues

Arnold, Ulli; Schmidt, Werner (eds.): *Barock in Dresden. Kunst und Kunstsammlungen unter der Regierung des Kurfürsten Friedrich August I. von Sachsen und Königs August II. von Polen, genannt August der Starke 1694–1733 und des Kurfürsten Friedrich August II. von Sachsen und Königs August III. von Polen 1733–1763*, catalogue of the exhibition organised by the Kulturstiftung Ruhrfoundation at the Villa Hügel in Essen, Leipzig 1986.

Avery, Charles; Radcliffe, Anthony; Leithe-Jasper, Manfred (eds.): *Giambologna. Ein Wendepunkt der europäischen Plastik*, catalogue of the exhibition at the Kunsthistorisches Museum Wien 1978/79, Vienna 1978.

Baumstark, Reinhold; Seling, Helmut (eds.): *Silber und Gold. Augsburger Goldschmiedekunst für die Höfe Europas*, catalogue of the exhibtion at the Bayerisches Nationalmuseum München, Munich 1994.

Baumstark, Reinhold (eds.): *Rom in Bayern. Kunst und Spiritualismus der ersten Jesuiten*, catalogue of the exhibition at the Bayerisches Nationalmuseum München, Munich 1997.

Distelberger, Rudolf: *Die Kunst des Steinschnitts. Prunkgefäße, Kameen und Commessi aus der Kunstkammer*, catalogue of the exhibition at the Kunsthistorisches Museum Wien, Vienna 2002.

Evans, Helen C.; Wixom, William D. (eds.): *The Glory of Byzantium. Art and Culture of the Middle Byzantine Era A.D. 843–1261*, catalogue of the exhibition at the Metropolitan Museum of Art New York, New York 1997.

Fučikova, Eliška u.a. (ed): *Rudolf II. and Prag. The Court and the City*, catalogue of the exhibition in Prague, Prague/London 1997.

Hoyer, Eva-Maria: *Sächsischer Serpentin. Ein Stein und seine Verwendung*, catalogue of the exhibtion at the Grassi Museum Leipzig, Leipzig 1995.

Кабинет драгоценностей Августа Силного. Из собрания Эленых Сводов, Дрезден (The Jewellery Cabinet of Augustus the Strong. From the Collection of the Grünes Gewölbe, Dresden), catalogue of the exhibtion at the Patriarchs' Palace, Kremlin, Moscow, Moscow 2006.

Kappel, Jutta: *Bauern, Händler, Komödianten und andere Leute. Die Sammlung barocker Elfenbeinfigürchen im Grünen Gewölbe zu Dresden*, catalogue of the exhibition at the Grünes Gewölbe at Museum Huelsmann Bielefeld, Bielefeld 2002.

Kappel, Jutta: *Bernsteinkunst aus dem Grünen Gewölbe*, catalogue of the exhibition in the Sponsel-Room at the Neues Grünes Gewölbe, Dresden Residenzschloss, Munich/Berlin 2005.

Kappel, Jutta (ed.): *Deutsche Steinschneidekunst aus dem Grünen Gewölbe zu Dresden*, catalogue of the exhibtion at the Deutsches Edelsteinmuseum (gemstone museum) Idar-Oberstein, at the Kunstgewerbemuseum (museum of applied art) der Staatlichen Museen zu Berlin and at the Dresden Residenzschloss 1998/99, Dresden 1998.

Königliches Dresden. Höfische Kunst im 18. Jahrhundert, catalogue of the exhibtion at the Kunsthalle der Hypo-Kulturstiftung München, Munich 1990.

Krahn, Volker (ed.): *Von allen Seiten schön. Bronzen der Renaissance und des Barock*, Skulpturensammlung SMPK, Berlin/Heidelberg 1995.

Kunsthistorisches Museum Wien (ed.): *Prag um 1600. Kunst und Kultur am Hofe Rudolfs II.*, catalogue of the exhibition at Villa Hügel, Essen and at the Kunsthistorisches Museum Wien, Freren 1988.

Marx, Harald; Kluth, Eckhard (eds.): *Glaube und Macht. Sachsen im Europa der Reformationszeit*, catalogue of the 2nd Sächsische Landesausstellung at Schloss Hartenfels, Torgau, 2 vols., Dresden 2004.

Schmidt, Werner; Syndram, Dirk (ed.): *Unter einer Krone. Kunst und Kultur der sächsisch-polnischen Union*, catalogue of the exhibition at the Residenzschloss Dresden, Leipzig 1997.

Seipel, Wilfried (ed.): *Bernstein für Thron und Altar. Das Gold des Meeres in fürstlichen Kunst- und Schatzkammern*, catalogue of the exhibition at the Kunsthistorisches Museum Wien (Alte Geistliche Schatzkammer), revised by Sabine Haag and Georg Laue, Milan 2005.

Seipel, Wilfried (ed.): *Exotica. Portugals Entdeckungen im Spiegel fürstlicher Kunst- und Wunderkammern der Renaissance*, catalogue of the exhibition at the Kunsthistorisches Museum Wien, Vienna 2000.

Siebenmorgen, Harald (ed.): *Leonhard Kern (1583–1662). Meisterwerke der Bildhauerei für die Kunstkammern Europas*, catalogue of the exhibtion at the Hällisch-Fränkisches Museum Schwäbisch Hall, Sigmaringen 1988.

Splendeurs de la cour de Saxe. Dresde à Versailles, catalogue of the exhibition at the Palace of Versailles, Paris 2006.

Staatliche Kunstsammlungen Dresden (ed.): *Restaurierte Kunstschätze aus Dresdner Museen*, catalogue of the exhibition at the Albertinum, Dresden 1990.

Stephan, Bärbel: *Balthasar Permoser hats gemacht*, catalogue of the exhibition at the Albertinum in Dresden, Dresden 2001.

Strozzi, Beatrice Paolozzi; Zikos, Dimitrios (eds.): *Giambologna, gli dei, gli eroi*, catalogue of the exhibition at the Museo Nazionale del Bargello Florence, Milan 2006.

Syndram, Dirk: *Die Juwelen der Könige. Schmuckensembles des 18. Jahrhunderts aus dem Grünen Gewölbe*, catalogue of the exhibition at the Sponsel-Room at the Neues Grünes Gewölbe in Dresden, Munich/Berlin 2006.

Syndram, Dirk; Woelk, Moritz; Minning, Martina (eds.): *Giambologna in Dresden – Die Geschenke der Medici*, catalogue of the exhibtion in the Sponsel-Room at the Neues Grünes Gewölbe in Dresden, Munich/Berlin 2006.

Syndram, Dirk; Weinhold, Ulrike: »*... und einen Leib von Perl.« Die Sammlung der barocken Perlfiguren im Grünen Gewölbe*, catalogue of the exhibition at the Grünes Gewölbe Dresden, Wolfratshausen 2000.

Syndram, Dirk; Scherner, Antje (eds.): *In fürstlichem Glanz. Der Dresdner Hof um 1600*, catalogue of the exhibition at the Museum für Kunst und Gewerbe (museum of applied art) Hamburg, Metropolitan Museum of Art in New York, Fondazione Memmo at the Palazzo Ruspoli in Rome, Gilbert Collection at Somerset House in London, Dresden/Milan 2004.

The Glory of Baroque Dresden. The State Art Collections Dresden, catalogue of the exhibtion at the Mississippi Arts Pavilion in Jackson/Mississippi, Munich 2004.

Wiedergewonnen. Elfenbeinkunststücke aus Dresden. Eine Sammlung des Grünen Gewölbes, catalogue of the exhibition at the Deutsches Elfenbeinmuseum (ivory museum) Erbach, Erbach 1995.

Literature

Alcouffe, Daniel: *Les Gemmes de la Couronne* (Musée du Louvre. Département des Objets d'art, Catalogue), Paris 2001.

Arbeteta Mira, Letizia: *El tesoro del Delfin. Alhajas de Felipe V recibidas por herencia de su padre Luis, gran delfin de Francia* (Museo Nacional del Prado), Madrid 2001.

Arnold, Ulli: *König August III. und die Juwelengarnituren des Grünen Gewölbes*, in: *Der stille König. August III. zwischen Kunst und Politik*, Dresdner Hefte 46, Dresden 1996, pp. 69 – 76.

Arnold, Ulli: *Die Juwelen Augusts des Starken*, Munich/Berlin 2001.

Arnold, Ulli: *Der historische Bestandsverlust an Silber im Jahre 1772. Ein Beitrag zur Geschichte der Schatzkammersammlung »Grünes Gewölbe«*, in: Jahrbuch der Staatlichen Kunstsammlungen Dresden, vol. 21, 1989/1990, pp. 55 – 63.

Aschengreen Piacenti, Kirsten: »*Beschreibung eines von Helffenbein gedrehten Kunststücks ... beneben desselben geistliche Bedeutung« von Marcus Heiden 1640*, in: Anzeiger des Germanischen Nationalmuseums Nürnberg, 1964, pp. 82 – 98.

Bäumel, Jutta: *Auf dem Weg zum Thron. Die Krönungsreise Augusts des Starken*, Dresden 1997.

Bock, Sebastian: *Ova struthionis. Die Straußeneiobjekte in den Schatz-, Silber- und Kunstkammern Europas*, Heidelberg 2005.

Boudon-Machuel, Marion: *François Duquesnoy (1597 – 1643)*, Paris 2005 (especially cat. nos. 62.2 – 62.7).

Distelberger, Rudolf: *Rosenwasserbecken und Kanne*, in: Dresdener Kunstblätter, published by the Staatliche Kunstsammlungen Dresden, vol. 4, Dresden 2004, pp. 254–257.

Ehmer, Angelika: Die Maucher. *Eine Kunsthandwerkerfamilie des 17. Jahrhunderts aus Schwäbisch Gmünd*, Schwäbisch Gmünd 1992.

Fransolet, Mariette: *François Du Quesnoy, sculpteur d'Urbain VIII, 1597–1643*, Académie royale de Belgique, Classe des Beaux Arts, Mémoires, 2e série, t. IX, fasc. I, Brussels, 1942 (especially p. 82 f. and p. 180, no. 43).

Fritz, Rolf: *Die Gefäße aus Kokosnuss in Mitteleuropa 1250–1800*, Mainz 1983.

Glaser, Gerhard: *Das Grüne Gewölbe im Dresdner Schloß als Weiterentwicklung der barocken Architekturidee des Spiegelkabinetts und als Ausgangspunkt gegenwärtiger Museumsgestaltung*, in: Jahrbuch der Staatlichen Kunstsammlungen Dresden, vol. 12, 1980, pp. 7–67.

Haag, Sabine: *»A Signed and Dated Ivory Goblet by Marcus Heiden«*, in: The J. Paul Getty Museum Journal, 24, 1996, pp. 45–53.

Hahnloser, Hans R.; Brugger-Koch, Simone: *Corpus der Hartsteinschliffe des 12.–15. Jahrhunderts*, Berlin 1985.

Heres, Gerald: *Dresdner Kunstsammlungen im 18. Jahrhundert*, Leipzig 1991.

Holzhausen, Walter: *Die Bronzen der kurfürstlich sächsischen Kunstkammer zu Dresden*, in: Jahrbuch der Preußischen Kunstsammlungen, vol. 54, Berlin 1933, Berlin 1, pp. 45–88.

Holzhausen, Walter: *Regesten über Leipziger Golschmiede*, in: Schröder, Albert: *Leipziger Goldschmiede aus fünf Jahrhunderten (1350–1850)*, Leipzig 1935, pp. 234–256.

Holzhausen, Walter: *Prachtgefäße, Geschmeide, Kabinettstücke. Goldschmiedekunst in Dresden*, Tübingen 1966.

Holzhausen, Walter: *Die Bronzen Augusts des Starken*, in: Jahrbuch der Preußischen Kunstsammlungen vol. 60, 1939, pp. 157–186.

Kappel, Jutta: *Das Bergkristallgefäß der Königin Jadwiga von Polen »in der Mitten mit einer Münchs Schrifft von schwarzen Buchstaben«*, in: Dresdener Kunstblätter, vol. 3/2000, Dresden 2000, pp. 76–84.

Kappel, Jutta: *Einblicke in die Brühlsche Elfenbeinsammlung*, in: Dresdener Kunstblätter, 4/2000, Dresden 2000, pp. 112–120.

Kappel, Jutta: *»Hier wird allzeit bleiben in Gunst und Hochachtung seine Kunst«. Zum 350. Geburtstag Balthasar Permosers*, in: Dresdener Kunstblätter, 6/2001, Dresden 2001, pp. 217–223.

Kappel, Jutta: *Elfenbeindrechselkunst am Dresdner Hof*, in: exhibition catalogue Hamburg, New York, Rome, London 2004/2005, pp. 176–179.

Kappel, Jutta: *Sächsische Serpentindrechselkunst*, in: exhibition catalogue Hamburg, New York, Rome, London 2004/2005, pp. 198–200.

Kappel, Jutta: *Mailänder Bergkristallgefäße in der Dresdner Schatzkammer*, in: exhibition catalogue Hamburg, New York, Rome, London 2004/2005, pp. 250–267.

Kappel, Jutta: *Zur Geschichte der Bernsteinsammlung des Grünen Gewölbes. »Kunststucklein von Adtsteinen«*, in: exhibition catalogue Dresden 2005, pp. 11–23.

Kappel, Jutta: *Der große Bernsteinschrank. »...etwas nie gesehenes und unschätzbahres...«*, in: exhibition catalogue Dresden 2005, pp. 27–37.

Kappel, Jutta: *Zwei Bernsteinschränke im Dienst der Diplomatie*, in: Laue, Georg (ed.), Bernsteinkostbarkeiten europäischer Kunstkammern, Munich 2006, pp. 74–85.

Kappel, Jutta; Weinhold, Ulrike: *Das Neue Grüne Gewölbe*, Munich/Berlin 2006.

Keller, Katrin (ed.): *»Mein Herr befindet sich gottlob gesund und wohl«. Sächsische Prinzen auf Reisen*, in: Deutsch-Französische Kulturbibliothek, vol. 3, Leipzig 1994.

Kerssenbrock-Krosigk, Dedo von: *Rubinglas des ausgehenden 17. und des 18. Jahrhunderts*, Mainz 2001.

Krahn, Volker: *Bemerkungen zu Giambolognas »Merkur«*, in: Dresdener Kunstblätter, published by the Staatliche Kunstsammlungen Dresden, vol. 4, Dresden 2004, pp. 237–240.

Laue, Georg (ed.): *Bernsteinkostbarkeiten europäischer Kunstkammern* (with essays by Viola Effmert, Sabine Haag, Jutta Kappel, Georg Laue, Bruno Platter and Silke Reiter), Munich 2006.

Lentz, Christel: *Der Glas- und Bergkristallschneider Christoph Labhardt und seine künstlerische Tätigkeit am Idsteiner Hof von 1671 bis 1679*, in: Nassauische Annalen 108/1997, pp. 107–130.

Lentz, Christel: *Ein Idsteiner Kunstwerk im Grünen Gewölbe zu Dresden*, in: Nassauische Annalen 111/2000, pp. 205–212.

Menzhausen, Joachim: *Das Grüne Gewölbe*, Leipzig 1968.

Menzhausen, Joachim: *Der Hofjuwelier Johann Heinrich Köhler als Restaurator*, in: Jahrbuch der Staatlichen Kunstsammlungen Dresden, vol. 5, Dresden 1965/66, pp. 91–99.

Menzhausen, Joachim: *Die zweite Bauperiode des Grünen Gewölbes 1727–1730*, in: Jahrbuch der Staatlichen Kunstsammlungen Dresden, vol. 8, 1970/71, pp. 117–127.

Menzhausen, Joachim: *Der Goldschmied Elias Geyer*, Schriftenreihe der Staatlichen Kunstsammlungen Dresden, Dresden 1971.

Menzhausen, Joachim: *Kurfürst Augusts Kunstkammer. Eine Analyse des Inventars von 1587*, in: Jahrbuch der Staatlichen Kunstsammlungen Dresden, vol. 17, 1985, pp. 21–29.

Menzhausen, Joachim: *Dresdener Kunstkammer und Grünes Gewölbe*, Leipzig 1977.

Mette, Hanns-Ulrich: *Der Nautiluspokal. Wie Kunst und Natur miteinander spielen*, Munich/Berlin 1995.

Peltz, Uwe: *»Das Bad des Apoll« – Modell oder Kopie?*, in: Dresdener Kunstblätter, published by the Staatliche Kunstsammlungen Dresden, vol. 47, Dresden 2003, pp. 253–260.

Philippovich, Eugen von: *Simon Troger und Matthias Kolb. Zwei Hauptvertreter des Kombinationsstils in der Elfenbeinkunst*, in: Kunst und Antiquitäten, IV/1981, pp. 27–32.

Richter, Ernst-Ludwig: *»D: Luthers Mund-Becher«*, in: Dresdener Kunstblätter, published by the Staatliche Kunstsammlungen Dresden, vol. 4, Dresden 2004.

Scherer, Christian: *Studien zur Elfenbeinplastik der Barockzeit*, in: Studien zur Deutschen Kunstgeschichte, 12th vol., Strasbourg 1897.

Scherner, Antje: *Bronzeplastik in der kurfürstlichen Kunstkammer*, in: Hamburg, New York, Rome, London 2004/2005, pp. 268–280.

Seling, Helmut: *Die Kunst der Augsburger Goldschmiede 1529–1868*, vol. 3, Munich 1980.

Seling, Helmut: *Der Doppelpokal von Hans Schebel*, in: Dresdener Kunstblätter, published by the Staatliche Kunstsammlungen Dresden, vol. 4, Dresden 2004, pp. 250–253.

Siebenmorgen, Harald (ed.): *Leonhard Kern (1588–1662). Neue Forschungsbeiträge*, Kataloge des Hällisch-Fränkischen Museums Schwäbisch Hall, vol. 2-Supplement, Sigmaringen 1990.

Sponsel, Jean Louis: *Führer durch das Grüne Gewölbe zu Dresden*, Dresden 1921 (2nd edition).

Sponsel, Jean Louis: *Das Grüne Gewölbe. Eine Auswahl an Meisterwerken der Goldschmiedekunst in vier Bänden*, Leipzig 1925 (vol. 1), 1928 (vol. 2), 1929 (vol. 3), 1932 (vol. 4).

Syndram, Dirk (ed.); Arnold, Ulli; Kappel, Jutta: *Das Grüne Gewölbe zu Dresden. Führer durch seine Geschichte und seine Sammlungen*, Munich/Berlin 1997 (2nd edition).

Syndram, Dirk: *Das Schloss zu Dresden. Von der Residenz zum Museum*, Munich/Berlin 2001.

Syndram, Dirk: *Der Pfälzer Löwe und Christian I. von Sachsen. Anmerkungen zu einem zurückerworbenen Kleinod*, in: Jahrbuch der Staatlichen Kunstsammlungen Dresden, vol. 27, Dresden 1998/99, pp. 7–14.

Syndram, Dirk: *Die barocke Lebenslust des Johann Melchior Dinglinger*, in: Butler, Karen; Krämer, Felix (eds.): *Jacobsweg. Festschrift zum 70. Geburtstag*, Rome 2006.

Syndram, Dirk: *Die Elfenbeindrechseleien im Grünen Gewölbe – Von der Maschinenkunst zum fürstlichen Sammlungsgegenstand*, in: *Wiedergewonnen. Elfenbeinkunststücke aus Dresden, Eine Sammlung des Grünen Gewölbes*, catalogue of the exhibition at the Deutsches Elfenbeinmuseum (ivory museum) Erbach, Erbach 1995, pp. 6–13.

Syndram, Dirk: *Die Schatzkammer Augusts des Starken. Von der Pretiosensammlung zum Grünen Gewölbe*, Leipzig 1999.

Syndram, Dirk: *Ein Denkmal für die Kunst. Der Obeliscus Augustalis im Grünen Gewölbe*, in: Kappel, Jutta: *Deutsche Steinschneidekunst aus dem Grünen Gewölbe zu Dresden*, catalogue of the exhibition at the Deutsches Edelsteinmuseum (gemstone museum) Idar-Oberstein, at the Kunstgewerbemuseum (museum of applied art) der Staatlichen Museen zu Berlin and at the Residenzschloss in Dresden, Dresden 1998, pp. 73–87.

Syndram, Dirk (ed.): *Naturschätze – Kunstschätze. Vom organischen und mineralogischen Naturprodukt zum Kunstobjekt*, Bielefeld 1991.

Syndram, Dirk: *Prunkstücke des Grünen Gewölbes zu Dresden*, Munich/Berlin 1997 (2nd edition).

Syndram, Dirk: *Prunkvolle Ordnung*, in: exhibition catalogue Hamburg, New York, Rome, London 2004/2005, pp. 282–286.

Syndram, Dirk: *Schatzkunst der Renaissance und des Barock. Das Grüne Gewölbe zu Dresden*, Munich/Berlin 2004.

Syndram, Dirk: *Serpentin – der drechselbare Schlangenstein*, in: Syndram, Dirk (ed.): *Naturschätze – Kunst-*

schätze. Vom organischen und mineralogischen Natur-produkt zum Kunstobjekt, Bielefeld 1991.

Syndram, Dirk: *Von fürstlicher Lustbarkeit und höfischer Präsentation. Die Kunstkammer und die Dresdner Sammlungen der Renaissance,* in: exhibition catalogue Hamburg, New York, Rome, London 2004/2005, pp. 54 – 69.

Theuerkauff, Christian: *Zum Werk des Monogrammisten B.G. (vor 1662 – nach 1680),* in: Aachener Kunstblätter, Aachen, 4 (1973), pp. 245 – 286.

Theuerkauff, Christian: *Anmerkungen zu Melchior Barthel,* in: Zeitschrift des Deutschen Vereins für Kunstwissenschaft, 41, Berlin 1987, pp. 71 – 117.

Ulferts, Gert-Dieter: *»Artefacta Eburata. Elfenbeinarbeiten von Marcus Heiden und Jeremias Bezolt in der Kunstkammer der Herzöge von Sachsen-Weimar«,* in: Niederdeutsche Beiträge zur Kunstgeschichte, 38, 1999, pp. 143 – 148.

Wagner, Franz: *Balthasar Grießmann (c. 1620 – 1706). Überlegungen zu einer Identifizierung des Monogrammisten B.G.,* in: Barockberichte, Salzburger Barockmuseum, 8/9, 1994, pp. 334 – 340.

Watzdorf, Erna von: *Johann Melchior Dinglinger. Der Goldschmied des deutschen Barock,* 2 vols., Berlin 1962.

Weinhold, Ulrike: *Emailmalerei an Augsburger Goldschmiedearbeiten von 1650 bis 1750,* Munich/Berlin 2000.

Weinhold, Ulrike: *Von »kunst und geschicklichkait«. Goldschmiedekunst am Dresdner Hof um 1600,* in: exhibition catalogue Hamburg, New York, Rome, London 2004/2005, pp. 206 – 249.

Weinholz, Gerda: *Zu Bergkristallarbeiten von Giovanni Battista Metellino,* in: Jahrbuch der Staatlichen Kunstsammlungen Dresden, vol. 6, 1967, pp. 131 – 138.

Acknowledgments

The publishers and authors would like to thank the following for their kind permission to reproduce photographs in this book:

Landesamt für Denkmalpflege Sachsen, Dresden:
Illustration 3 (Plansammlung, Inv. no. M 6.I.Bl.29), illustration 6 (reproduction photograph: Riedel, 1970), illustration 23 (Pfauder, 1974), illustration 21
Sächsisches Staatsarchiv – Hauptstaatsarchiv Dresden: Illustration 17 (Geheimes Kabinett, Loc. 896, Sachen das Grüne Gewölbe, Deßen ... betr., fol. 37 r), illustrations 16, 18
SLUB/Dept. Deutsche Fotothek:
Illustrations 7, 12 (Wolff), illustration 8 (reproduction after a photograph by Max Fischer), illustration 11 (Steuerlein), illustrations 5, 9, 24, 25
Staatliche Kunstsammlungen Dresden, Bildarchiv Grünes Gewölbe: Illustration 2, 28 (Jürgen Karpinski), illustrations 1, 4, 10, 20, 27
Staatliche Kunstsammlungen Dresden, Kupferstich Kabinett: Illustration 26 (Herbert Boswank), illustration 19

Photographs of objects from the Grünes Gewölbe by Jürgen Karpinski. Copyright to all the illustrations not listed here: Staatliche Kunstsammlungen Dresden.

Authors

Dirk Syndram (DS)
Jutta Kappel (JK)
Ulrike Weinhold (UW)

The Historic Grünes Gewölbe at Dresden

The Deutsche Nationalbibliothek lists this publication in the Deutsche Nationalbibliografie; detailed bibliographical information is available on http://dnb.dnb.de

Editorial Director:
Katharina Stauder

Project Editor:
Christine Nagel

Translation:
Ulrich Boltz
Dr. Richard Gary Hooton

Production:
Jens Möbius

Typography and Cover Design:
Dorén + Köster, Berlin

Layout:
Typographik Anette Klinge, Gelnhausen

Reproduction:
LVD, Berlin

Printed and bound by:
DZA Druckerei zu Altenburg GmbH, Altenburg

2. unveränderte Auflage
© 2014 Staatliche Kunstsammlungen Dresden,
Grünes Gewölbe
Deutscher Kunstverlag Berlin Munich

ISBN 978-3-422-07286-2